A Dissident Voice

Studies in the
Postmodern Theory of Education

Shirley R. Steinberg
General Editor

Vol. 418

The Counterpoints series is part of the Peter Lang Education list.
Every volume is peer reviewed and meets
the highest quality standards for content and production.

PETER LANG
New York • Washington, D.C./Baltimore • Bern
Frankfurt • Berlin • Brussels • Vienna • Oxford

ANTONIA DARDER

A Dissident Voice

Essays ON Culture, Pedagogy, AND Power

PETER LANG
New York • Washington, D.C./Baltimore • Bern
Frankfurt • Berlin • Brussels • Vienna • Oxford

Library of Congress Cataloging-in-Publication Data

Darder, Antonia.
A dissident voice: essays on culture, pedagogy, and power / Antonia Darder.
p. cm. — (Counterpoints: studies in the postmodern theory of education; v. 418)
Includes bibliographical references and index.
1. Critical pedagogy—United States. 2. Biculturalism—United States.
3. Educational sociology—United States. 4. Educational equalization—United States.
5. Social justice—United States. I. Title.
LC196.5.U6D37   379.2'60973—dc23   2011021142
ISBN 978-1-4331-1400-7 (hardcover)
ISBN 978-1-4331-1399-4 (paperback)
ISBN 978-1-4539-0152-6 (e-book)
ISSN 1058-1634

Bibliographic information published by **Die Deutsche Nationalbibliothek.**
Die Deutsche Nationalbibliothek lists this publication in the "Deutsche
Nationalbibliografie"; detailed bibliographic data is available
on the Internet at http://dnb.d-nb.de/.

Cover art by Antonia Darder

The paper in this book meets the guidelines for permanence and durability
of the Committee on Production Guidelines for Book Longevity
of the Council of Library Resources.

© 2011 Peter Lang Publishing, Inc., New York
29 Broadway, 18th floor, New York, NY 10006
www.peterlang.com

Printed in the United States of America

Voices of dissent have nothing left to lose. Everything has been stripped away already by literary and governmental entities determined to control, contain and silence dissenting voices. All that remains is truth, pride, courage, and voices that will not be silenced no matter what bully tactic may be applied.

—G. TOD SLONE

Article 19: Everyone has the right to freedom of opinion and expression; this right includes freedom to hold opinions without interference and to seek, receive and impart information and ideas through any media and regardless of frontiers.

—UNIVERSAL DECLARATION OF HUMAN RIGHTS (1848)

To all the dissident women of my time, whose revolutionary passion inspired a poor barrio girl to dream of a world where love, freedom, and justice prevail—if only we could reclaim the courage of Eve and bite the *forbidden* apple.

 # Acknowledgments

Acknowledgments are always tricky business, for there is never enough space to thank all the people who have made it possible to write and produce a volume that spans 20 years of work. Nevertheless, beyond the many brilliant students and colleagues who have supported my work over the years, there are a few people in particular who are directly associated with the production of this book that I wish to thank.

First and foremost, I thank Shirley Steinberg, who for the last three years has patiently nudged me to produce this book of collected writings. It is truly only because of her stubborn persistence and genuine belief in my scholarship that this book exists. *Gracias hermana*, both for your affirmation and solidarity—no truer gift could be received.

I also want to thank my editor at Peter Lang, Chris Myers, who immediately welcomed the idea and provided me, throughout the process, hands-on support and encouragement. It was a real joy to work with you, Chris.

Many thanks also go to Jessica Slovak, Imani Harris, and Velviet Zang for their kind assistance in the preparation of the manuscript. Your rapid and invaluable help with the nuts-and-bolts of scanning and converting original articles and chapters left me speechless. I couldn't have move as quickly in the preparation of this work without you.

On a more personal note, I want to thank my children, Gabriel, Christy, and Kelly, whose love, understanding, and generosity always amaze me. And special thanks for the great inspiration I receive from my granddaughters, Jessica, Naomi, Sofia, and Hope. Girls, Nani prays that you will inherit a better world, because of the struggles undertaken by the dissident women of your time. I love you.

Table of Contents

Foreword

Artist, Scholar, Poet, Teacher, Activist...Sister to the World

How does one *preface* such a woman as Antonia Darder? In a few short paragraphs, I will attempt to share with readers just who this deeply layered and talented entity is. I can't begin with a chronological accounting of just how I came to know Antonia; I only remember that she has been in my consciousness for many years. It was, however, through her writing that I first met her and became introduced to the most significant woman in the then-new growth of critical pedagogy. When I did actually meet Antonia, I was met with love, warmth, and the abrazos, she is so quick to give. Antonia envelops those she meets with arms open and shares with them the universe. One does not encounter Antonia, one is invited in...to her paintings, her poetry, her speeches, her books, her advocacy.

Antonia advocates for humanity, for the aesthetic, the rigorous intellectual, the ecological, and for knowledge. Her lifeworld is critical in her understanding of the energies and knowledges we must protect in the wake of the power mongering which we confront on a daily basis. She grounds her work in her deeply theoretical and nuanced understanding of Marx and Freire, and adds to it the decades of voices of those who have also been birthed from those traditions. Never quickly conceived, Antonia's work is crafted with a fusion of her social theoretical knowledge, her own lived experiences, and her vision of what could be.

She infuses her paintings and poetry with those voices from past, present, and future, always acknowledging where she has been, is, and will be. Her ontological presence is clear, and her art is infused with the histories of those she continues to advocate for. Antonia is part of the world, she does not see the world as surrounding her. It is this humility that most personifies the spirit of Paulo Freire, in that she does not expect attention and adoration....She is a worker above all else, constantly pushing the boundaries and borders to make room for those who have no advocate. Her rewards are her work.

Speaking with a voice from the ages, from the barrios out of which she came, Antonia moves seamlessly into worlds of the child, the youth, the poor, the ill, and the student. She informs all those she encounters, and does not look back to see who noticed. This book isn't merely a book. It is a collection of efforts from an amazing woman who sees through the illusions of many who claim a critical pedagogy (those who miss looking through the looking glass to imagine what could be), who names what must be named, and who, without apology, stands up for those who have no one else to stand for them. The pages of this volume fill us with those emotions we must have to be critical pedagogues: love, indignation, freedom, humility, confidence, politics, art, and above all...hope.

Please feel in my words the depth of admiration and love that I have for this woman, mi hermana. Feel also the transfer of the deep and radical love that Joe Kincheloe had for Antonia. This preface could not be completed with my acknowledging that the most important man, the love in my life, is present as I write these words, knowing that Antonia was una hermana de Joe, and indeed it was he who introduced us. His love and admiration for Antonia brought me to her, and I have relished our friendship for these many years.

This book is the culmination of years of thought, work, and activism by a woman who is clearly, a leading voice and guiding force in critical pedagogy. I invite you into this volume, to share firsthand what must be read and used...the voice and commitment of Antonia Darder.

Shirley R. Steinberg,
University of Calgary

The Making of a Dissident Voice

An Introduction

> You do not become a 'dissident' just because you decide one day to take up this most unusual career. You are thrown into it by your personal sense of responsibility, combined with a complex set of external circumstances. You are cast out of the existing structures and placed in a position of conflict with them. It begins as an attempt to do your work well, and ends with being branded an enemy of society.
>
> VÁCLAV HAVEL (1990)

Dissident voices emerge from historical conditions of political crisis, social disruption, and economic betrayal. As social agents of revolutionary ideas, dissidents embrace a commitment to historical struggle as a life vocation. Those who emerge from the anguish of poverty and dispossession know only too well the need to be ever-vigilant and conscious of how political power in society is exercised. Such dissidents exist in direct opposition to myths of modernity that would have us believe that our world can only be genuinely known through dispassionate inquiries and transcendent postures of scientific neutrality.

Instead, dissidents refuse to be extricated from the flesh and, thus, immerse ourselves fully into the blood and guts of what it means to be alive, awake, and in love with the world. As such, political grace becomes an imperative of struggle. Grace, here, is not employed as a religious concept, but rather it is constitutive of an affective and communal power that ruptures our alienation, in the wake of neoliberal devastation. Instead of the boredom, isolation, and banality of contemporary mainstream life, dissidents seek places of imagination, possibilities, and creativity from which to live, love and dream anew.

However, the journey is arduous, and dissidents must be constantly self-vigilant and formidably prepared to contend with a variety of obnoxious contentions and veiled obstructions that, consciously or not, serve as effective roadblocks to the wider dissemination of radical ideas and revolutionary visions. This is to say, that unless one is born into or in alliance with the ruling class, the journey to voice for most dissidents is an extremely precarious one. Many come dangerously close to losing heart, mind, body, soul—losses which can effectively disable dissident passion, make uncertain our faith, shed doubt on our intentions, and thus, immobilize the transgressive power of dissenting voices—voices absolutely essential to democratic life.

In a climate of marginalization, systematic silencing, and brutal assaults to our personhood, relationships are not easy terrain for dissident voices, given that these can often become tainted by the ripe stink of competition, jealousy, dismissal, ridicule, or mean-spirited gossip. In a world of alienating competition and wholesale consumption, the dissident voice that demands justice is easily marked as lunatic, renegade, or an enemy of the state. To remain sane and not lose heart in such an atmosphere requires much more than just the willingness to do battle out in the field. It demands a willingness to also wage battle within, to wrestle our personal demons to the ground instead of projecting them onto the political arena. Yet, even then, the dissident is not absolved of being pathologized or maligned. Given the rocky terrain, political commitment to dissent can develop in some, well-worn emotional muscles, so that love, courage, persistence, and solidarity can sustain us upright, as we dust ourselves off each time we fall and begin the journey anew.

Dissidence Is Not a Performance!

Celebrity culture has leached into every aspect of our culture, including politics...

—CHRISTOPHER HEDGES (2010A)

Political dissidents are not performers, rock stars, or celebrities. The very ego-mechanisms that drive such compulsions are in direct conflict with the political aims of dissent. For while celebrity performers, anchored in the profit motives of the entertainment industry, fancy themselves as great contributors to humanity, the feet of political dissidents are constantly held to the fire, with few resources to stave off public slander or institutional thrashing. As Hedges (2010a) so rightly argues,

> Celebrities have fame free of responsibility. The fame of celebrities…disguises those who possess true power: corporations and the oligarchic elite. Magical thinking is the currency not only of celebrity culture, but also of totalitarian culture. And as we sink into an economic and political morass, we are still controlled, manipulated, and distracted by the celluloid shadows on the dark wall of Plato's cave. The fantasy of celebrity culture is not designed simply to entertain. It is designed to keep us from fighting back (33).

In contrast, dissidents are anchored to revolutionary possibilities that demand both intellectual discipline and irrepressible courage to speak the unspeakable, to stand alone if necessary, and to accept the material and emotional consequences of tramping over hegemony's "holy" ground.

Unfortunately, in the deeply privatizing, bootstrapped, and consuming neoliberal culture of the day, even university professors and public intellectuals seem more invested in what Warren Susman (cited in Hedges, 2009) terms the "new culture of personality" than the responsibility to remain ever vigilant and in contestation with forces of oppression and injustice that threaten to dehumanize our bodies and our souls. Hedges (2009), in *Empire of Illusion: The End of Literacy and the Triumph of Spectacle,* distinguishes the difference between the nature of dissidents, who have nothing to gain from their political actions other than to remain true to the power of their convictions, and the nature of the elite performer class who easily moves from one glossy political fad to the other, devoid of political substance or a clear vision of class struggle or social transformation. He writes, "The old production-oriented culture demanded…character. The new consumption-oriented culture demands personality. The shift in values is a shift from a fixed morality to the artifice of presentation. The old cultural values of thrift and moderation honored hard work, integrity, and courage. The consumption-oriented culture honors charm, fascination, and likeability. The social role demanded of all in the new culture of personality [is] that of a performer." (51)

To reduce the actions and the role of political dissidents to performance or to a personality gone amuck conveniently deters and ignores the need for substantive and sustained engagements with injustice. As such, the hegemonic phenomenon of the culture industry functions to veil deeper political questions and ethical concerns that must be raised—questions and concerns that expose the hypocrisy and contradictions at work in the very fabric of American institutions and US democracy. Hence, true to Marxist wisdom, the ruling ideas of our society continue to be those of the ruling class, no matter the democratizing rhetoric of our new social networked society. And beliefs or theories to the contrary are simply wishful delusions or deliberate camouflage that belies what history had taught us. In the words of Frederick Douglass first written in 1857, "If there is no struggle there is no progress. Those who profess to favor freedom and yet depreciate agitation...want crops without plowing up the ground, they want rain without thunder and lightning. They want the ocean without the awful roar of its many waters.... Power concedes nothing without a demand. It never did and it never will (Douglass, 2009, 32)."

Dissidents and Power

> The dissident is not seeking power...has no desire for office and does not gather votes...does not attempt to charm the public... offers nothing and promises nothing. [She] can offer, if anything, only [her] own skin-and [she] offers it solely because [she] has no other way of affirming the truth [she] stands for. [Her] actions simply articulate [her] dignity as a citizen, regardless of the cost.
>
> —VÁCLAV HAVEL (1990)

In postmodern renditions of a decade ago, it seemed that the location of power had suddenly flattened—power was everywhere and nowhere. The pretense that all metanarratives should be disposed seemed to signal a new epoch in democratizing theory. However, for some radicals, this philosophical whim seemed a dangerous proposition in a world where capitalism's internationalizing force had well preserved the majority of wealth and power overwhelmingly in the hands of a few. Hence, to speak of power outside of a larger revolutionary anti-capitalist struggle serves, inadvertently, only as diversionary intellectual tryst. Hence, issues of power do remain at the heart of radical dissident voices. However, this power is not in pursuit of established power but rather as a call for the reinvention of what Havel refers to as "genuine power."

Yet, it should be noted that it is precisely a lack of concern for established power and an uncompromising commitment to the transformation of social power that ultimately renders dissident voices suspect and in need of silencing. In a world where self-interest and individualistic pursuit seem paramount, a dissident can seem quite the odd bird, facilitating workplace mobbing or institutional consensus for dismissal. At least, this has been the case in my life. And despite all the assertions to the contrary of those who in the past have silenced my voice, as Havel argues, I have held no economic, cultural, or political power that would render my ideas or my presence of any real threat to any establishment. The only power I hold and have held is the power of my words, the substance of my political convictions, and the passion that resides within my soul. But, of course, for the dissident these are the weapons, whether words are used against the tyranny of individuals, against the injustice of corporations, or against the impunity of the state.

To say, however, that dissidents hold no power, does not mean we are afflicted victims or powerless casualties of oppression, but rather that dissidents recognize, if we are to remain in integrity with our political convictions and respect the dignity of our humanity, then we must, first and foremost, acknowledge the futility of striving to enter into the domain of hegemonic power, which illegitimately resides in the hands of the wealthy and their faithful managers and performers—all who, wittingly or unwittingly, dictate through their callous pretensions and white-washed morality who shall have leisure and who shall toil, who shall live and who shall die.

Thus, a life of dissent requires us to expel the "success myths" of capital that pollute the ivy-covered halls of academia and to reject the warped and distorted privileges of power, preserved and doled out to the obedient servants of the empire. And as such, dissident voices reject the incarceration of our minds and bodies, by the neat and orderly colonizing rationale that conserves the hegemonic order. True to this commitment, radical dissidents rail against the most underhanded crime against humanity—namely, sentencing the majority of the world's population to a life of wretched poverty and dependence and then, blaming them collectively for their "moral ineptitude" or "cultural deficiency."

Perhaps I became a dissident because of my very intimate knowledge of what it means to be seen as deficient—racialized, gendered, and economically dispossessed at every stage of my life, from impoverished child, welfare mother, "paraprofessional," and finally my entrance into the fully certified "professional" class. And along this journey, I was subjected to the degrading remarks of nurses who cackled about the 16-year-old "Spanish" girl in labor; to waiting upon the mercy of a church basket to feed my children; to sitting in a welfare office dejected and shamed for my poverty; to hearing the veiled surprise of principals each time one of my children tested "gifted"; to listening to the nursing instructor who wanted me investigated because she could not believe that I produced such a well-written final study; to receiving the news, after the fact, about anonymous student letters accusing me of "reverse racism" sent in opposition to my tenure; to hearing a liberal "diversity" colleague explain why she could not stand up in my defense when I was unjustly hazed by members of my department; and to witnessing a dean summarily reduce my 25 years of scholarship to the realm of "opinion."

To be constantly at the receiving end of racialized prejudice, class exploitation, gendered marginalization, and political disempowerment is wearing to every aspect of our lives. No doubt it is meant to push us back into our appropriate places in the veiled caste order of racialized, gendered, homophobic ideals of perfect bodies. And unfortunately very often these tactics are overwhelmingly effective in coercing acquiescence or withdrawal, should one fall prey to indifference, apathy, cynicism, or despair.

Dissidents, however, seem to be those who have had enough. Ya basta! has been the rallying cry of farmworkers, Zapatistas, and Chicana and Chicano revolutionaries alike—dissident movements of people who could no longer remain complacent about the injustice or accept the prescribed domestication of the powerful and wealthy. Moreover, to say "enough is enough" prompts dissidents to speak with faith of revolutionary possibilities and to challenge with conviction myths of exceptionalism that effectively preserve all forms of inequalities and social exclusions.

Dismantling Exceptionalism

And when our white sisters
radical friend see us
in the flesh
not as a picture they own,
they are not quite as sure
If
they like us as much.
We're not as happy as we look
on
their
wall.

—JO CARRILLO (1981)

Intellectuals or politicians who come from impoverished racialized communities often are commodified by conservatives as proof that anyone can succeed if only they are sufficiently intelligent and willing to lift themselves up by the bootstraps. Middle-class liberals, on the other hand, seem to love the idea of our presence, but are often ambivalent about our participation, particularly when our expressed concerns fall outside of the exceptional notions of their ideal. Dominant myths of exceptionalism not only shroud the debilitating impact of meritocratic ideals but also support the notion that schooling and other aspects of American life are indeed democratic, despite the persistence of deafening inequalities. Yet, what those of us who have been commodified as *spectacles of equality* know only too well is that the politics of exceptionalism objectifies and defines from the outside, both the exceptions and those who are deemed otherwise.

Such tainted perspectives fail to contend with longstanding inequalities at work in the intellectual formation of poor and working class students, particularly those from racialized cultures who enter school bright and enthusiastic but speaking a different language. Yet, with all of the hoopla of evidence-based research of No Child Left Behind and, now, Race to the Top, the national educational discourses have effectively narrowed and thus, readily perpetuate anti-democratic practices of high stakes testing and assessment in public schools. As a consequence, important political and scientific discourses alike are silenced, if they do not benefit the prevailing neoliberal rationale of meritocracy that fuels exceptionalism.

On a more personal level, my own dissidence can be linked to my battle against being objectified and commodified as an exception. By so doing, I have managed to remain more firmly anchored to an organic aesthetic and collective sensibility as a Puerto Rican working-class woman, who recognizes that it is by an inexplicable accident of history that I sit here now and write these words. That is to say, that it is not some exceptionalism that empowers my political discourse or passionate commitment but rather, as my friend Barbara Richardson would say, *there but for the grace of God go I.* There are millions of poor and working-class people around the world, fettered in prisons or enslaved by conditions not of their own making; citizens of the planet, formally educated or not, who ponder and dream of a world where justice and democracy prevail, not simply as a rhetorical veil of capital but, as an unexceptional living praxis of everyday life.

The Language of Dissidence

> When I speak of knowledge...I am speaking of that dark and true depth which understanding serves, waits upon, and makes accessible through language to ourselves and others. It is this depth within each of us that nurtures vision.
>
> —AUDRE LORDE (1981)

There is no doubt that dissidents must speak consistently across many language forms to give voice to that knowledge that previously had been silenced. As for me, I know not when exactly I surrendered to a deep passion that beckoned me to speak of unspoken suffering, lest it remain incarcerated in fixed bourgeois fantasies of "the other." For some of us there is no escape from this task; there is no going back into the safety of anonymity, no matter how much one might fantasize the return during moments of anguish. Once the unknown die is cast, the dissident is compelled to speak or else have entire parts of one's soul forever cut off by wicked panic and consternation—even if it results in the shedding of public tears. For such tears, born of rage and shame, serve as cleansing salve for fettered souls. They are another language of the repressed body, unleashed to counter the dispassionate sensibilities of those who can afford to distance themselves from the anguish of the dispossessed.

Hence, the language of dissidence must be wide and far-reaching, for injustice cannot be permitted to escape from the radar of political vigilance. Moreover, developing a sense of comfort across the language forms of the privileged and not so privileged is essential to listening and learning with others, in any public or private space. And none of this ever requires speaking over people's heads or disrespectfully "dummying down" political discourse, believing that this is the only way in which the young or those of modest means might find it intelligible. Instead, for me it has meant accepting responsibility for making my meaning clear even when using language that is more at home in the university classroom than on the streets of the barrio in which I grew up. Nevertheless, what I know from my personal experience is that language, just like political struggle, is communal. And thus, it is most powerfully understood and learned within the material conditions that inform it and most powerfully cracks open privilege when used to speak of suffering or tangible possibilities of everyday life.

Years ago, I had an experience in Boston that began to assist me to understand the value of a being able to move comfortably across language communities, which generally remain segregated by both class apartheid and racism. All on the same day, I delivered a keynote for a teacher's conference at Wellesley College, spoke with Community Fellows students at the Massachusetts Institute of Technology, spoke at a school assembly with Boston youth, and then, in the evening participated in a dialogue with parents of color in Roxbury. My comrade and colleague Angela Cook accompanied me that day as I navigated the city to and from these very different public spheres. At the end of the day, Angela and I were finally "chilling" and talking about the day's events. In the course of our dialogue, Angela spoke about the power of the experience—not so much the content of these presentations but the fact that the same concepts were repeated in very different arenas and yet, in each setting my words were understood and the response was overwhelmingly affirmative.

This experience showed me that in the process of my political formation, as I was forced to move back and forth from spaces of poverty to those of privilege, my dissident voice had somehow helped me remain open to the variety of ways in which people speak the "true depth" of their wisdom. Hence, if people lent an ear, no matter who they were, I saw this as a privilege they extended me; and, as such, I had a responsibility to make clear my words rather than arrogantly expect them to conform to some peculiar discourse style. As a consequence, faith in our mutual capacity to understand one another remained intact. Moreover, remaining open and present to experiencing others also makes my connection with their ideas, concerns and questions far more significant than simply communicating my own. However, I must confess that in many highly politically charged arenas of university life, I've not been as successful in exchanges of the heart and mind as I was with the parents that beautiful evening in Roxbury. For in highbrow academic arenas, I am the one who is expected to conform rigidly to a narrow language and rationality that betrays my very soul. Perhaps with time, I may be more able to call forth the cooler reflective elements of intellect. For now, I remain far more confident in the powers of the flesh to expose political repression than to depend exclusively on the windmills of my mind.

Dissidence in the Flesh

When you defend your ideas in public, you then have to make an effort to live accordingly.

—PAULO COELHO

Mine is a dissidence of the flesh. Hence, I seek to speak publically only those words for which I am prepared to struggle for and to live by. And this seems a far lesser danger, at least for the moment, than that of many historical dissidents the world over, whose consequences have included incarceration and even death for their political convictions. Thus, it is happenstance that as I complete this introduction, Myanmar's military government has just released the dissident it considers an archrival—democracy leader and Nobel Peace Prize Laureate, Aung San Suu Kyi, who has been jailed or under house arrest for most of the last 21 years. Stories like that of Aung San Suu Kyi make me wonder why it is that we as a nation, with far greater possibilities for dissent than most, still remain crippled in the face of oppression, unable to enact a historical breakthrough that can awakens us from our morbid slumber.

No doubt, there is always a physical and emotional price to be paid for one's unwillingness to be silenced or repressed even in our so-called democratic nation. Ethel and Julius Rosenberg and Sacco and Vanzetti were U.S. dissidents who paid with their flesh. Many political prisoners who remain in U.S. prisons today are a direct result of the activities of the FBI's counter-intelligence program, COINTELPRO, directed against U.S. dissidents. According to J. Soffiyah Elijah (2002),

> Hundreds of members of the Puerto Rican Independence Movement, The Black Panther Party, The Young Lords, The Weather Underground, Student for a Democratic Society (SDS), The Republic of New Africa (RNA), The Student Non-Violent Coordinating Committee (SNCC), Members of the American Indian Movement, (AIM), The Chicago Movement, The Revolutionary Action Movement (RAM), peace activists, and everyone in between were targeted by COINTELPRO "for neutralization" (130–131).

Others who refuse to pretend that there is *no elephant in the room* can also suffer consequences less physically destructive but yet severely scarring to the psyche. More often than not, workplace repression is deliberate and orchestrated; meant to shut down dissent and preserve the structures of inequality so prevalent to the bureaucratic norms of both private and public institutions. In such contexts, one quickly discovers that the quality of labor or the quantity of credentials will seldom protect dissidents from repression—particularly those from working-class and racialized communities who are already perceived as second class. Hence, political dissidents live with the knowledge that they are never immune from the repressive forces of organizational paranoia or national hysteria, which can blindside without a moment's notice should a threat to the established order, real or imagined, rear its ugly head.

Hence, one cannot be naïve, for inherent in the labor of radical dissidents is an oppositional stance against the repressive forces of capital and exclusionary policies of the state. Hence, dissidents are not to be trusted. This is not because we are untrustworthy, but rather because we can be trusted to disrupt bourgeois etiquettes of civility, if need be, to push back attitudes or actions that are fundamentally destructive to democratic life—no matter where or who is in leadership. The struggle against oppression for true dissidents is not an individual matter but rather in concert with a larger political project that informs the transgressions and disruptions of dissent. It is precisely this collective and communal agenda of struggle that makes the ways of radical dissidents fully unintelligible to both their conservative and liberal peers. This is particularly so within academia, where an allegiance to the working class and anti-imperialist agenda is regarded as vulgar or

passé; and where *activist scholarship* is frowned upon as lacking rigor and dangerously steeped in practical concerns.

Moreover, why should an intellectual with a secure position and good pay ven-
ture into the danger zones of such unstable terrain? Such are the attitudes that prevail among collegial circles, when one not only writes about liberation but seeks
to embody liberation as a living praxis. Within the university, dissident praxis is
generally met with suspicion. Within our communities, university dissidents can
also be met with suspicion. However, one of the overarching axioms of being a
dissident is that struggle seems to choose the dissident, as much as the dissident
chooses struggle.

At some point in the making of a dissident, one reaches a point of no return;
not because one feels compelled by comrades or forced by foes to do so, but
because one comes to understand that our greatest political agency, as individuals and communities, resides not in our perfection of ideas or the correctness of
our actions but in our on-going commitment to struggle for our humanity and our
uncompromising courage—particularly when we must commit to facing our own
human follies. Hence, dissidents must struggle to abide in the love and solidarity of community, even during difficult moments. For dissidents, probably more
than most people, actually need committed comrades, who with their clarity and
strength both support and challenge us to rethink, to re-feel, and to reinvent our
praxis, in light of the ever-partial nature of knowledge and the ever-changing conditions of history.

Dissidents as Subjects of History

It is in the knowledge of the genuine conditions of our lives that
we must draw our strength to live and our reasons for acting.
—SIMONE DE BEAUVOIR

Radical dissidents have little choice other than to remain anchored as subjects of
history. Thus, any moment of life is but a very partial, minute rendering of personal and collective history, as is any book or article or speech or poem or work
of art. In seeing oneself, others, and the world as ever historical, the radical dissident can be freed both from the fascistic compulsion to achieve perfection and the
underlying deception that anything produced at any given moment is somehow
the *ultimate end all*.

Paulo Freire understood well the importance of holding this view of ourselves
in history, in that such a view actually works to support a deeper faith in others

and in the possibility of social transformation. If the world in which we live is a collective rendering of both our affective and material conditions, then the possibility of creating a different world can also be found in our collective hands. To participate in such an endeavor, however, demands we seek an integral quality in our work and our lives—one that is attained by our willingness to be touched by the preciousness of life, not as sappy sentimentalism but as political necessity. It is from such an ecologically motivated politics that we can labor to reconstruct and reenact relations of power that confirm the wide-ranging complexity and vital diversity of our human existence.

The ideas put forth in this introduction are simply to provide the reader of this collection a small glimpse into an ever-evolving politics and pedagogy that, step by step, have shaped the evolution of my political consciousness over the last 35 years. In those years, I've walked through a variety of unwelcoming and hostile social spheres. In the process, I have waged a multitude of battles with those who would repress my right to speak and to enact an emancipatory vision of education—a vision that, as Eagleton (2003) so rightly argues, neither abandons the romantic soulfulness of our humanity nor the realistic dimensions of our battered world. For, it is in the dialectical tension of these two essential dimensions of our existence, that dissidents find fertile ground for imagination, passion, creativity, friendship, solidarity and revolutionary love.

Unfortunately, dissidents who hold steady such a dialectical vision are often branded rebels with the least provocation. To judge a dissident as somehow defiant for defiance's sake is far simpler than to critically grapple with the deeper ethical questions being raised. Moreover, as Hedges (2010b) contends in his essay, "Calling All Rebels,"

> The power structure and its liberal apologists dismiss the rebel as impractical and see the rebel's outside stance as counterproductive. They condemn the rebel for expressing anger at injustice. [They] call for calm and patience. They use the hypocritical language of spirituality, compromise, generosity, and compassion to argue that the only alternative is to accept and work with the systems of power. The rebel, however, is beholden to a moral commitment that makes it impossible to stand with the power elite. The rebel refuses to be bought off...aware that virtue is not rewarded.

As these words suggest, many battles waged by dissidents are lost. So it has been true in my own life as well, but nevertheless, my voice and my passion have remained intact and true to my convictions. Hence, this collection of transdisciplinary writings represents my efforts over the last 20 years to name a variety of conditions of racialized life, so that from that place we "might draw our strength to live and our reasons for acting." This, of course, is not to suggest that what I have written here is somehow irrefutable "truth," but rather that this collection is offered as a variety of examples of small historical moments in one dissident's endeavor to make meaning out of suffering; and by so doing, remain open to the revolutionary possibilities of a transformed future.

REFERENCES

Carillo, J. (1981). And When You Leave, Take Your Pictures with You in C. Moraga and G. Anzaldúa (eds.). *This Bridge Called My Back*. New York: Kitchen Table Women of Color Press.

Douglass, F. (2009). *Narrative of the Life of Frederick Douglass, an American Slave, Written by Himself: A New Critical Edition*. San Francisco: City Lights Publishers.

Eagleton, T. (2003). *Figures of Dissent*. London: Verso.

Elijah, J. S. (2002). The Reality of Political Prisoners in the United States: What September 11 Taught Us about Defending Them in *Harvard Black Letter Law Journal*, Vol. 18, (129–137).

Havel, V. (1990). *Living in Truth*. London: Faber & Faber.

Hedges, C. (2009). *Empire of Illusion: The End of Literacy and the Triumph of Spectacle*. Toronto: Knopf Canada.

Hedges, C. (2010a). Celebrity Culture and the Obama Brand. *Tikkun* 25(1): 33.

Hedges, C. (2010b). Calling All Rebels in *Truth Dig*. See: http://www.truthdig.com/report /item/ calling_all_rebels_20100308/

Lorde, A. (1981). An Open Letter to Mary Daly in C. Moraga and G. Anzaldúa (eds.) *This Bridge Called My Back*. New York: Kitchen Table Women of Color Press.

PART I.
Politics of Biculturalism

A BICULTURAL RIDDLE

I live on the borders
because it is the only place
where they speak my name,
it is the only place where
two worlds meet
yet never meet,
where I am not asked
to pledge allegiance
to any world,
where I can see
all that I am without shame.

But let no one be fooled
for this place is haunted
by the wicked ghosts who creep
in the dark and are fed fat on
fears, self-doubts, and uncertainties;
political correctness seldom visits here,
it becomes too confused and twisted

I walk at different times
upon each delineated rim,
my legs cannot always stretch across
to make the bridge,
they are too short to span the distance;
but in the strain of it all,
I learn what is mine here,
and what is mine there.

But my life cuts across
many danger zones,
for I never know
when I might be told
that I do not belong here
or that I do not belong there;
at moments well-meaning people
insist that I renounce those parts
of me that are much too light,
or much too dark.

But I have come to learn that
to live among difference and conflict
always brings great contradiction;
it is a dance of incongruency,
my body responds to a multitude
of environmental stimuli, as if
I could claim ownership to one
and easily disclaim the other

The salsa queen sings in my world
as loudly as does Marvin Gaye,
Madonna, and the Temptations;

I savor Buñel's films, as easily
as those of Woody Allen or Truffaut.

I eat with equal gusto arroz con pollo,
as I do quiche and croissants.

I sit in meetings with harvardites,
as I sit with the barrio folks
on lazy afternoons in the park.

The sounds of Spanish beckon my soul,
as the sounds of English move my mind.

I am fed by multicolored mothers,
I am caressed by multicolored fathers.

And all of these
I contain within
the complex borders
of my double-vision,
of my two worldness,
of my twin beings,
of this place where
I am never quite who
I appear to be.

—ANTONIA DARDER (1990)

CHAPTER 1

A Critical Theory
of Cultural Democracy

Education has to be linked to forms of self and social empowerment if the school is to become...a force in the ongoing struggle
for democracy as a way of life.

—HENRY GIROUX (1988B),
Schooling and the Struggle for Public Life

In examining the link between culture and power, it becomes quite evident that in
order to move toward a genuinely liberatory form of education there must exist in
theory and practice an emancipatory political construct on which to build a critical bicultural pedagogy. This is particularly true given the asymmetrical power
relations in American society and the disproportionate number of injustices suffered by students of color in the public schools. Significant to this discussion is the
notion of student voice and empowerment and the conditions required for bicultural students to develop their bicultural voice and to actually experience a process of empowerment in the classroom. In more specific terms, there must exist a
democratic environment where the lived cultures of bicultural students are critically integrated into the pedagogical process. Keeping these principles in mind, a

critical theory of cultural democracy emerges as part of a language of possibility and hope.

In the same spirit of human equality and social justice that is so clearly found in John Dewey's (1916) writings on democratic schooling and in the work of Henry Giroux (1988a) on critical democracy, a critical theory of cultural democracy seeks to function as an educational construct that can transform the nature of classroom life. Above all, it represents a concerted effort to awaken the bicultural voice of students of color and cultivate their critical participation as active social agents in the world. This is particularly essential in light of the many social forces of domination at work in the lives of bicultural students.

A philosophy of *cultural democracy* was first defined by Mexican-American educators Manuel Ramirez and Alfredo Castañeda (1974). Their notion is based primarily on the principle that every individual has the right to maintain a *bicultural identity*. Since the critical theory of cultural democracy to be developed in this chapter is an effort to expand on some of the ideas formulated in the original theory, the meaning of biculturalism and its implications for establishing a culturally democratic environment must first be considered as a necessary part of a culturally emancipatory discourse.

Biculturalism

Biculturalism speaks to the process wherein individuals learn to function in two distinct sociocultural environments: their primary culture, and that of the dominant mainstream culture of the society in which they live. It represents the process by which bicultural human beings mediate between the dominant discourse of educational institutions and the realities that they must face as members of subordinate cultures. More specifically, the *process of biculturation* incorporates the different ways in which bicultural human beings respond to cultural conflicts and the daily struggle with racism and other forms of cultural invasion.

It is essential that educators recognize that, just as racism constitutes a concrete form of domination directly experienced by people of color, biculturalism specifically addresses the different strategies of survival adopted by people of color in response to the dynamics of living in constant tension between conflicting cultural values and conditions of cultural subordination. Although the responses may bear a similarity to those that result from conditions of class oppression, an analysis of biculturalism cannot be reduced simply to notions of class conflict. The "attack on culture is more than a matter of economic factors. [I]t differs from the class situation of capitalism precisely in the importance of culture as an instrument of domination" (Blauner, 1972, p. 67). Thus, simply to consider the lived experiences of bicultural populations as only dictated by forces related to class conflict is to fall into a reductionistic theoretical trap that trivializes and distorts the struggles for equality of people of color in the United States.

In examining the notion of biculturalism, it is of major significance that, since the early 1900s, writers, educators, and social theorists of color have made references in their work to the presence of some form of dual or separate socialization process among their own people. These references have included a variety of constructs used to describe the personality development, identity, or traits of non-Whites socialized in a racist society: double consciousness (Du Bois, 1903); double vision (Wright, 1965); bicultural (Valentine, 1971; deAnda, 1984; Ramirez & Castañeda, 1974; Red Horse et al., 1981; Solis, 1980; Rashid, 1981); diunital (Dixon & Foster, 1971); multidimensional (Cross, 1978); and other references that closely resemble notions of duality and twoness (Memmi, 1965; Fanon, 1967; Kitano, 1969; Hsu, 1971; Sue & Sue, 1978).

These studies of Black, Latino, Asian, and Native American populations clearly indicate that a bicultural phenomenon is present in the development of members from subordinate cultures. They also support the notion of biculturalism as a mechanism of survival that constitutes forms of adaptive alternatives in the face of hegemonic control and institutional oppression. Further, these alternatives must be understood as forms of resistance that may—or may not—function in the emancipatory interest of the individuals who utilize them in their lives. In order to understand better the role of biculturalism in relation to a theory of cultural democracy, it is helpful to examine some of these studies more closely.

Charles Valentine (1971) was one of the first social theorists to consider the concept of a *bicultural model of human development*, based on his work with Black children. His work represents an early attempt to expand on the *cultural difference model* and to challenge directly and displace the *cultural deprivation model*, which has failed to portray with accuracy the socialization process of children of color in the United States. Valentine suggests that bicultural groups undergo a dual socialization process that consists primarily of enculturation experiences within one's culture of origin (subordinate culture), in addition to less comprehensive but significant exposure to the socialization forces within the dominant culture. In reference to this notion of development, he writes,

> The idea of biculturation helps explain how people learn and practice both mainstream culture and ethnic culture at the same time. Much intragroup socialization is conditioned by ethnically distinct experience, ranging from linguistic and other expressive patterns through exclusive associations like social clubs and recreational establishments to the relatively few commercial products and mass media productions designed for ethnic markets. Yet at the same time, members of all [subordinate cultures] are thoroughly enculturated

in dominant culture patterns by mainstream institutions, including most of the contents of the mass media, most products and advertising for mass marketing, the entire experience of public schooling, constant exposure to national fashion, holidays, and heroes. (Valentine, 1971, p. 143)

Diane deAnda's (1984) efforts to examine the bicultural process and to explain the differences found among bicultural individuals have led her to suggest six factors that she argues have an influence on the level of biculturalism in the individual.

1. The degree of overlap or commonality between the two cultures with regard to norms, values, beliefs, perceptions, and the like;
2. The availability of cultural translators, mediators, and models;
3. The amount and type (positive and negative) of corrective feedback provided by each culture regarding attempts to produce normative behaviors;
4. The conceptual style and problem-solving approach of the bicultural individual and their mesh with the prevalent or valued styles of the majority culture;
5. The individual's degree of bilingualism; and
6. The degree of dissimilarity in physical appearance from the majority culture, such as skin color, facial features, and so forth.

The major conceptual difference between Valentine's and deAnda's models of biculturalism lies in the manner in which the individual is considered to interrelate with the two distinct cultures. Whereas Valentine's model of biculturalism perceives the process as resulting from the bicultural individual stepping in and out of two separate and distinct cultures, deAnda's argues that the bicultural experience is possible only because an overlap exists between the two cultures. The more overlap there is between the two cultures, the more effective the bicultural process of dual socialization.

The bicultural world of Mexican-American children is described by Ramirez and Castañeda (1974) as encompassing the realities that Mexican-American children must learn in order to function effectively in the mainstream of the American cultural community, and to continue to function effectively in and contribute to the Mexican-American cultural community. They characterize this phenomenon as follows:

If a Mexican-American child has been raised during his [or her] preschool years in the sociocultural system characteristic of the traditional Mexican American community, the socialization practices pertaining to (1) language and heritage, (2) cultural values, and (3) teaching [and cognitive] styles will be unique to that system, and the child will have developed a communication, learning, and motivational style which is appropriate to it. At the same time the child begins his experience in the public schools he is required to relate to a sociocultural system whose socialization practices pertaining to language and heritage, cultural values, and teaching [and cognitive] styles are different from those experienced during his preschool years. In effect, it is a new cultural world which he must come to explore and understand. At the same time, he must continue to explore, understand, and learn to function in the heretofore familiar sociocultural system...represented in his home and community. These demands placed on many Mexican American children in one sense constitute the reality of a bicultural world. (p. 29)

In addition, Ramirez and Castañeda posit a summary of characteristics for what they term *traditional, dualistic, and atraditional communities.* The schematic presentation for their framework incorporates the categories of general community characteristics; the degree of identification with the family, community, and ethnic group; the definitions of status and roles; the religious ideology espoused; and the preferred cognitive mode. Individuals from *traditional* communities hold a strong Mexican worldview, speak Spanish as their primary language, have a field-sensitive cognitive style, espouse a strongly Catholic ideology, and tend to live in relative isolation from the mainstream culture. Those individuals, who are said to be *dualistic* incorporate cultural values from both the Mexican and Anglo-American cultures, are bilingual, Catholic, utilize mixed cognitive styles, and live in more ethnically heterogeneous communities. *Atraditional* individuals maintain an Anglo-American orientation, speak English exclusively, are field independent, Protestant, and live in communities that are predominantly Anglo-American. In addition, Ramirez and Castañeda attribute the diversity observed in Mexican-American communities to these seven variables:

1. distance from the Mexican border;
2. length of residence in the United States;
3. identification with Mexican, Mexican-American, or Spanish-American history;
4. degree of American urbanization;
5. degree of economic and political strength of Mexican-Americans in the community
6. degree of prejudice; and
7. degree of contact with non-Mexican-Americans.

Ramirez and Castañeda also view the notion of bicognitive functioning as a most important goal in the development of bicultural human beings. This not only relates to the issue of cognitive flexibility but also to the fact that functioning effectively in two cognitive styles allows bicultural students to participate more fully in both their culture and the mainstream American culture, which can then help them to achieve a strong bicultural identity. Consequently, the concept of *bicognitive development* is a vital component of the Ramirez and Castañeda methodology, which evaluates both teachers and students in terms of field-sensitive and field-dependent cognitive styles. This assessment is primarily conducted with instruments that measure preferential modes in terms of cultural values, relational styles, incentive motivation, and other behavioral and attitudinal criteria.[1]

Based on his work with Black children, Hakim Rashid (1981) defines biculturalism as "the ability to function effectively and productively within the context of America's core institutions while simultaneously retaining [an] ethnic identity" (p. 55). He strongly argues that biculturalism is an essential developmental process if children of subordinate cultures are to develop the ability to cope with the racism and classism that permeate American society. Related to this view, Rashid posits the notion that biculturalism should also be considered an important component of the cognitive and behavioral repertoire of all American children, "for it is only through recognition of the need for biculturalism that a foundation for true multiculturalism [in society] can be built. When children have developed the ability to survive and thrive within the context of their own culture as well as that of the broader society, a genuine appreciation for the variety of cultures that comprise America is the next step." (Rashid, 1981, p. 61)

A *theory of biculturality* is described by indigenous psychologist Arnoldo Solis (1980, 1981), based on his work with Chicano populations. He defines "biculturality" (biculturalism) in an individual as the result of existing in and adapting to two cultures having substantial dissimilarity. Solis argues that the more similar the cultures, the less the degree of biculturality; and on the other hand, the more the dissimilarity between the two cultures, the greater the degree of biculturality. For Solis, the dynamics of biculturation are considered to begin when the dominant culture exerts increasing influence on the subordinate culture to accommodate and assimilate to the dominant culture's value, language, and cognitive style. At this point, a dynamic of resistance is said to develop, which causes the individual to experience cultural crisis. Within this construct, the process of biculturation is viewed as an attempt to reestablish the intrapsychic harmony of the primary culture that is threatened by the tensions arising as a result of pressure by the dominant culture to renounce subordinate cultural values. The resolution of the *bicultural* crisis is brought about through a series of developmental stages whereby the individual becomes increasingly able to recognize the value of and is able to utilize adaptive functions from both cultures in a harmonious manner (Solis, 1981).

Although there exist some differences in the manner in which these bicultural theorists have conceptualized the notion of biculturalism, it is nonetheless evident from this discussion that an understanding of what constitutes the dynamics of biculturalism is essential to any model of education that is designed to meet the needs of students of color. This is particularly true since what has often been missing (although often mentioned) from many theories of bicultural education is 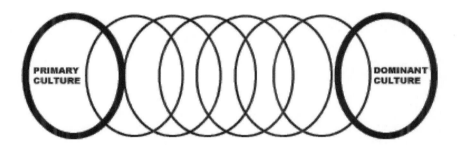 a serious confrontation of the power relations that shape the nature of how bicultural students respond to the tension of cultural conflicts and the pressure to assimilate so highly prevalent in traditional American schools. Hence, a notion of biculturalism must not be reduced to an absolute determined moment or a linear developmental stage. On the contrary, its critical dimension must be emphasized through its representation of bicultural existence as a complex process encompass-

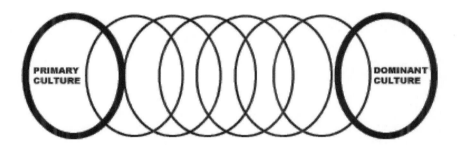

FIGURE 1.1: The Biculturation Process Represented along a Dialectical Continuum

ing all the conscious and unconscious contradictory, oppressive, and emancipatory responses that can be found along a continuum that moves, conceptually, between the primary culture and the dominant culture (see Figure 1.1).

Educators who possess this dialectical understanding of biculturalism will be better equipped to assist their students of color in critically examining their lived experiences in an effort to reveal genuinely the impact that cultural domination has on their lives. Further, given the nature of cultural domination and resistance, the process of biculturation can also be understood as patterns of responses that are shaped by the manner in which bicultural students react, adjust, and accommodate to the emotional anxiety and physical stress that result from a constant cultural dissonance. These response patterns can be perceived in a more critical manner when understood in terms of an axis relationship between culture and power that, on one hand, moves between the dominant and subordinate cultures and, on the other hand, moves between the forces of dominance and resistance (see Figure 1.2).

There are four major response patterns related directly to the biculturation process: alienation, dualism, separatism, and negotiation. Responses categorized

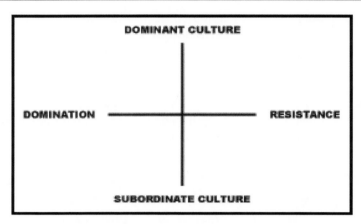

FIGURE 1.2: Axis Relationship between Culture and Power

under *cultural alienation* reflect those that suggest an internalized identification with the dominant culture and a rejection of the primary culture. Some examples of alienation responses include a bicultural student's preference for identifying herself/himself as American, refusal to speak Spanish, belief in the inferiority of the primary culture, and denial of the existence of racism. A *cultural dualist* (or nonnegotiation) response pattern is informed by a perception of having two separate identities: one that is identified with the primary cultural community, and one that is related to acceptance of mainstream institutional values. An example of a dualist response is found among members of an all-Black social club who espouse the dominant culture's elitist bourgeois ideology. The *cultural separatist* response pattern identifies those responses related to remaining strictly within the boundaries of the primary culture while rejecting adamantly the dominant culture. A cultural nationalist group's responses geared toward complete self-sufficiency for its members outside of the dominant culture represent an example of this mode. The *cultural negotiation* response pattern reflects attempts to mediate, reconcile, and integrate the reality of lived experiences in an effort to retain the primary cultural identity and orientation while functioning toward social transformation within the society at large. Examples of cultural negotiation are present in community struggles for bilingual education programs in schools. It must be stressed that these patterns lie within a social domain that can be conceptualized as a *sphere of biculturalism* (see Figure 1.3).

As such, these four patterns reflect modes of engagement that are directly influenced by the power relations that result from the axis relationship between power and culture. Within this sphere of biculturalism, student responses can also be considered with respect to the degree that they support a context of *bicultural*

FIGURE 1.3: Sphere of Biculturalism

affirmation. For example, cultural alienation and cultural separatism responses move the individual away from bicultural affirmation responses. In this sense, alienation responses tend to move the bicultural student more exclusively toward the context of the dominant culture while cultural separatism responses tend to move the student more exclusively toward the primary (subordinate) cultural context.

On the other hand, cultural dualism and cultural negotiation responses, which result from some effort to contend with the reality of both the dominant and subordinate cultural realities, are more likely to result in moving the student toward bicultural affirmation. However, it is critical that educators remain cognizant of the fact that the forces of hegemony are constantly at work in shaping the realities that constitute the bicultural existence. Hence, just as with other response modes, bicultural affirmation responses may or may not necessarily result in supporting the emancipatory interests of bicultural students. Nonetheless, it is safe to say that bicultural affirmation response patterns may hold the greatest emancipatory possibility with respect to the struggle for cultural democracy in the schools.

Also vital to an understanding of biculturalism is recognition of the relationship that exists between cultural response patterns, modes of engagement (thinking), and cultural identity (see Figure 1.4). Here again, it is helpful to utilize the

Cultural Response Pattern	Mode of Engagement	Cultural Identity	
		Individual	Social
Alienation	Absolute	Dominant	Dominant
Dualism	Dichotomized	Primary	Dominant
Separatism	Absolute	Primary	Primary
Negotiation	Critical	Primary	Bicultural

FIGURE 1.4: Relationship of Cultural Response Pattern, Modes of Engagement, and Cultural Identity

four previously discussed response patterns to illustrate the dynamics inherent in the relationship between these three variables. In addition, the variable of cultural identity is presented with respect to both an individual and a social sub-category.

Cultural alienation and separatist responses, commonly reflective of a mode of engagement, associated with absolute thinking,[2] generally seek to negate, elimi-nate, or move away from the tension, conflict, and contradictions that result from cultural differences. This mode of engagement reinforces a form of cultural iden-tity that is also absolute or total in nature. Hence, an alienation response pattern is commonly associated with individuals who espouse an exclusive identification with the dominant culture, while cultural separatism response patterns are associ-ated with individuals who hold an exclusively primary cultural identity. A dichoto-mized mode of engagement generally results in dualism response patterns, which are likely to result from a cultural identity that is also dichotomized between the primary culture and the dominant culture. It is important to note that, although the dualist context acknowledges the existence of both cultures, its dichotomized mode of engagement also results in undialectical responses due to its efforts to avoid or deny the tension and contradictions that result from cultural conflicts. Cultural negotiation response patterns most commonly result from a critical mode of engagement that seeks to contend with the tension and contradictions inher-ent in cultural differences and conflicts. This mechanism functions to affirm a bicultural social identity, while reinforcing a solid individual identification with the primary culture.

Although these categories can assist educators to understand better the dynamics of the biculturation process, it is critical to remember that these pat-terns are not fixed. Given the contradictory nature of human consciousness and the complexity of the survival mechanisms that motivate these response patterns, bicultural students will exhibit many different variations of responses, depending on the level of their primary cultural socialization, the degree of their bilingualism, their consistent association with other bicultural students, the teacher's cultural orientation, the degree of peer pressure, institutional constraints, and other socioeconomic variables.

It is readily apparent that some of the response patterns described above incorporate principles set forth by the various bicultural theories discussed previously. But what the critical bicultural perspective proposed here attempts to do is to challenge the reductionistic and deterministic influences that shape the earlier theories of biculturalism. If educators are to meet the pedagogical needs of bicultural students, it is essential for them to recognize the ideological underpinnings that shape bicultural responses and the contradictions and tensions that result from students' efforts to survive in the midst of serious forms of educational oppression.

It is important that educators recognize that, whether or not a student from a subordinate culture perceives herself or himself as a *bicultural being*, the fact that the individual is raised within the sociocultural and class constraints dictated by the dominant culture places the student, from a sociopolitical standpoint, in a culturally subordinate position. It is the pervasive quality of hegemonic control that so often obscures the truth of this reality, particularly for those bicultural individuals who perceive themselves as adjusting successfully to the social constraints through their identification with the culture of the oppressor (Freire, 1970). This clearly points to the need for educators to examine critically bicultural responses in terms of resistance, particularly when these responses fall to result in behaviors, attitudes, or relationships that empower bicultural students by preparing them to engage as subjects in their world.

As a consequence of traditional pedagogical theories and practices, bicultural students often face isolation, alienation, and despair in public schools, because there exist few opportunities for these students to reflect together on their lived experiences and to explore critically how these experiences relate to their participation in the larger society and to their process of emancipation. Instead, student voices are silenced as "the discourse of the other" is systematically ignored in the process of schooling (Giroux, 1988a). If the bicultural voice is to be awakened and students of color are to become active social agents in the world, educators must create the conditions for a genuine form of cultural democracy to take root in the classroom.

A Philosophy of Cultural Democracy

In an effort to develop a critical theory of cultural democracy, it is useful to examine first Ramirez and Castañeda's (1974) philosophy of cultural democracy for the bilingual classroom. One of the primary objectives of their work is to challenge the negative effects of the Anglo conformity/assimilation ideology of the melting pot theory, which—by implication—reduces all other cultural forms to one of inferior value, status, and importance. Hence, their notion of cultural democracy argues that

> ...an individual can be bicultural and still be loyal to American ideals. Cultural democracy is a philosophical precept which recognizes that the way a person communicates, relates to others, seeks support and recognition from his [sic] environment...and thinks and learns. [Cognition] is a product of the value system of the home and community. Furthermore, educational environments or policies that do not recognize the individual's right, as guaranteed by the Civil Rights Act of 1964, to remain identified with the culture and language of his cultural group, are culturally undemocratic. (Ramirez & Castañeda, 1974, p. 23)

More specifically, a philosophy of cultural democracy argues for the right of each individual to be educated in her or his own language and learning style, which, according to Ramirez and Castañeda, has been found to be associated with one's language community. This also implies that every child has the right to maintain a bicultural identity—that is, the right to retain their identification with her or his culture of origin while simultaneously adopting American values and lifestyle. This philosophy encourages institutions to develop learning milieus, curriculum materials, and teaching strategies that are sensitive to the child's cultural orientation, and thus language and cognitive styles (Hernandez, 1976).

Further, the education of bicultural students within the context of a culturally democratic environment is considered by Valverde (1978) to support five specific purposes for students and the school:

1. reducing language and educational disabilities through the opportunity to learn in one's native language;
2. reinforcing the relations of the school and the home through a common bond;
3. projecting the individual into an atmosphere of personal identification;
4. giving the student a base for success in the field of work;
5. preserving and enriching the cultural and human resources of a people.

In contrast to the exclusionist Anglo conformity view, Ramirez and Castañeda characterize the culturally democratic environment as one that:

1. considers the student's language, heritage, cultural values, and learning styles as educationally important;
2. views the home culture as determining unique communication, relational, incentive motivational, and cognitive styles and utilizes these styles as a basis for teacher training;

3. recognizes the child's personality as acceptable and as a means whereby the child can explore new cultural forms related to communication, human relations, incentive motivation, and cognition;
4. works to change the educational style of the school through greater parent participation, new teaching strategies, curriculum development, and assessment of techniques; and *how?*
5. holds as one of its major goals the child's formation of a bicultural identity.

Despite the many contributions of the Ramirez and Castañeda philosophy of cultural democracy to the field of bicultural education and its promise as a politicizing educational construct, it nonetheless lacks many of the critical qualities essential to the education of bicultural students as members of a subordinate culture. The deficits of the model are most apparent in the fact that it can too easily deteriorate into a positivist instrumentalist modality that perceives culture as predictable, deterministic, neutral, oversimplified, and at moments even relativistic in nature. And although it argues for changing the cultural realities of classrooms, it fails to address critically the necessary shift in power relationships required in schools and society in order to involve bicultural students in an active process of empowerment, one that can assist them to effectively find their voice and support their development of collective identity and political solidarity.

Critical Democracy and the Process of Schooling

In an effort to expand on the emancipatory intent of Ramirez and Castañeda's philosophy of cultural democracy, it would be helpful to examine the concept of *critical democracy*, particularly as it relates to the process of schooling. This would provide the critical dimension that is missing in the work of Ramirez and Castañeda and would be useful in specifically addressing the relationship of democracy to the notions of student participation and solidarity, as well as the development of voice in the process of schooling.

The term "democracy" is derived from the Greek words *demos* and *kratos*, meaning rule by the people or the many; in addition, because there were so many poor in Greece, it was taken to mean rule by the poor. Hence, despite the fact that democracy seldom has been equated with overt social conflict, historically it has never been realized without a struggle, and that struggle has always been related to social and economic equality (Arblaster, 1987). Even today, the American struggle for democracy and equality, particularly in the classroom, continues to be reflected along the lines of social class and cultural struggle.

The recognition of democracy as a site of struggle is significant to the issue of cultural democracy, where the struggle is focused specifically on the issue of culture and power and on who controls cultural truths. Unfortunately, democracy often has been reduced simplistically to an unqualified principle of majority rule, while minority groups are ignored as a part of the society at large. When this occurs—and consequently minority interests, views, and convictions are disregarded in the institutional process of decision-making, and certain groups are permanently relegated to a minority position—such a democracy is likely to become unstable and lose legitimacy in the eyes of its citizens. This results because democracy cannot function where there does not exist a sense of common will or common interest, and this cannot develop where a foundation of social and economic equality is missing. Arblaster (1987) addresses this need more specifically in his writings on democracy:

> [Democracy] needs a foundation not only of shared values but also of shared experience, so that people identify with the political system to which they belong, and can trust its procedures and outcomes. This means not only that those procedures are seen and felt to be fair. It is also necessary that no significant minorities feel themselves to be permanently excluded from power and influence; that groups and individuals sense that they are roughly equal in their ability to influence the outcome of communal policymaking; and that those outcomes embody what people recognize to be the general interests of society rather than merely the combination or balance of the interests of various particular and organized groups or specific interest. (p. 78)[3]

From this perspective, it can be better understood why the gross and excessive forms of inequality that exist in the process of American schooling threaten the coherence of society and hence negate the principles of equality, of which democracy is an expression. It also clearly supports the notion that the contradiction between an espoused theory of democracy and a lived experience of inequality (and the obvious diffusion of power that results) is greatly responsible for the growing social tensions existing in the relationship between subordinate cultural groups and the public schools, whose pedagogical aim centers around the perpetuation of cultural domination and technocratic control. And as a further consequence, it is precisely this form of social disequilibrium that also functions effectively to prevent the concrete development of a genuine common interest and a spirit of solidarity among different groups in society. John Dewey, in writing about democratic schooling, addresses the impact that this form of inequality has on students:

> In order to have a large number of values in common, all members of the group must have an equitable opportunity to receive and to take from others. There must be a large variety of shared undertakings and experiences. Otherwise, the influences which educate some into masters educate others into slaves. And the experience of each party loses in mean-

ing when the free interchange of varying modes of life experience is arrested.... [This] lack of free equitable intercourse which springs from a variety of shared interests makes intellectual stimulation unbalanced.... The more activity is restricted to a few definite lines—as it is when there are rigid class [cultural] lines preventing adequate interplay of experiences—the more action tends to become routine on the part of the class at a disadvantage, and capricious, aimless, and explosive on the part of the class having the materially fortunate position. (Dewey, 1916, pp. 84–85).

Dewey also argues strongly that schooling in the United States should function as a primary vehicle for students to develop an ethical foundation for their participation in the process of democracy and a critical understanding of democracy as a moral ideal from which to establish a sense of community and struggle for such principles as freedom, liberty, and common good. But in order for schools to meet this challenge, Dewey proposes that educators create environments where there is a clear recognition of mutual interest as the basic factor in social control, and where there is a commitment to enter into a continuous form of readjustment through meeting the new situations produced by a variety of social discourses. He believes this to be an essential step in deconstructing the "fear of intercourse with others" by permitting conflict between students to occur so as to enable them to learn from each other and thereby expand their understanding of the world. In this context, Dewey defines democracy as

...primarily a mode of associated living, of conjoint communicated experience. The extension in space of the numbers of individuals who participate in an interest so that each has to refer [her or] his own action to that of others and to consider the action of others to give point and direction to his own is equivalent to the breaking down of those barriers of class, race, and national territory which kept men [and women] from perceiving the full import of their activity. These more numerous and more varied points of contact denote a greater diversity of stimuli to which an individual has to respond; they consequently put a premium on variation in his action. They secure a liberation of powers which remain suppressed as long as the invitations to action are partial, as they must be in a group which in its exclusiveness shuts out many interests. (Dewey, 1916, p. 87)

This notion of schools as apprenticeships in democracy is also shared by Freire (1978). In his work, Freire points to the "habit of submission" that curtails subordinate classes from seeking to integrate themselves with reality, which, he argues, results from their undeveloped capacity for critical thought—a phenomenon of socially conditioned dependency and a lack of experience with participation in the democratic process. He argues that it is only through participation in an educational climate in which open dialogue is fostered that students can develop the skills for critical engagement with their world and a genuine sense of participation in a common life. Thus, Freire posits this axiom: Without dialogue, self-government cannot exist. Here, he speaks to the notion of the free and creative consciousness that results from dialogue indispensable to authentically democratic environments. He elaborates on the relationship of democracy and this idea of "transitive consciousness":

> Democracy requires dialogue, participation, political and social responsibility, as well as a degree of social and political solidarity.... Before it becomes a political form, democracy is a form of life, characterized above all by a strong component of transitive consciousness. Such transitivity can neither appear nor develop except as men [and women] are launched into debate, participating in the examination of common problems. (Freire, 1978, pp. 28–29)

From this discussion it also becomes evident that a student's ability to participate and enter into dialogue within the classroom and, as a result, participate in a democratic social process in the world is also critically connected to the development of voice—that is, voice as it relates to the variety of ways by which students actively participate in dialogue and attempt to make themselves heard and understood, as well as the manner in which they define themselves as social beings. Giroux describes this concept of student voice in the following manner:

> Voice refers to the principles of dialogue as they are enunciated and enacted within particular social settings. The concept of voice represents the unique instances of self-expression through which students affirm their own class, culture, racial, and gender identities. A student's voice is necessarily shaped by personal history and distinctive lived engagement with the surrounding culture. The category of voice, then, refers to the means at our disposal—the discourses available to use—to make ourselves understood and listened to, and to define ourselves as active participants in the world.... The concept of voice...provides an important basis for constructing and demonstrating the fundamental imperatives of a critical democracy. (Giroux, 1988a, p. 199)

The notion of student voice is fundamental to the struggle for democracy and equality in the classroom, particularly as it relates to the development of voice in students of color. It is connected to the control of power and the legitimation of specific student discourses as acceptable truths or rejected fallacies, and consequently determines who speaks and who is silenced. Also significant to this discussion is the reality that, when bicultural students are consistently silenced by teachers, they often are trapped in classrooms with teachers who not only prevent them from finding their voice, but who also thwart their contextual understanding of how what they are learning in the classroom can be used to transform their lives. As a result, they are conditioned into a state of dependency on a system that they do not understand and are unable to influence because they lack the critical skills necessary to participate and the social and self empowerment to make their needs, interests, and concerns heard. This, then, leads to a form of social isolation that prevents the development of a sense of community and solidarity, and that negates any possibility for a genuine process of democracy to take place in society.

Giroux, greatly concerned with the question of voice, speaks to the kind of environment teachers must cultivate in the classroom to prevent the silencing of students:

> Organize classroom relationships so that students can draw on and confirm those dimensions of their own histories and experiences that are deeply rooted in the surrounding community,...assume pedagogical responsibility for attempting to understand the relationships and forces that influence students outside the immediate context of the classroom,...develop curricula and pedagogical practices around those community traditions, histories, and forms of knowledge that are often ignored within the dominant school culture,...create the conditions where students come together to speak, to engage in dialogue, to share their stories, and to struggle together within social relations that strengthen rather than weaken possibilities for active citizenship [and democracy]. (Giroux, 1988a, pp. 199–201)

What emerges from this discussion on democracy and the process of schooling are the fundamental principles on which to develop further a critical theory of cultural democracy. Central to any theory that seeks to speak to the notion of democracy in the classroom is the requirement that it address seriously the themes of student participation, solidarity, common interest, and the development of voice. It is not enough to focus on specific cultural and/or cognitive determinants or questions related to curricular content. This is not to say that certain aspects of these educational concerns are not vital to a bicultural pedagogy, but rather to emphasize that these alone will not necessarily ensure a democratic environment. If bicultural students are to become competent in the democratic process, they must be given the opportunities to experience it actively as it gradually becomes a part of their personal history. But this can only be accomplished if a culturally democratic educational environment exists; one in which students may participate actively and freely, and where they will receive the consistent support and encouragement required for them to develop their bicultural voice so they may learn to use it toward their social empowerment and emancipation.

The Awakening of the Bicultural Voice

The concept of voice constitutes one of the most important democratic essentials related to the process of student empowerment and the ability to participate in and influence the manner in which power is relegated in society—so much so that any theory of cultural democracy must specifically consider the development of voice as it relates to the pedagogical needs of bicultural students. This is particularly significant given the forces of hegemony and cultural invasion at work in the manner that bicultural students perceive themselves, their communities, and their ability to participate in the world.

As suggested in the previous section, students can only develop their voice through opportunities to enter into dialogue and engage in a critical process of reflection from which they can share their thoughts, ideas, and lived experiences with others in an open and free manner. Herein, lies a primary requirement that so often is missing in the classroom experience of bicultural students. This generally occurs because the dominant pedagogy of American schools predominantly reflects the values, worldview, and belief system of the dominant culture's middle and upper classes, while it neglects and ignores the lived experiences of subordinate cultures. Hence, students of color are silenced and their bicultural experiences negated and ignored, while they are systematically educated into the discourse of the dominant culture—an ethnocentric ideology that perceives the discourse of the other as inferior, invaluable, and deficient in regard to the aims of American society. This manifests itself in various forms of cultural invasion that, consciously or unconsciously, teach bicultural students to deny their lived cultures and their bicultural voice, and to take on uncritically the ideology of the dominant culture.

In light of the hegemonic forces active in the hidden curriculum and in classroom relations, the bicultural voice can seldom develop within the school context unless students of color receive the opportunity to enter into dialogue with one another. It is primarily through the dynamics of the *bicultural dialogue* that students can come together to reflect on the common lived experiences of their bicultural process and their common responses to issues of cultural resistance, alienation, negotiation, affirmation, and oppression. In this way, bicultural students can begin to break through the rigidly held perspectives that can result when those who hold power inauthentically name their experience for them. Also important to this process is the role of the bicultural educator who functions as guide, model, and support, and who facilitates the critical (and often fearful) journey into the previously prohibited terrain of the bicultural discourse—a discourse that is often only felt or sensed, and seldom articulated.

Despite this pedagogical need, most teachers of color, unfortunately, repeat the educational patterns they experienced as children and later learned in teacher education programs. Hence, what generally occurs in most classrooms is the silencing of the bicultural experience by teachers who have been trained to concentrate their efforts on creating an inauthentic climate of cohesion, conformity, and harmony. In so doing, they fail to involve bicultural students in their own learning and to provide opportunities for them to enter into dialogue regarding the cultural conflicts and social contradictions they experience in the classroom and in their communities.

It is precisely in meeting the student's need to participate in bicultural dialogue with others that the bicultural teacher can most provide assistance in facilitating the process across this terrain of struggle, and thus cultivate through a critical process with students a spirit of possibility and empowerment. Bicultural educators who have found their own voice can provide an effective *bicultural mirror*, which may validate, support, and encourage students through this process during moments of cognitive disequilibrium, and help them discover a language that accurately describes the feelings, ideas, and observations that previously have not fit into any of the definitions of experience provided by the dominant educational discourse. Above all, this represents a critical effort to assist students in integrating themselves as complete human beings in the world by recognizing the truths embedded in their personal reflections and the substance of their everyday lives—in essence, to awaken the bicultural voice. The development of voice and social empowerment go hand in hand as bicultural students peel away the layers of oppression and denial, undergo a deconstruction of the conditioned definitions of who they are, and emerge with a sense of their existence as historically situated social agents who can utilize their understanding of their world and themselves to enter into dialogue with those who are culturally different.

At this point, it is imperative to note that this does not mean that the bicultural voice is the only voice bicultural students need. But it does suggest that it represents a major step toward their self-empowerment, because it is the voice most intimately linked to their personal identity. Further, it is by way of the bicultural voice that students can develop the self-empowerment required to participate in the collective public voice—a voice that must be built around a collaborative effort and commitment of the many to examine critically their collective lived experiences so that together they might discover the common good. In this manner, bicultural students can also develop the ability, confidence, and desire to acknowledge the similarities, honor the differences, examine the possibilities, and struggle openly with a genuine spirit of solidarity in the context of a multicultural society.

The role of the White educator in the development of the bicultural voice is also significant to this discussion, in that often the White teacher is one of the few people from the dominant culture with whom bicultural students have any contact with on a regular basis. Consequently, the White teacher can become for the bicultural student the primary reflection of not only the public institutions, but also the society at large. How conscious teachers are of this phenomenon, as well as the histories and stories of the bicultural communities in which bicultural students reside, is fundamental to their ability to assist students in developing their voice. White educators who are working with bicultural students must first come to acknowledge their own limitations, prejudices, and biases, and must be willing to enter into dialogue with their students in a spirit of humility and with respect for the knowledge that students bring to the classroom.

Despite how well-meaning many teachers may be, often it is at this juncture of power (and control) that they fail bicultural students. This commonly occurs because any genuine acknowledgment of one's limitations is closely related to letting go of the control (power) associated with knowing (or holding authority), and in the process permitting the student to teach the teacher (Freire, 1970). This process truly requires the teacher to share the power more equitably and, in so doing, to empower the student through critically engaging, challenging, affirming, and incorporating into the classroom the knowledge that the bicultural student has about self and community. The emphasis here is placed on the recognition that the White critical educator has much to learn from as well as to teach bicultural students in the context of a culturally democratic classroom. From students, teachers can discover what bicultural people feel, think, dream, and live, while the teachers can provide for their students the opportunity to develop their critical thinking skills, examine their histories, reflect on the world, and engage with the dominant educational discourse as free social agents who are able to influence and transform their world.

Most important to any educational theory of cultural democracy is recognition by the educator—regardless of her or his class, race, or ethnic identity—of the emancipatory needs of working class students of color. In order for bicultural students to develop critical skills in the classroom, there must first be present a culturally democratic environment where these students can find the opportunities to participate freely with others as they learn the forms of knowledge, values, and social practices necessary to understand how society works, where they are located in it, and what inequities exist. It is fundamental that educators remain conscious of the fact that bicultural students shape and are shaped not only by their cultural values but also by their constant struggle to survive within the myriad of cultural contradictions they face in society every day.

Given the different elements introduced in this discussion, what is readily evident is the need to integrate a critical model of bicultural pedagogy built on the foundation of a cultural democracy that not only speaks to issues of particular cultural values and the development of cognitive styles, but also critically addresses the awakening of the bicultural voice and the development of a social consciousness of struggle and solidarity that will prepare bicultural students to undertake the democratic responsibility of participation in their world, morally committed to the liberation and empowerment of all people.

REFERENCES

Arblaster, A. (1987). *Democracy*. Minneapolis: University of Minnesota Press.

Blauner, R. (1972). *Racial Oppression in America*. New York: Harper & Row.

Cole, M., and S. Scribner (1974). *Culture and Thought*. New York: John Wiley & Sons.

Cross, W. E. (1978). "The Thomas and Cross Models on Psychological Nigrescence: A Literature Review." *Journal of Black Psychology* 4: pp. 13–31.

Cummins, J. (1986). "Empowering Minority Students: A Framework for Intervention," *Harvard Educational Review* 56:1 1,18–36.

deAnda, D. (1984). "Bicultural Socialization: Factors Affecting the Minority Experience." *Social Work* 29:2; pp. 101–07.

Dewey, J. (1916). *Democracy and Education*. New York: Free Press

Dixon, V., and Foster, B. (1971). *Beyond Black or White*. Boston: Little Brown.

Du Bois, W. E. B. (1903). *The Souls of Black Folk*. Chicago: A. C. McClurg.

Fanon, F. (1967). *Black Skin, White Masks*. New York: Grove Press.

Freire, P. (1970). *Pedagogy of the Oppressed*. New York: Seabury Press.

Freire P. (1978). *Education for Critical Consciousness*. New York: Seabury Press.

Giroux, H. (1990). "The Politics of Postmodernism: Rethinking the Boundaries of Race and Ethnicity," *Journal of Urban and Cultural Studies* 1:1; 5–38.

Giroux, H. (1988a). *Teachers as Intellectuals*. Westport: Bergin and Garvey.

Giroux, H. (1988b). *Schooling and the Struggle for Public Life*. Minneapolis: University of Minnesota Press.

Giroux, H. (1981). *Ideology, Culture, and the Process of Schooling*. Philadelphia: Temple University Press.

Goldenberg, A. (1987). "Low-Income Hispanic Parents' Contribution to Their First Grade Children's Word Recognition Skills." *Anthropology and Education Quarterly* 18:3; 149–79.

Gramsci, A. (1971). *Selections from* Prison Notebooks. New York: International Publications.

Held, 1980. *Introduction to Critical Theory*. London: Heinemann.

Hernandez, C., et al. (1976). *Chicanos: Social and Psychological Perspectives*. St. Louis: Mosby.

hooks, b. (1989). *Talking Back*. Boston: South End Press.

Horkheimer, M. (1972). *Critical Theory: Selected Essays*. New York: Herder & Herder.

Hsu, F. (1971). *The Challenge of the American Dream: The Chinese in the United States*. Belmont, CA: Wadsworth.

Jay, M. 1973. *The Dialectical Imagination*. Boston: Little Brown,.

Kitano, H. (1969). *Japanese-Americans: The Evolution of a Subculture*. Englewood Cliffs, NJ: Prentice-Hall.

Kozol, J. (1990). "The New Untouchables," *Newsweek*, Special Issue: 48–53.

Memmi, A. (1965). *The Colonizer and the Colonized*. Boston: Beacon Press.

Phillips, C. (1988). "Nurturing Diversity for Today's Children and Tomorrow's Leaders," *Young Children* 43:2; 42–47.

Ramirez, M., and Castañeda, A. (1974). *Cultural Democracy: Bicognitive Development and Education.* New York: Academic Press

Rashid, H. (1981). "Early Childhood Education as a Cultural Transition for African-American Children," *Educational Research Quarterly* 6:3; 55–63.

Red Horse, J.G., et al. (1981). "Family Behavior of Urban American Indians." In R. Dana, ed., *Human Services for Cultural Minorities.* Baltimore: University Park Press.

Simon, R. (1988). "For a Pedagogy of Possibility," *Critical Pedagogy Networker* 1; 1–4.

Solis, A. (1980). "Theory of Biculturality." *Calmecac de Aztlan en Los* 1:1; 7–12.

Solis, A. (1981). "Theory of Biculturality." *Calmecac de Aztlan en Los* 2:1; 36–41.

Sue, S., and Sue D. W. (1978). "Chinese-American Personality and Mental Health." *Amerasia Journal* 1:2; 36–49.

Valentine, C. (1971). "Deficit, Difference, and Bicultural Models of AfroAmerican Behavior." *Harvard Educational Review* 41:2; 137–57.

Valverde, L. (1978). *Bilingual Education for Latinos.* Washington, DC: Association for Supervision and Curriculum Development.

Wright, R. N. (1953). *The Outsider.* New York: Harper & Row.

NOTES

1. Ramirez and Castañeda (1974) have included in their text *Cultural Democracy: Bicognitive Development and Education* an "Appendix C: Field-Sensitive-Independent Behavioral Observation Instruments: Child and Teacher," which includes field cognitive assessment tools for use in teacher and student evaluations. The primary purpose of these instruments is to assist educators in determining the degree to which a child may be bicognitive and, from the results, planning a program to increase the child's cognitive flexibility.

2. *Absolute thinking* for the purposes of this discussion is related to a view of a social reality as a totality or whole. This mode of engagement with the world is clearly sustained by the ideological tenets of identity thinking. The Frankfurt School has addressed this notion of *identity thinking* in its work related to culture. A discussion of the Frankfurt School's views on this theme can be found in "Materialism and Metaphysics," in *Critical Theory: Selected Essays* (Horkheimer, 1972); *The Dialectical Imagination* (Jay, 1973); and *Introduction to Critical Theory* (Held, 1980).

3. For an excellent investigation into the definition, historical nature, and principal ideas related to the nature of democracy, see *Democracy* by Anthony Arblaster (1987).

CHAPTER 2

The Politics of Biculturalism

Culture and Difference in the Formation
of *Warriors for Gringostroika*
and *The New Mestizas*

There is a whisper within you that reminds me of who I am...

—GUILLERMO GOMEZ-PENA (1993)

The dormant areas of consciousness are being activated,
awakened.

—GLORIA ANZALDÚA (1987)

The yearning to remember who we are is a subject that is rarely discussed in the
realms of traditional academic discourse. It is not easily measured or observed
by the standard quantification of scientific inquiry, nor is it easily detected in the
qualitative dimension of focus groups and ethnographic research methods. It is a
deeply rooted quality, obscured by layers upon layers of human efforts to survive
the impact of historical amnesia induced by the dominant policies and practices
of advanced capitalism and postmodern culture.

For these reasons, efforts to articulate a conclusive politics of biculturalism
is a highly complex and messy endeavor. Yet it is significant to note that even the
naming of such a phenomenon clearly is linked to an experience of listening to

"the whisper within" and giving voice to an unspoken, yet ever-present memory of difference—"dormant areas of consciousness" that must be awakened. This view is readily supported by the fact that despite countless studies and writings about people of color by white researchers, none names or engages the experience of two-worldness or double consciousness. It was not until scholars of color, such as Du Bois (1903), Fanon (1967), Valentine (1971), Ramirez & Castañeda (1974), Solis (1980), Rashid (1981), Red Horse (1981), deAnda (1984), Buriel (1984), and others began to posit specific theoretical frameworks grounded in their own community histories and cultural knowledge that notions of biculturalism began to appear in the discourse of the social sciences and historical studies. These scholars of color during the last thirty years have made significant contributions to an understanding of biculturalism. As a consequence, there has been a slowly, but consistently, emerging body of work that has attempted to give voice to a variety of explanations of bicultural processes and identities. These efforts, to a greater or lesser degree, have discussed the societal and psychological impact of living between two world views. In more recent years, a new wave of critical scholars of color (Darder, 1991; Akinyela, 1992; Millan, 1993; and Romay, 1993) in different disciplines has also begun to address the notion of biculturalism in their work.

Toward a Critical Theory of Biculturalism

The story never stops beginning or ending. It appears headless and bottomless for it is built on differences (p. 2).
—TRINH MINH-HA (1989)

Within a critical theoretical tradition, biculturalism must be understood as a contested terrain of difference. It is upon this highly complex and ambiguous ground that subordinate groups create both a private and public space in which to forge battle with the faces of oppression, while flying high their banners of cultural self-determination. Biculturalism as a critical perspective acknowledges openly and engages forthrightly the significance of power relations in structuring and prescribing societal definitions of truth, rules of normalcy, and notions of legitimacy which often defy and denigrate the cultural existence and lived experiences of subordinate groups.

The story of where, when, and how biculturation processes and identities begin, move, and end is generally a difficult one to recount, given the historical and contextual dimensions which shape the particular survival requirements of different groups at any given moment in their histories. This is to say that each subordinate group grapples with the effects of cultural imperialism according to the manner in which geographical, political, social, and economic forces shape and influence the efforts of members of a group to resist, oppose, negotiate, or even accept passive or voluntary assimilation into the dominant group.

Further, given the wide-reaching effects of advanced capitalism and a deeply rooted tradition of cultural oppression and domination in the United States, African Americans, Chicanos, Puerto Ricans, Native Americans, Asians, and other subordinate cultural groups for the most part exist in a hybridized state. This is to say that their histories of forced interaction with the dominant culture have required consistent forms of adaptational behaviors which have, in many instances, eroded, restructured, and reconstructed the language system, cultural beliefs, and social traditions of these groups.

Michael Omi and Howard Winant (1983a) argue that throughout most of the history of the United States, the discourses of subordinate cultures received very little political legitimacy. "However democratic the United States may have been in other respects, with respect to racial [and cultural] minorities it may be characterized as having been to varying degrees despotic for much of its history" (p. 55). Given a collective history of social marginalization, exploitation, cultural invasion, powerlessness, and systematic violence,[1] all subordinate cultures in this country currently experience an advanced state of hybridization. Understanding this phenomenon requires that we acknowledge the deep historical consequences of being driven out of the dominant political space and relegated to a subordinate position. Black, indigenous, and mestizo communities across the United States evolved over the last four hundred years through their efforts to survive conditions of oppression, develop alternative structures, and resist annihilation of cultural knowledge and traditions.[2]

It cannot be denied that patterns of cultural, economic, and political oppression have been repeated in the international arena wherever European colonizers and their descendants have appropriated the land and resources of indigenous populations. Usurping the people's natural resources, destroying their economic and agricultural self-sufficiency, placing the children in foreign educational environments, devaluing the language community, and interfering with the generational transmission of spiritual knowledge are all common strategies of cultural imperialism. As such, every subordinate cultural group in the United States, to one extent or another, has been required to contend with the destructive impact of all or some of these strategies. Most insidious are the established relationships of domination and dependency which, despite ongoing and persistent group efforts to resist cultural oppression, further complicate the struggle to affirm the cultural integrity and self-determination of subordinate cultural groups.

Rethinking Ethnicity and the Formation of Identity

> We will not remain the same. Either we re-make ourselves or we
> will be remade by others (p. 24).
>
> —GONZALO SANTOS (1992)

In many respects, biculturalism entails an ongoing process of identity recovery, construction, and reconstruction driven by collective efforts of subordinate cultural groups to build community solidarity, engage tensions surrounding nationality differences, revitalize the boundaries of subordinate cultures, and redefine the meaning of cultural identity within the current social context (Nagel, 1994). Further, this phenomenon is influenced by the persistent efforts of those who have been historically marginalized to establish a sense of place from which to struggle against relations of domination. Along the same lines, Stuart Hall (1990a) argues that a notion of ethnicity is required in order to truly engage the relationship between identity and difference.

> There is no way, it seems to me, in which people of the world can act, can speak, can create, can come in from the margins and talk, can begin to reflect on their own experience unless they come from some place, they come from some history, they inherit certain cultural traditions. What we've learned about the theory of enunciation is that there's no enunciation without positionality. You have to position yourself somewhere in order to say anything at all...the relation that peoples of the world now have to their own past is, of course, part of the discovery of their own ethnicity. They need to honor the hidden histories from which they come. They need to understand the languages which they've been taught not to speak. They need to understand and revalue the traditions and inheritances of cultural expression and creativity. And in that sense, the past is not only a position from which to speak, but it is also an absolutely necessary resource in what one has to say (p. 19).

Hall's use of the term *ethnicity* provides us with a framework upon which to rethink the analytical value of ethnicity with respect to biculturalism, particularly as it relates to identity formation. This requires a dialectical reading of ethnicity[3] that, first of all, retrieves the category from the political opportunism and academic domain of neo-conservatives, and secondly, challenges the failure of critical scholars to conceptualize the liberatory dimensions of this category in more fully class-specific terms. Thus, a critical definition of ethnicity is one that engages, in both concept and articulation, a politics of difference and class specificity within the context of a changing economy and postmodern world.

On Essentialism

> I voice my ideas without hesitation or fear because I am speaking,
> finally, about myself (p. 189).
>
> —JUNE JORDAN (1992)

In conventional critical debates about culture, there is generally a tremendous uneasiness when there is any effort made to seriously explore notions of cultural consciousness and the merits of knowledge that is rooted in the lived cultural experience of marginalized communities.[4] Often this uneasiness seems to stem most directly from an overarching commitment to protect Western assumptions of individualism, objectivity, and universal truth which deceptively conceal institutionalized structures of entitlement and privilege embedded in critiques of identity politics that, intentionally or unintentionally, function as "the new chic way to silence…marginal groups" (hooks, 1994, p. 83). And though it is true that cultural groups are not entities that exist apart from individuals, neither are they just arbitrary classifications of individuals by attributes which are external to or accidental to their cultural identities.

> Group meanings partially constitute people's identities in terms of the cultural forms, social situations, and history that group members know as theirs, because their meanings have been either forced upon them or forged by them or both. Groups are real not as substances, but as forms of social relations…. A person's sense of history, affinity, and separateness, even the person's mode of reasoning, evaluation, and expressing feelings, are constituted partly by her or his group affinities (Young, 1990, pp. 44–45).

Along with the traditional academic anxiety over obliterating the individual as subject are the overzealous denouncements of essentialism whenever scholars of color attempt to grapple with those actual experiences of cultural identity rooted in social and material conditions of racialized relations—experiences that, more often than not, reinforce a strong sense of cultural consciousness and solidarity among members of subordinate cultural communities. There is an expectation that they abdicate the power of their experience, without concern for the fact that "only the powerful can insist on a neat separation between the thought and reality…a separation that serves them well" (Sampson, 1993, p. 1227). It is not surprising then to note that often critiques of essentialism embody the mistaken dichotomous notion that inquiry focused on subordinate life experiences automatically precludes recognition of in-group differences and cultural change, and amounts to nothing more than the act of reducing culture to a theory of reifying collectivity. As a consequence, scholars of color whose research engages cultural questions in their own communities are often marginalized by the "enlightened" mainstream of their disciplines, while those who are deemed more "open-minded" by Eurocentric standards are permitted to play freely in the arena of intellectual thought.

At this point, it is imperative to stress that I am not suggesting that subjective interpretations of lived experience alone can suffice in the struggle to overcome and transform structural conditions of domination, whether in theory or practice.

And further, it cannot be denied that claims to exclusive "authority" derived solely from lived experience can be misused to silence and undermine the possibility of dialogue. Yet, despite these possible dangers, we must find the manner to incorporate in our intellectual work those ways of knowing that are rooted in experience. hooks (1994) addresses eloquently this idea in the following passage from her essay "Essentialism and Experience."

> Though opposed to any essentialist practice that constructs identity in a monolithic, exclusionary way, I do not want to relinquish the power of experience as a standpoint on which to base analysis or formulate theory. For example, I am disturbed when all the courses in black history or literature at some colleges and universities are solely taught by white people, not because I think that they cannot know these realities but that they know them differently. Truthfully, if I had been given the opportunity to study African American critical thought from a progressive black professor instead of the progressive white woman with whom I studied...I would have chosen the black person. Although I learned a great deal from this white woman professor, I sincerely believe that I would have learned even more from a progressive black professor, because this individual would have brought to the class that unique mixture of experiential and analytical ways of knowing—this is, a privileged standpoint. It cannot be acquired through books or even distanced observation and study of a particular reality. To me this privileged standpoint does not emerge from "the authority of experience" but rather from the passion of experience, the passion of remembrance (p. 90).

Cultural Consciousness and Decolonization

> Whereas the colonized usually has only a choice between retraction of his being and a frenzied attempt at identification with the colonizer, the [decolonized] has brought into existence a new, positive, efficient personality, whose richness is provided... by his certainty that he embodies a decisive moment of [cultural] consciousness (p. 103).
>
> —FRANTZ FANON (1964)

It is impossible to arrive at an emancipatory politics of biculturalism without questions of cultural consciousness and knowledge derived from lived experience receiving a rightful place within critical discourses on culture and difference. Likewise, the reality of subordinate groups cannot be sufficiently grasped without a foundational understanding of culture as an epistemological process that is shaped by a complex dialectical relationship of social systems of beliefs and practices which constantly moves members between the dynamic tension of cultural preservation and cultural change. This is to say that no culture (particularly within the Western postmodern context of advanced capitalism) exists as a fixed, static, or absolute entity, since culture, and hence cultural identity, is a relationally constituted phenomenon, activated and produced through constant social negotiation between others and one's own integration in the daily life and history of the community (Epstein, 1987). "It is something that happens over time, that is never absolutely stable, that is subject to the play of history and the play of difference" (Hall, 1990a, p. 15).

Nevertheless, forms of cultural consciousness, grounded in collective memories of historical events, language, social traditions, and community life, exist. This collective experience of affinity that emerges from such forms of cultural knowledge is often echoed in historical discursive accounts of African Americans, Latinos, Native Americans, and Asian Americans in this country. For example, it is not unusual for a person who identifies ethnically with the Latin American cultural experience to readily discuss the differences in affinity experienced when immersed within a Spanish-speaking versus an English-speaking context. This experience of affinity is a powerful connecting and perpetuating force in the lives of members of subordinate cultural groups—a force so strong that it continues to play a significant role in supporting a politics of identity, resistance, self-determination, and cultural nationalism among members of historically disenfranchised cultural communities worldwide.

In light of this, it is no wonder that all strategies of colonial oppression, to one extent or another, function to interfere with cultural community beliefs and practices that foster cultural integrity and cohesion among colonized subjects (Fanon, 1964). This process of cultural subjugation continues within the current so-called post-colonial era. This is readily evident in a multitude of economic, political, legal, educational, and religious institutional policies and practices in the United States aimed at furthering the assimilation process of subordinate groups. More specifically, we see it at work today in the forging of trade agreements that solidify the labor market's exploitation of workers of color, English-only initiatives to interfere with the advancement of bilingualism, covert and overt educational strategies that support cultural domination, laws to prevent particular religious activities of groups who exist outside Judeo-Christian traditions, the current inflammatory politics of immigration control as evidenced in California's passage of Proposition 187, and the worldwide commodification of subordinate cultural forms as multinational profit ventures.

There can be no question that biculturalism in the United States has evolved from a set of conscious and unconscious adaptational strategies to preserve significant dimensions of cultural knowledge and collective identity, adapt to changing material conditions, and resist institutional forms of psychological and physical violence (Young, 1991). In many respects, the bicultural process reflects what Frantz Fanon (1963) describes as a process of decolonization where "the meeting of two forces, opposed to each other by their very nature, which in fact owe their originality to the sort of substantiation which results from and is nourished by [the political and economic context of domination]." Biculturalism can then best be understood as incorporating the complex multilayered realities that shape a people's cultural and material struggle for survival. It is a phenomenon that "is born of violent struggle, consciousness raising and the reconstruction of identities" (West, 1993, p. 15), and one that is most intensely felt within those subordinate cultural contexts that most greatly differ from the established social beliefs, expectations, and norms of the dominant group. As such, subordinate communities continue to be stigmatized by both external and internalized perceptions of inferiority and deficit, whereby their members are, for the most part, viewed as inadequately prepared or socially unfit to enter mainstream American life.

Growing Poverty and the Evasion of Class

[P]olitical [economic] questions are disguised as cultural ones,
and as such become insoluble (p. 149).
—ANTONIO GRAMSCI (1971)

At this juncture, it must be stressed that the dominant culture and its fabrication of the American middle-class mainstream are clearly driven by the political economy of advanced capitalism, with its overwhelming emphasis on the interests of the marketplace and its "tendency to homogenize rather than diversify human experience" (Wood, 1994, p. 28). Even more important is the recognition that postmodern mechanisms of cultural domination in the United States and abroad are most directly linked to the domination of multinational firms and new international divisions of labor. The impact of these rapidly changing and deepening economic and class relations serves to perpetuate the embroilment of subordinate cultural communities in a fierce struggle for economic survival with fewer and fewer possibilities of self-sufficiency. And despite the growing number of professionals of color and the glossy image portrayal of their success, the majority of American institutions, with their accompanying resources, continue to be overwhelmingly controlled by a cadre of elite white males who are, slowly but steadily, being joined by their female counterparts. The consequences have resulted in an actual decrease in the proportional wealth and resources of communities of color over the last thirty years (Children's Defense Fund, 1994).[5] This widening economic gap is directly linked to what Xavier Gorostiaga (1993) characterizes as the "dominant fact of our age—growing poverty" (p. 4). In his analysis of a 1992 United Nations report, he explains:

> [T]hroughout the world the last decade has been characterized by the rise of inequality between the rich and the poor....In 1989 the richest fifth controlled 82.7 percent of the revenue; 81.2 percent of the world trade; 94.6 percent of commercial loans; 80.6 percent of internal savings and 80.5 percent of investment. If in terms of distribution the panorama is untenable, it is equally so regarding resources: The rich countries possess approximately one-fifth of the world population but consume seventy percent of world energy, seventy-five percent of the metals, eighty-five percent of the timber, and sixty percent of the food. Such a pattern of development...is only viable in the degree to which the extreme inequality is maintained, as otherwise the world resources would be exhausted. Therefore, *inequality is not a distortion of the system. It is a systematic prerequisite for growth and permanence of the present system* (p. 4, author's emphasis).

It is the tendency to ignore or overlook this "systematic prerequisite" of capitalism in discussions of culture, difference, and identity politics in the United States that motivates Ellen Meiksins Wood (1994) to question why "having recognized the complexities, diversities, and multiple oppressions in the so-called postmodern world, we can't also recognize that capitalism is not only dominant but massively present in every aspect of our lives and in all our 'identities'" (p. 28). Wood's critique rightfully challenges class-blind notions of cultural identity and argues that identity politics decontextualized from material conditions only limits and narrows the impact of such discourse upon the deep structures of economic inequality. Further, the absence of class discourse in the politics of marginalized communities in no way lessens the exigencies of class struggle. In fact, "since the discourse of justice is intimately tied to class, ethnicity, race, and gender, the absence of one of its most salient components—class"—(Aronowitz, 1992, p. 59) foredooms the transcultural solidarity required to effectively address the plight of economically dispossessed people, not only in this country but around the world. Stanley Aronowitz (1992), in his writings on working-class identity,[6] sheds light on this issue. The American evasion of class is not universal. We have no trouble speaking of ourselves as a "middle class" society or, indeed, endowing the economically and politically powerful with the rights and privileges of rule. American ideology identifies the middle class with power and, in its global reach, has attempted to incorporate manual workers into this family. The anomaly of the large and growing working poor, some of whom are hungry, others homeless and, indeed, the increasing insecurity suffered not only by industrial workers but also professional and clerical employees in the service sector, make some uneasy but have, until recently, failed to faze the ongoing celebration. Or, to be more accurate, class issues are given other names: crime, especially drugs; teen age pregnancy and suicide; homelessness and hunger; chronic "regional" unemployment that is grasped as an exception to an otherwise healthy national economy (p. 71).

The Media and Ideological Distortions of Difference

> Mass media in the United States exploit...representations of race and racialized contact in various ways daily: angry black folks doing violence, somebody—usually a young black man—dying (p. 173).
>
> —BELL HOOKS (1990)

It is impossible to fully grasp the social formation of ideological distortions about class, "race," and gender in the postmodern world if we ignore the overwhelming impact of today's accelerated media and communications technology. Through its captivating influence on "mental production" and its false presentation of democratic cultural differentiation, the media increasingly give shape to new forms of postmodern repression while sustaining common-sense approval for their capitalist representations. Within the structured relationships between the media and the ideas they extend forth to the public, the ideological function is deceptively concealed. Hall and his colleagues (1978) explain this relationship in terms of Marx's basic proposal that "the ruling ideas of any age are the ideas of its ruling class."

> [The] dominance of the "ruling idea" operates primarily because, in addition to its ownership and control of the means of production, this class also owns and controls the means of "mental production." In producing their definition of social reality and the place of "ordinary people" within it, they construct a particular image of society which represents particular class interests of all members of society; this class's definition of the social world provides the basic rationale for those institutions which protect and reproduce their "way of life." This control of mental resources ensures that theirs are the most powerful and "universal" of the available definitions of the social world. Their universality ensures that they are shared to some degree by the subordinate classes [and cultures] of the society (p. 59).

The media, with a highly centralized and almost monolithic structure, provide an essential link between the ruling ideology of the dominant culture and the society at large (Winston, 1982). In a society such as the United States where most of the people do not have any direct access to nor power over the bulk of decisions that affect their lives, the media play a powerful legitimating role in the social production of mass consensus. And although it may be argued that the power of the media is not absolute, in that there frequently exist counter-ideologies and definitions which challenge its legitimacy by way of dissident voices,

many emergent counter-definers however have no access to the defining process at all...
[for] if they do not play within the rules of the game, counter-spokesmen [*sic*] run the risk
of being defined out of the debate (because they have broken the rules of reasonable opposition).... Groups which have not secured even this limited measure of access are regularly
and systematically stigmatized, in their absence, as "extreme," their actions systematically
deauthenticated by being labeled as "irrational" (Hall et al., 1978, p. 64).

Oppositional Consciousness

This means locating the structural causes of unnecessary forms
of social misery, depicting the plight and predicaments of demor-
alized and depoliticized citizens caught in market-driven cycles
of therapeutic release...and projecting alternative visions, anal-
yses, and actions that proceed from particularities and arrive at
moral and political connectedness (p. 35).

—CORNEL WEST (1992)

It is against such a backdrop of societal contradictions and mainstream cultural
complexities that subordinate cultural groups must endeavor to rethink past strategies for cultural survival that now prove ineffective and to discover new ground
upon which to carry out political projects of resistance and negotiation. This also
includes the need to forge a new consciousness of opposition, in light of assimilationist postmodern rhetoric and right-wing conservative backlash.[7]

In the face of wide social and economic inequalities, biculturalism as a political construct must move beyond simple notions of individual psychological theories of identity, liberal paradigms of pluralism, and unproblematic notions of two
distinct cultural world views interacting. Instead a genealogy of biculturalism must
be theoretically grounded in the historical intricacies of social formations that
emerge from the collision between dominant/subordinate cultural, political, and
economic relations of power which function to determine the limits and boundaries of institutional life in this country. Given the hegemonic nature of American
institutions, marginalized communities must develop the ability to negotiate and
navigate through the current social complexities and co-opting nature of postmodern conditions of cultural domination. This requires a mode of oppositional
consciousness that depends on the ability to read actual situations of power and to
choose and adopt tactics of resistance that are best suited to push against the different forms of power configurations that shape actual experiences of injustice and
inequality. Chela Sandoval (1991), in her work on U.S. Third World feminism and
oppositional consciousness, describes this as a "differential mode of oppositional
consciousness" which provides members of subordinate groups with

enough strength to confidently commit to a well-defined structure of identity...enough flexibility to self-consciously transform that identity according to the requisites of another oppositional ideological tactic, if readings of power's formation require it; enough grace to recognize alliances with others committed to egalitarian social relations and race, gender, and class justice, when their readings of power call for alternative oppositional stands (p. 15).

In historical struggles against cultural oppression, bicultural communities have oftentimes joined together, albeit not always smoothly or easily, to oppose practices of social injustice directed against those groups in the United States who have been perceived consistently as unentitled to a rightful place within the mainstream. These coalitions and movement organizations have generally been primarily founded upon bicultural affinities of struggle rooted in the shared historical opposition of African Americans, Latinos, Asians, and Native Americans to cultural, class, and gender subordination. As the "nature" of postmodern social oppression presents itself in a more highly sophisticated, differentiated, and confusing manner, there is a greater necessity for members of subordinate groups to incorporate a differential mode of oppositional consciousness in order to build expanding alliances of struggle. Such alliances can serve as vehicles by which to more effectively identify and challenge actual relations of power at work and to select more effective modes of intervention that are directed toward actualizing an alternative vision of both institutional and community life.

Racialization and Notions of Difference

[W]here cultural difference is represented as natural and immutable, then it has all the qualities signified by the notion of biological difference, with the result that the distinction between racism and nationalism seems to have been dissolved (p. 100).
—ROBERT MILES (1993)

As discussed earlier, expressions of bicultural affinity among members of subordinate cultural groups are generally linked to experiences of difference and the role that difference plays in the social construction of both dominant and subordinate attitudes, beliefs, and practices in the United States. This is particularly at play when both dominant and subordinate groups struggle to challenge racism and the problematic inherent in notions of "race relations"; for the manner in which these notions are commonly used, more often than not, implies "an acceptance of the existence of biological differences between human beings, differences which express the existence of distinct, self-producing groups" (Miles, 1993, p. 2). Robert

Miles (1993), in his book, *Racism After Race Relations,* challenges this racialization of groups by arguing that all forms of racism "are always mediated by and through other structures and social relations, the most important of which are class relations and the political reality of the nation state" (pp. 12–13). Therefore as relations of economic domination intensify worldwide, subordinate cultural groups must not fall into the trap of defining cultural differences as a "race problem" or a "race struggle." Instead what must be confronted is

> the problem of racism, a problem which requires us to map and explain a particular instance of exclusion, simultaneously in its specificity and in its articulation with a multiplicity of other forms of exclusion. Hence, we can now confront the fundamental issues concerning the character and consequences of inequality reproduced by and in contemporary capitalist social formations, freed from a paradigm which finds an explanation for that inequality within the alleged "nature" of supposedly discrete populations rather than within historical and so humanly constituted social relations (Miles, 1993, p. 23).

From this vantage point, we must also understand notions of "race identity and difference" as politically formed rather than embedded in the color of the skin or a given nature (Hall, 1990a, 1990b). In other words, to identify as Black or Chicano is not so much a question of color as it is a question of cultural, historical, and political differences. Hence, to conceptualize accurately the social construction of bicultural identity formation requires an understanding of the process of racialization. In other words, the theoretical foundation of a politics of biculturalism challenges the "common sense" discourse of "race" and problematizes its utility as an analytical category. This summons a bold analytical transition from the politics of "race" to recognizing the centrality of racism and racialization in the interpretation of exclusionary practices.

Life on the Border

> The prohibited and forbidden are its inhabitants. Los atravesados live here: The squint-eyed, the perverse, the queer, the troublesome, the mongrel, the mulatto, the half-breed; in short, those who cross over, pass over, or go through the confines of the "normal" (p. 3).
>
> —GLORIA ANZALDÚA (1987)

The transcultural dimensions of biculturalism must then be situated within a continually changing process of cultural identity formation, as much as within complex human negotiations for social and material survival. The place where these processes and negotiations evolve and shift, construct and reconstruct, is what Homi Bhabha (1990) terms "the third space." It is also in his discussions of the third space that Bhabha engages the "process of hybridity." Hybridity here does not represent a relativist notion of culture, but instead challenges the global structures of domination which shape the lives of subordinate groups and creates a space for new formations of cultural identity to take hold. "This process of hybridity gives rise to something different, some thing new and unrecognizable, a new area of negotiation of meaning and representation" (p. 211).

It is then this "process of hybridity" that constitutes one of the central characteristics of border existence where the border itself becomes a political terrain of struggle and self-determination. Lawrence Grossberg (1993) expounds on the nature of this "in-between" place by engaging the work of Gloria Anzaldúa, *Borderlands/La Frontera: The New Mestizo.*

> Here the subaltern is different from the identities on either side of the border, but they are not simply the fragments of both. The subaltern exists as different from either alternative in the place between colonizer and the (imagined) precolonial subject or, in Gloria Anzaldúa's borderland, between the Mexican and the American: "A border land is a vague and undetermined place created by the emotional residue of an unnatural boundary.... People who inhabit both realities...are forced to live in the interface between the two."... Anzaldúa describes the third space as "a shock culture, a border culture, a third culture, a closed country" (p. 97).

In the safety of the "third space," notions of bicultural identity are constructed, deconstructed, and reconstructed anew, all while negotiating the tension of ongoing interactions with social and material conditions of subordination. This suggests "a form of border crossing which signals forms of transgression in which existing borders forged in domination can be challenged and redefined" (Giroux, 1992, p. 28). In short it is a "transborder" experience of identity that "is involved in constantly struggling to emerge from the bottom-up" (Santos, 1992, p. 16).

In many respects at its very core, this "bottom-up" act of challenging and redefining reflects an effective strategy of cultural survival that Trinh Minh-ha (1992) terms "displacing."

> Displacing is a way of surviving. It is an impossible truthful story of living in-between regimes of truth. The responsibility involved in this motley in-between living is a highly creative one; the displacer proceeds by increasingly introducing difference into repetition. By questioning over and over again what is taken for granted as self-evident, by reminding oneself and the others of the unchangeability of change itself. Disturbing thereby one's own thinking habits, dissipating what has become familiar and clichéd, and participating in the changing of received values—the transformation (without master) of the selves through one's self.... Strategies of displacement defy the world of compartmentalization and the system of dependence it engenders, while filling the shifting space of creation with a passion named wonder (pp. 332–333).

The meaning and complexity of this culture of hybridity, transgressing nature, and bottom-up displacement that shapes and enlivens a critical politics of biculturalism are fiercely echoed in the border culture manifesto of Guillermo Gomez-Pena's *Warrior for Gringostroika.*

> Border culture means boycott, complot, ilegalidad, clandestinidad, contrabando, transgresion, desobediencia, binacional; en otras palabras, to smuggle dangerous poetry and Utopian visions from one culture to another, desde alia, hasta aca. But it also means to maintain one's dignity outside the law. But it also means hybrid art forms for new content-in-gestation...to be fluid in English, Spanish, Spanlish, and Ingefiol, 'cause Spanglish is the language of border diplomacy.... But is [sic] also means transcultural friendships and collaborations among races, sexes, and generations. But it also means to practice creative appropriation, expropriation, and subversion of dominant cultural forms...a multiplicity of voices away from the center... to return and depart once again...a new terminology for new hybrid identities (p. 43).

Bicultural Re-presentations and a Solidarity of Difference

The insidious colonial tendencies we have internalized—and that express themselves in sadistic competition for money and attention, political cannibalism, and moral distrust—must be overcome. We must realize that we are not each other's enemies and that the true enemy is currently enjoying our divisiveness (p. 62).

—GUILLERMO GOMEZ-PENA (1993)

The bicultural re-presentations of Gomez-Pena and Anzaldúa, as the *warrior for gringostroika* and the *new mestiza,* unmistakably emerge from the passion of experience, the power of reflection, and the courage to act. From these examples, we can glimpse at the face of revolutionary commitment—a grounded commitment to struggle against any and all forms of theory or practice that imprison our minds and incarcerate our hearts. Collectively these bicultural re-presentations call forth not only themes of opposition to dominant structures and cultural forms that impede the humanity and liberation of subordinate subjects, but also signal new ways of perceiving our dialectical capacities to transform the social and material conditions of our communities. It is through their vibrant discourses of simultaneous deconstruction and reconstruction, undoing and redoing, embracing and releasing, that we find the hidden seeds of self-determination and catch glimpses of the possibilities awaiting us, possibilities that are given birth through our courage to transgress the antiquated "sacred cows" of profit and privilege, and that join us together in a solidarity of difference—a solidarity that is ever mindful of the manner in which

> Institutionalized rejection of difference is an absolute necessity in a profit economy which needs outsiders as surplus people. As members of such an economy, we have all been programmed to respond to the human differences between us with fear and loathing and to handle that difference in one of three ways: ignore it, and if that is not possible, copy it if we think it is dominant, or destroy it if we think it is subordinate. But we have no patterns for relating across human difference as equals. As a result, those differences have been misnamed and misused in the service of separation and confusion (Lorde, 1992, pp. 281–282).

Audre Lorde's words strongly reflect one of the most important questions we must openly acknowledge and consistently address in our efforts to establish a solidarity of difference. How do we move across a multiplicity of subjectivities rooted in both material conditions and diverse orientations that historically shape our world views? For example, so often we hear people, even within bicultural communities, bemoan the "loss of community." Yet, if the truth be told, a return to the good old days of such an imagined community actually would require returning to a simpler, unproblematic vision of community—a vision that, in fact, was often theorized in monolithic and solely essentialist terms and enacted through exclusionary practices that precluded the full participation of women, poor and working class people, gays, lesbians, and those perceived as "racially" inferior.

As critical beings we must consistently recognize the dangers of falling into the hidden traps of both absolutely exclusionary (assimilationist) and relativistically inclusive (liberal pluralist) theories and practices. A solidarity of difference instead challenges us to actively struggle across human differences within the ever-present dialectical tension of inclusionary/exclusionary personal and institutional realities and needs. For the purpose is not to obscure or obliterate differences or diminish and destroy cultural self-determination in the search for "common values"; rather, our greatest challenge is to negotiate the on-going construction and reconstruction of relations of power and material conditions that both affirm and challenge our partialities in the interest of cultural and economic democracy, social justice, human rights, and revolutionary love.

Conclusion

The theoretical foundation for a politics of biculturalism posited upon these pages represents, above all, one effort to articulate a dialectical reading of issues that are central to extending our political understanding of culture and difference and the impact of these forces upon the identity formation of members from subordinate communities. In so doing, this has entailed (1) a reexamination of notions of identity and ethnicity; (2) the reclamation of the power of experience in the construction of cultural knowledge; (3) the reconsideration of colonization, decolonization, and the development of cultural consciousness; (4) the reinstitution of class relations and material conditions as central to identity formation; (5) the distorting impact of the media on social perceptions of difference; (6) a move away from race-based specificity to a clear focus on racism and racialization; (7) an engagement with transcultural notions of border existence; and (8) the necessity for a solidarity of difference as a significant strategy of struggle against the forces of domination that shape our world.

Most importantly, this work embodies a recognition that critical bicultural scholars must engage actively and persistently with the political challenges faced by our communities—not through simplistic platitudes of hope, but rather the committed intellectual discipline and critical practice required to boldly imagine and bring into existence a world that up to now has existed only in our dreams.

REFERENCES

Akinyela, M. (1992). "Critical Africentricity and the Politics of Culture," *Wazo Weusi (Think Black)* (Fall). Fresno: California State University.

Anzaldúa, G. (1987). *Borderlands/La Frontera: The New Mestizo*. San Francisco, CA: Aunt Lute.

Aronowitz, S. (1992). *The Politics of Identity: Class, Culture, Social Movements*. New York: Routledge.

Bhabha, H. (1990). "The Third Space." In J. Rutherford (ed.), *Identity, Community, Culture Difference*. London: Lawrence and Wishart.

Buriel, R. (1984). "Integration with Traditional Mexican-American Culture and Socio-cultural Adjustment." In J. Martinez (ed.), *Chicano Psychology*, 2nd ed. New York: Academic Press.

Children's Defense Fund. (1994). *The State of America's Children Yearbook*. Washington, D.C.

Cohen, J. (1993). *Q'eros: The Shape of Survival*. New York: Mystic Fire Video.

Darder, A. (1991). *Culture and Power in the Classroom: A Theory for a Critical Bicultural Pedagogy*. Westport: Bergin and Garvey.

deAnda, D. (1984). "Bicultural Socialization: Factors Affecting the Minority Experience," *Social Work* 29:2 101–7.

Du Bois, W.E.B. (1903). *The Souls of Black Folk*. Chicago: A.C. McClurg.

Epstein, S. (1987). "Gay Politics, Ethnic Identity: The Limits of Social Constructionism," *Socialist Review* 17 (May–August): 9–54.

Fanon, F. (1964). *Toward the African Revolution*. New York: Grove.

Fanon, F. (1963). *Wretched of the Earth*. New York: Grove.

Fanon, F. (1967). *Black Skin, White Masks*. New York: Grove.

Giroux, H. (1992). *Border Crossings*. New York: Routledge.

Gomez-Pena, G. (1993). *Warrior for Gringostroika*. St. Paul, MN: Graywolf Press.

Gorostiaga, X. (1993). "Is the Answer in the South?" Paper presented at the international seminar "First World Ethics and Third World Economics: Christian Responsibility in a World of Plenty and Poverty," Sigtunn, Sweden.

Gramsci, A. (1971). *Selections from* The Prison Notebooks. New York: International Publishers.

Grossberg, L. (1993). "Cultural Studies and/in New Worlds." In C. McCarthy and W. Crichlow (eds.), *Race, Identity, and Representation in Education*. New York: Routledge.

Hall, S. (1990a). "Ethnicity: Identity and Difference." *Radical America* 13, no. 4: 9–20.

Hall, S. (1990b). "Cultural Identity and Diaspora." In J. Rutherford (ed.), *Identity, Community, Culture, Difference*. London: Lawrence and Wishart.

Hall, S., et al. (1978). *Policing the Crisis*. London: Macmillan.

hooks, b. (1994). *Teaching to Transgress*. New York: Routledge.

hooks, b. (1990). *Yearnings*. Boston: South End Press.

Jordon, J. (1992). *Technical Difficulties*. New York: Vintage Books.

Lorde, A. (1992). "Age, Race, Class, and Sex: Women Redefining Difference." In R. Ferguson et al. (eds.), *Out There: Marginalization and Contemporary Culture*. New York: New Museum of Contemporary Art.

Luttwak, E. (1993). *The Endangered American Dream*. New York: Simon and Schuster.

Miles, J. (1993). *Racism after Race Relations*. London: Routledge.

Millan, D. (1993). "The Chicano Collective Bicultural Consciousness: Identity and the Politics of Race." In A. Darder (ed.), *Bicultural Studies in Education: The Struggle for Educational Justice*. Claremont, CA: Institute for Education in Transformation/Claremont Graduate School.

Minh-ha, T. (1992). "Cotton and Iron," In R. Ferguson et al. (eds.), *Out There: Marginalization and Contemporary Culture*. New York: New Museum of Contemporary Art.

Minh-ha, T. (1989). *Woman Native Other*. Indianapolis: Indiana University Press.

Nagel, J. (1994). "Constructing Ethnicity: Creating and Recreating Ethnic Identity and Culture." *Social Problems* 41, no. 1 (February): 152–76.

Omi, M., and H. Winant. (1983a). "By the Rivers of Babylon: Race in the United States" (Part 1), *Socialist Review* 13, no. 5: 31–65.

Omi, M., and H. Winant. (1983b). "By the Rivers of Babylon: Race in the United States" (Part 2). *Socialist Review* 13, no. 6: 35–68.

Ramirez, M., and A. Castañeda. (1974). *Cultural Democracy: Bicognitive Development and Education*. New York: Longman.

Rashid, H. (1981). "Early Childhood Education as a Cultural Transition for African-American Children," *Educational Research Quarterly* 6, no. 3: 55–63.

Red Horse, J., et al. (1981). "Family Behavior of Urban American Indians." In R. Dana (ed.), *Human Services for Cultural Minorities*. Baltimore, MD: University Park Press.

Roberts, S. (1993). *Who We Are: A Portrait of America*. New York: Random House.

Romay, E. (1993). "Policy Implications for the United States through Mexican Immigration Bilingual Teachers' Experiences of Bilingual-Bicultural Education: A Participatory Research Process." Ph.D. dissertation, University of San Francisco.

Sampson, E. (1993). "Identity Politics: Challenges to Psychology's Understanding," *American Psychologist* 48, no. 12 (December): 1219–30.

Sandoval, C. (1991). "U.S. Third World Feminism: The Theory and Method of Oppositional Consciousness in the Postmodern World," *Genders* 10 (Spring): 1–24.

Santos, G. (1992). "Somos RUNAFRIBES? The Future of Latino Ethnicity in the Americas," *National Association of Chicano Studies Annual Conference Proceedings.*

Solis, A. (1980). "Theory of Biculturality," *Calmeccac de Atzlan en Los* 2:1 36–41.

Valentine, C. (1971). "Deficit, Difference, and Bicultural Models of Afro-American Behavior," *Harvard Educational Review* 41:2;137–57.

West, C. (1993). *Race Matters.* Boston: Beacon Press.

West, C. (1992). "The New Politics of Difference." In R. Ferguson et al. (eds.), *Out There: Marginalization and Contemporary Culture.* New York: New Museum of Contemporary Art.

Winston, M. (1982). "Racial Consciousness and the Evolution of Mass Communications in the United States," *Daedalus* 8: 171–82.

Wood, E.M. (1994). "Identity Crisis," *In These Times* (June 13): 28–29.

Young, I.M. (1990). *Justice and the Politics of Difference.* Princeton, NJ: Princeton University Press.

NOTES

1. See Iris Marion Young's (1991) text *Justice and the Politics of Difference* for an excellent critical analysis of the sociopolitical contexts that shape the histories of subordinate cultural groups in the United States.

2. Although there no longer exist cultural groups in the United States untouched by the dominant artifacts, structures, and economic relations of power, the beginning stages of this hybridization process can be observed in indigenous cultures that exist in remote regions of the world. One such example is the culture of the Q'eros in Peru. The Q'eros are the remaining community of people in the Peruvian highlands who are the direct descendants of the Inca. To flee the violent rampage of the conquistadors in the 1500s and to protect their way of life, the Q'eros fled into the Andes, living virtually in isolation for five hundred years. It is only recently that the Q'eros have begun to have some contact with the West. Government projects to assimilate the Q'eros into the mainstream of Peruvian life have taken the form of setting up farm collectives and Spanish-language educational programs for the children. As the Q'eros begin to have greater contact with the West, it is expected that a way of life conserved for hundreds of years will undergo dramatic reconstruction, if not be lost altogether. This is already evident in those members of the Q'eros who have moved into the cities, only to face harsh conditions of poverty and very few opportunities for a better life amid the Peruvian mainstream (Cohen, 1993).

3. For a more extensive and thought-provoking discussion of ethnicity, see "Ethnicity: Identity and Difference" and "Cultural Identity and Diaspora," by Stuart Hall (1990a, 1990b); and Stanley Aronowitz's (1992) *The Politics of Identity*.

4. See chapter 6, "Essentialism and Experience," in *Teaching to Transgress*, by bell hooks (1994) for an incisive discussion and critique of Diana Fuss's *Essentially Speaking: Feminism, Nature, and Difference*, particularly with respect to the manner in which Fuss problematizes student voices that she characterizes as speaking from the "authority of experience."

5. According to the Children's Defense Fund yearbook, *The State of America's Children*: In 1992, more children lived in poverty than in any year since 1965; the share of family income received by the poorest one fifth of families shrank to 4.4 percent in 1992, while the share going to the richest one fifth reached 44.6 percent. In *Who We Are: A Portrait of America*, among other income inequities, Roberts (1993) shows that despite an increase in total Black families who earn more than $50,000 (from 7 percent to 15 percent), the total number of Black families earning under $5,000 has risen from 8 percent in 1967 to 12 percent in 1990. Edward Luttwak (1993) bemoans the "Third-Worldization" of America in his book *The Endangered American Dream*. He writes: "America's slide toward Third World conditions is even now being prepared by the sheer force of demography: the proportion of poor Americans is increasing, the concentration of wealth in the hands of the richest one percent is also increasing, and the proportion of Americans in between who have enough wealth and income to claim genuine middle-class status is therefore in decline" (153). Luttwak also provides the following figures: between 1979 and 1990, the number of workers below the poverty line nearly doubled, from 7.8 million to 14.4 million; the combined net worth of the richest 1 percent was greater than the total net worth of the bottom 89.9 percent of all American families, at $5.2 trillion.

6. For an eloquent discussion of the history of working-class identity, see *The Politics of Identity: Class, Culture, Social Movements*, a text by Stanley Aronowitz (1992).

7. Michael Omi and Howard Winant (1983b) in their essay "By the Rivers of Babylon: Race in the United States (Part II)," provide an informative and useful discussion of the New Right's "programmatic attempts to limit the political gains of the minority movement (and its successors) by reinterpreting their meanings." In their work, the authors outline several of the major currents in the rearticulation process that have fueled the right-wing conservative backlash in the United States.

CHAPTER 3

Institutional Research as a Tool for Cultural Democracy

[W]hen we notice that our social institutions are driven by the larger political contexts in which they are embedded, we are forced to acknowledge that the content of our research and the methods we use are likewise subject to the prevailing political forces.

—KENWYN SMITH (1990, P. 121)

American educational institutions are currently struggling to contend with the widespread demographic changes that are sweeping this country. As the population of people of color increases in the United States, it is becoming far more difficult to maintain the facade of cultural equality without dramatically increasing the number of students, faculty, and administrators of color on college and university campuses. Yet cultural equality is not only about numbers. It is, foremost, about an institution's ability to embrace a culturally democratic view of life that not only supports participation by all constituents, but also provides avenues for different cultural voices to be heard and integrated within the changing culture and history of the institution.

This struggle for cultural democracy cannot be defined merely in terms of social justice paradigms that focus solely on the redistribution of material and non-material benefits within the academy. Such a transformation must also address the ideological tenets and philosophical contradictions that have historically structured academic environments to benefit an elite group, while systematically marginalizing the participation of "the other"—people of color, women, gays and lesbians, and the working class (Young, 1990).

Most importantly, institutional change in the interest of cultural democracy cannot take place without major shifts in the manner in which school life is organized, academic issues are framed, education is actualized, and research is conducted (Smith, 1990; Crossen, 1988; Jaramillo, 1988; Loo and Rolison, 1986; Sanders, 1987). Although each of these areas of change is equally significant and vital, this chapter will specifically consider issues related to institutional research and its potential role in promoting an ethos of cultural democracy in higher education.

Institutional research, as a tool of traditional organizations, has often contributed to the perpetuation of asymmetrical power relations and the subordination of groups existing outside the mainstream. Inextricably linked to organizational values, beliefs, and practices defined by the structure of Western scientific thought, institutional research has served to make acceptable decontextualized and victim-blaming views of culturally diverse students—students who, more often than not, have found it difficult to succeed within the traditional structure of American higher education.

For example, test scores are widely used by college and university researchers to make conclusions about the future success of students of color. Their academic ability and potential are often determined by the scores they receive on standardized tests, even though these tests reflect the norms of the dominant culture and class. Moreover, the knowledge required to score well on such tests is generally achieved by means of the students' exposure to certain educational conditions. These conditions include the availability of well-prepared teachers, challenging instructional approaches, higher teacher expectations, adequate educational materials and equipment, and significant home educational resources—the very conditions that have been historically denied to the large majority of students from disenfranchised communities. Yet such differences in context are usually ignored; instead, students who score poorly on standardized tests are judged less capable or less motivated—a practice that places the fault for lower scores directly on the student.

Institutional values and practices that sustain racism, sexism, classism, and homophobia in educational settings have perversely shaped and defined the nature of institutional governance, hiring practices, academic standards, testing and assessment, curriculum design, faculty-student interactions, financial priorities, and what is deemed legitimate research. As a consequence, traditional institutional research on diversity unwittingly supports institutional conditions that perpetuate:

- Simplistic perceptions of discrimination by failing to distinguish those acts of discrimination that function in the interest of exclusion and those that function in the interest of diversity
- A view of women and people of color as deficient
- An overemphasis on the "special" attributes of people of color to justify their entry into the institution
- Admitting too few people of color to enact an actual culture of diversity
- Insufficient services for promoting the success of disenfranchised students, faculty, and staff
- Hostility toward alternative cultural spheres that promote cultural integrity
- The silencing of discourse that fails to adhere to the Eurocentric ideal of dispassionate objectivity
- An absence of knowledge of students' histories and community realities
- The collusion of white students, white faculty, and white administration resistant to institutional change
- Fragmentation of subordinate group leadership to forestall institutional change
- Arguments of "political correctness" to abdicate social responsibility to struggle for equality
- Research-driven classifications (for example, "Hispanic" or "minority") that obscure the extent to which diversity actually exists within educational institutions.

Critique of Traditional Research Values

Educational conditions promoting inequality have been made possible by the underlying philosophical assumptions that inform traditional research methodology, namely, the acceptance of a dualistic, objective, value-free, hierarchical, and instrumental perspective regarding knowledge. It is a view that sees human beings as separate from nature, and thus as objectifiable, observable, quantifiable, predictable, and controllable. Through objectifying human beings into "things," human behavior can be treated as if it existed according to a predetermined set of universal rules, independent of the contexts in which the behavior takes place. Knowing the universal causes and effects provides the instrumental basis on which to effectively intervene and manipulate the flow of events, to bring about a desired control over the environment (Fay, 1987).

Traditional research has emerged from an authoritarian context bent on the prediction of the environment for the purpose of controlling and dominating its evolution, with an emphasis on the hierarchical categorization and compartmentalization of human experience. As a consequence, the belief exists that to conduct legitimate research, to produce legitimate knowledge, requires distancing "oneself emotionally from the rest of life" (Slater, 1991, p. 99). Both Philip Slater (1991) and Page Smith (1990) speak against this "rationalism of science."

> [T]he vaunted rationalism of science is often merely a guise for the zealous suppression of feeling which authoritarianism has always demanded.... The most irrational of all beliefs is the belief in rationalism...and the most subjective of all delusions is the belief that objectivity is possible. [Slater, 1991, p. 991

> [T]here is no such thing as "value-free" thought or research; those who act sincerely on such a premise deceive the world and, more dangerously, themselves.... The notion of value-free inquiry of social research without reference to social ends is the bugaboo of escapist science. [Smith, 1990, p. 161]

Other aspects of traditional educational research include a tendency toward reductionism, an overemphasis on the search for universals and homogeneity, and ethnocentric bias. These tendencies have resulted in the production of decontextualized knowledge, limiting the attention given to the unique impact of cultural, gender, and class influences in the attitudes and behaviors of students from subordinate cultures. Gordon, Miller, and Rollock (1990) perceive this neglect as "probably the result of androcentric, culturocentric, and ethnocentric chauvinism in Euro-American and male-dominated production of social science knowledge. We refer to this chauvinism as communicentric bias: The tendency to make one's own community the center of the universe and the conceptual frame that constrains all thought" [p. 15].

Research and Social Power

Without doubt, institutional relations of power are always at work in the manner in which traditional research is defined, implemented, and utilized within educational environments. In other words, the primary purpose of traditional research and the cultural values that inform it is directly related to the production of knowledge; and this knowledge is intimately linked to questions of social power. Michel Foucault (1977) describes this relationship between knowledge and power:

> Truth is a thing of this world: it is produced only by virtue of multiple forms of constraints. And it induces regular effects of power. Each society [culture] has its regime of truth, its "general politics" of truth: that is, the types of discourse which it accepts and makes function as true; the mechanism and instances which enable one to distinguish true and false statements; the means by which each is sanctioned; the techniques and procedures accorded value in the acquisition of truth; the status of those who are charged with saying what counts as true. [p. 131]

The emphasis on objectivity and value-free knowledge can readily be understood from the standpoint of preserving the integrity of the status quo. It is generally those who are most protective of current conditions who most adamantly insist on institutional research that reflects a neutral and objective perspective and who, likewise, respond with great suspicion to research results that challenge the existing relations of power. Further, this emphasis on objective and value-free research functions to veil the implicit control the dominant culture holds over subordinate populations. Slater (1991) addresses this phenomenon and its consequences:

> It is easier for those who are satisfied with things as they are to appear neutral, unemotional, and unmotivated. The motivational impetus of those who seek change is more visible. They are more likely to be seen as "shrill" or "strident."...Those who seek change—those who attempt to challenge [explicitly] the powers that be—must speak louder in order to be heard at all, and the demand for a quieter, "more objective" voice is an effective way to silence them.... [And] when dissenting voices grow in numbers, authoritarian [institutions] will often stave off change by calling for further study. [p. 100]

Slater's comments point to the manner in which institutional research is used to prevent movement and to subvert institutional transformation. Instead of utilizing institutional resources for necessary organizational change, time, money, and human expertise are diverted to abstract research tasks that in and of themselves change nothing. It is as if change could somehow be pretended or magically actualized through the technocratic accumulation of volumes of "scientific" research reports. Frank Fisher (1985) describes the power of such "technocracy": The power of technocracy is based on a positivistically oriented empirical conception of knowledge, which is reflected in a growing inventory of operational techniques such as cost-benefit analysis, operations research, systems analysis, strategic planning and computer simulations. Emphasizing the tenets of value-neutral objectivity, empirical operationalism and professional expertise, modern technocracy stands or falls with the ideology of scientism [p. 232).

In summary, what is clearly missing in the traditional perspective concerning institutional research is an acknowledgment of the manner in which culture and power intersect to support a view of research that is apolitical and ahistorical. The standards and norms assigned and the approach utilized are encapsulated in a belief in the existence of universal values and an ideal of individualism and assimilation. These function to perpetuate a view of research that is not only devoid of critical insight, but that reduces knowledge into abstract parts and perceives ideas as useful only to the extent that they produce actions that sustain the status quo. By so doing, traditional research reinforces the homogenizing intent of the dominant culture, while negating the cultural reality of subordinate groups; perpetuates a deficient view of women and people of color, while positioning the researcher as neutral and objective; denies the political nature of the research process, while assuming a moral posture of superiority; defines what constitutes legitimate knowledge, while ignoring the impact of sociopolitical contexts on such a value judgment; and de-emphasizes issues of social class and sexual orientation, while the hidden values reproduce social class inequality and compulsory heterosexuality.

Institutional Responses to Cultural Diversity

All educational institutions are fundamentally grounded on a set of values and beliefs that inform the manner in which they engage with questions of cultural diversity. All educational institutions enact an organizational culture that enhances or deters the process of cultural diversification. Institutional research on diversity must address the manner in which cultural democracy is stifled and truncated in the interest of preserving the existing organizational dynamics of power at work. Toward this end, it is valuable to assess the manner in which institutions respond to questions of cultural diversity. For purposes of discussion, most institutional responses to cultural differences can be considered in terms of an organizational power continuum that moves from traditional to culturally democratic, with liberal and multicultural reference points existing in between:

Traditional—Liberal—Multicultural—Culturally Democratic

In creating this framework, certain fundamental assumptions are clearly at work. First, culture incorporates all the implicit and explicit relationships and interactions that impart a sense of continuity and integrity to community life, despite individual differences. In as much as shared cultural beliefs, values, mores, and assumptions strongly shape individual and organizational practices and responses of a group, the environmental conditions in which groups live and work also impact their cultural practices and responses. Hence, efforts to contend with issues related to cultural differences in a reductionistic and decontextualized manner can easily lead to distortions of reality and major flaws in the subsequent prescription of institutional practices. Second, race, class, gender, and sexual orientation constitute subcategories of culture and thus represent differentiating systems of belief within the particular worldview. All cultural communities must contend with the underlying cultural assumptions that shape their prevailing views related to each of these dimensions of life. Third, racism, classism, sexism, and homophobia exist as interlocking spheres of institutional oppression that are driven by institutional practices (carried out by individuals) supporting what Iris Marion Young (1990) calls the "five faces of oppression": exploitation, marginalization, powerlessness, cultural invasion, and violence.

Also significant to the following analysis of institutional responses to diversity is a critical view of power. Such a view encompasses a notion of power as existing everywhere, forever at play when people come together. Thus, power is perceived as a social phenomenon that occurs between and among people—never in a vacuum. What institutions do, as much as what they do not do, affects the lives of their constituents, because institutions exercise power through decisions that lead to particular actions and consequences. Most importantly, power must be understood with respect to the impact that actions and their consequences have on particular groups. What are the consequences of institutional research, policies, practices, and standards? Who benefits the most from particular kinds of research, policies, practices, and standards? Who benefits the least? Whose voices are heard and whose participation is valued? These are useful questions for unveiling the power dynamics at work within an institution and identifying possibilities for creating the conditions for social justice and equality.

The remainder of this chapter will provide a framework to consider the manner in which four different institutional paradigms—here termed *traditional, liberal, multicultural,* and *culturally democratic*—engage the issues of cultural diversity and how they might inform institutional research.

The Traditional Institution

The values of the traditional institution support a view of culture as a depoliticized and neutral construct. In such an institution cultural differences, for the most part, are denied and are not considered legitimate. Hence, when cultural differences between people surface much effort is made to label them as an individual phenomenon. Any effort to openly address cultural differences between groups is viewed as suspect, generating much talk and concern about divisiveness and tribalism. This response is supported by an ideology that reinforces the notion of American culture as a "melting pot" and a belief in cultural amalgamation, social Darwinism ("survival of the fittest"), and the doctrine of Manifest Destiny (an ostensibly benevolent policy of American imperialistic expansion).

The value system within a traditional organization places a great deal of emphasis on unity, conformity, and homogeneity, on the one hand, and on the ideal of individualism and a "boot-strap" mentality, on the other. To support the utmost possibility of unity, conformity, and homogeneity, power relations are highly centralized and marked by a strong hierarchical and authoritarian governance structure. This strong homogenizing effort results in positions of power being held almost exclusively by members of the dominant group. Little action, if any, is taken to address issues of diversity; these are generally ignored or dealt with in a manner that forces conformity. As a consequence, subordinate groups are generally excluded from participation and perceived as deficient, even to the point of being considered genetically inferior. Moreover, traditional institutions are marked by strong xenophobic attitudes regarding the use of languages other than English anyplace other than in the foreign language classroom.

The expressed purpose of research at traditional institutions is to produce "objective" knowledge that is focused upon prediction of conditions and subsequent interventions, with the goal of better managing or controlling the institutional environment through more effective control of its constituents. In the area of diversity, research is focused upon identifying deficits in subordinate groups and determining ways to facilitate widespread societal assimilation. This research is often found at work in vocational tracking of working-class students, women students, and students of color, particularly within the community college system, a practice that is considered to be the most effective educational approach to remediating problems caused by presumed poor academic achievement. Simultaneously, this approach meets the demands of the labor market. Generally, the underlying perspective here is that "diversity is viewed as deviance; and differences are viewed as deficits" (Gordon, Miller, and Rollock 1990, p. 15).

The Liberal Institution

Liberal institutions view culture as primarily an apolitical and decontextualized phenomenon that is readily identified as the experience of Latinos, African Americans, and other subordinate cultural groups. Cultural differences are considered to legitimately exist in the world, but their social importance is minimized or they are viewed as exotica. When cultural differences are addressed within such a context, the goal is to reveal the human similarities that unite all people. This approach is driven by an ideological foundation that is often described as "color-blind"—an ideology steeped in a belief in universalism, assimilation, and a notion that all human beings are essentially the same "under the skin."

Liberal, like traditional, institutions place an emphasis on unity and conformity by highlighting the similarities among people, and place an even greater emphasis on the uniqueness of the individual. Such values reinforce power relations that remain highly centralized, although they also lead to a more liberal hierarchical and authoritarian governance structure than is found at traditional institutions. As a consequence, those in middle management positions may gain more influence and control within the organization. Most of the positions of power are held by members of the dominant culture, but people of color are generally brought into the organization at entry or service levels. The belief that there are few people of color who are qualified for professional positions highlights discussions related to hiring, as does concern about finding the "right fit."

When the liberal organization chooses to address cultural differences, the extent of change is at a very basic content level, leading to the "adding-on" of cultural artifacts that are symbolic of diversity (for example, ethnic art on the walls, ethnic food in the cafeteria, and other forms of window dressing). People of color are both seen and treated with benevolence and are granted the possibility of becoming equal to members of the dominant culture, if they can overcome their cultural environments. Victim-blaming attitudes are often hidden beneath the organization's drive and passion to help the "disadvantaged and deprived." As a consequence, these attitudes support a missionary mentality. There is some acceptance of language diversity but, without question, English is considered the most important language.

The liberal institution must contend with oppositional responses to its liberalism from conservative members of the institution or the larger community. Opposition is generally most prominent among those who hold a strongly xenophobic and ethnocentric view of life in the United States. Most of their concerns are strongly linked to the need to be reassured that their own privileges and entitlements as members of the dominant culture will not be jeopardized.

Liberal institutional research strongly reflects most of the apolitical and ahistorical tenets of traditional research, with a similar emphasis on prediction and control of the environment. Much of the research on cultural diversity is focused on discovering the similarities and differences between the dominant and subordinate groups. The similarities are used by these institutions to promote an assimilationist ideal and efforts to integrate. Differences are studied primarily to identify areas that require intervention to assist students of color to perform as well as members of the dominant culture. There is some development of descriptive ethnographic approaches that function to generate popular narratives about subordinate groups.

The Multicultural Institution

The multicultural institution views culture as a legitimate and significant determinant of individual identity, but the focus remains on members of subordinate cultural groups. Cultural differences are generally acknowledged and strong diversity rhetoric permeates the institutional discourse. Cultural differences are addressed in an effort to find ways to limit the increased tensions that result from an increasingly diverse institutional environment. The prevalent ideology within the multicultural institution is shaped by a belief in "fair and equal" representation and cultural pluralism.

The multicultural institution places a greater emphasis on shared common values, as the distribution of power begins to shift as an increasing number of members of subordinate groups enter the institution. As a consequence, the multicultural institution is marked by its greater decentralization of power and greater liberalizing of the traditional governance structures to accommodate differences. Despite these changes, undercurrents of unity and conformity are still at work challenging proposals for dramatic structural change. The majority of power positions are still held by members of the dominant culture, but more efforts are made to recruit and hire members from subordinate cultures. People of color hold some positions of power, but generally the higher his or her position, the greater the expectation that he or she will express and demonstrate loyalty to the dominant group's multicultural notion of shared common values and an integrationist discourse.

Within the multicultural institution there are many visible adaptations and a variety of efforts to address issues related to cultural difference. Much effort is also made to appear "culturally conscious" and to incorporate obvious material representations of the institution's commitment to diversity. Some new positions and departments are created to address the expanding needs of the newer members and constituents of the institution. People of color are welcomed into the culture of the institution, so long as they are able to function within the prescribed multicultural vision of those who hold power. It is not unusual for "acceptable" people of color to be utilized in efforts to neutralize those who hold strong radical positions of cultural integrity and who openly acknowledge the existence of cultural conflicts between groups. This practice can cause some fragmentation of leadership among subordinate groups. There is greater acceptance of language differences, but some ambivalence still remains as to the viability and effectiveness of multilingual societies.

Oppositional responses to change from mainstream constituents increase as cultural differences produce tension, conflict, and ambiguity within the institutional environment. Those who have lived within a context of privilege and entitlement now express anger and fear of "losing ground." This can result in backlash efforts by conservatives coupled with a growing hostility toward affirmative action and claims of "reverse racism" when actions are carried out in the interest of diversity. Often institutional transformative efforts are fragmented by those who feel the need to appease any opposition voiced by powerful business, government, church, or political groups.

The research perspective of multicultural institutions most often reflects an acceptance of alternative approaches to producing knowledge. Nonetheless, there still is a strong underlying concern about questions of objectivity and professional distance. As a consequence, some researchers express concerns regarding the validity of diversity studies conducted by women or people of color. Although there is a greater willingness to contend with issues of inequity, often the research continues to reflect a perception of culturally diverse student populations as deficient and in need of compensatory programs. Some elements of cultural relativism and determinism are often present in research on diversity issues at multicultural institutions. The persistence of these views results from the failure of researchers to engage the impact of power in the formation of subordinate cultural values and practices. Institutional tensions surface as people of color collide with power structures that, for the most part, are of the dominant culture. As diversity increases, educational researchers also tend to aggregate groups due to limited numbers and then utilize the results to make group generalizations. Such practices inadvertently lead to distortions in research conclusions and flawed recommendations that perpetuate cultural subordination, despite well-intentioned efforts.

The Culturally Democratic Institution

Within the culturally democratic institution culture is viewed as an integral and fundamental component of the collective, as well as crucial to the individual identity of all human beings. Cultural differences among people are understood and accepted as inherent in any environment that is governed by a strong culturally diverse population. Cultural differences are engaged as common and ongoing occurrences, with tolerance for ambiguity, conflict, and uncertainty. The strengths and limitations of all cultural perspectives that exist within the institution and in society at large are accepted.

The culturally democratic ideological foundation of the institution is shaped by the belief that culture and power are linked and must be understood within the context of historical struggles for voice, participation, and self-determination. This foundation is not only understood with respect to abstract ideals but also in relation to community struggles for the improvement of material conditions. The institutional emphasis is placed on creating conditions for social justice and cultural equality through a dialogical view of working values that are continuously defined and redefined by the historical context and social realities in which people function. Instead of a static notion of specific "shared values," what is shared is the willingness to create working values that can inform institutional decision making.

The distribution of power within a culturally democratic institution is defined in terms of maximum possibilities for structural decentralization. There is greater shared influence and control among the members of the institution. In the interest of social justice and equality, the decentralization of institutional power is also connected to a structure of centralized power in which representative views of all groups are engaged. Multiple spheres within the institution are created to provide the opportunity for expression of cultural integrity and diversity, and for cross-cultural dialogue, decision making, and social action to take place. Within the culturally democratic institution positions of power are redefined in politically equitable, representative, and fair terms, as determined by the social context in which the institution functions. Consequently, people of color hold many positions of leadership, particularly where the interests of specific cultural communities are involved.

The extent of institutional change reflects policies that ensure an ongoing and consistent system of equity. There is greater latitude for the open expression and practice of diversity. The rhetoric diminishes due to an internalized acceptance of cultural differences that is reflected in widespread institutional practices. New and more fluid institutional structures can emerge that support the wider participation of the institution's constituents and the communities it serves.

People of color, just like their white counterparts, are perceived as active "owners" of the institutions. Hence, all are actively involved in shaping the institutional culture as equal participants in the process. Diversity among people of color is recognized and understood as part of the human conditions of all groups. Language differences are accepted and efforts are maximized to cultivate and support multilingualism as a positive and commonplace phenomenon. This view supports the establishment of effective multilingual programs and services that support and encourage the academic success of bilingual and immigrant students.

Oppositional responses to change are expected to exist on a continuous basis, as ongoing themes of privilege, entitlement, subordination, and domination surface for all groups, depending on the particular contexts and specific decisions and actions being taken during the historical evolution of a particular institution.

Research methods within a culturally democratic institution are expected to produce knowledge that supports the emancipatory intent of the institution. To facilitate the production of such knowledge, interdisciplinary team research approaches that incorporate a historical, political, and culturally contextualized view of knowledge are utilized. The utilization of diverse approaches to the study of institutional diversity can assist institutions to understand the relationships that exist across the spectrum of human experiences, particularly concerning issues related to social injustice.

In addition, a participatory approach that begins and ends with those who are the subjects of study is strongly encouraged. This approach encourages participants to be involved in the planning and development of the study, the collection of data, the final analysis of the information gathered, and the development of a set of recommendations for institutional action. This research methodology conveys a vision of empowerment by returning to the participants what truly belongs to them, namely, their voice and self-determination. Inherent in this approach is not an attempt to learn about people, but to come to know with them the reality that challenges them. Through this process, research participates in the discovery of those actions that will function to transform institutional conditions that limit and prevent the enactment of a culturally democratic process (Darder, 1992).

Research in the Interest of Cultural Democracy

Research and its function within an institutional environment are closely linked to the values, beliefs, and practices that are held by those in power. How questions of diversity are framed and defined, the questions that are asked or ignored, and the consequences of institutional research on the lives of subordinate groups are all guided by the prevailing political forces at work. Research in the interest of cultural democracy must be shaped and defined by principles supporting social justice.

In contrast to traditional research that reduces human beings to quantifiable objects in order to predict and control behavior, culturally democratic research begins with the view that human beings participate actively in producing meaning and knowledge in their ongoing interactions with the environment. Research cannot be perceived as a neutral and objective function, but instead must be viewed as an active historical, cultural, and political process of knowledge production. Research must function as a tool for appropriating the codes and cultural symbols of institutional power in an effort to transform institutional environments in the interest of cultural democracy.

Culturally democratic research stimulates constituents to reflect critically upon their world, cultural values and practices, and personal histories so that they may better understand themselves and the social relations of power that affect their lives and shape their social participation. Such research must demystify the artificial limits that are imposed by racism, sexism, classism, and homophobia, by fostering acceptance and understanding of different forms of cultural systems that shape and define diverse communities. Research that supports culturally democratic life must reinforce a language of possibility while acknowledging the human experience of despair that can arise when people must contend daily with the impact of social and economic injustice.

Research in the interest of cultural democracy enables participants to recognize and name their own realities and to understand and assert their own voices within the multitude of discourses present in any institutional environment. It is in essence a critical form of research that stimulates creativity, risk taking, doubting, and questioning in the interest of social justice and equality, while affirming and challenging the strengths and limitations of particular social conditions and institutional realities.

In such a process of study, the researcher can never be perceived as neutral. There is recognition that knowledge production is always informed by the values and interests of all the participants. It is expected that researchers make their values explicit and make consistent efforts to understand how their values shape their work (Gordon, Miller, and Rollock, 1990). In this way, researchers who carry out their work in the interest of cultural democracy can function as social advocates, facilitating a production of knowledge that is committed to the creation of institutional conditions where people find their voices and their rightful places as full and equal participants.

REFERENCES

Crossen, P. (1988). "Four-Year College and University Environments for Minority Degree Achievement," *Review of Higher Education.*11:4: 356–82.

Darder, A. (1991). *Culture and Power in the Classroom.* Westport:Bergin and Garvey.

Darder, A. (1992). "Problematizing the Notion of Puerto Ricans as 'Underclass': Toward a Decolonizing Study of Poverty," *Hispanic Journal of Behavioral Sciences* 14: 1: 144–56.

Fay, B. (1987). *Critical Social Science.* Ithaca: Cornell University Press.

Fisher, F. (1985). "Critical Evaluation of Public Policy: A Methodological Case Study." In F. Forester (ed.), *Critical Theory and Public Life*. Cambridge, MA: MIT Press.

Foucault, M. (1977). *Power/Knowledge: Selected Interviews and Other Writings*. New York: Pantheon Books.

Gordon, E., F. Miller, and D. Rollock (1990). "Coping with Communicentric Bias in Knowledge Production in the Social Sciences," *Educational Researcher* 19:3: 14–19.

Jaramillo, M. (1988). "Institutional Responsibility in the Provision of Educational Experiences to the Hispanic-American Female Student." In T. McKenna and F.I. Ortiz (eds.), *The Broken Web*. Encino, CA: Floricant Press.

Loo, C., and G. Rolison (1986). "Alienation of Ethnic Minority Students at a Predominantly White University," *Journal of Higher Education* 57: 1: 59–77.

Sanders, D. (1987). "Cultural Conflicts: An Important Factor in the Academic Failures of American Indian Students," *Journal of Multicultural Counseling and Development* 15: 2: 81–90.

Slater, P. (1991). *A Dream Deferred*. Boston: Beacon Press.

Smith, D. (1990). "The Challenge for Diversity: Implications for Institutional Research." In M. T. Nettles (ed.), *The Effect of Assessment on Minority Student Participation*. New Directions for Institutional Research, no. 65. San Francisco: Jossey-Bass.

Smith, K. (1990). "Notes from the Epistemological Corner: The Role of Projection in the Creation of Social Science," *Journal of Applied Behavioral Science* 26:1:119–27.

Smith, P. (1990). *Killing the Spirit: Higher Education in America*. New York: Penguin Books.

Young, I. (1990). *Justice and the Politics of Difference*. Princeton, NJ: Princeton University Press.

PART II.
From "Race" to Racism

RICAN-WOMAN-MADNESS IS JUST
ANOTHER WORD FOR LOVE

Rican-woman-madness
is just another word for love,
she is born of the chains of slavery
and the genocidal history of the taino
brushing furiously against
the backdrop of spanish barbarism

She is a fighter, warrior blood
oozes through her veins, fills
her womb and exists willfully
through the pounding of her heart

She will have no qualms about
throwing out the man she loves,
if he comes swinging at her
with the metaphoric machete
of a hateful tongue

No man who has loved a rican woman
can forget the wicked lustfulness
and blessed grace of her sensuality,
she makes love in the living

In her sacred land of histerica
(as we are often proclaimed),
no human emotion is denied,
all are welcomed and pursued
for the sheer pleasure of their sensation
rip roaring from our toes to the
ends of our frizzified rican hair

Rican woman's rage runs deep,
but her love runs deeper,
she is the sensibilities of the
moon, sky, and earth combined,
they penetrate into the very core
of all lives natural existence
transmitting and receiving

a million and one universal vibrations
coming and going all at the same time

The rican woman is a wild woman,
it is true that she has been colonized
by the rabid thieves who stole her land,
and twisted her history to unrecognizable
proportions, but still and yet,
she refuses to be colonized in the spirit
and she will surely kill to protect
the integrity of the people's song

But be not the fool and make no mistakes,
the rican woman is about life and death,
if you desire death she will surely comply
with the fury of the betrayed on a killing
	rampage,
if you desire life, she will clearly oblige
with her sweet and wild rican-woman-mad-
	ness ways

The rican woman
does not hold her tongue,
she will not permit you to toy
with the passion of her existence,
she refuses submission,
she will speak loudly until
she is buried underground,
and then she will return
to haunt you in your dreams

The magical whiff of her presence
refuses to leave the scene once she is gone,
it will stay upon your clothes,
it will saturate your hair,
it will permeate your very being,
she will never let you forget that she exists

So don't be deceived
by the rican assimilated versions
who curtsey and roll around in the
bureaucratic red tape in disguise,
underneath the white-washed facade
hides a wild island spirit
that will not be domesticated,
weeping ceaselessly to be released

Rican woman embraces her power as
the motherhood of all creations,
and she will follow the sweet sounds
of her children or her lover calling
"aye mamita" to the ends of the world
In her negrita self, she is a vessel of love
and shimmering, unadulterated truth,
her truth is of radiant ebony black,
she is not of the sterilized, sophisticated
purity of the etherealized white light,
she is about gutsy, grimy, earthy truth,
the kind that is found beneath the thickness
of old toenails, in the very pit of underarms,
within the folds of fleshy skin, and between
the musty scent of warm full thighs,
her's is a truth of no return, no compromise,
that liberates and frees enslaved black
and brown brothers and sisters who weep
and pray to yemaya and chango in the dark

Rican-woman-madness is just another form
     of love
that is so easily misunderstood, feared, and
tyrannized by those who do not know how to
read the vital signs of a
     rican-woman-madness,

a love that lives in the midst of anguish and
     joy,
all wrapped up together in the urgency and
delight of her salsa island gyrations

Rican woman is a volcano,
her anger is legitimate
for she is tired of the bullshit
cover-up reality of a so-called
culturally diverse rhetorical world,
her struggle is legitimate
for she cannot live in a world of pretense
and colorized marginalization,
her love is legitimate,
for she cannot live in a world of lies

Rican-woman-madness
is just another word for love,
a love that needs open, flowing life in
all its shapes and far reaching dimensions,
a love that will accept nothing but today and
refuses to be appeased with translucent
promises of tomorrow,
a love that will no longer tolerate the forces
of human cruelty and injustice,
a redemptive love that is completely
stripped naked and fully present
just for the asking,
(if you dare).

—ANTONIA DARDER (1983)

CHAPTER 4

The Establishment of Liberatory Alliances with People of Color

What Must Be Understood

> Decolonization involves profound transformation of self, community, and governance structures. It can only be engaged through active withdrawal of consent and resistance to structures of psychic and social domination.
> —CHANDRA TALPADE MOHANTY (2003)

The voice expressed in my poetry and scholarship is a voice informed by a critical engagement with the impact that a history of living at the margins has had upon my life as a colonized, working-class Puerto Rican woman. It speaks also of the difficulties of so many people of color with whom I have worked, served, and struggled, in the midst of our commonalities and differences. To go from voicelessness to voice is always a precarious journey, when one must constantly brush against those colonizing attitudes and practices that objectify and belittle, even within contexts that promise us voice and participation.

My life, like so many others, has been a maze of whirling experiences of political and personal disappointments and heartaches. In the course of my journey, I have come to a place where I can see no possibility of liberation unless we are willing to abandon worn-out traditional protocols and practices that continue to be informed by deceptive and twisted views of our humanity. Instead, we must embrace a politics that is grounded upon a willingness to challenge openly those values, attitudes, and practices within our schools and communities that perpetuate oppression, injustice, and human suffering. I suggest here a politics that can engage with the material truth; our differences are not just a matter of social construction, but are very real material and affective differences, shaped by the brutalities of capital and a history of state-sanctioned impunity. Despite how uncomfortable this may be for our liberal comrades, the truth is that there are some populations, and hence their members, who are fundamentally more oppressed than others in America. And this is so, despite political, philosophical, psychological, or metaphysical notions designed to prove our "sameness" under the skin. This incessant search for sameness, consciously or unconsciously, allows the state to shun its political responsibility to move more expediently toward altering the current conditions of inequality that shape the lives of the majority of people of color in this society and around the world. Of course, to do so would require our national leaders to also contend with the huge conflicts and contradictions that remain at the heart of mainstream life.

I speak of these things, however, not only from my historical experiences as a working-class woman of color, but also from my understanding of our colonized histories. This is an understanding born of critical reflection, dialogue, and political practice with others, within and outside a racialized existence. As such, these critical encounters across difference and sameness have deeply strengthened my resolve to speak from the authority of my own life. Notwithstanding, critical study of Paulo Freire's writings and those of other critical education theorists, as well as my practice with many radical activists, artists, and educators, have given shape to my consciousness and political understanding of what is still required to launch a radical educational movement in the United States. I am very grateful for the manner in which Freire's *Pedagogy of the Oppressed* (1971), in particular, provided me the language to name deeper conditions of oppression that had been silenced, but the greatest meaning his work had for me came within relationships of community struggle.

Hence, it has been through a multitude of encounters that I have come to the perspective I now hold and share with you—a perspective that certainly is not held by all people of color, a perspective for which I have been seen as angry and harsh by some or naive and foolish by others, even some who themselves claim to speak in the name of the oppressed. And yet, I submit to you that mine is a perspective that echoes the suffering, frustration, and rage of the disenfranchised working class and people of color in this country.

Critique of Multiculturalism

> Multiculturalism became an ideology of conservatism, of pre-
> serving the status quo intact, in the face of a real desire to move
> forward.
>
> —ARUN KUNDANI (2002)

I would like to begin with a brief critique of what I see occurring under the auspices and rhetoric of multiculturalism. Most of the work that has emerged out of
traditional theories of multiculturalism has simply replicated, albeit in a more
sophisticated manner, a melting pot philosophy—a philosophy that is devoid of
understanding of or respect for the cultural integrity of oppressed populations and
that is driven by an obsessive need to construct a false sense of social unity and
sameness without addressing the social conditions that have fueled intense cultural and class divisions in this country for centuries.

Lip service is paid to inequity, yet most theories of multiculturalism do little to directly challenge or alter the existing relations of power and structures of
privilege, and, thus, the underbelly of this society remains unchanged. The ruling members of the dominant culture still retain the majority of decision-making
power in the world, including the world of multiculturalism, whose discourse principally emanates from a Eurocentric worldview, laced with xenophobia and superiority. Meanwhile, liberatory interventions on behalf of dispossessed communities
remain at the margins of public policy debates. And efforts to change this long-
standing phenomenon can elicit suspicion from mainstream officials, given the
potential disruption that policies of equity can cause the status quo.

All the while, academic notions of "multiple worldviews" and the "fragmented
postmodern self" unwittingly serve to reproduce a new layer of universalizing discourses of the self and the "other," which conveniently perpetuate ideological colonialism within teacher education programs and classrooms across the country. At
times, even promising theoretical concepts such as "border crossers" or "border
intellectuals" can be appropriated and commodified to legitimate subtle—and
not so subtle—forms of racism and cultural invasion in the education of subordinate populations. This speaks of a cultural invasion that is enacted through an
academic disrespect for the cultural boundaries and integrity that are vital to the
survival of colonized populations in the face racism, class oppression, and gender
and sexual discrimination.

I argue that such a phenomenon is fueled by an arrogant refusal to acknowledge the limitations of one's subject position as a dominant cultural being and, as
a consequence, the failure to grapple with the limitations of mainstream perspec-

tives, particularly when such dominant views seek to name and define the experience of the "other"—experiences that clearly exist *outside* of the cultural and historical purview of the dominant group. Hence, repeatedly we see white scholars who draw liberally on the cultural knowledge and history of the "other," without much concern for the need to understand accurately the cultural genealogies that inform cultural meanings or fuel their intended purpose. And all of this is done in the name of scientific study or cultural studies research, which often serves only to confuse matters more, while dismissing or neglecting the right of indigenous voices to speak for ourselves.

Just as perverse is the manner in which assimilative ideals are reinforced in American schools through liberal practices that are executed in the name of diversity and multiculturalism. This is most blatantly observed in the way that power relations are structured within the process of schooling. Despite thirty years of multicultural reforms, those who hold institutional power have remained constant, with few opportunities created for those who have been historically marginalized to influence the transformation of institutional life—unless, of course, the person of color is willing to dance to the tunes of an assimilative band.

The consequence is that despite the rhetoric of cultural diversity in schools, colleges, and universities across this country, institutional support for change exists primarily as abstract ideal, written down in lovely mission statements or pronounced with fervor at public gatherings on "diversity." Meanwhile, people of color in the university, for example, are repeatedly forced to struggle under conditions of "collegial adversity," to carve out the alternative opportunities and counterhegemonic spaces necessary to influence organically the direction of emancipatory ideas, if any transformative practices are to unfold.

Another example of this phenomenon is observed in the suspicions and objections that quickly surface when working-class educators and parents of color clamor for the need for more bicultural and bilingual teachers in public schools to teach their children. In such cases, well-meaning folks from the dominant culture become agitated, arguing against essentialism, rather than contending with their underlying fears. Given the current hierarchical structure of education, to make changes that would increase teachers of color would, in turn, reduce the number of teaching posts for white educators in the field—particularly for those with little experience or interest in further preparing themselves to teach working-class students of color in culturally relevant and meaningful ways. Instead, many of these teachers who object most loudly seem smitten by their own privileged belief in themselves as good teachers for *all* children. Thus, many of the teachers and educators from the dominant culture are hard pressed to accept that there might be very important cultural pedagogical knowledge that can best be provided by teachers who come from the same communities as the children themselves. And this can remain so, even when carefully progressive white teachers in the field can make important contributions to the education of our children.

Further, institutional practices implemented in response to multicultural directives have also worked to instrumentalize and commodify people of color as tokens within education and other spheres of society. As a consequence, practices of tokenism have functioned to not only prevent the full development of our voices and participation but to limit and compromise the integrity of our work with our students and our communities. Moreover, tokenism allows mainstream institutions to perpetuate a self-congratulatory stance while simultaneously limiting both the political and cultural diversification of its leadership. What is especially revealing about this commonplace practice is that, despite all the proclamations of diversity, there persists a veiled belief in the innate deficiency of people of color and thus an excessive concern for and vigilance of our competence, moral worth, and loyalty to the institution.

Harmful institutional practices of "workplace mobbing" can also be closely linked to systematic efforts to limit the possibility for leadership by people of color. This is most prevalent when our cultural communication styles and political views make those in power feel uncomfortable or threatened, particularly if there is the possibility of influencing colleagues, students, or others in the larger community. Furthermore, during times of institutional political conflict, those in power will remind us that there are many kinds of "difference," as if we ourselves were not aware of heterogeneity in our own communities. At such times, those in authority conveniently hide behind discourses of diversion rather than willingly address institutional issues that thwart cultural democracy. And often it is at this juncture that more "acceptable" people of color are recruited to neutralize any radicalizing voices in the ranks.

Many classroom practices, in particular, are driven by the persistent hegemonic values that undergird the prescribed multicultural curriculum. In other words, I'm referring to the use of cultural artifacts and celebrations stripped of their cultural meanings and disembodied of their revolutionary intent. And even more problematic is the use of a multicultural curriculum without ever challenging pedagogical practices and relationships that perpetuate racism, class oppression, and other forms of social inequalities.

Finally, mainstream institutional practices that function to undermine cultural democracy in order to protect the legitimacy of the academy must be exposed. This is the case despite university departments that "tolerate" liberal and even radical discourses in the name of academic freedom, while structurally reproducing conservative meritocratic practices related to faculty hiring and promotion, student admissions criteria, classroom structures, research methodologies, program development, and so on—all implicated in the process of racialization.

Limitations of the Critical Pedagogy Movement in the United States

The first need of a free people is to define their own terms.

—KWAME TURE (1967/2007)

I would like to examine briefly what I believe are some of the limitations of the critical pedagogy movement in the United States, with respect to addressing the educational concerns of communities of color, despite its progressive foundations. First, there has been a tenacious refusal to engage seriously with questions of cultural difference and cultural conflicts beyond a class analysis, which, although central, can inadvertently permit critical pedagogical discourses to adhere to a dominant Eurocentric and patriarchal worldview. This absence, in turn, marginalizes and silences critical voices forced to contend constantly with dynamics of cultural conflict and oppositional tensions inherent to a racialized existence.

Second, the intellectual leadership of the critical pedagogy movement has been primarily in the hands of white males who determine, solely from their particular subject position, whose work is to be deemed legitimate and whose work is deemed questionable. Often these decisions are directly in concert with their own comfort or discomfort with discourses of difference or their own capacity (or lack of capacity) to comprehend the logic of cultural formations of racialized and gendered subjects—particularly if they are women of color, who not only negotiate daily issues of poverty but also must contend with the oppressive forces of racism and sexism that weigh heavily upon our life circumstances and our mobility as both everyday citizens and critical intellectuals in a field where we had hoped to find acceptance and solidarity.

Another major concern among people of color is the manner in which the critical pedagogy movement has supported the construction of theory devoid of lived experience. Unfortunately, this has weakened, rather than strengthened, the power of this movement. To address this concern requires a delimiting of a pedagogy that can actually speak to the flesh and blood of oppression. This is a critical pedagogy that is able to grapple with the actual conditions and consequences of human suffering today and can tolerate the pain, anger, and frustration in the voices of Blacks, Chicanos, Puerto Ricans, Native Americans, and other oppressed people—folks who took to heart the word *liberation*, replete in the critical pedagogy literature. The absence of an organic approach, where people of color name their own terms, negatively impacts the building of alliances across our differences. And, more to the point, it puts into question the solidarity of critical theorists who many times unwittingly shut down the critique of women and people of color trying to address for themselves the historical abuses and repression of disenfranchised communities.

Linked to all this has been the perpetuation of an elitist criterion for assigning value and status to individuals within this movement with respect to their legitimate role as intellectuals. As such, the quantity of books you have written seems to assign one greater value as an intellectual, despite limited experiences outside of the academic realm; while those who have spent their lives toiling "in the trenches" of community and labor activism but who have written little are viewed as somehow less intellectual, hence less politically legitimate in their discursive accounts of political struggle and oppression.

And just as disturbing are the racialization and marginalization of different cultural styles of speaking and different ways of naming conditions of inequality. This happens so often that for people of color to remain in integrity with our cultural ways of knowing and being can actually place us at risk of being labeled "too intense," "too emotional," or "too angry" by the very people who profess acceptance of differences, solidarity with anti-racism, and commitment to democratic participation. Hence, the message that is clearly given is that there still exists one correct and universal way to think critically and to speak intelligently about questions of racism within this movement in order to be heard and treated with respect.

A New Politics of Liberation

> Our struggle for liberation has significance only if it…has as a fundamental goal the liberation of all people.
>
> —BELL HOOKS (1999)

If we are to create a political movement that is above all committed to anti-racism and anti-imperialism, then we must embrace a new politics of liberation that truly encompasses the participation of all people. And to do so calls for a politics that can assign as much significance to what people say or write as to what they practice and live in their everyday lives. This is not to suggest a criterion of purity—for everyone has experienced their share of mistakes and failures—but rather that we must make a greater effort to face our mistakes, through an ongoing commitment to struggle within ourselves and with one another to live with greater integrity with the words of liberation we write and speak.

I recognize that we do not live in a world that easily permits us to be honest and open. Yet, to live a politics of liberation, we must be willing to struggle precisely for such a world. It asks of us to discontinue our lifeless infatuation with the safety of the abstract, despite its illusion of comfort, and, instead, to embrace more fully the knowledge that emerges from the ordinary of everyday life, in the spaces where people live, eat, work, love, suffer, and die. And this, of course, means that we need a critical pedagogical movement where racialized people can anchor our critical praxis both to our contemporary conditions of struggle and to our historical knowledge of survival, which often looks very different from that of the dominant culture.

In a society like that of the United States, enacting a politics of liberation is next to impossible unless we come to terms with the tremendous power inherent in our ability to act and engage collectively as consciously grounded cultural beings—the very power that those with wealth and privilege would have us thwart and stifle in ourselves. To come to the table as free cultural citizens, we must know who we are within the context of American society and the conditions that have shaped our histories. This also requires an acknowledgment of the fundamental strengths and limitations of our social locations, with respect to our ability to know and transform the world. In so doing, we can come closer to understanding the cultural knowledge and histories that inform our ideas, while also recognizing that to know one another as comrades we must be involved in ongoing dialogue and political labor together.

Hence, the most powerful political discourses are best generated organically through the intimacy of solidarity that emerges from our mutual emancipatory labor. This is in contrast to those who believe that the power of transformation is primarily dependent on the articulation of texts. This is not to say that written insights about economic inequalities, social exclusions, or theories of liberation are not significant references that can supplement in important ways our understanding of the world, but rather that the written word alone will never constitute the centrality of emancipatory struggle for the transformation of the world—this can only happen in the realm of human encounters in the flesh.

This perspective represents both a subjective and an objective dance with life; it is a critical form of both study and relationships that begins and ends ultimately with ourselves *and* one another. As such, we accept responsibility for our thoughts, ideas, beliefs, and the practices that emerge from these. It is a politics that calls for a clear purpose and commitment to a vision of social justice and equality and to an ongoing examination and reexamination of our lives with respect to both the short- and long-term consequences of our actions. For wherever we are headed, individually and collectively, is always intimately linked to the steps that we choose to take in our present efforts. Thus, *the means does not justify the ends*, but rather the means will shape the ends. And, as such, we must be courageously intolerant and uncompromising when it comes to human suffering and injustice.

Rules of Engagement for Building Alliances across Difference

> What we share with the allegedly impenetrable other is just this overlapping of strangenesses; and it is this, rather than some mutual mirror-imaging of egos which has to become the basis of genuine encounter. Always seeing the other as others is partly a way of avoiding this unnerving recognition, just as attending consistently to the margins is usually a way of implying that there are no conflicts to be found at the centre.
>
> —TERRY EAGLETON (2003)

What does this all mean for building alliances with people of color who are engaged in liberatory struggle? What are the rules of engagement across the inequalities of racism and other forms of injustice? The above suggests a variety of issues that must be examined and critically engaged in political efforts to build alliances across the differences that exist between members of racialized communities and those from the mainstream. This is done in the hope that we might actually catch a glimpse of this "overlapping of strangenesses" we share, rather than holding one another hostage to the "mutual mirror-imaging of egos" that debilitate our capacity for love and solidarity.

Given the center of gravity for this discussion, the following suggestions are grounded in decades of efforts by racialized communities to establish solidarity across cultural differences with comrades from the dominant culture. These represent a sort of shorthand *terms of engagement* that must be understood if we are to move forward more effectively in our political work to transform schools.

Members from the dominant culture and class must struggle to overcome their internalized and normalized ideas and practices of entitlement and privilege. Often unexamined attitudes and practices, informed by social norms of bias and prejudice, are perpetuated in the most unconscious, inadvertent, and subtle ways. Breaking out of this racializing habitus demands humility and a willingness to stop and listen when such actions are challenged by those who experience the brunt of racism.

There is a need to fully interrogate and challenge the meaning of "equality" and "democratic participation" with respect to the actual values and practices that shape organizational and institutional life. To do so requires nothing less than a willingness by those from the dominant culture and class to surrender their control over vital resources—space, money, decision-making power, and influence—in the interest of reconfiguring existing conditions of inequity in the flesh. Without a commitment to democratizing the distribution of wealth and power, words of social justice ring as hypocrisy.

Those from the dominant culture and class must cease naming our experience for us, outside of our participation. Instead, if they sincerely wish to express solidarity for the self-determination of people of color and support anti-racism and anti-imperialism, then they must work to use their privilege and influence to support, in concrete ways, our struggles for a place to work, speak, and affirm our existences as first-class citizens of this nation and to participate, as equals, in the building of a new world.

There must be an active commitment by those from the dominant culture to work in their own communities and to challenge forms of injustice that result from racism, classism, sexism, homophobia, disablism, and other forms of institutional oppression, for all forms of oppression are inextricably linked to the overarching consequences of a political economy that chews up our hearts to feed the fat royal beast of capital.

Relationships of difference must emerge from a place of honesty and courage, in order to assist each one of us in accepting that no one is ever capable of knowing it all. Thus, to know the world more fully, we need one another, just as to change the world we need one another. And here again is the capacity to approach political relationships across differences with humility, dignity, and respect not only for the universalisms we share as human beings, but also for the cultural particularisms that are deeply rooted to histories of genocide, enslavement, and colonization.

Moreover, those from the dominant culture and class must come to a deep realization that oppressed and racialized subjects will struggle for self-determination and liberation, with or without the commitment and participation of those from the dominant culture and class. And as such, nothing less than an uncompromising respect for our social agency and self-determination must be at the heart of the matter.

And so, there must exist a clear understanding by all that the struggle of disenfranchised people is not one that is limited to the domain of the academy or the realm of pristine ideology, but rather must be part and parcel of a greater political emancipatory vision, one that is linked consistently to the material conditions that shape our lives and the lives of our communities.

Conclusion

These words spring forth from decades of living with compromise and tolerance, waiting for the promises of the civil rights era to unfold; witnessing the unnecessary suffering of children, women, and men of color; responding to the brutal consequences of incarceration, poverty, isolation, alienation, and violence; contending with the disastrous impact of well-meaning and well-intentioned multicultural educational efforts; and tempering my rage at the wholesale perpetuation of white class privilege here and abroad, in the name of justice and democracy.

The time has come for no more compromise, no more superficial solutions or policies of appeasement. Our political actions must be open, clear, direct, and fully committed to a world where we can exist free from the brutality of racism—and this begins with each one of us, through our lived purpose, courage, and commitment, to refuse nothing less than liberation in our daily lives. For it is in the ordinary existences of the everyday that the revolutionary principles of critical pedagogy must be firmly rooted, and it is in the everyday that the ongoing struggle for our humanity must be waged.

REFERENCES

Eagleton, T. (2003). *Figures of Dissent*. London: Verso, p. 4.

Freire, P. (1971). *Pedagogy of the Oppressed*. New York: Continuum.

hooks, b. (1999). *Ain't I a Woman: Black Women and Feminism*. Boston: South End Press, p. 13.

Kundani, A. (2002). *The Death of Multiculturalism*. Institute of Race Relations (available at: http://www.irr.org.uk).

Mohanty, C.T. (2003). *Feminism without Borders*. Durham, NC, and London: Duke University Press, p. 7.

Ture, K. (Stokely, Carmichael) (2007). *Stokely Speaks: From Black Power to Pan-Africanism*. Chicago: Lawrence Hill Books, p. 65.

CHAPTER 5

Shattering the "Race" Lens

Toward a Critical Theory of Racism

With Rodolfo Torres

Race has become the lens through which is refracted all of society's problems.

—KENAN MALIK (1996)[1]

The truth is that there are no races…. The evil that is done by the concept and by easy—yet impossible—assumptions as to its application. What we miss through our obsession . .. is, simply, reality.

—KWAME ANTHONY APPIAH (1995)[2]

In recent years, "race"[3] has been the focus of theoretical, political, and policy debates. Dramatic national and international changes, both economic and political, have created conditions in which, on the one hand, racialized structures, processes and representations are more intricate and elusive; yet, on the other hand, the historically entrenched inequalities persist. The changing socioeconomic conditions in the United States present immense challenges and opportunities for anti-racist activists and social science scholars to rethink the nature of contemporary racialized inequality. With President Bill Clinton's recent "race initiative" commencement address at University of California, San Diego, and the acrimonious debates on affirmative action, language policy, and immigration, it is more evident now than ever before that there is a need for a critical theory of racism that can assist us to better understand the complex issues associated with the increasing racialization of American society.

"Race," though a key concept in sociological discourse and public debate, remains problematic. Policy pundits, journalists, and conservative and liberal academics alike all work within categories of "race" and use this concept in public discourse as though there is unanimity regarding its analytical value. However, like all other component elements of what Antonio Gramsci[4] called common sense, much of the everyday usage of "race" is uncritical. Gramsci argues that human beings view the world from a perspective that contains both hegemonic forms of thinking and critical insight. As such, notions of common sense are "rooted in cultural folklore but at the same time are enriched with scientific ideas and philosophical opinions, which enter into ordinary daily life."[5] Racialized group conflicts are similarly advanced and framed as a "race relations" problem, and presented largely in Black/White terms.

A prime example of this confusion is the analysis of the causes of the 1992 Los Angeles riots. In the aftermath of the riots, academics and journalists analyzed the riots as a matter of "race relations"—first it was a problem between Blacks and Whites, then between Blacks and Koreans, and then between Blacks and Latinos, and back to Blacks and Whites. The interpretation of the riots as a "race relations" problem failed to take into account the economic restructuring and the drastic shifts in demographic patterns that have created new dynamics of class and racialized ethnic relations in Los Angeles.[6] These new dynamics include increasing changes in the ethnic composition of the city and a dramatic shift from a manufacturing-centered economy to one based on light manufacturing, service industries, and information technologies—urban dynamics intricately linked to "the globalizing pressure of capitalism to abandon the will to social investment within the national-domestic sphere."[7]

The Question of Identity Politics

[W]e work with raced identities on already reified ground. In the context of domination, raced identities are imposed and internalized, then renegotiated and reproduced. From artificial to natural, we court a hard-to-perceive social logic that reproduces the very conditions we strain to overcome.

—JON CRUZ (1996)[8]

Over the last three decades, there has been an overwhelming tendency among social science scholars to focus on notions of "race." Over the last three decades, there has been an overwhelming tendency among a variety of critical scholars to focus on the concept of "race" as a central category of analysis for interpreting the social conditions of inequality and marginalization.[9] As a consequence, much of the literature on subordinate cultural populations, with its emphasis on such issues as "racial inequality," "racial segregation," "racial identity," has utilized the construct of "race" as a central category of analysis for interpreting the social conditions of inequality and marginalization. In turn, this literature has reinforced a racialized politics of identity and representation, with its problematic emphasis on "racial" identity as the overwhelming impulse for political action. This theoretical practice has led to serious analytical weaknesses and absence of depth in much of the historical and contemporary writings on racialized populations in this country. The politics of busing in the early 1970s provides an excellent example that illustrates this phenomenon. Social scientists studying "race relations" concluded that contact among "Black" and "White" students would improve "race relations" and the educational conditions of "Black" students if they were bused to "White" (better) schools outside their neighborhoods.[10] Thirty years later, many parents and educators adamantly denounce the busing solution (a solution based on a discourse of "race") as not only fundamentally problematic to the fabric of African American and Chicano communities, but an erroneous social policy experiment that failed to substantially improve the overall academic performance of students in these communities.

Given this legacy, it is not surprising to find that the theories, practices, and policies that have informed social science analysis of racialized populations today are overwhelmingly rooted in a politics of identity, an approach that is founded on parochial notions of "race" and representation which ignore the imperatives of capitalist accumulation and the existence of class divisions within racialized subordinate populations. The folly of this position is critiqued by Ellen Meiksins Wood[11] in her article entitled "Identity Crisis," where she exposes the limitations of a politics of identity which fails to contend with the fact that capitalism is the most totalizing system of social relations the world has ever known.

Yet, in much of the work on African American, Latino, Native American, and Asian populations, an analysis of class and a critique of capitalism is conspicuously absent. And even when it is mentioned, the emphasis is primarily on an undifferentiated plurality of identity politics or an "intersection of oppressions," which, unfortunately, ignores the overwhelming tendency of capitalism to homogenize rather than to diversify human experience. Moreover, this practice is particularly disturbing since no matter where one travels around the world, there is no question that racism is integral to the process of capital accumulation. For example, the current socioeconomic conditions of Latinos and other racialized populations can be traced to the relentless emergence of the global economy and recent economic policies of expansion, such as the North American Free Trade Agreement (NAFTA). A recent United Nations report by the International Labor Organization confirms the negative impact of globalization on racialized populations. By the end of 1998, it was projected that one billion workers would be unemployed. The people of Africa, China, and Latin America have been most affected by the current restructuring of capitalist development.[12] This phenomenon of racialized capitalism is directly linked to the abusive practices and destructive impact of the "global factory"—a global financial enterprise system that includes such transnational corporations as Coca-Cola, Walmart, Disney, Ford Motor Company, and General Motors. In a recent speech on "global economic apartheid," John Cavanagh,[13] co-executive director of the Institute for Policy Studies in Washington, D.C., comments on the practices of the Ford Motor Company.

> The Ford Motor Company has its state-of-the-art assembly plant in Mexico...where because it can deny basic worker rights, it can pay one-tenth the wages and yet get the same quality and the same productivity in producing goods.... The same technologies by the way which are easing globalization are also primarily cutting more jobs than they're creating.

The failure of scholars to confront this dimension in their analysis of contemporary society as a racialized phenomenon and their tendency to continue treating class as merely one of a multiplicity of (equally valid) perspectives, which may or may not "intersect" with the process of racialization, are serious shortcomings. In addressing this issue, we must recognize that identity politics, which generally gloss over class differences and /or ignore class contradictions, have often been used by radical scholars and activists within African American, Latino, and other subordinate cultural communities in an effort to build a political base. Here, fabricated constructions of "race" are objectified and mediated as truth to ignite political support, divorced from the realities of class struggle. By so doing, they have unwittingly perpetuated the vacuous and dangerous notion that the political and economic are separate spheres of society which can function independently—a view that firmly anchors and sustains prevailing class relations of power in society.

Ramon Grosfoguel and Chloe S. Georas posit that "social identities are constructed and reproduced in complex and entangled political, economic, and symbolic hierarchy."[14] Given this complex entanglement, what is needed is a more dynamic and fluid notion of how we think about different cultural identities within the context of contemporary capitalist social formations. Such a perspective of identity would support our efforts to shatter static and frozen notions that perpetuate ahistorical, apolitical, and classless views of culturally pluralistic societies. How we analytically accomplish this is no easy matter. But however this task is approached, we must keep in mind Wood's concern:

> We should not confuse respect for the plurality of human experience and social struggles with a complete dissolution of historical causality, where there is nothing but diversity, difference and contingency, no unifying structures, no logic of process, no capitalism and therefore no negation of it, no universal project of human emancipation.[15]

Hence, if we are to effectively challenge the horrendous economic impacts of globalization on racialized communities, we must recognize that a politics of identity is grossly inept and unsuited for building and sustaining collective political movements for social justice and economic democracy. Instead, what we need is to fundamentally reframe the very terrain that gives life to our political understanding of what it means to live, work, and struggle in a society with widening class differentiation and ever-increasing racialized inequality. Through such an analytical process of reframing, we can expand the terms by which identities are considered, examined, and defined, recognizing racialized relations of power are fundamentally shaped by the profound organizational and spatial transformations of the capitalist economy.

A Critique of Race Relations

> If "race relations" are a feature of contemporary society, it seems obvious that academics should study them. But the casual observer could equally well conclude from personal observation that it is "obvious" that the sun circulates around the earth. In order to believe otherwise, it is necessary to confront personal experiences with analytical reasoning and forms of rational measurement. In other words, "obviousness" is a condition which depends upon the location of the observer and the set of concepts employed to conceive and interpret the object.
>
> —ROBERT MILES (1993)[16]

There has been a tendency in postmodern and poststructuralist views of the antiracism project and "race relations" to neglect or ignore profound changes in the structural nature and dynamics of U.S. capitalism in place of obvious or common-sense appraisals of racialized inequality. This same tendency is also evident in much of the recent scholarship on cultural politics and social difference. At a time when a historical materialist analysis of capitalism is most crucially needed, many social theorists and radical educators seem reticent to engage the very idea of capitalism with any analytical rigor or methodological specificity. Yet, recent structural changes in the U.S. political economy and the increasing cultural diversity of America have made the issue of racism much more complex than ever before.

Rather than occupying a central position, these historical socioeconomic changes serve merely as a backdrop to the contemporary theoretical debates on the meaning of "race" and representation in contemporary society, debates that, more often than not, are founded on deeply psychologized or abstracted interpretations of racialized differences and conflicts. This constitutes a significant point of contention, given the dramatic changes in U.S. class formation and the demographic landscape of major urban centers. These changing conditions have resulted in major shifts in perceptions of social location, prevailing attitudes, and contemporary views of racialized populations. More so than ever, these socioeconomic conditions are linked to transnational realities shared by populations of Mexico, Taiwan, the Caribbean, and other "developing" countries, despite specific regional histories which gave rise to particular sociocultural configurations, configurations that are fundamentally shaped within the context of the ever-changing global economy.

Recent works in cultural studies, multicultural education, and critical pedagogy have brought new critical perspectives to the study of racism and cultural differences within society. U.S. scholars such as Cornel West, Michael Omi, Howard Winant, bell hooks, Henry Giroux, and others have attempted to recast the debate on the nature of "race" and racism and its implications for social change and educational reform. More specifically, these scholars discuss the concept of "race" within the larger context of changing social and economic conditions and posit "race" as both a social construct and fluid analytical category, in an effort to challenge static notions of "race" as a biologically determined human phenomenon. Although it cannot be denied that these provocative and eloquent works represent a challenge to the mainstream analysis of "race relations" and have made contributions to our understanding of the significance of racism and anti-racist struggles, they have failed to reconceptualize the traditional social science paradigm that relies on the reified category of "race." In the final analysis, the conceptual framework utilized by these scholars is entrenched in the conventional sociology of "race relations" language.

Nowhere has this theoretical shortcoming been more evident than in the contemporary multicultural education debate—a debate that has widely informed the development of postmodern educational theory today. Despite an expressed "transformative" intent, much of the multicultural education literature has only peripherally positioned public education within the larger context of class and racialized class relations. Noticeably absent from much of the writings of even critical multicultural educators is a substantial critique of the social relations and structures of capitalism and the relationship of educational practices to the rapidly changing conditions of the U.S. political economy. The absence of an analysis of the capitalist wage-labor system and class relations with its structural inequalities of income and power represents a serious limitation in our efforts to construct a theory and practice of democratic life.

A lack of imagination in multicultural education discussions is also highly evidenced by a discourse that continues to be predominantly anchored in the Black-White framework that has for over a century shaped our thinking and scholarship related to social group differences. One of the most severe and limited aspects of the Black-White framework to the future of the anti-racist project is its tendency (albeit unintentionally) to obstruct or camouflage the need to examine the particular historical and contextual dimensions that give rise to different forms of racisms around the globe. Further, the conflation of racialized relations into a Black-White paradigm, with its consequential rendering of other subordinate cultural populations to an invisible or "second-class oppression" status, has prevented scholars from engaging with the specificity of particular groups and delving more fully into the arena of comparative ethnic histories of racism and how these are ultimately linked to class forms of social inequalities.

The habitual practice of framing social relations as "race relations" in discussions of students from subordinate cultural communities obfuscates the complexity of the problem. Here educational theorists assign certain significance to "racial" characteristics rather than attributing student responses to school conditions and how these are shaped by the structure of society and the economic and political limitations which determine the material conditions under which students must achieve. The unfortunate absence of this critique veils the real reasons why African American, Latin American, and other "minority" students underachieve, perform poorly on standardized tests, are over-represented in remedial programs and under-represented in gifted programs and magnet schools, and continue to drop out of high school at alarming rates. As a consequence, educational solutions are often derived from distorted perceptions of the problem and lead to misguided policies and practices. The politics of busing in the early 1970s discussed earlier in this chapter provides an excellent example of this phenomenon of distortion.

Although some would be quick to object to our critique, we can see the above also at work in the manner in which many education scholars have focused their studies in racialized communities. Overall, studies with minority students have placed an overwhelming emphasis on cultural and linguistic questions tied to

academic achievement. This is illustrated by the large body of education literature that focuses on the cultural difference of "language minority" students, while
only marginally discussing the impact of racialized inequality and class position on identity and cultural formations, as if somehow the problems of African
Americans, Latinos, Native Americans, and other students from subordinate cultural populations can be resolved simply through the introduction of culturally
relevant curriculum or the enactment of language policy. Moreover, it is this limited view of the problem that most informs the recent political debates between
supporters of bilingual education and California's Proposition 227 (also known as
the Unz Initiative or English for the Children).

From "Race" to Racialization

> For three hundred years black Americans insisted that "race" was
> no useful distinguishing factor in human relationships. During
> those same three centuries every academic discipline...insisted
> that "race" was the determining factor in human development.
> TONI MORRISON (1989)[17]

As Morrison implies, unproblematized "common sense" acceptance and use of
"race" as a legitimate way to frame social relations have been highly prevalent in
the social sciences. The use of this term, for example, among Chicano scholars in
the 1960s can be linked to academic acts of resistance to the term "ethnicity" and
theories of assimilation which were generally applied to discuss immigration populations of European descent. In efforts to distance Chicano scholarship from this
definition and link it to a theory of internal colonialism, cultural imperialism, and
racism, Chicanos were discussed as a colonized "racial" group in much the same
manner that many radical theorists positioned African Americans. Consequently,
the term's association with power, resistance, and self-determination has veiled
the problematics of "race" as a social construct. Protected by the force of cultural
nationalist rhetoric, "race" as an analytical term has remained a "paper tiger"—
seemingly powerful in discourse matters but ineffectual as an analytical metaphor, incapable of moving us away from the pervasive notion of "race" as an innate
determinant of behavior.

In these times, we would be hard-pressed to find a progressive scholar who
would subscribe to the use of "race" as a determinant of specific social phenomena associated with inherent (or genetic) characteristics of a group. Yet the use of
"race" as an analytical category continues to maintain a stronghold in both aca-

demic and popular discourse. What does it mean to attribute analytical status to the idea of "race" and use it as an explanatory concept in theoretical discussions? The use of "race" as an analytical category means to position it as a central organizing theoretical principle in deconstructing social relations of difference as these pertain to subordinate cultural populations.

Notwithstanding provocative arguments by left theorists such as Adolph Reed Jr., who unequivocally assert that "Race is purely a social construction; it has no core reality outside a specific social and historical context…its material force derives from state power, not some ahistorical 'nature' or any sort of primordial group affinities,"[18] there is an unwillingness to abandon its use. Yet, it is this persistent use of "race" in the literature and research on African Americans, Latinos, and other culturally subordinated populations that perpetuates its definition as a causal factor. As such, the notion of "race" as a social construction "only leads us back into the now-familiar move of substituting a sociohistorical conception of race for the biological one…that is simply to bury the biological conception below the surface, not to transcend it."[19] Hence, significance and meaning are still attributed to phenotypical features rather than to the historically reproduced processes of racialization. This ultimately serves to conceal the underlying causes of material conditions experienced by racialized groups that are determined by complex social processes, one of which is premised on the articulation of racism to effect legitimate exclusion.[20]

This process of racialization is at work in the disturbing "scientific" assertion that "race" determines academic performance made by Richard J. Herrnstein and Charles Murray in their book *The Bell Curve*.[21] Their work illustrates the theoretical minefield of perpetuating such an analytical category in the social sciences and the potential negative consequences on racialized groups. The use of the term "race" serves to conceal the truth that it is not "race" that determines academic performance, but rather, that academic performance is the outcome of an interplay of complex social processes, one of which is tied to the articulation of racism (and its subsequent practices of racialization) to effect exclusion in the classroom and beyond.

It is within the historical and contemporary contexts of such scholarship that differences in skin color have been and are signified as a mark which suggests the existence of different "races." As a consequence, a primary response among many progressive activists and scholars when we call for the elimination of "race" as an analytical category is to reel off accusations of a "color-blind" discourse. This is not what we are arguing. What we do argue is that the fixation on skin color is not inherent in its existence but is a product of signification. This is to say, human beings identify skin color to mark or symbolize other phenomena in a variety of social contexts in which other significations occur. As a consequence, when human practices include and exclude people in light of the signification of skin color, collective identities are produced and social inequalities are structured.[22]

Moreover, it is this employment of the idea of "race" in the structuring of social relations that is termed racialization. More specifically, Miles in his book *Racism* defines this process of racialization as

> those instances where social relations between people have been structured by the signifi-
> cation of human biological characteristics in such a way as to define and construct differ-
> entiated social collectivities...the concept therefore refers to a process of categorization, a
> representational process of defining an Other (usually, but not exclusively) somatically.[23]

Hence, to interpret accurately the conditions faced by subordinate cultural populations requires us to move from the idea of "race" to an understanding of racialization and its impact on class formations. This summons a bold analytical transition from the language of "race" to recognizing the centrality of racism and the process of racialization in our understanding of exclusionary practices that give rise to structural inequalities.

Toward a Plurality of Racisms

> [T]he presumption of a single monolithic racism is being
> replaced by a mapping of the multifarious historical formula-
> tions of racisms.
>
> —DAVID THEO GOLDBERG[34]

In order to address these structural inequalities, an analytical shift is required, from "race" to a plural conceptualization of "racisms" and their historical artic-ulations with other ideologies. This plural notion of "racisms" more accurately captures the historically specific nature of racism and the variety of meanings attributed to evaluations of difference and assessments of superiority and inferi-ority of people. Conversely, to continue our engagement of racism as a singular ideological phenomenon fails to draw on the multiplicity of historical and social processes inherent in the heterogeneity of racialized relations. This is to say, for example, that the notion of "White supremacy" can only have any real meaning within populations whose exploitation and domination are essentialized based on skin color. As such, this view severs the experience of African Americans, for instance, from meaningful comparative analysis with those racialized populations whose subordination is predicated on other social characteristics.

Consequently, "White supremacy" arguments cannot be employed to ana-lyze, for example, the racialization of Jews in Germany during the 1930s, or Gypsy populations in Eastern Europe, or the Tutsi population in the Congo. Closer to home, the concept of "White supremacy" sheds little light on what is happening in Watts and South Central Los Angeles between the Korean petite-bourgeoisie and the African American and Latino underclass or reserve army (to use a more traditional concept!). Instead, what we are arguing for is a plural concept of racism that can free us from the "Black/White" dichotomy and, in its place, assert the historically shifting and politically complex nature of racialization. More specifically, it is a pluralized concept of racism that has relevance and analytical utility in comprehending the political economy of racialized relations in South Central Los Angeles as well as the larger sociocultural landscape that can, beyond this analysis, link the economic structures of oppression in this local context to the global context of racialized capitalism. Most importantly, we argue that the problems in racialized communities are not about "race" but rather about the intricate interplay between a variety of racisms and class. It is for this reason that we do not believe that scholars should not be trying to advance a "critical theory of race."[35] A persistence in attributing the idea of "race" with analytical status can only lead us further down a theoretical and political dead end. Instead, the task at hand is to deconstruct "race" and detach it from the concept of racism. This is to say, what is essential for activists and social science scholars is to understand that the construction of the idea of "race" is embodied in racist ideology that supports the practice of racism. It is racism as an ideology that produces the notion of "race," not the existence of "races" that produces racisms.[36]

Hence, what is needed is a clear understanding of the plurality of racisms and the exclusionary social processes that function to perpetuate the racialization of members from culturally and economically marginalized communities. Robert Miles convincingly argues that these processes can be analyzed within the framework of Marxist theory without retaining the idea of race as an analytical concept.

> Using the concept of racialization, racism, and exclusionary practices to identify specific means of effecting the reproduction of the capitalist mode of production, one is able to stress consistently and rigorously the role of human agency, albeit always constrained by particular historical and material circumstances, in these processes, as well as to recognize the specificity of particular forms of oppression.[37]

Miles's work also supports the notion that efforts to construct a new language for examining the nature of differing racisms requires an understanding of how complex relationships of exploitation and resistance, grounded in differences of class, ethnicity, and gender, give rise to a multiplicity of ideological constructions of the racialized Other. This knowledge again challenges the traditional notion of racism as predominantly a Black/White phenomenon and directs us toward a more accurately constructed and, hence, more politically and analytically useful way to identify a multiplicity of historically specific racisms.

We recognize that there are anti-racist scholars who cannot comprehend a world where the notion of "race" does not exist. Without question, mere efforts to undo and eliminate the idea of "race" as an analytical category in the social sciences is insufficient to remove its use from the popular or academic imagination and discourse of everyday life. Moreover, in a country like the United States, filled with historical examples of exploitation, violence, and murderous acts rationalized by popular "race" opinions and scientific "race" ideas, it is next to impossible to convince people that "race" does not exist as a "natural" category. So, in Colette Guillaumin's words, "Let us be clear about this. The idea of race is a technical means, a machine, for committing murder. And its effectiveness is not in doubt."[38] But "races" do not exist. What does exist is the unrelenting idea of "race" that fuels racisms throughout the world.

The Need for a Critical Theory of Racism

> Moreover, language presents us with resources for the construction of meanings which reach out towards the future, which point to possibilities that transcend our experience of the present.... And those fighting for liberation from oppression and exploitation will invariably find within language words, meanings and themes for expressing, clarifying, and coordinating their struggle for a better world.
>
> —DAVID MCNALLY (1997)[39]

In considering a shift from the study of "race" to the critical study of racism, what is clear is that we need a language by which to construct culturally democratic notions of sociopolitical theory and practice. This entails the recasting and reinterpretation of social issues in a language with greater specificity, which explicitly reflects an international anti-racist notion of society. Such a language must unquestionably be linked to global histories of social movements against economic inequalities and social injustice. Although we fully recognize that theoretical language alone will not necessarily alter the power relations in any given society, it can assist us to analytically reason more accurately and, thus, to confront more effectively how power is both practiced and maintained through the systematic racialization of subordinate populations. As such, a critical language of racism can provide the foundation for developing effective public policies that are directly linked to liberatory principles of cultural and economic democracy.

In summary, we deny any place for the use of "race" as an analytical concept and support efforts to eliminate all conceptions of "race" as a legitimate entity or human phenomenon. We believe that the future struggle against racism and capitalism must at long last contend with the reality that

> There are no "races" and therefore no "race relations." There is only a belief that there are such things, a belief which is used by some social groups to construct an Other (and therefore the Self) in thought as a prelude to exclusion and domination, and by other social groups to define Self (and so to construct an Other) as a means of resisting that exclusion. Hence, if it is used at all...."race" should be used only to refer descriptively to such uses.[40]

In light of this, we posit a critical conceptualization of racism with which to analyze both historical and contemporary social experiences and institutional realities. Insofar as such a concept, whether employed in social investigation or political struggle, reveals patterns of discrimination and resulting inequalities, it raises the question: What actions must be taken to dismantle these inequalities? This in turn requires nothing less than to confront racism in all its dimensions head-on. At the risk of being redundant, we must emphasize once again that rejecting "race" as having a real referent in the social world does not mean denying the existence of racism, or the denial of historical and cultural experiences predicated on a specific population's particular struggle against racism. Rather, a critical theory of racism represents a bold and forthright move to challenge common-sense notions of "race" that often lead not only to profound forms of essentialism and ahistorical perceptions of oppression but also make it nearly impossible to dismantle the external material structures of domination that sustain racialized inequalities in schools and the larger society.

Further, we recognize the empirical reality that people believe in the existence of biologically distinct races. This can be captured analytically by stating that people employ the idea of "race" in the construction and interpretation of their social worlds. Similarly, we acknowledge that it is a common practice among the oppressed to invert the experience of exploitation. This is to say that negative notions of "race" linked to racist ideology are turned on their head and employed to fuel political movements among racialized populations. Social activists and scholars are not obliged to accept the common-sense ideas employed in the social world and use them as analytical concepts. The whole tradition of critical/ Marxist analysis highlights the importance of developing an analytical framework that penetrates the surface and reified realities of social relations. (See, for example, Marx's discussion of the distinction between phenomenal forms and essential relations, his discussion of reification, and his discussion of method in the Introduction to the *Grundrisse der Kritik der politischen Okonomie*[41] [1939].) In keeping with this tradition, we focus on racism as an analytical concept—a concept that has a real object in the social world, namely an ideology with a set of specific characteristics informed by economic imperatives—and we only refer to the idea of "race" when people use the notion in their everyday genres, utilizing it to make social distinctions based on the significance that is attached to differences between populations.

Finally, unlike scholars who argue resolutely for a critical theory of "race," we seek a critical language and conceptual apparatus that makes racism the central category of analysis in our understanding of racialized inequality, while simultaneously encompassing the multiple social expressions of racism. Undoubtedly, this entails the development of a critical language from which activists and scholars can reconstruct theories and practices of contemporary society that more accurately reflect and address capitalist forms of social and material inequities that shape the lives of racialized populations. Most importantly, we are calling for a critical theory of racism that can grapple with a radical remaking of democracy in the age of a globalized post-industrial economy. There are many who have proclaimed the death of the socialist project, but we argue that its renaissance is close at hand and will be articulated through a language that is fueled by the courage and passion to break with those hegemonic traditions on the left that fail to support a democratic vision of life for all people.

NOTES

1. K. Malik, *The Meaning of Race: Race History, and Culture in Western Society* (New York: New York University Press, 1996), 34.

2. K.A. Appiah, "The Uncompleted Argument: Du Bois and the Illusion of Race," in L. Bell and D. Blumenfeld (eds.), *Overcoming Racism and Sexism* (Lanham, MD: Rowman and Littlefield, 1995), 75.

3. Quotation marks are used around the word "race" not only to distinguish it as a social construct but to question the legitimacy of its descriptive and analytical utility. Following the example of British sociologist Robert Miles we agree that the use of "race" as an analytical concept disguises the social construction of difference, presenting it as inherent in the empirical reality of observable or imagined biological differences. For more on this issue, see Miles, *Racism* (London: Routledge, 1989) and *Racism after "Race Relations"* (London: Routledge, 1993). For an insightful note on the use of quotation marks and the "racial" logic of the practice itself, see M.F. Jacobson, *Whiteness of a Different Color: European Immigrants and the Alchemy of Race* (Cambridge, MA: Harvard University Press, 1998), ix, x.

4. A. Gramsci, *Selections from the Prison Notebooks* (New York: International Publications, 1971).

5. A. Darder, *Culture and Power in the Classroom* (Westport, CT: Bergin and Garvey, 1991), 42.

6. V. Valle and R.D. Torres, "The Idea of Mestizaje and the 'Race' Problematic: Racialized Media Discourse in a Post-Fordist Landscape," in A. Darder (ed.), *Culture and Difference* (Westport, CT: Bergin and Garvey, 1995), 139–53.

7. Jon Cruz, "From Farce to Tragedy: Reflections in the Reification of Race at Century's End," in A.F. Gordon and C. Newfield (eds.), *Mapping Multiculturalism* (Minneapolis: University of Minnesota Press, 1996), 29.

8. Ibid., 35.

9. Some contemporary examples of this scholarship can be found in C. West, *Race Matters* (Boston: Beacon Press, 1993); b. hooks, *Killing Rage: Ending Racism* (1995); M. Omi and H. Winant, *Racial Formation in the United States: From the 1960s to the 1980s* (New York: Routledge, 1993); and H.L. Gates, Jr., *Loose Canons: Notes on the Culture Wars* (New York: Oxford University Press, 1992).

10. Gordon Allport's *The Nature of Prejudice* (Reading, MA: Addison-Wesley, 1954) and Kenneth Clark's *Prejudice and Your Child* (Boston: Beacon Press, 1955) strongly influenced the intellectual rationale and public policy decisions that instituted the busing solution in the United States.

11. E.M. Wood, "Identity Crisis," *In These Times* (June 1994): 28–29.

12. Associated Press, Geneva, report released by the United Nations' International Labor Organization, entitled "Unemployment Will Reach 1 Billion Worldwide by Year's End," on Sunday, September 28, 1998.

13. J. Cavanagh, "Global Economic Apartheid" (transcript from a speech delivered in Takoma Park, Maryland, September 19, 1996), 2, available through Alternative Radio. Boulder, Colorado. Dr. Cavanagh is a specialist in international trade, economics, and development and is coauthor with Richard J. Barnet of *Global Dreams: Imperial Corporations and the New World Order* (New York: Simon and Schuster, 1994).

14. R. Grosfoguel and C.S. Georas, "The Racialization of Latino Caribbean Migrants in the New York Metropolitan Area," *Centro: Focus en Foco* 1–2, no. 8 (1996): 193.

15. E. Meiksins Wood, *Democracy against Capitalism: Renewing Historical Materialism* (New York: Cambridge University Press, 1995), 263.

16. Miles, *Racism after "Race Relations,"* 1.

17. T. Morrison, "Unspeakable Things Unspoken: The Afro-American Presence in American Literature," *Michigan Quarterly Review* 28:1 (Winter 1989): 3.

18. A. Reed Jr., "Skin Deep," *Village Voice* 24 (September 1998), 22.

19. Appiah, "The Uncompleted Argument," 74.

20. R. Miles and R.D. Torres, "Does 'Race' Matter? Transatlantic Perspectives on Racism after 'Race Relations,'" in Vered Amit-Talai and Caroline Knowles (eds.), *Re-situating Identities: The Politics of Race, Ethnicity and Culture* (Peterborough, Ontario: Broadview Press, 1996), 32.

21. R.J. Herrnstein and C. Murray, *The Bell Curve: Intelligence and Class Structure in American Life* (New York: Free Press, 1994).

22. Miles and Torres, "Does 'Race' Matter?," 75.

23. Miles, R., *Racism* (London: Routledge, 1989).

24. M. Wieviorka, "Is It Difficult to Be an Anti-Racist?," in P. Werbner and T. Modood (eds.), *Debating Cultural Hybridity: Multicultural Identities and the Politics of Anti-Racism* (London: ZED Books, 1997), 40.

25. Fifty years after the publication of *Caste, Class, and Race* (New York: Doubleday, 1948) many continue to attribute Marxist analytical status to the work of Oliver C. Cox. Yet we argue that this is misleading, in that Cox, who retained race as the central category of analysis in his work, remained staunchly anchored in a "race relations" paradigm.

26. O.C. Cox, *Caste, Class, and Race* (1948: reprint New York: Monthly Review Press, 1970), 319.

27. C.W. Mills, *The Racial Contract* (Ithaca, NY: Cornell University Press, 1997), 76.

28. A. Davis, "Gender, Class, and Multiculturalism: Rethinking Race Politics," in A.F. Gordon and C. Newfield (eds.), *Mapping Multiculturalism* (Minneapolis: University of Minnesota Press, 1996), 43.

29. P. Gilroy, "*There Ain't No Black in the Union Jack": : The Cultural Politics of Race and Nation.* (Chicago: University of Chicago Press, 1991), 9.

30. J. Baldwin, "On Being White...and Other Lies," in David Roediger (ed.), *Black on White: Black Writers on What It Means to Be White* (New York: Schocken, 1998), 178.

31. b. hooks, *Talking Back* (Boston: South End Press, 1989), 112–13.

32. F. Anthias and N. Yuval-Davis, *Racialized Boundaries: Race, Nation, Gender, and Color and Class and the Anti-racist Struggle* (New York: Routledge, 1992), 15.

33. M. Radin, cited in C. Harris, "Whiteness as Property," in David Roediger (ed.), *Black on White: Black Writers on What It Means to Be White* (New York: Schocken, 1998), 107.

34. D.T. Goldberg, *Anatomy of Racism* (Minneapolis: University of Minnesota Press, 1990), xiii.

35. For recent scholarly works that focus on "critical theories of race," see Richard Delgado (ed.), *Critical Race Theory: The Cutting Edge* (Philadelphia: Temple University Press, 1995); K. Crenshaw et al. (eds.), *Critical Race Theory: The Key Writings That Formed the Movement* (New York: New Press, 1995); and A.K. Wing, *Critical Race Feminism: A Reader* (New York: New York University Press, 1997); as well as writings by Michael Omi and Howard Winant, including *Racial Conditions* (Minneapolis: University of Minnesota Press, 1994).

36. C. Guillaumin, *Racism, Sexism, Power, and Ideology* (London: Routledge, 1995).

37. Miles, *Racism after "Race Relations,"* 52.

38. Guillaumin, *Racism, Sexism,* 107.

39. D. McNally, "Language, History, and Class Struggle," in E.M. Wood and J.B. Foster (eds.), *In Defense of History: Marxism and the Postmodern Agenda* (New York: Monthly Review Press, 1997), 40–41.

40. Miles, *Racism after "Race Relations,"* 42.

41. K. Marx, *Grundrisse der Kritik der politischen Okonomie* (Moskau: Verlag fur Fremdsprachige Literatur, 1939).

CHAPTER 6

What's So Critical
about Critical Race Theory?

A Conceptual Interrogation

With Rodolfo Torres

Racism as it operates socially, in no way assumes an explicit theory of "race."

— PIERRE-ANDRE TAGUIEFF 2001, 197

Over the last half-century considerable attention has been paid to issues related to "race" and "race relations" in the social sciences, humanities, and legal studies. The debates intensified first with the groundbreaking *Brown v. Board of Education* case in 1954 and then again with the civil rights movements of the 1960s. The current debates are beginning to intensify once more as critical race theorists[1] not only retain the idea of "race" but further entrench it as a central category of analysis. Hence, the early "race" paradigm has become the new orthodoxy, retaining symbolic and political utility for many. This is evident in even more progressive articulations of "race" such as *The Miner's Canary,* a highly acclaimed book by Lani Guinier and Gerald Torres (2002) that enlists race as a political space within the context of what they term "a political race project."

Before continuing any further, we wish to acknowledge and commend such efforts to make sense of the problematics associated with "race" within U.S. society. However, we seek to raise different questions regarding the foundational theories that shape these arguments and, more importantly, to question the analytical limitations of "race" with respect to the formation of a critical social science and execution of progressive social policies.

Critical race theory emerged as an offshoot of critical legal theory. Legal scholars in this tradition argued that legal theory had historically failed to engage in a critical analysis of society and, by so doing, continued to function as a fundamental tool of oppression that ultimately benefited the state. Not long after, critical legal theory was critiqued by black critical legal scholars such as Derrick Bell, Patricia Williams, Randall Kennedy, Lani Guinier, and others who pointed to the failure of critical legal scholars to engage questions of "race" within the framework of the alternative views they posited. The result was the forging of a subdivision of critical legal theory that is now called critical race theory.

Latino critical legal scholars such as Gerald Torres and Richard Delgado, in concert with Latino scholars in education and other disciplines, followed suit by developing a field of study today known as Latino critical race theory, or LatCrit, to address similar issues within the context of Latino life in the United States. Similar critical race theory began to evolve among Asian American scholars with the work of Mari Matsuda, often considered one of the founders of the field.

Grounded in the belief that "much of the national dialogue on race relations takes place in the context of education" (Roithmayr, 1999, 1), African American and Latino scholars such as Gloria Ladson-Billings, Daniel Solórzano, Dolores Delgado Bernal, and Laurence Parker began to infuse their arguments in education policy with critical race theory. Their key argument was the uncompromising insistence that "race" should occupy the central position in any legal, educational, or social policy analysis. Given the centrality assigned to "race," "racial" liberation was embraced as not only the primary but as the most significant objective of any emancipatory vision of education or the larger society.

The Centrality of "Race"

There is no question but that the issues raised by critical race theorists in education, policy studies and the social sciences are significant to our understanding of the conditions that plague racialized student populations in U.S. schools today. However, one of our major concerns with the use of critical race theory to buttress educational-political debates of racialized oppression or racism is directly linked to the use of "race" as the central unit of analysis. Coupled with an uncompromising emphasis on "race" is the conspicuous absence of a systematic discussion of class and, more importantly, a substantive critique of capitalism.

Let us be more specific here. In contending with questions of "race" and institutional power, references are indeed made to "capitalism" or "class"[2] in some works by critical race theorists and, in particular, Latino critical race theorists, who acknowledge that "attention to class issues has been...a pending, but as yet underdeveloped, trajectory in the future evolution of LatCrit theory and the consolidation of LatCrit social justice agendas" (Iglesias, 1999, 64).[3] However, these efforts to explore the ways in which socioeconomic interests are expressed in the law or education are generally vague and undertheorized. Because of this lack of a theoretically informed account of racism and capitalist social relations, critical race theory has done little to further our understanding of the political economy of racism and racialization. In addition, much of critical race theory's approach is informed by ambiguous ideas of "institutional racism" or "structural racism," which, as Miles (1989) points out, are problematic due to the danger of conceptual inflation.

Our aim here is not to dismiss this important body of work but to point out an important analytical distinction we make in our intellectual and political project. Our analysis of racism in contemporary society begins with the capitalist mode of production, classes, and class struggle. The mode of production, which is the site of class relations, is the point of departure in our interrogation of racism as an ideology of social exclusion. In contrast, critical race scholars attribute constitutive power to the American legal system itself. Hence, the "relative autonomy" of legal institutions is invoked to stress the power of "race" and to set their work apart from critical legal scholars, who "could not come to grips with the continuing problems of deeply embedded racism" (Guinier and Torres, 2002, 34). We maintain that the legal system (the state) is located in a given economic context and is shaped by the imperatives of capital.[4]

Our critique, then, is tied to the continued use of the traditional language of social theory, which has always been inadequate in problematizing notions of "race" in both research and popular discourse. In essence, we argue that the use of "race" has been elevated to a theoretical construct, despite the fact that the concept of "race" itself has remained under-theorized. Hence, to employ alternative constructs derived from legal theory to shape arguments related to educational policy and institutional practices, although well meaning and eloquent, is like beating a dead horse. No matter how much is said, it is impossible to enliven or extend the debate on educational policy with its inherent inequalities by using the language of "race."

Even a brief overview of the most prominent writings in critical race theory shows how little movement there has been in furthering our understanding of the concept or redirecting the debate. Overall, most of the work is anchored in the popular intersectionality argument of the poststructuralist and postmodernist era, which maintains that "race," gender, and class should all receive equal attention in our understanding of society and our development of institutional policies and practices. More recently, Guinier and Torres (2002), in an apparent effort to push through the limits of the intersectionality argument, proposed to advocate for what they term "racial literacy" from which "to identify patterns of injustice that link race to class, gender, and other forms of power." (29) Despite their innovative use of "race," its traditional analytical use remains intact.

Our concerns with critical race theory go beyond the desire to construct intellectual abstractions. Rather, our concerns are grounded in political questions such as: Where exactly does an anti-race theory of society lead us in real political struggles for social justice, human rights, and economic democracy? How do we launch a truly universal emancipatory political project anchored primarily upon a theory of "race"? Where is a critique of capitalism or an explicit anti-capitalist vision in a critical theory of "race"? Can we afford to overlook the inherent existence of a politics of identity in the foundational views that led to the construction of critical race theory? We are also troubled by the confusion with respect to the terms critical race theorists use to frame their analysis.

In this context, it is important to distinguish between how we understand the construct of "race" and its genesis. In our analysis, "race," simply put, is the child of racism. That is to say, racism does not exist because there is such a thing as "race." Rather, notions of "race" are a fundamental ideological construction of racism or a racialized interpretation of phenotypically and, may we add, regionally different human beings. The process of racialization, then, is at work in all relations in a capitalist society. Alternatively, we might say that the empire is not built on "race" but on an ideology of racism—this being one of the primary categories by which human beings are sorted, controlled, and made disposable at the point of production.

Hence, the experience of alienation is shaped along a variety of variables, one of which is that of racialization or racialized class relations. Racism is one of the primary ideologies by which material conditions in society are organized and perpetuated in the service of capitalist accumulation. This is why, to repeat, the empire is not built on "race" but on a variety of ideologies (of which racism is one) that justify the exploitation and domination of populations deemed as "Other" so as to conserve the capitalist social order.

We also seek to interrogate the idea of "race" as culture. For example, instead of linking the notion of culture to class relations which emerge at the point of production, or to the relations of production in which human beings exist and survive, critical race theorists link culture to the idea of "race"—an idea that historically has been associated with phenotypical traits. In the new "race" orthodoxy, phenotypical traits remain central to social construction, shared histories, and social narratives defined by experiences that are phenotypically determined. Miles (1989) associates this discourse of "race" to the process of signification:

> [W]hen the idea of "race" is employed, it is the result of signification whereby certain somatic characteristics are attributed with meaning and are used to organise populations into groups which are defined as "races." People differentiated on the basis of the signification of phenotypical features are usually also represented as possessing certain cultural characteristics, with the result that the population is represented as exhibiting a specific profile of biological and cultural attributes. The deterministic manner of this representation means that all those who possess the signified phenotypical characteristics are assumed to possess the additional characteristics. (71)

Narrative and Storytelling as Method

The process of signification is at work in the emphasis that critical race theory places on "experiential knowledge" (Delgado, 1995; Ladson-Billings, 1999). Robin Barnes (1990) notes that "Critical race theorists…integrate their experiential knowledge, drawn from a shared history as 'Other' with their ongoing struggles to transform a world deteriorating under the albatross of racial hegemony" (1864–65). In concert with this privileging of experience, critical race theory employs narratives and storytelling as a central method of inquiry to "analyze the myths, presuppositions, and received wisdoms that make up the common culture about race and that invariably render blacks and other minorities one-down" (Delgado, 1995, xiv). The results of this storytelling method are theorized and then utilized to draw conclusions meant to impact public policy and institutional practices.

The narrative and storytelling method employed by critical race theorists sought to critique essentialist narratives in law, education, and the social sciences. In place of a systematic analysis of class and capitalist relations, critical race theory constructs "race"-centered responses to Eurocentrism and white privilege. Delgado Bernal (2002) affirms the validity of this position, arguing that

> Western modernism is a network or grid of broad assumptions and beliefs that are deeply embedded in the way dominant Western culture constructs the nature of the world and one's experiences in it. In the United States, the center of this grid is a Eurocentric epistemological perspective based on White privilege. (111)

The narrative method based on this perspective "has become especially successful among groups committed to making the voice of the voiceless heard in the public arena" (Viotti da Costa, 2001, 21). However, despite an eagerness to include the participation of historically excluded populations, scholars who embrace the poetics of the narrative approach often "fail to challenge the underlying socioeconomic, political and cultural structures that have excluded these groups to begin with and have sustained the illusion of choice" (Watts, 1991, 652). Thus, the narrative and storytelling approach can render the scholarship antidialectical by creating a false dichotomy between objectivity and subjectivity, "forgetting that one is implied in the other, [while ignoring] a basic dialectical principle: that men and women make history, but not under the conditions of their own choosing" (Viotti da Costa, 2001, 20).

We agree that "cultural resources and fund of knowledge such as myths, folk tales, *dichos, consejos,* kitchen talk, [and] autobiographical stories" (Delgado Bernal, 2002, 120) employed by critical race theory can illuminate particular concrete manifestations of racism. However, we contend that they can also prove problematic in positing a broader understanding of the fundamental macrosocial dynamics which shape the conditions that give rise to the "micro-aggressions" (Solórzano, 1998) of racism in the first place. In an incisive critique of the narrative approach, Emilia Viotti da Costa (2001) argues,

> The new paths it opened for an investigation of the process of construction and articulation of multiple and often contradictory identities (ethnic, class, gender, nationality and so on), often led to the total neglect of the concept of class as an interpretive category.... What started as...a critique of Marxism, has frequently led to a complete subjectivism, to the denial of the possibility of knowledge and sometimes even to the questioning of the boundaries between history and fiction, fact and fancy. (19)

Robin Kelley, in his book *Yo' Mama's DisFUNKtional* (1997), offers the following illuminating and sobering commentary regarding the limits of personal experience and storytelling:

> I am not claiming absolute authority or authenticity for having lived there. On the contrary, it is because I did not know what happened to our world, to my neighbors, my elders, my peers, our streets, buildings, parks, our health, that I chose not to write a memoir. Indeed, if I relied on memory alone I would invariably have more to say about devouring Good and Plentys or melting crayons on the radiator than about economic restructuring, the disappearance of jobs, and the dismantling of the welfare state. (4–5)

Hence, we believe the use of critical race theory in education and the social sciences in general, despite authors' intentions, can unwittingly serve purposes that are fundamentally conservative or mainstream at best. Three additional but related concerns with the storytelling narrative method are also at issue here. One is the tendency to romanticize the experience of marginalized groups, privileging the narratives and discourses of "people of color," solely based on their experience of oppression, as if a people's entire politics can be determined solely by their individual location in history. The second is the tendency to dichotomize and "overhomogenize" both "white" people and "people of color" with respect to questions of voice and political representation (Viotti da Costa, 2001). And the third, anticipated by C. L. R. James in 1943,[5] is the inevitable "exaggerations, excesses and ideological trends for which the only possible name is chauvinism" (McLemee, 1996, 86). Unfortunately, these tendencies, whether academic or political, can result in unintended essentialism and superficiality in our theorizing of broader social inequalities as well as the solutions derived from such theories.

Yet, truth be told, prescribed views of humanity are seldom the reality, whatever be their source. Human beings who share phenotypical traits seldom respond to the world within the constraints of essentialized expectations and perceptions. Hence, any notion of "racial" solidarity "must run up against the hard facts of political economy...and enormous class disparities" within racialized communities (Gates, 1997, 36). This is why Gilroy (2000) warns against "short-cut solidarity" attitudes that assume that a person's political allegiance can be determined by his or her "race" or that a "shared history" will guarantee an emancipatory worldview. For this reason, we argue that such declarations, though they may sound reasonable, commonsensical, or even promising as literary contributions, have little utility in explaining "how and why power is constituted, reproduced and transformed" (Viotti da Costa, 2001, 22).

Identity Politics and the Mantra of Intersectionality

Since the 1970s, much of the progressive literature on subordinate cultural populations has utilized the construct of "race" as a central category of analysis for interpreting social conditions of inequality and marginalization. In turn, this literature has adhered to a perspective of "race" as identity. This "raced" identity has received overwhelming attention in both the sociological and political arenas. Unfortunately, the unrelenting emphasis on "identity" unleashed a barrage of liberal and conservative political movements that unwittingly undermined the socialist project of emancipation in this country and abroad. Radical mass organizations that had once worked to spearhead actions for economic democracy, human rights, and social justice were crippled by the fury. In the midst of the blinding celebratory affirmations of identity, neoliberal efforts to seize greater dominion over international markets proliferated, and globalization became the policy buzzword of U.S. economic imperialism at the end of the twentieth century.

Given this legacy, it is not surprising that many of the theories, practices, and policies that inform the social science analysis of racialized populations today are overwhelmingly rooted in a politics of identity. Consequently, this approach—steeped in deeply insular perspectives of "race" and representation—has often ignored the imperatives of capitalist accumulation and the presence of class divisions among racialized populations, even though, as John Michael (2000) reminds us, "identity categories and groups are always [racialized] and gendered and inflected by class" (29).

As we have previously stated, much of the literature on critical race theory lacks a substantive analysis of class and a critique of capitalism. And when class issues are mentioned, the emphasis is usually on an undifferentiated plurality that intersects with multiple oppressions. Unfortunately, this "new pluralism" fails to grapple with the relentless totalizing dimension of capitalism and its overwhelming tendency to homogenize rather than to diversify human experience (Wood, 1994).

Strongly influenced by a politics of identity, critical race theorists incorporate the intersectionality argument[6] to refer to their examination of race, sex, class, national origin, and sexual orientation and how the combination of these identities plays out in various settings (Delgado and Stefancic, 2001). This school of thought, common to progressive scholarship, generally includes a laundry list of oppressions (race, class, gender, homophobia, and the like) that are to be engaged with equal weight in the course of ascribing pluralized sensibilities to any political project that proposes to theorize social inequalities. Hence, inadvertently in the name of recognizing and celebrating difference and diversity, this analytical construct reduces "the capitalist system (or the 'economy') to one of many spheres in the plural and heterogeneous complexity of modern society" (Wood, 1995, 242).

Wood argues that the intersectionality argument represents a distorted appropriation of Antonio Gramsci's notion of "civil society," which was explicitly intended to function as a weapon against capitalism by identifying potential spaces of freedom outside the state for autonomous, voluntary organization and plurality. However, as used by many on the left to link multiple oppressions to specific plural identities, the concept has been stripped of its unequivocal, anticapitalist intent. Wood speaks to the danger inherent in this analytical twist.

> Here, the danger lies in the fact that the totalizing logic and the coercive power of capitalism is reduced to one set of institutions and relations among many others, on a conceptual par with households or voluntary associations. Such a reduction is, in fact, the principal distinctive feature of "civil society" in its new incarnation. Its effect is to conceptualize away the problem of capitalism, by disaggregating society into fragments, with no overarching power structure, no totalizing unity, no systemic coercion—in other words, no capitalist system, with its expansionary drive and its capacity to penetrate every aspect of social life. (Wood, 1995, 245)

This denial of the totalizing force of capitalism does not simply substantiate the existence of plural identities and relations that should be equally privileged and given weight as modes of domination. The logic of this argument fails to recognize that "the class relation that constitutes capitalism is not, after all, just a personal identity, nor even just a principle of 'stratification' or inequality. It is not only a specific system of power relations but also the constitutive relation of a distinctive social process, the dynamic of accumulation and the self-expansion of capital" (Wood, 1995, 246).

Furthermore, such logic ignores the fact that notions of identity result from a process of identification with a particular configuration of historically lived or transferred social arrangements and practices tied to material conditions of actual or imagined survival. The intersectionality argument fails to illuminate the manner in which commonly identified diverse social spheres or plural identities exist "within the determinative force of capitalism, its system of social property relations, its expansionary imperatives, its drive for accumulation, its commodification of all social life, its creation of the market as a necessity, and so on" (Wood, 1995, 246).

There is no question but that racism as an ideology is integral to the process of capital accumulation. The failure to confront this dimension in an analysis of contemporary society as a racialized phenomenon or to continue to treat class as merely one of a multiplicity of (equally valid) perspectives, which may or may not "intersect" with the process of racialization, is a serious shortcoming. In addressing this issue, we must recognize that even progressive African American and Latino scholars and activists have often used identity politics, which generally glosses over class differences and/or ignores class contradictions, in an effort to build a political base. Constructions of "race" are objectified and mediated as truth to ignite political support, divorced from the realities of class struggle. By so doing, race-centered scholars have unwittingly perpetuated the vacuous and dangerous notion that politics and economics are two separate spheres of society which function independently—a view that firmly anchors and sustains prevailing class relations of power in society.

Separation of the Political and Economic

One of our greatest concerns with the way notions of "race" and "race relations" have evolved over time, including the most recent arguments for a critical race theory, is the fact that political and economic spheres continue to remain separate in traditional analytical treatments of "race." In shedding light on the impact of such a practice, we turn once again to the work of Wood (1995) who argues that "there has been a tendency to perpetuate the rigid conceptual separation of the 'economic' and 'political' which has served capitalist ideology so well ever since the classical economist discovered the 'economy' in the abstract and began emptying capitalism of its social and political content" (19).

In essence, Wood attempts to reveal the way this false separation of the political and economic has served to obscure and distort our understanding of the fragmentation of social life within capitalism. Michael Parenti's (1995) work similarly exposes the class-driven interests of the economy hidden under its abstraction.

> The economy itself is not a neutral entity. Strictly speaking, there is no such thing as "the economy." Nobody has ever seen or touched the economy. What we see are people engaged in the exchange of values, in productive and not such productive labor, and we give an overarching name to all these activities, calling them "the economy," a hypothetical construct imposed on observable actualities. We then often treat our abstractions as reified entities, as self-generating forces of their own. So we talk about the problems of the economy in general terms, not the problems of the capitalist economy with a specific set of social relations and a discernable distribution of class power. The economy becomes an embodied entity unto itself. (81)

Traditional and popular conceptual formations utilized down to the present day to define "race" within the United States have likewise concealed the deeply embedded relationship between racism and class. For this reason, Miles and Brown (2003) assert that one of the major analytical tasks before us is "the historical (as opposed to abstract theoretical) investigation of the interpolation of racialisation and racism in political and economic relations" (137).

The separation of economic and political spheres was underscored in the civil rights movements of the 1960s and 1970s. Although these movements sought to address the impoverished material conditions of African Americans and other economically oppressed populations, their emphasis on a liberal, rights-centered political agenda undermined the development of a coherent working-class movement in the United States. Unfortunately, the opposition to a class-based politics, resulting from an ideological separation of economic and political spheres, solidified the division between economic and political action—a division inherent in capitalist appropriation and exploitation. As Wood (1995) suggests, "This 'structural' separation may, indeed, be the most effective defense mechanism available to capital" (20).

Our opposition to the separation of political and economic spheres is in concert with Marx's notion that the ultimate secret of capitalist production is a political one. The key to Marx's argument is that the well-camouflaged continuity between what we term economic and political spheres be exposed. In Marxist analysis, the economy is viewed as a set of social relations. This view is in sharp contrast with classical views of the economy that "fail to treat the productive sphere itself as defined by social determinations and in effect deal with society 'in the abstract'" (Wood, 1995, 22). Consequently, when theories of "race," racism, and other forms of inequality are informed by liberal perspectives of the economy, their critical edge is eroded, and they are easily assimilated into mainstream ideologies that retreat from class concerns.

Contrary to such perspectives, we argue for a materialist understanding of the world in which we grapple forthrightly with the impact of racism upon our lives. This entails understanding two significant principles of analysis. The first requires us to engage the social relations and practices by which human beings interact with nature and which are thereby implicated in producing the life conditions we are seeking to remedy. And second, we seek a historical understanding of human life that recognizes all products of social activity and all social interactions between human beings as material forces. All social forms, including those that sustain racism, as well as other forms of social inequalities, are products of a particular social system of production. Wood (1995) sheds light on this relationship by linking the mode of production to questions of power relations and exploitation.

> A mode of production is not simply a technology but a social organization of productive activity, and a mode of exploitation is a relationship of power. Furthermore, the power relationship that conditions the nature and extent of exploitation is a matter of political organization within and between contending classes. In the final analysis the relation between appropriators and producers rests on the relative strength of classes, and this is largely determined by the internal organization and the political forces with which each enters into the class struggle. (27)

Hence, all forms of social inequality are defined by class relations or motivated by the persistent drive to perpetuate class inequality within the context of the capitalist state, a phenomenon perpetuated by the ongoing construction and reconstruction of capitalist class relations. Thus, racism is operationalized through racialized class relations. Sexism is operationalized through gendered class relations. Heterosexism is operationalized through homophobic class relations. All these function in concert to sustain cultural, political, and economic stratification within societies at large.

To reiterate, everything functions within the context of material conditions— whether one is talking about psychological, corporeal, or spiritual dimensions of culture. We understand culture as a social phenomenon produced at the point of production through the particular configuration of social-material relations found within the nation-state, which include the particularities of the region's historical, social-material arrangements and organization.

Given this perspective, class is implicated in all social arrangements of oppression, including racism. Nothing occurs without implicating the material conditions that shape the way individuals and groups locate themselves (and are located) in the context of the body politic of the nation-state. What, then, is the motivating force for the construction of particular social arrangements, whether these are marked by physical, national, or ideological signifiers? Simply put, it is the exploitation and domination of the majority of the population in the interest of sustaining the power of capital. This is inextricably tied to retaining dominion over the world's populations and natural resources by the ruling elite.

Capitalist class relations, both anchored in and camouflaged by the precepts of modernity, are constructed in the historical, social-material milieu of each nation-state at the moment of colonization, by way of the introduction of capitalist modes of production into each region. Consequently, questions of the economy and politics are inextricably linked and cannot be separated. Hence, to speak of the political sphere as being separate from the economic is to create a false abstract notion that fundamentally serves the interests of capitalist relations and the accumulative drive for capital and power by the few. This abstract separation conceals the unjust accumulation of capital and power—an accumulation sustained by asymmetrical relations tied to class and firmly anchored to the social practices of racism, sexism, homophobia, ethnocentrism, and other forms of social inequality.

White Supremacy and the Intractability of Racism

James Baldwin argues, in his 1984 essay "On Being 'White'... and Other Lies," "No one was white before he/she came to America. It took generations, a vast amount of coercion, before this became a white country" (Baldwin, 1998, 178). Baldwin's words clearly point to the artificial construction of a "black-white" paradigm for organizing power in America. We argue that this racialized construction of power was (and continues to be) predicated upon the political economic imperatives of capitalism, rather than an essentialized and intractable white supremacy.

Although a goal of critical race theory is to eliminate "racial oppression" as part of a larger effort to end all forms of oppression (Tate, 1997), a central tenet of this perspective is that "race" is an essential reality of life and racism a permanent feature of social relations in the modern world. Hence, critical race theorists and their supporters uncompromisingly adhere not only to a belief in the existence of "races" but also to the "normalcy" of racism. For example, Ladson-Billings (1999) explains that critical race theory begins with the view that

> racism is "normal, not aberrant, in American society" (Delgado, 1995, xiv).... Indeed,
> Bell's major premise in Faces at the Bottom of the Well (1992) is that racism is a permanent
> fixture of American life. Thus, the strategy becomes one of unmasking and exposing rac-
> ism in its various permutations. (12)

This belief in the permanence of racism is coupled with the notion of white supremacy in the literature on critical race theory. Major writings in the field (Wing, 1997; Crenshaw et al., 1995; Delgado, 1995; Bell, 1992) highlight two central unifying ideas. The first is to understand how a "regime of white supremacy and its subordination of people of color have been created and maintained in America" (Crenshaw et al., 1995, xiii); and the second is "to change the bond that exists between law [or institutions] and racial power" (Ladson-Billings, 1999, 14). It is important to note that, although mention is made of changing the law and other societal institutions such as schools, the change is first and foremost concerned with the idea of "racial power," preserving the centrality of "race."

Hence, in their efforts to sort out the complexities of "race" problems in America, critical race theorists and many prominent intellectuals place an emphasis on the notion of white supremacy. For example, Villenas, Deyhle, and Parker (1999) speak of education as "the greatest normalizer of White supremacy" (48). The writings of bell hooks illustrate the common use in critical race theory of the term "white supremacy" when addressing the racialized inequalities suffered by African Americans. In *Talking Back* (1989) hooks explains the shift in her language.

> I try to remember when the word racism ceased to be the term which best expressed for me the exploitation of black people and people of color in this society and when I began to understand that the most useful term was white supremacy...the ideology that most determines how white people in this society perceive and relate to black people and other people of color. (112–13)

hooks's explanation illustrates both her belief in the existence of a "white" ideology that has "black" people as its primary object (despite her mention of "people of color") and the reification of skin color as the most active determinant of social relations between "black" and "white" populations. The persistence of such notions of racialized exploitation and domination privileges one particular form of racism while ignoring the historical and contemporary oppression of populations who have been treated as distinct and inferior "races" without the necessary reference to skin color.

Moreover, white supremacy arguments essentialize "black-white" relations by inferring that the inevitability of skin color ensures the reproduction of racism in the "postcolonial" world, where "white people" predominantly associate "black people" with inferiority. Delgado Bernal (2002) expresses this view in her discussion of a "Eurocentric perspective" when she writes: "Traditionally, the majority of Euro-Americans adhere to a Eurocentric perspective founded on covert and overt assumptions [of] White supremacy" (111).

This view fails to recognize the precolonial origins of racism, which were structured in Europe by the development of nation-states and capitalist relations of production. "The dichotomous categories of Black as victims, and Whites as perpetrators of racism, tend to homogenize the objects of racism, without paying attention to the different experience of men and women, of different social classes and ethnicities" (Anthias and Yuval-Davis, 1992,15). As such, there is little room to link, with equal legitimacy and analytical specificity the continuing struggles against racism by Jews, Romas, the Irish, immigrant workers, refugees, and other racialized populations of the world (including Africans racialized by Africans) to the struggle of African Americans.

Theories of racism based on racialized ideas of "white supremacy" ultimately adhere to a "race relations" paradigm. Thus, these theories anchor racialized inequality to the alleged "nature" of "white people" and the psychological influence of "white ideology" on both "whites" and "blacks" rather than to the complex nature of historically constituted social relations of power and their material consequences. In light of this, hooks's preference for "white supremacy" (although, more recently, she links it to both patriarchal and capitalist formations) represents a perspective that, despite its oppositional intent and popularity among activists and critical race scholars, fails to advance an understanding of the debilitating structures of capitalism and the nature of class formations within a racialized, gendered world. More specifically, the struggle against racism and class inequality cannot be founded on either academic or popularized notions of "race" or "white supremacy"—notions that ultimately reify and "project a 'phantom objectivity,' an autonomy that seems so strictly rational and all-embracing as to conceal every trace of its fundamental nature" (Radin, cited in Harris, 1998, 107). Rather than working to invert racist notions of racialized inferiority, antiracist scholars and activists should seek to develop a class-based critical theory of racism.

Our contention with the critical race theorists is that they remain silent about capitalist production relations in the midst of their often-repeated intersectionality mantra of class, race, and gender. However, it is not our intention to resurrect the race-versus-class debate of the last several decades. Instead, we seek to place the political, economic, and ideological process of capitalist social relations at the center of an understanding of racialized inequalities. Moreover, we find no theoretical or empirical reasons for legitimizing the ideological notion of "race" or "white supremacy" by promoting these ideas as central analytical categories. On the contrary, as Balibar (1991) suggests, an "after race" position must be something more substantial. It must challenge "the idea that there is *no end to racism in history*" (18).

Reframing the Politics of Racism

In order to begin reframing the politics of racism, it is necessary to construct a new language with which to articulate the conditions of exclusion, exploitation, and domination in the world. As activists and social scientists, we must begin this effort in our scholarship and our political practice by deconstructing "common sense categories and [setting] up rigorous analytic concepts in their place. Here, it appears to us that an excessively vague use of the vocabulary of race should be rejected, and that one should resist the extensions which banalise the evil, or remove its specificity" (Wieviorka, 1997, 40). More specifically, we must begin by shattering our "race fixation."

However, despite the dangerous distortions that arise from the use of "race" as a central analytical category, most scholars seem unable to break with the hegemonic tradition of its use in the social sciences. Our efforts to problematize the reified nature of the term "race" and eliminate it as a metaphor in our work are met with resistance, even by progressive intellectuals of all communities. This resistance is expressed through anxiety, trepidation, and anger. Even merely questioning the existence of "races" is often met with greater suspicion than liberal notions that perpetuate a deficit view of "race."

Oliver Cox, in his 1948 treatise on "race relations," for example, posits that "it would probably be as revealing of [negative] interracial attitudes to deliberate upon the variations in the skeletal remains of some people as it would be to question an on-going society's definition of a race because, anthropometrically speaking, the assumed race is not a *real* race" (Cox, 1959, 319).[7] Similarly, in a more recent work, *The Racial Contract*, Charles Mills (1997) argues that "the only people who can find it psychologically possible to deny the centrality of race are those who are racially privileged, for whom race is invisible precisely because the world is structured around them, whiteness as the grounds against which the figures of other races—those who, unlike us, are raced—appear" (76).

Inherent in these commentaries is the refusal to consider that the denial of "races" does not imply the denial of racism or the racist ideologies that have been central to capitalist exploitation and domination around the globe. The failure to grasp this significant analytical distinction ultimately stifles the development of a critical theory of racism, one with the analytical depth to free us from a paradigm that explains social subordination (or domination) by the alleged "nature" of particular populations.

Visceral and uncritical responses to eliminating the concept of "race" are often associated with a fear of delegitimizing the historical movements for liberation that have been principally defined in terms of "race" struggles, or progressive institutional interventions that have focused on "race" numbers to evaluate success. Although understandable, such responses demonstrate the tenacious and adhesive quality of socially constructed ideas and show how these ideas, through their historical usage, become commonsense notions that resist deconstruction. The dilemma for scholars and activists in the field is well articulated by Angela Davis (1996).

> "Race" has always been difficult to talk about in terms not tainted by ideologies of racism, with which the notion of "race" shares a common historical evolution. The assumption that a taxonomy of human populations can be constructed based on phenotypical characteristics has been discredited. Yet, we continue to use the term "race," even though many of us are very careful to set it off in quotation marks to indicate that while we do not take seriously the notion of "race" as biologically grounded, neither are we able to think about racist power structures and marginalization processes without invoking the socially constructed concept of "race." (43)

Consequently, "race" has been retained as "an analytical category, not because it corresponds to any biological or epistemological absolutes, but because of the power that collective identities acquire" (Gilroy, 1991, 9). This power requires that racialized identities be accepted as commonplace and as central to political struggle, despite the constructed limitations that belie their utility.

Terry Eagleton (2000) asserts, "There can be no political emancipation for our time which is not at some level indebted to the Enlightenment" (65). In agreement, we posit that reframing a politics of racism requires us to rethink one of the fundamental critiques of the Enlightenment made by many progressive theorists, including those at the forefront of critical race theory. The demise of the metanarratives in the late twentieth century cleared the way for the "new pluralism." Tied to this politics of diversity was the eradication of any assumptions that supported the existence of universal principles of rights sufficiently undifferentiated to accommodate diverse identities and lifestyles. The increasing fragmentation of social relations and personal identities were thought to require more complex pluralistic principles that recognized the plurality of oppressions or forms of domination. The socialist emancipatory project was rejected in favor of what was considered to be the more inclusive category of democracy, a concept that essentially treats all oppressions equally. These theories were posited as being more in tune with the complexity of human diversity than those that "privileged" class relations or "reduced" all oppressions to class struggle.

However politically progressive such a view might seem, its results were disastrous to the development of a truly expansive emancipatory movement and the forging of an economically democratic society. As Eagleton (2000) reminds us,

> A classless society can be achieved only by taking class identifications seriously, not by a liberal pretense that they do not exist. The most uninspiring kind of identity politics are

those which claim that an already fully fledged identity is being repressed by others. The more inspiring forms are those in which you lay claim to an equality with others in being free to determine what you might wish to become. Any authentic affirmation of difference thus has a universal dimension. (66)

In the absence of this "universal dimension," social movements principally grounded in identity politics—despite appalling material inequalities—resulted in an uncritical acceptance of capitalist expansion.

Consequently, the final years of the twentieth century were marked by one of the greatest moments of capitalist expansion, shrouded in the rhetoric of globalization—an economic expansionism carried out with few political restraints or legal reprisals by the myriad of identity movements all busy vying for their piece of the pie. While the new pluralism aspired to create a democratic community that could embrace and celebrate all social formations of difference—with its mantra of "race, gender, and class"—it failed to acknowledge the possibility that these differences could also encompass relations of exploitation and domination. Thus, advocates of the "new pluralism" failed to recognize several deadly fundamental realities of class relations: 1. it can exist only within structures of inequality; 2. all social oppressions are fundamentally linked to class within the context of capitalist relations of power; and 3. differences within groups also "proliferate along the obvious axes of division: gender, age, sexuality, region, class, wealth and health... [challenging] the unanimity of racialized collectivities" (Gilroy, 2000, 24).

The "new pluralism" opened the door to the carte blanche dismissal of class analysis and the unbridled impact of capitalism on people's lives. In its place, hidden narratives of distinct collectivities evolved along with essentialized notions that often shaped new forms of social tyranny for those perceived as "Other" within the context of antiracism. In the name of conserving the right to difference and oppositionality, such narratives also eroded the sustained solidarity of diverse sectors of the population both from within and without. Underpinning these movements was the goal of stripping away the Enlightenment metanarrative of universal humanity. Without this metanarrative, as Jeffrey Isaac (1992) argues, theory lost its sense of purpose: "If there are no metanarratives, no underlying reasons for us to do what we should do then the theorist or political writer is under no obligation to offer such reasons in support of his or her proposal. Theory then becomes rhetoric, or poetry, or perhaps a game in which the writer's will to power or self-expression becomes his or her primary motivation" (8–9).

Instead, we firmly believe that to reframe the politics of racism in society today requires a willingness to resurrect the Enlightenment tradition within a historical process as posited by Marx. "By putting a critique of political economy in place of uncritical submission to the assumptions and categories of capitalism, he made it possible to see within it the conditions of its suppression by a more humane society" (Wood, 1995, 177). These categories of political economy devised and articulated by Marx are requisite conceptual tools in understanding racism in contemporary capitalist societies. One of the major objectives of this volume and in particular this chapter has been to show that the retention of "race" as a discursive or analytic category is seriously problematic. Moreover, an attempt to develop a "critical theory of race" or a LatCrit methodology will in effect reproduce a specious concept which has no theoretical or analytical value. Also, the widely employed notion of *intersectionality* is equally problematic where a multitude of oppressions and identities are assigned "equivalent" explanatory power outside class relations. As we posit in our introduction, to treat the category of class as just another "ism" as many LatCrit writers do is simplistic and misguided. The concept of class is located within production relations and represents a very different and unique structural feature in a capitalist political economy.

As we have attempted here, the terrain occupied by critical race and LatCrit scholars must and can be contested. The task for all anti-racist scholars is to focus on *racism as an ideology* and *racism as a relation of production*. Such an interrogation requires a renewed historical materialist method informed by Marx's writings, most notably the preface to *A Contribution to the Critique of Political Economy*. Thus, this analysis leads us to locate the capitalist mode of production at the center of a theory of racism and class inequality. Finally, the theoretical argument that we offer is that any account of contemporary racism(s) and related exclusionary practices divorced from an explicit engagement with racialization and its articulation with the reproduction of capitalist relations of production is incomplete. The continued neglect by critical race theorists to treat with theoretical *specificity* the political economy of racialized class inequalities is a major limitation in an otherwise significant and important body of literature.

REFERENCES

Anthias, Floya and Nica Yuval-Davis in association with Harriet Cain. 1992. *Racialized Boundaries: Race, Nation, Gender, and Color and Class and the Anti-racist Struggle.* London: Routledge.

Baldwin, James, 1998. "On Being White...and Other Lies." In David Roediger (ed.), *Black on White.* New York: Schocken.

Balibar, Etienne. 1991. "Es gibt keinen Staat in Europe: Racism and Politics in Europe." *in New Left Review* 186: 5-19.

Barnes, Robin, 1990. "Race Consciousness: The Thematic Content of Racial Distinctiveness in Critical Race Scholarship." *Harvard Law Review*, 103, 1864–1871.

Bell, Derrick, 1992. *Faces at the Bottom of the Well.* New York: Basic Books.

Cox, Oliver, 1959. *Caste, Class and Race: A Study in Social Dynamics.* New York: Monthly Review Press.

Crenshaw, Kimberlé, Neil Gotanda, Gary Peller, and Kendal Thomas (eds.). 1995. *Critical Race Theory: The Key Writings That Formed the Movement.* New York: New Press.

Davis, Angela. 1996. "Gender, Class and Multiculturalism" in *Mapping Multiculturalisms.* Avery F., Gordon and Christopher Newfield (eds.) Minneapolis and London: University of Minnesota Press.

Delgado, Richard.1995. *Critical Race Theory: The Cutting Edge.* Philadelphia: Temple University Press.

Delgado, Richard and Jean Stefancic. 2001. *Critical Race Theory.* New York: New York University Press.

Delgado Bernal, Dolores. 2002. "Critical Race Theory, Latino Critical Theory, and Critical Raced-Gendered Epistemologies: Recognizing Students of Color as Holders and Creators of Knowledge." *Qualitative Inquiry* 8(1): 105–26.

Eagleton, Terry. 2000. *The Idea of Culture.* Oxford: Blackwell.

Garcia, Ignacio. 1997. *Chicanismo: The Forging of a Militant Ethos among Mexican Americans.* Tucson: The University of Arizona Press.

Gates, Henry Louis, Jr. 1997. *Thirteen Ways of Looking at a Black Man.* New York: Random House.

Gilroy, Paul 1987. *"There Ain't No Black in the Union Jack": The Cultural Politics of Race and Nation.* London: Hutchinson.

———. 1991. *"There Ain't No Black in the Union Jack": The Cultural Politics of Race and Nation.* Chicago: University of Chicago Press.

———. 2000. *Against Race: Imagining Political Culture Beyond the Colorline.* Cambridge, MA: Harvard University Press.

Guinier, Lani and Gerald Torres. 2002. *The Miner's Canary: Enlisting Race, Resisting Power, Transforming Democracy.* Cambridge, MA: Harvard University Press.

Iglesias, Elizabeth M. 1998. "Out of the Shadow: Marking Intersections in and between Asian Pacific American Critical Legal Scholarship and Latina/o Critical Theory.: *Third World Law Review* 19: 349-83.

hooks, bell. 1989. *Talking Back.* Boston: South End Press.

Harris, Cheryl. 1998. "Whiteness as Property." In David Roediger, *Black on White: Black Writers on What It Means to Be White.* New York: Schocken Books.

Isaac, Jeffrey C. 1992. *Arendt, Camus, and Modern Rebellion.* New Haven, CT: Yale University Press.

Kelley, Robin. 1997. *Yo' Mama's DisFUNKtional.* Boston: Beacon Press.

Ladson-Billings, Gloria. 1999. "Just What Is Critical Race Theory, and What's It Doing in a Nice Field Like Education?" In *Race Is—Race Isn't: Critical Race Theory and Qualitative Studies in Education.* Donna Deyhle, Laurence Parker and Sofia Villenas (eds.). Boulder, CO: Westview.

Marx, Anthony W. 1998. *Making Race and Nation: A Comparison of South Africa, the United States, and Brazil.* Cambridge, MA: Cambridge University Press.

McLemee, Scott. 1996. *C.L.R. James on the "Negro Question."* Jackson: University Press of Mississippi.

Michael, John. 2000. *Anxious Intellects.* Durham, NC: Duke University Press.

Miles, Robert. 1989. *Racism.* Key Ideas series. London: Routledge.

Miles, Robert and Malcolm Brown. 2003. *Racism* (2d ed.). London: Routledge.

Mills, Charles. 1997. *The Racial Contract.* Ithaca: Cornell University Press.

Parenti, Michael. 1995. *Against Empire.* San Francisco: City Lights Books.

Roithmayr, Daria (1999). "Introduction to Critical Race Theory." In Laurence Parker, Donna Deyhle, and Sofia Villenas, eds., . Boulder, CO: Westview Press.

Solórzano, D. 1998. "Critical Race Theory, Race, and Microaggressions, and the Experience of Chicana and Chicano Scholars." *International Journal of Qualitative Studies in Education,* 11: 121–36.

Taguieff, P. 2001. *The Force of Prejudice: On Racism and Its Doubles.* Minneapolis: Minnesota University Press.

Tate, William F. 1997. "Critical Race Theory and Educational: History, Theory, and Implications." In Michael Apple, ed., *Review of Research in Education,* no. 22: 195–250. Washington, DC: American Educational Research Association.

Villenas, Sofiia, Donna Deyhle, and Laurence Parker. 1999. "Critical Race Theory and Praxis: Chicano(a)/ Latino(a) and Navajo Struggles for Dignity, Education Equity, and Social Justice." In Laurence Parker, Donna Deyhle, and Sofia Villenas, eds., *Race Is—Race Isn't: Critical Race Theory and Qualitative Studies in Education.* Boulder, CO: Westview.

Viotti da Costa, Emilia. 2001. "New Publics, New Politics, New Histories: From Economic Reductionism to Cultural Reductionism—In Search of Dialectics." In *Reclaiming the Political in Latin American History: Essays from the North.* Gilbert M. Joseph (ed.). Durham and London: Duke University Press.

Watts, Steven. 1991. "The Idiocy of American Studies: Poststructuralism, Language and Politics in the Age of Self-Fulfillment." *American Quarterly,* December, 652.

Wieviorka, Michel. 1997. "Is It Difficult to Be an Anti-Racist?" In Puina Werbner and Tariq Modood (eds.), *Debating Cultural Hybridity: Multicultural Identities and the Politics of Anti-Racism.* Atlantic Highlands, NJ: ZED.

Wing, Adrien Katherine. 1997. *Critical Race Feminism: A Reader.* New York: New York University Press.

Wood, Ellen Meiksins. June 1994. "Identity Crisis." In *These Times* : 28–29.

———1995. *Democracy Against Capitalism: Renewing Historical Materialism.* New York: Cambridge University Press.

NOTES

1. For scholarly works that focus on "critical race theories,' see Richard Delgado, *Critical Race Theory: The Cutting Edge* (1995); Kimberlé Crenshaw, Neil Gotanda, Gary Peller, and Kendal Thomas, eds., *Critical Race Theory: The Key Writings That Formed the Movement;* Mari Matsuda, Charles Lawrence, Richard Delgado, and Kimberlé Crenshaw, *Words That Wound: Critical Race Theory, Assaultive Speech, and the First Amendment* (1993); as well as writings by Michael Omi and Howard Winant, including *Racial Conditions* (Winant 1994).

2. Recent efforts to bring "class" into the debate are a positive conceptual and theoretical development. But we caution our colleagues not to fall into the trap of just adding "class" to the equation of other identities. As we argue in this volume, there is a need to sort out the salient theoretical underpinnings of an approach to class-based analysis that recognizes struggle and conflict as a means of social change. In these chapters, we attempt to specify the meaning of a Marxist-informed class-based approach that views class and classes in capitalist society in terms of their structural position within production relations. The Marxist theory of modes of production is central and necessary to this project of deracialization in capitalist society.

3. Also see the article by Elizabeth M. Iglesias (1998), "Out of the Shadow: Marking Intersections in and between Asian Pacific American Critical Legal Scholarship and Latina/o Critical Theory," where she issues a call "for LatCrit theory to move beyond abstract race/class debates by centering political economy and the production of class hierarchies" (95).

4. Care must be taken not to speak of the state and capital in monolithic terms, as they are sometimes at odds. See Ralph Miliband's (1998) *Divided Societies: Class Struggle in Contemporary Capitalism* and Nico Poulantzas's (1973) *Political Power and Social Classes* for competing views of the state in capitalist societies, though both would agree on the heterogeneity of capital and the state.

5. C.L.R. James addresses the "Negro Question" in the Historical Developments of the Negroes in American Society" (1943), which was "originally circulated within the Workers' Party as a memorandum dated 30 December 1943. It was submitted to the 1944 National Convention of the Workers' Party, and first published as "Negroes and the "Revolution: Resolution of the Minority' in the *New International*, January 1945" (McLemee, 1996, 149). Although James identifies the "dangers" of the "chauvinisms of the oppressed" in this essay, he makes a case that "the only way to overcome them is to recognize its fundamental progressive tendency and to distinguish sharply between chauvinisms of the oppressed and the chauvinism of the oppressor" (McLemee, 1996, 86). However, more than sixty years later, what we have learned from a myriad of antiracism struggles, rooted in nationalism and identity politics is that chauvinism of any persuasion ultimately confines, restricts, and delimits the political solidarity required to challenge the totalizing impact of capitalism in this country and around the world.

6. One of the most significant theoretical contributions made during the post-civil rights era regarding questions of racialized identities was formulated by radical feminists of color who presented the most sophisticated articulations of the intersectionality argument, with its often cited mantra of "race, class, and gender."

7. More than fifty years after the publication of *Caste, Class and Race* by Doubleday in 1948, many scholars continue to attribute Marxist analytical status to the work of Oliver Cox. We argue that this is misleading because Cox, who retained "race" as the central category of analysis in his work, remained staunchly anchored in a "race relations" paradigm.

PART III.
Culture, Schooling, and Difference

OF STRUGGLE AND REFLECTION

A wave of confusion hits
as i look to sort out
the truth of my existence,
the essence of my life,
a bilingual, bicultural woman
is what i am, so i am told,
and in retrospect i see
the kaleidoscopic rearrangements
from this to that,
from here to there,
trying to find out
just who the hell i am.

i am a small child,
proud of boricua roots,
soy puertorriqueña,
naci en las isla,
i would enthusiastically proclaim
to the response of white faces.

i am a school child,
trying to hard to learn,
to learn that english well,
for quickly i saw
that the ticket for travel
in this strange world
was the white way
of my teachers
who would smile
when i was a good girl.

i am an adolescent,
in search of identity, value, worth,
with no consciousness or guidance
of the changes bombarding my mind,
the last person i want to be like is mami
with her thick accent
and loud conversation,
the last thing i want
is to live the barrio,
push, push, push,
for the assimilated look,
dye my hair,
shave my legs,
shield the sun,
put down all the old fashion stuff
and backward ways of jibaros,
break away from home,
search for a white name,
get high with a white man.

i am confrontation,
why do you put that shit on your hair,
who do you think you are anyway,
can't you speak spanish,
noooooooooooooooo,
gee, you're sure not like the rest,
oh, thank you,
hide the accent,
sorry, you people don't do well
in professional programs,

what??????????
folks jam me up and
realization comes so slow on the outside
with ulcers on the inside,
why do i think white people
are better, smarter, more hip,
why did i leave my family, the barrio,
i start to fight myself.

i am validation,
and i begin to feel
for me and all brown faces
and the sounds of my music
resurrect like old time friends,
just waiting for me to know
that i don't have to
look white, talk white,
or smell white to be,
hallelujah!
i begin to find la jibarita
who stood up with pride
and told the world
i am puerto rican,
born on the island,
and i am proud.

i am rebuilding,
as i go to regain
the lost treasures of
my ancestors and childhood,
give them to my children,
and leave behind the bullshit
of melting pots and color blinds,
to lift my head and say
i am not the same as you white man,
for this is my history,
these are my roots,
here is my heart,
and none of them had
a god damn thing to do
with your fucking mayflower.[1]

—ANTONIA DARDER (1983)

---

1. When I was in third grade, a teacher forced us to write 200 times (in the traditional use of "stan-
    dards") *My forefathers came over from England on the Mayflower*. Although at the time I was
    unable to articulate my childhood awareness that this was not *my* history, the silent discomfort
    it produced settled in my body and resurfaced, unexpectedly, in the final stanza of this poem.

CHAPTER 7

Education in the Age of "Globalization" and "Difference"

> What excellence is this that manages to coexist with more than a billion inhabitants of the developing world who live in poverty, not to say misery? Not to mention the all but indifference with which it coexists with "pockets of poverty" and misery in its own, developed body. What excellence is this that sleeps in peace while numberless men and women make their home in the street, and says it is their own fault that they are on the street? What excellence is this that struggles so little, if it struggles at all, with discrimination for reasons of sex, class, or race?
>
> —PAULO FREIRE (1994)

As these words illustrate, Paulo Freire was deeply conscious of the myriad of illusions that masquerade within modern society as justice, freedom, autonomy, and democracy. At a time when the United States touts its agenda of "excellence" for the democratization of the world, what we find is greater economic inequality on the planet than ever in recorded history. As the major world power, the United States has effectively extended its dominion through an ideology of modernization, technological dominance, military superiority and its stronghold on the world's political economy. There was a time when this would have been publicly denounced as outright imperialism or capital monopoly, but now it travels under the more palatable euphemism of "globalization."

The closing years of the twentieth century resulted in major changes in the socioeconomic landscape of U.S. society—changes that potentially could herald greater class conflict and social unrest than U.S. modern history has ever known. Nowhere are these changes more evident than in California, where large populations have been directly affected by the impact of economic restructuring, "postindustrial" conditions of urban life, and the "globalization" of the economy. Moreover, these represent significant material changes that must be considered within the context of educational reform debates currently taking place. Yet despite a blatant concentration of wealth and its harsh impact on subordinate populations, schools continue to view contemporary social conflicts and conditions of inequality as if their primary causes were the intellectual deficiencies or psychological problems of individual students or their parents. By so doing, they ignore the structural conditions of social injustice and economic inequality at work in the process of schooling.

Paulo Freire (1970, 1993) recognized very clearly how public schooling is implicated in the perpetuation of cultural invasion and economic domination. He understood that in order to comprehend the pervasive nature of late capitalism and its rapidly changing cultural maps, class relations, gender patterns of discrimination, and racialized exploitation, teachers must recognize how schools function undemocratically, in complicity with the political economy. More specifically, schools play an important role in the process of capital accumulation as they organize student populations in an economic hierarchy and officially carry out an unfair system of meritocracy that ultimately functions to legitimate the ideological formations necessary for the reproduction of inequality (Apple, 1995).

Hence, schools are sites of ideological struggle and contestation, where the values of the marketplace are cultivated, nurtured, and reinforced. There are ideological tensions clearly at work in the educational debates related to affirmative action, vouchers, charter schools, bilingual education, and student and teacher assessment. Generally speaking, however, these issues are hotly debated without serious attention given to their direct connection to economic restructuring, the dismantling of the middle class, the increasing polarization of wealth, and the subsequent racialization of populations.

For example, a key issue raised in many discussions related to the problems with public education today is the concern over increasing immigration and the subsequent changing demographics of many inner-city schools. Yet if we look at this issue with a more critical lens, we will discover that inner-city schools have consistently educated diverse populations of students. Thus, educating diverse student bodies or meeting the needs of diverse communities is not the central impetus for the concern. Rather, the true source of the concern is the growing realization that immigrant populations are not going away, they are not assimilating as predicted, and they can no longer be ignored. Moreover, the number of people seeking both documented and undocumented entry into the United States more than likely will increase in the coming years. In fact, these numbers have consistently remained high for a variety of reasons, not the least of which is the impact of the last fifty years of U.S. foreign policy in Southeast Asia and Latin America and the accelerated movement toward economic "globalization."

During the 1990s, economic policies such as the North American Free Trade Agreement (NAFTA) had a debilitating effect on the labor participation in the United States of Latinos, African Americans, and other workers through the swift transfer of factories to countries in Latin American and the Pacific Rim. Even more disconcerting is the ever-increasing rate of poverty in the United States and the failure of schools to contend with changing class formations and their impact on the academic needs of students in poor communities. Consequently, many teachers, content with trite, psychological notions of student failure, fail to engage with the fundamental historical practices of domination and exploitation that perpetuate social, political, and economic relationships of inequality.

It seems that few teachers are prepared to grapple with the impact of the widening gap between the rich and poor on the lives of the students who sit in their classrooms. Yet, according to the latest U.S. Census Bureau, 20.5 percent of the 70 million children in the United States live in poverty. And although there is an alarmingly disproportionate representation of children from subordinate cultural communities, 62.5 percent of all poor children are identified as "white." It is also significant to note that almost 70 percent of all poor children live in families in which one or both parents work. Yet public educational policy regarding poor students—often made by people who themselves have never seen a hungry day in their lives—continues to perpetuate false portrayals of the actual conditions that are responsible for poverty in the first place.

These false portrayals of poverty result from the particularly American predisposition to evade the question of class inequality. Rather than address the structural inequalities that underlie the plight of economically disenfranchised people, social commentators psychologize, pathologize, or demonize the poor, then systematically categorize them as criminals, drug addicts, homeless people, juvenile delinquents, or the chronically unemployed (Aronowitz, 1992).

The Politics of Racism and Economic Inequality

The politics of racism and economic inequality is at the heart of the social conditions that oppressed communities face. Since its inception, the United States has always been a multicultural and multilingual nation-state, yet a denial and negation of class inequalities and cultural differences have long been reflected in the alienating values and practices of most private and public institutions, including churches, schools, and social welfare organizations. For over two hundred years there has been a fierce assimilative drive at work in America. Under its influence the doctrine of Manifest Destiny was conceived and practiced to the detriment of colonized and enslaved populations who were socially and economically exploited as cheap labor and reserve armies. Simply stated, the worst consequence of such a practice is the shameful creation of economic dependency. The forceful ideology of capitalism, justified by the politics of racism, has fueled widespread global economic conquest under the guise of "freedom and democracy" or the banner of "human rights" (Clairmont, 1995). In concert with economic dependency, such rhetoric has instilled in both dominant and subordinate populations the socially destructive notion that there is only one legitimate way of being an acceptable and "free" human being. What has been ignored is the manner in which class formations and mainstream beliefs, attitudes, and values are deeply anchored within dominant cultural and class expectations—expectations defined by the interests of the economically and politically powerful and carried out by the country's most inconspicuous moral leaders—namely, teachers.

In the arena of social services, "healthy" is the ubiquitous euphemism for normalcy and its implicit expectations of cultural conformity and homogeneity. Hence, institutional expectations of conformity reinforce the notion that for a working-class family to be deemed "healthy," its members must fit within the prescribed roles that sustain both the labor force and the marketplace. "Good" families are expected to adhere to the norms of patriarchal structures and capitalist interests. Meanwhile, poor and working-class people, along with members of subordinate ethnic communities, are expected to passively follow the institutional rules established for them by the dominant society—even when these rules are blatantly unfair and unequal and perpetuate human suffering.

The history of the U.S. health, education, and welfare system is filled with heart-wrenching examples of the dominant society's class-based, ethnocentric responses to cultural differences and working-class sensibilities—responses that, subsequently, led to the imposition of practices of conformity on families from subordinate populations—practices that often reinforced the loss of cultural identity through subtle and not-so-subtle forms of assimilation. This is well illustrated by the experiences of Native American children who were taken from their families on the reservation and placed in boarding schools or foster homes, had their hair cut, and their language and cultural rituals prohibited by the interventions of well-meaning social service agencies—all done, of course, for the good of the children.

And although federal laws and policies supposedly outlawing discrimination based on "race" have been in place for over fifty years, similar interventions have been carried out in African American and Latino communities, grounded in dominant-class perceptions of the parents in these communities as dirty, immature, neglectful, aggressive, or feeble-minded—all deemed legitimate reasons for intervening. What is even more disconcerting is the manner in which these racialized perceptions continue to be reflected in the policies and practices of education, health, and welfare agencies across the country.

Such class-bound, racialized perceptions of "difference" were clearly at work in the drafting of the 1996 Welfare Law that virtually eliminated the economic safety net for millions of children. These perceptions also drive the unrelenting emphasis that public schools have placed on bilingual transition programs for language minority students, despite the wealth of data (including government studies) that document its detrimental impact on academic achievement. Even more recently, in California, these perceptions fueled the racialized public debates and the strong anti-immigrant climate that led to the passage of Proposition 187 to prohibit education, health, and social services to undocumented immigrant children and their families; the overreaction of the public to the Oakland School Board's effort to include Ebonics in the public school curriculum; and the rhetoric, including the bogus title "English for the Children," used in the campaign to pass Proposition 227 (the Unz Initiative), whose aim was to dismantle bilingual education.

In *Shifting Fortunes: The Perils of the Growing American Wealth Gap* (1999), Collins and his colleagues argue that while the government "generously subsidizes those who don't need any help with building assets," the poor are being stripped of their safety net. The authors report that "an estimated $125 billion in federal subsidies are directed to corporations in the form of loopholes, direct cash transfers and subsidized access to public resources" (62), even though corporate profits totaled 4.5 trillion last year. This amount is equivalent to the paychecks of over 50 million working Americans (Collins et al., 1999). Nor can we ignore a heavily funded scientific community that has no compunction about spending over $350 million on a single Mars project, while millions of people starve from famine and the consequences of war.

Given such examples of economic inequality and racialized injustice in contemporary society, teachers must become more cognizant of the alienating conditions faced by poor ethnic communities—conditions that are indelibly linked to historical events that position members of subordinate populations very differently from members of the ruling class. Consider just for a moment the manner in which the historical experience of slavery (forced unpaid labor) continues to impact the overall economic conditions of African Americans. Or how the betrayal of the 1848 Treaty of Guadalupe Hidalgo, which explicitly "respected and guaranteed the civil and property rights of Mexicans" remaining in the United States after the Mexican-American War (San Miguel and Valencia, 1998, 354), continues to be at work in the inadequate education available for Chicanos in the Southwest today. Or the negative impact of "Operation Bootstrap" in Puerto Rico during the 1950s, which resulted in the sterilization of almost 35 percent of Puerto Rican women. Or how the political atrocities and economic expenditures of the Vietnam War continue to affect the lives of Vietnamese American families, or the families of soldiers seriously wounded or killed in the war, or Latino and African American working-class families, who suffered the greatest proportion of casualties.

Similarly, we need to recognize that events that are taking place today in Bosnia or Chiapas or Nigeria or the Middle East are not solely the result of regional struggles. Conflicts in these regions are closely tied to the manner in which industrial development and U.S. "postindustrial" interests have exercised global control of mass populations, influencing the economic and political climates in these parts of the world. These interests are the ones that are sustained by the values and practices that shape educational institutions. In other words, the traditional values and expectations of many health, education, and welfare agencies are inextricably tied to the same interests and values that on one hand support the "globalization" of U.S. corporate "common culture" and on the other sustain deepening economic inequalities here and abroad. Moreover, as an industry, the education, health and welfare system historically has functioned as a formidable buffer between the ruling elite and the disenfranchised.

"Globalization" and the Free Market

At this juncture, it is helpful to note that "globalization" has become the new buzzword for economic imperialism and its ruthless mechanisms to maximize capital accumulation. It seems to have become the "dominant political, social, economic issue of our era" (McChesney, 1998, 1). Consequently, everyone has begun to use this term, even when speaking about issues which were once domestic concerns. Everything is talked about as global-labor rights, housing issues, citizens' rights, and even education. Such ubiquitousness requires that we ask whether the global term functions primarily to obscure the problems of local politics and debilitate the value of local struggles or whether it can shed some light on the conditions we're facing in urban centers today. It seems it is wise here not to fall into dichotomized notions and recognize that both are inherently possible, given the nature of these times.

What is meant by "globalization"? The earth's diverse societies are being arranged and united in complicated ways by global capitalism through a politics of "global convergence." Robert W. McChesney (1998, 1) defines "globalization"[1] as

> The process whereby capitalism is increasingly constituted on a transnational basis, not only in the trade of goods and services but, even more important, in the flow of capital and the trade in currencies and financial instruments. The dominant players in the globalization are the world's few hundred largest private corporations, which have increasingly integrated production and marketing across national borders over the past decade.

McChesney (1998, 2) also points out that there has been considerable debate as to "just how advanced this globalization process is, or is likely to become, as well as its political implications."

In response, some might want to rally to the "postmodernized" notion that the current economy reflects a grand epochal shift. Ellen Meiksins Wood, however, in "Modernity, Postmodernity or Capitalism?" (1998, 47), argues that what we are seeing is not a major shift in the logic of capitalism, but rather "the consequences of capitalism as a comprehensive system...capitalism itself reaching maturity."

So, although there might be some new forms, new rhythms, new impetuses in the globalizing process of capital or "universalization of capitalism" (Wood, 1998, 47), for the majority of populations around the world the so-called "global economy" began in 1492. "In their histories, the centuries of conquest and economic colonization were integral to the rise of industrial capitalism in Europe and North America, but the returns were never really shared with them. In fact, the global economy long ago consigned most regions of the world to lowly status as commodity producers" (Greider 1997, 19).

Some of the consequences of the last decade of global capitalist expansionism include high profit and sales with low human labor requirements. These consequences have resulted in much of the current labor needs being met by technology and a dramatic shift in the number of workers required; the downsizing or closure of companies in the United States with corporate transfers of historically well-paying manufacturing jobs to "cheap labor" manufacturing centers around the world; and the U.S. shift from an industrial to a postindustrial economy predicated on what many are calling the Information Age and the knowledge society, an age that is defined by a new international division of labor. Workers are the biggest losers, having "lost substantial control over their labor markets and terms of employment" (Greider, 1997, 24) and their purchasing power, while salaries and benefits of top executives, consultants, and advisors have soared. Decentralization of control has resulted in corporations becoming global webs, with stakeholders becoming a large diffused group, spread over the world—less visible, less accountable, and less noisy than national stakeholders. The modern welfare state with "the social protections that rich nations enacted to ameliorate the harsh inequalities of industrial capitalism, is now in peril. [Corporate emphasis is on] maximizing returns on capital without regard to national identity or political or social consequences" (ibid., 25), while the "Third World" grows more and more economically dependent as a consequence of imposed economic systems, industrial exploitation of natural resources, and obligatory participation in the global market.

What U.S. capitalism has effectively produced is what John Cavanaugh (1996) terms "global economic apartheid," for of the 100 largest economies in the world, 51 are now global corporations. The Ford Motor Company is bigger than the economy of South Africa, and Wal-Mart is bigger than the economies of 161 countries. The top 200 companies have been job destroyers, wielding enormous power but creating few jobs. The heads of these companies use the phrase "global village" and other such celebratory rhetoric of "difference" to impress on us how they're bringing people together as workers and consumers. But while the profits of "difference" are being happily celebrated, "the characteristics of the global cultural system...suggest that its massive inequities remain both potent and deeply rooted" (Golding, 1998, 70).

Meanwhile, the United States remains the dominant force of culture production—homogenizing the experience of 90 to 95 percent of the world's people through music, movies, and other cultural outlets. Transnational corporations such as Nike use free-trade zones in Mexico, the Philippines, and the Caribbean Basin where workers are paid 5 to 10 percent of what people would be paid in the United States and child labor—common practices of these global factories—is rampant. There is no question but that "globalization" is about the power inherent in the "new" flexible capitalist modes of production and accumulation and the control of life—a control of life that has widened the gap between the rich and the poor. Xavier Gorostiaga wrote, in a 1993 United Nations report entitled "Is the Answer in the South?":

> Throughout the world the last decade has been characterized by the rise of inequality between the rich and the poor.... In 1989 the richest fifth controlled 82.7 percent of the revenue; 81.2 percent of the world trade; 94.6 percent of commercial loans, 80.6 percent of internal savings and 80.5 percent of all investments. If in terms of distribution the panorama is untenable, it is equally so regarding resources. The rich countries possess one fifth of the world's population but consume 70 percent of world energy, 75 percent of the metals, 85 percent of the timber, and 60 percent of the food. Such a pattern of development...is only viable in the degree to which the extreme inequality is maintained, as otherwise the world resources would be exhausted. Therefore, inequality is not a distortion of the system. It is a systematic prerequisite for growth and permanence of the present system (4).

Yet it is this tendency to overlook the "systemic prerequisite" of capitalism in discussions of "cultural difference" or cultural identity that permits the construction and imposition of deceptive myths related to notions of "difference"—myths that function to preserve and deepen the institutional structures of "cultural invasion" and the social processes of racialization (Darder and Torres, 2004).

Given, then, the disastrous implications of an intensifying "globalized" political economy, both locally and abroad, educators need to understand the impact of capitalism around the world and link it to the local conditions that exist in their schools and communities. There is no question but that capitalism is advanced upon contradictory terrain, and does not function as simple imposition. Instead, the notion of society as a collection of possessive individuals is reinforced, and any serious sense of the common good is marginalized. This is advanced effectively through the dynamics of the "free market" ideology.

The forces of the marketplace and the interest of corporations also drive educational rhetoric and classroom curricula. This was apparent in corporate America's response to the 1983 Nation at Risk report, which alleged that public schooling was a fiasco. It was a response that overwhelmingly emphasized school improvement as a matter of the national economy—if schools failed, the economy would crumble (Molner, 1996). Consequently, in today's world, schools are often considered to be economic engines. Unfortunately, schools generally function in the interest of the marketplace rather than serving as a democratizing influence upon local economies. Take, for instance, language policies and their relationship to the economy. While Sacramento is busy setting up mandates for the implementation of a phonics curriculum in the schools, the marketing divisions of corporations that publish phonics texts and materials are revving their engines for multi-million-dollar sales. Democracy too has become principally tied to the creation of conditions of "free consumer choice" in an unfettered market. Hence, democracy is no longer a political concept but an economic metaphor. In the same way, education and its democratizing purpose is lost to the wiles of market-driven educational solutions such as the privatization of education—one of the most dangerous threats facing public schools today. Through the rhetoric of "consumer choice" prevalent in the privatization debate, capitalism articulates a classless, homogenous society of consumers, all existing within a common, transcendent culture (Apple, 1995). In a similar manner, the "pluralism" of the marketplace appropriates conflicting cultural forms, ideas, and images, in order to guarantee its own expansion. Rupturing the ideological bubble that insulates this false notion that democracy equals capitalism seems to be one of the most difficult tasks that teachers face when working with students, colleagues, and parents. Exposing the hidden values, beliefs, and practices of a political economy that greedily seeks maximum returns on capital, with little concern for human life or the sustainability of the planet, is key to rethinking democratic schooling. Teachers cannot disregard the manner in which transnational capital whips around the world placing a neck hold on the economies of "developing" nations. Simultaneously, the market appropriates whatever shred of cultural capital as can be commodified to appease the cultural industry's fabricated hunger for chic ethnic paraphernalia—whether clothing, food, music, art, or spiritual artifacts. In the process, the consumptive wiles of one third of the world's population reign over the subsistence of the other two thirds, condemning millions to conditions of subhuman material existence.

The Disposable and Expendable

Although it may seem very unfamiliar or terribly uncomfortable at moments, teachers who say they are committed to antiracist struggle and social justice must become fully conscious to what is perhaps America's most concealed truth—an all-consuming capitalist system that is everywhere at work in sustaining, perpetuating, and exacerbating all forms of social discrimination, economic exploitation, cultural invasion, and systematic violence against women, gays and lesbians, working-class people, and racialized populations. Freire often argued that "racism and sexism [are] very much linked to capitalist production.... I don't see the possibility of overcoming racism and sexism in a capitalist mode of production" (Shor and Freire, 1987, 167). What exists in the United States is a political economy nourished and bolstered by an ideology of power relations and a class structure that render members of disenfranchised groups virtually disposable and expendable.

This ideology of disposability is at work in a variety of contemporary examples of urban life. For instance, when a Euro-American professional woman was raped and killed in Cambridge, Massachusetts, there was a public outcry by the Boston community in response to this crime. The police and community had to do something! This seemed like a logical response. However, this was a sharp contrast to the Boston community's lack of concern for the three poor African American women who had been raped and killed the week before in Roxbury, a predominantly low-income African American neighborhood. The latter can only be considered a logical response within a context in which poor African American women are considered expendable.

In public schools the ideology of disposability is evident in the mania of high-stakes standardized testing, where tests acknowledged to be flawed are used to make inaccurate and inappropriate decisions about the fate of millions of students across the nation. The results of these tests are linked to the practice of student retention and nonpromotion—a practice that has consistently been shown to result in long-term negative effects to student achievement and loss of educational resources and opportunities. Retention rates are higher for African American, Latino, and other children from poor families. And of all students who are retained, 50 percent are more likely to not graduate from high school. Hence, early in their lives these children are officially classified and tracked, rendering them members of a disposable and expendable class. What is completely unconscionable from a social and economic-justice perspective is not only the perpetuation but overwhelming revival that standardized testing has been undergoing during the last decade.[2] Hence, early in their lives, these children are officially classified and tracked, which renders them members of the disposable and expendable class.

It is impossible to consider the issue of populations deemed disposable and expendable without discussing the prison industrial complex. The U.S. prison population is now over 2 million—the largest incarceration rate in the world. This constitutes 25 percent of the entire world's prison population, although the United States has less than 5 percent of the world's population. During the 1990s the prison population grew at a greater rate than in any earlier decade in recorded history (see Justice Policy Institute, 2000). In California, in particular, greater and greater numbers of Latinos, African Americans, and working-class men and women are being incarcerated by a society that has systematically rendered them disposable—disposable because they are problematic to capital accumulation.

An attempt to make sense of this growing phenomenon from a perspective that focuses only on the deviant psychological health or immorality of particular individuals or, worse, on racialized cultural explanations of criminal behavior is sheer fallacy. Instead, teachers must make the connection between the increasing imprisonment of working-class men and women and the control by transnational corporations of everyday life. Never in the history of the United States have workers been subjected to more corporate mergers and movements of companies to foreign countries. These moves resulted in an overwhelming number of layoffs and terminations during one of the most profitable economic eras of all time—an era of enormous profits for the 10 percent of the population who reaped almost 90 percent of the benefit, while real wages for the majority of U.S. workers declined (Collins et al., 1999).

Often, educators are incredulous or find it distasteful and disturbing to be confronted with these issues head-on, given the sense of powerlessness that difficult social and economic issues elicit in most people. However, we must fully recognize that as long as any group of people is deemed disposable or expendable, any popularized American notion of "liberty and justice for all" will remain nothing but a myth—or, in the words of Donaldo Macedo, a "big lie" (1994, 9). It is, in fact, he argues, a "pedagogy of big lies" that perpetuates a process of schooling in which the majority of students are so domesticated with fragmented and disconnected knowledge that they are left virtually uneducated and with little access to the political and economic spheres of society.

In light of traditional educational policies concerning testing, assessment, curriculum, second-language acquisition, and promotion that blatantly perpetuate the systemic marginalization of subordinate groups, it seems nearly impossible to envision how teachers might begin to break through the hegemonic forces at work. This is particularly difficult when teachers fail to embrace a revolutionary ethic of civic responsibility and social value for all people, irrespective of culture, gender, economic status, sexual orientation, physical ability, or age. Such forms of social consciousness must be actively cultivated and nourished within classrooms through critical dialogues and social relationships that reshape our perceptions and interactions with one another and the world in which we must survive as teachers and students. Through an educational practice that encourages ongoing questioning and the development of critical social thought, teachers and their students can engage critically the profound social, political, and economic issues at work in their lives. It is through such a process of critical inquiry that links can also be made between the increasing profit and wealth of transnational corporations and the growing numbers of economically disenfranchised people here and around the globe. Through such inquiry, teachers can come to understand the cause of poverty as structural, rather than accepting simplistic and fallacious interpretations of poverty to explain why students from particular communities are more likely to do poorly in school, drop out, be incarcerated, or end up pregnant and on welfare. This shift in consciousness represents a fundamental step in redefining our politics and constructing a new vision of schools and the society.

Racism and the Imaginary Middle

The relationship that exists between racism, class conflict, and the construction of the mythical "normal" or "healthy" child, adolescent, or adult should be of grave concern to teachers of all educational levels. Paulo Freire referred to this phenomenon as the necessity to "mythicize the world" in fixed categories that serve to perpetuate the subjugation and cultural invasion of oppressed populations. He saw this as an extension of the "banking" concept of education, which, in conjunction with paternalism, considers marginal those

> who deviate from the general configuration of a "good organized and just society." The oppressed are regarded as the pathology of the healthy society, which must therefore adjust these "incompetent and lazy" folk to its own patterns by changing mentality. These

marginals need to be "integrated," "incorporated" into the healthy society that they have "forsaken" (1970, 60–61).

Hence, a critical view of schooling must unveil and openly challenge the manner in which ideologies of racism and class conflict function to distort the realities and conditions of working-class students, particularly those who come from subordinate cultural communities. It is important to note how differing forms of racism are often produced through the perpetuation of racialized language in the conceptual development of public policies and practices within both public and private institutions. Essentialized language is produced through false dichotomous notions of black/white existence that fail to engage substantively with the diversity of social, political, and economic realities that make up racialized populations. Further, such language is given meaning within the dominant belief system that shapes the practices of public and private institutions—a belief system that for centuries has functioned to effectively exclude the democratic participation of subordinate populations through the process of racialization (Darder and Torres, 1999).

More specifically, "racialization" refers to those instances where social relations between people are structured by the significance that is given to specific human biological characteristics, particularly when such significance is used to define, categorize, and construct meaning about different social groups (Miles, 1993)—for example, when skin color is perceived to signify a whole array of psychological, cultural, and social information. This information is then utilized to construct reified interpretations of the character of individuals from different cultural communities. Yet those who are from subordinate cultural communities know that our communities are never monolithic. Moreover, the color of one's skin does not guarantee one's intelligence, skill, competency, personality, or, for that matter, politics. Along the same lines, Paulo Freire (1997) argued against the notion that racism is

> inherent to the nature of human beings.... We "are" not racist; we "become" racist, and we can also stop being that way. The problem I have with racist people is not the color of their skin, but rather the color of their ideology. Likewise, my difficulty with the "macho" does not rest in their sex, but in their discriminatory ideology. Being racist or macho, progressive or reactionary, is not an integral part of human nature (85–86).

Unfortunately, even today with the abundance of information available, most teachers working within oppressed communities still back substantive knowledge related to the manner in which discriminatory ideologies related to political, economic, and cultural policies and practices influence the lives of students in their classrooms. This is particularly disturbing when teachers must confront daily the negative impact of social and economic injustice on the lives of students who have been historically marginalized, solely because of their skin color, the material conditions of their parents, or the communities in which they reside.

This is particularly the case for teachers who practice in large urban centers. Despite the great War on Poverty of the sixties, segregation and distress rates in urban centers such as New York, Chicago, Detroit, Cleveland, Los Angeles, and Philadelphia continue to increase, as residents must grapple with stagnant wages, the loss of jobs, the elimination of welfare benefits, and fewer vocational training opportunities (Wilson, 1997). And despite a significant improvement in the educational attainment across all communities—including students from extreme poverty areas—during the last thirty bears, there is more poverty today in many of these cities than there was in 1968 (Cisneros, 1993).

The Impact of the Media

Over the course of the twentieth century the media have come to occupy an increasingly central role in the formation of individual and collective identities and in shaping the aesthetics and politics of a generation. In today's world, it is impossible for teachers to fully grasp the insidious process of racialization, sexism, and other forms of ideological distortions without noting the overwhelming impact of the media on the manner in which students come to make sense of their world. Through their captivating influence and fictitious representations of "difference," the media function effectively to sustain through commonsense approval the ideology of social and economic domination. "In a society such as [that of] the United States where most of the people do not have any direct access to nor power over the bulk of decisions that affect their lives, the media play a powerful legitimating role in the production of social consensus" (Darder, 1995b, 10).

Hence, the role of the media in the perpetuation of class-bound and racialized attitudes cannot be overlooked in our understanding of schooling or how students perceive their world and the relationships they forge in the classroom and the larger community. This reality has reached such blatant proportions that even a simple analysis of Disney[3] movies, teen flicks, or music industry products easily reveals the insidious market values and interests of capitalist America. These are the values and interests that actively shape and influence the attitudes and behaviors of young consumers and give meaning to fabricated ideals that are deceptively proselytized by the monopoly of the mass media.

From popularized cartoon images to the values of family sitcoms to the "cool" representations of athletes and movie stars, students are barraged daily with conflicting notions of who they should strive to be. Simultaneously, the hidden culture of the "imaginary ideal" powerfully influences the way teachers think and talk about "smart students," "caring parents," or "loving homes." Unfortunately, the problematic nature of such homogenizing discourse generally goes unquestioned within public schools, despite its influence on how teachers view students and how schools assess and evaluate the legitimacy of student knowledge, skills, worth, and potential.

Inherent in the mainstream popular gaze is a class-based and racialized view of "difference." When mainstream references to "man" or "woman" are made, the reference is always to a "white man" or "white woman" who is further ascribed with a "natural" set of acceptable, and often superior, traits. On the other hand, those who are considered "the other" are distinguished by the use of specific class-based or racialized categories. Obvious examples of this aspect of racialization are found in mainstream newspapers where reporters must identify people who are not "white" by using some sort of ethnic label (black mothers, Korean parents, Hispanic children, Filipino workers, etc.). A very similar dynamic is at work concerning class assumptions. Categories that immediately suggest class difference generally include "high-risk children," "latch-key kids," "illegal aliens," or "underclass populations." The racialized and class-bound images perpetuated by such language, and the values that inform its use, give students some very clear messages about their particular place in the socially constructed hierarchy of American life.

It is vitally important that teachers recognize how the media function as a subtle and not-so-subtle means of defining and shaping our innermost desires and dreams—which, more often than not, are linked directly to the interests of the marketplace. As we embark on the twenty-first century, corporate interests of greed and consumption are enjoying a field day even with what at one time were considered counterhegemonic or revolutionary images, artifacts, and symbols. This is exemplified by the worldwide marketing of, for instance, rap music, which as marketed only faintly mimics the political, cultural, and class origins of resistance of African American street youth. This is true also of the polished and packaged images of civil rights leaders, Third World revolutionaries, cultural celebrations and rituals, or exotic vacations in Third World "island paradises." These lucrative "multicultural" products serve to create the illusion that there truly exists greater acceptance of diversity and deference and increasing social freedom and equality—all because a small percentage of the privileged world population can freely sell and consume multiculturalism, to their little hearts' content.

What teachers cannot ignore is that a people's culture is not a fashion statement. It embodies meaningful collective knowledge about how communities have struggled to survive, work, love, and dream. It often contains significant historical remnants of cultural capital that potentially can inspire and motivate students toward greater social agency, political resistance, and community self-determination. But not surprisingly, it is precisely this revolutionary dimension that is stripped away from the fashionable products and images that are peddled on the big screen, on MTV, in popular magazines, and in slick educational materials—all sold under the rubric "celebrating diversity."

Privilege and Entitlement

Americans are subject to political manipulation, exploitation, and complicity with an oppressive system of privilege and entitlement based on gender, skin color, sexual orientation, and other discriminatory signifiers (Macedo, 1993). Implicated in this process are public schools that function to reproduce, as well as maintain, privilege by taking dominant-culture knowledge forms and content and defining it as legitimate knowledge to be preserved and transmitted. In this way, schools play a fundamental role in assisting in the accumulation of cultural capital and serving as one of the primary modes of production for the cultural commodities required by U.S. corporate society. Moreover, through the creation of jobs and the implementation of market-driven curricula, schools perpetuate commodity knowledge as economically essential products. Hence, the school's role in the accumulation process allows for the creation of reserve workers and cultural capital required to sustain the U.S. global economy.

The construction and institutionalization of racialized stereotypes in both the academic and popular imagination protect the established privilege and entitlement of those who hold political and economic power. These stereotypes are generally built and perpetuated against the backdrop of a mainstream belief in an "ideal." From the vantage point of privilege, racialized stereotypes are conceived according to the level of phenotypic and behavioral differences that supposedly exist between those who are considered outside the norms of appropriate behavior. As inferred earlier, those who deviate are deemed genetically inferior or culturally defective—judgments inherent in perceptions of the disenfranchised as too loud, hyperactive, oversexed, weak, passive, too emotional, hysterical, too intense, or just plain lazy.

The failure of teachers to acknowledge entitlements and privileges that come from the color of one's skin or one's class, gender, or sexual orientation powerfully obstructs their capacity to break through mythic illusions of diversity and forge a critically democratic vision of schooling and American life. Such denial of entitlement and privilege also perpetuates alienating beliefs within the educational system of what is legitimate knowledge, classroom practice, and teacher-student relationships. To be considered a legitimate or valuable educator or student requires the willingness to conform to a standard and protocol rooted in the dominant cultural and class values of the educational system. It is this set of values which also then determines whether a student or teacher will be considered a "good fit" within most institutions.

Furthermore, the perpetuation of universal psychological norms by which all students are evaluated is generally coupled with an expectation that those who are culturally different, rather than the schools, should change. Hence, persistent deficit notions of those perceived to be outside the mainstream abound, with often rigid and alienating expectations of what teachers, students, or parents must do, or how they must change, to "merit" additional educational resources or opportunities. In his writings on cultural identity and education, Freire exposes the ideological roots of such expectations.

> The dominant class, then, because it has the power to distinguish itself from the dominated class, first rejects the differences between them but, second, does not pretend to be equal to those who are different; third it does not intend those who are different shall be equal. What it wants is to maintain the differences and keep distance and to recognize and emphasize in practice the inferiority of those who are dominated (1998b, 71).

Consequently, assimilative expectations of conformity often veil a virulent discourse of what Freire called "false generosity" (1970), a feigned benevolent concern for the well being of culturally diverse or poor students that works to strip away their sense of identity and social power, often interfering with their very ability to act on their own behalf. The loss of self-determination and academic motivation that can result from difficult experiences with educational institutions constitutes one of major causes for students' dropping out of high school or withdrawing from colleges and universities. Unfortunately, this is a social phenomenon that is linked to their further disempowerment, particularly when their failure to "become educated" seriously impedes their full participation in the labor force and community life.

Again, there is no question but that the media are major culprits in perpetuating debilitating notions and false racialized images of class entitlement and privilege. Examples of this are highly prevalent in the media's portrayal of poor ethnic communities. Although the majority of people on welfare are Euro-American, a favorite portrayal of recipients is the large African American woman with many children, living in poor conditions. Along the same line, African American and Chicano youth are often portrayed as violent "gang-bangers," notwithstanding the fact that less than 10 percent of these youths are actually involved in gangs (Vigil, 1997). Hence it is not surprising to learn that an African American youth is six times more likely to be incarcerated than a white peer, even when the latter has had similar charges brought against him and neither youth a prior record; nor that minority youths are more likely than white youths who commit comparable crimes to be referred to juvenile court, be detained, face trial as adults, and be jailed with adults (National Council on Crime and Delinquency, 2000).

A Brief Comment on Political Backlash

As teachers become more conscious of social and economic injustice and move to engage critically with the inequalities so prevalent within public schools, they must not naively overlook the politics of political backlash. The response to losing power as a consequence of shifting entitlement and privilege within schools can elicit a feeling of threat or displacement among teachers, administrators, parents, and even students who identity principally with mainstream ideology and traditional institutional values. This can result in further political backlash that expresses itself as fear that the "other" is "taking over," irrespective to how the "other" is identified. Paulo Freire addressed this concern as he sought to consider critically the impact r shattering the oppressor/oppressed contradictions that result when traditional hierarchical relations of power become more equalized.

> But even when the contradiction is resolved authentically by a new situation established by the liberated laborers, the former oppressors do not feel liberated. On the contrary, they genuinely consider themselves to be oppressed. Conditioned by the experience of oppressing others, any situation other than their former seems to them like oppression. Any restriction on this way of life, in the name of the rights of the community, appears to the former oppressors as a profound violation of their individual rights (Freire, 1970, 43).

Unfortunately, such responses are not rare whenever women, working-class people or communities of color are perceived as making too many gains or inroads into the decision-making process and the control of resources.

Given the nature of backlash politics, one common tactic in schools is to make exaggerated requests for justification or proof that one's teaching practice or academic knowledge is legitimate—that one is truly worthy of equal standing. The institutional expectation of exaggerated proofs of legitimacy is a prevalent theme that is often privately discussed by both teachers and students from subordinate class and ethnic communities. The alienation so often experienced by teachers who are perceived as "other" is well illustrated when they find themselves in schools where they are a lone voice among their coworkers, administrators, or parents who adhere to the prescribed values of the dominant culture. Often in such a context, teachers are questioned incessantly about every aspect of their practice or details of their decisions that do not comply with what are considered acceptable mainstream methods, even when a teacher has been hired specifically to function as an "ethnic representative" of a particular community.

In such school settings, it seems beyond the capacity of many administrators, coworkers, or parents to believe that these teachers who seem so "different" are adequately competent to determine alternative practices on the basis of their cultural and class understanding of their students—knowledge that others in the institution may not possess. This generates further hiring debates, for example, as to whether minority teachers are actually required to serve students who come from diverse communities. These highly biased and uncritical responses are often rooted in hidden racialized notions of intelligence and aptitude as well as fears of job displacement. Most disconcerting is how these responses can serve to obstruct the ability of teachers from subordinate communities to carry out appropriate educational strategies and alternatives, based on an understanding of particular cultural histories as well as of the conditions of economic marginalization that their students face daily.

This example also illustrates the manner in which backlash politics is driven not only by an ideology of racism but by the potential class or economic impact of expanding institutional opportunities to diverse populations. Hence, teachers cannot neglect the fact that if a revolutionary practice is to be central to our vision of schooling, it can only be actualized in conjunction with a struggle for a radical shift in the current distribution of power and wealth. In the absence of such a redistribution of power and resources, the politics of pluralism, diversity, or antiracism constitutes only an illusion, an empty rhetoric, a mystified politics of deception.

The Need for a Critique of Capitalism

Given the changing dimensions of the political economy and its impact on schooling, Paulo Freire recognized the tremendous need for educators to infuse their teaching with a critique of capitalism. He argued that "criticism of the injustice within the capitalistic system must be strong" (1997b, 77–78). To launch such a critique, capitalism must be exposed as the most totalizing system of social relations the world has ever known. For it is precisely this totalizing dimension that renders capitalism unique and so difficult to challenge (Wood, 1996, 1998). As a consequence, most teachers find it very difficult to even comprehend, let alone effectively critique, the way capitalism shapes and controls their teaching, as well as the educational experiences of students in this country.

Forging a substantive critique requires that teachers unveil class-bound values inherent in education materials, classroom practices, and public policy, through dialogue and study. This is to say that teachers must come to comprehend with greater clarity and specificity how the dynamics of class formation function to structure the social conditions of all institutions, including schools. Through developing this knowledge, teachers can begin to infuse their work in schools, cities, and communities with a more substantive critique of capitalism and develop democratic strategies for intervention that will challenge the structural conditions of class and racialized inequalities. More important, educators together can rethink their current understanding of public policies directed toward the erosion of linguistic democracy, immigration rights, the dismantling of affirmative action, and the revival of standardized testing and high school exit examinations within the context of a class analysis of schooling. By so doing, they will not only develop the language and strategies to effectively counter the tirades of the political right, but effectively construct and articulate new possibilities for democratic schooling. This task is best accomplished when teachers understand patterns of distribution and redistribution that produce relations of exploitation within schools (McLaren, 2000).

A well-formulated critique of capitalism is also essential to understanding the complex relationship between schools and community development. Through the lens of such a critique, teachers can challenge more skillfully policies and practices that impact their students, parents, and community in oppressive ways. Here it is useful to note that cultural forms within social organizations are never simply mysterious unexplained creations but are always linked to particular relations of power. This is why the question of power is essential to our understanding of schooling: its patterns of distribution seriously impact all aspects of our personal and social lives (Naiman, 1996). In engaging the question of power, Paulo Freire seldom minced words when it came to defining the institutional objective of his pedagogy. "This struggle is a fight for power. Perhaps to be more exact, it is a fight for the reinvention of power" (1993, 124). His vision entailed the reconstruction of power relationships that could break through those reified processes of alienation and allow us to recognize ourselves as full human beings.

Associated then with this view of power is a basic premise of the classroom as a workplace, teachers as workers who are integrated into the local economy, and parents as workers immersed in the context of "globalization." From this radical perspective, teachers can perceive more readily that the material conditions in which parents live and work frequently provoke particular responses to their environment. The choices parents make are influenced by their class position. Yet teachers seldom seem to note that working-class parents often see the relationship between schools and work more narrowly, given class constraints. There are material forces at work that shape parents' sense of opportunities and limitations for themselves and their children within the larger social structure. Consequently, more times than not, the expectations parents have of schools and their children's academic future are also linked to their class position.

In light of all this, teachers must work collectively to enter into relationships of solidarity and struggle with parents, teachers, and students. Through the formation of such relationships, collective efforts can be made toward changing material conditions within communities. This is a significant contrast to the fact that one good teacher in a school cannot eliminate plant closures, loss of economic benefits, or change oppressive public policies or practices alone. The transformation of schools—a critical process that must be aimed at overcoming the social and economic injustices of society—requires a collective political struggle that can only be waged successfully through our collective efforts.

Building Social Movements

Paulo Freire believed till his death that "to change what we presently are, it is necessary to change the structures of power radically" (1997b, 80). Yet this did not "presuppose an inversion of the oppressed-oppressor poles; rather it intends to reinvent, in communion, a society where exploitation and the verticalization of power do not exist, where the disenfranchised segments of society are not excluded or interdicted from reading the world" (Macedo and Freire, 1998, 9). To accomplish such a "communion," Freire encouraged progressive educators to forge groups of struggle founded on his critical Utopian notion of "unity within diversity." For Freire, the inability to establish alliances across the "reconcilable" differences only serves to preserve the structures of domination and exploitation. Hence, he urged in *Pedagogy of the Heart* (85):

> The "different" who accept unity cannot forgo unity in their fight; they must have objectives beyond those specific ones of each group. There has to be a greater dream, a Utopia the different aspire to and for which they are able to make concessions. Unity within diversity is possible, for example, between antiracist groups, regardless of the group's skin color. In order for that to happen, it is necessary for the anti-racist groups to overcome the limits of their core racial group and fight for radical transformation of the socioeconomic system that intensifies racism.

In the spirit of Freire's dream, teachers need to create alliances across cultural communities and class positions that are firmly grounded in a process that can help us overcome our lack of democratic experience through participation, while superseding the irrational and dehumanizing hegemonic forces that prevail. Such a process requires that we remain ever cognizant of the increasing significance of class and the specificity of capitalism as a system of social and political relations of power; one where all forms of social injustice exist within particular social formations, where power is not equitably distributed, and where the struggle for power is in constant flux and change. Hence, part of the task is to rescue the concept of power from its diffused and immeasurable position "where power is everywhere and no where, back to where the possibility of collective political action remains possible" (Naiman, 1996, 16). In so doing, we become better prepared to contend with such issues as livable wages, adequate health care, welfare reform, affordable housing, and equal education—all issues that are acutely influenced by the political economy.

Moreover, through the creation of alliances, progressive teachers can participate in counterhegemonic political projects that do not dichotomize their work as cultural workers and social activists. Instead, such participation supports their work within schools while simultaneously providing the opportunity to collectively take positions on current educational issues that directly impact their teaching practice, such as school vouchers, charter schools, teacher certification, high school graduation exams, literacy, and bilingual education. In addition, through alliances where a solidarity of differences is cultivated, teachers from diverse communities and class positions can work together to create unifying, albeit heterogeneous and multifaceted, anticapitalist political strategies to counter conservative efforts to destroy public schooling. Most important, such community relationships of struggle can support teachers as they fight together to break out of the paralysis that has been plaguing the left for years. Through social-movement organizations, teachers can boldly move together to build an alternative vision of schooling in this county—a vision that must be connected to a larger political project of liberation.

History has repeatedly shown that significant institutional change can truly take place only as a result of collective work within social-movement organizations. True, legal and policy strategies have had some impact, but ultimately the collective pressure of the masses has had the greatest impact in quickly mobilizing these forces. Despite political and economic efforts to render the masses voiceless through the fabricated confusion of false cultural representations and the imposition of crippling myths, teachers working together can restore and empower the public will to take back our lives and our communities. Within such a context of solidarity, we can powerfully reanimate political self-determination and with courage speak out boldly in defiance of social and economic injustice. Through our collective participation, teachers can discover the means to channel the fears, guilt, rage, and despair into productive action. Through the building of ethical communities for struggle and change, we can develop the critical strength, reflective ability, political knowledge, social commitment, personal maturity, and solidarity across our differences necessary to reinvent our world. But most important, as Freire consistently stressed, we must restore the inalienable rights of what it means to have full citizenship.

Yes, citizenship—above all in a society like ours, of such authoritarian and racially, sexually, and class-based discriminatory traditions—is really an invention, a political production. In this sense, one who suffers any of these discriminations, or all of them at once, does not enjoy the full exercise of citizenship as a peaceful and recognized right. On the contrary, it is a right to be reached and whose conquest makes democracy grow substantially. Citizenship implies freedom—to work, to eat, to dress, to wear shoes, to sleep in a house, to support oneself and one's family, to love, to be angry, to cry, to protest, to support, to move, to participate in this or that religion, this or that party, to educate oneself and one's family, to swim regardless in what ocean of one's country. Citizenship is not obtained by chance: It is a construction that, never finished, demands we fight for it. It demands commitment, political clarity, coherence, decision. For this reason a democratic education cannot be realized apart from an education of and for citizenship (1998b, 90).

The strength of such communities, as Freire imagined them in *Pedagogy of the Heart*, is their fundamental capacity to establish, cultivate, and support humanizing relationships, while teachers collectively struggle for social and economic justice. Through their participation in such relationships, teachers can break down the debilitating alienation and isolation they often experience within public schools. In the process, they begin to find the freedom to embrace all aspects of their humanity more fully and openly—the pain, the suffering, the fear, the disappointments, the uncertainties, the pleasures, the joy, and the dreams—and by so doing, to discover the political power generated by our collective humanity.

Paulo Freire held that a critical vision for the future is impossible without a sense of hope, firmly anchored in the knowledge that there exists "no historical reality which is not human" (1970, 125). Only through a praxis of hope can alliances across differences be forged—alliances sufficiently strong for teachers and students to "learn together, teach together, be curiously impatient together, produce something together and resist the obstacles" (1998a, 69) that prevent the full expression of our humanity and steal our place as subjects of history. In *Pedagogy of Freedom*, Freire again connected the relationship of hope to the possibility of historical transformation.

Hope is a natural, possible and necessary impetus in the context of our unfinishness. Hope is an indispensable seasoning in our human, historical experience. Without it, instead of history we would have pure determinism. History exists only where time is problematized and not simply a given. A future that is inexorable is a denial of history (69).

There is no question that in today's world, no authentic form of democratic life is possible for the future without a revolutionary praxis of hope that works both for the transformation of social consciousness on one hand and the reconstruction of social structures on the other. Freire urged us to think of political strategies and state policies that humanize the culture of global capital as it lands in our locality. But the struggle is not only ideological. Social policy has real economic and social consequences for the poor and marginalized, and for the rich and middle class. "The consequences are not just symbolic. They shape people's lives and their place in the material world" (Carnoy, 1997, 16). For Freire, our true vocation never entailed that we should live as agents of capital or "detachable appendages of other people's dreams and desires" (McLaren, 1997b, 153). Rather, he embraced and cherished the hope and possibility that we could exist as full human beings, with the freedom to live passionately with an "increasing solidarity between the mind and hands" (Freire, 1997b, 33).

Living a pedagogy of love in our classroom and our communities defies the prescriptive formulas and models of the past, calling for the "reinvention" of our radical vision not only of schooling but of American society—a vision of a society that is unquestionably shaped by a democratic commitment to human rights, social justice, and a radical redistribution of wealth and power. It is a revolutionary vision of society that calls for the eradication of all forms of human suffering and oppression; and inspired by radical hope, openly challenges and rejects the cruel fatalism of poverty arguments among the elite that echo the familiar biblical adage "The poor will always be amongst us." Instead, it courageously declares that the poor are necessary and inevitable in the context of economic domination and human exploitation. Paulo Freire argued forcefully that poverty, racism, sexism, heterosexism, and other forms of discrimination are not natural traits of our humanity. Instead, these conditions exist as "naturalized" aberrations, invented within history by human beings. And because this is so, oppression in all its faces can be "reinvented" out of existence (1997, 308).

Most important, Freire was convinced that schools are significant sites of struggle and that teachers, who embrace an ethical responsibility as citizens and subjects of history, are in an ideal position to collectively fight for the reinvention of the world.

> Within an understanding of history as possibility, tomorrow is problematic. In order for it to come, it is necessary that we build it through transforming today. Different tomorrows are possible…. It is necessary to reinvent the future. Education is indispensable for this reinvention. By accepting ourselves as active subjects and objects of history, we become beings who make division. It makes us ethical beings (1997b, 55).

Although the task before us may often seem insurmountable, we are fortunate to find in Paulo Freire's life and work precious words that breathe life into our revolutionary visions of teaching and learning—a revolutionary vision that is uncompromisingly grounded in an *armed love*. He firmly held, as did Che Guevara before him, that it is this revolutionary love which fuels our political commitment to liberation and ultimately must embody our work in schools and society. For through this love, we not only prevent "nihilism and despair from imposing their own life-denying inevitability times of social strife and cultural turmoil (McLaren, 2000, 171), we incarnate the history we are now making together with the passion, beauty and joy of liberation.

REFERENCES

Apple, M. (1995). *Education and Power.* London: Routledge.

Aronowitz, S. (1992). *The Politics of Identity: Class, Culture, and Social Movements.* New York: Routledge.

Carnoy, M. (1997). "Foreword." In P. Freire, *Pedagogy of the Heart.* New York: Continuum.

Cavanaugh, J. (1996). "Global Economic Apartheid." Speech aired and distributed by Alternative Radio, Boulder, Colorado.

Cisneros, H. (1993). *Interwoven Destinies: Cities and the Nation.* New York: Norton.

Clairmont, F.F. (1995). *The Rise and Fall of Economic Liberalism.* Mapusa, India: The Other India Press/Third World Network.

Colins, Chuck, et al., eds. 1999. *Shifting Fortunes: The Perils of the Growing American Wealth Gap.* United for a Fair Economy.

Darder, A. (1995a). "Bicultural Identity and the Development of Voice." In J. Frederickson and A. Ada (eds.), *Reclaiming Our Voices: Bilingual Education, Critical Pedagogy, and Praxis.* Ontario: C.A.B.E.

Darder, A. (1995b). *Culture and Difference.* Westport, CT: Bergin and Garvey.

Darder, A., and P. Torres (forthcoming). *21st Century Racism.* New York: New York University Press.

Darder, A., and R. Torres (1999). "Shattering the Race Lens: Toward a Critical Theory of Racism." In M. Kenyatta and R. Tai (eds.), *Critical Ethnicity: Countering the Waves of Identity Politics.* New York: Rowman and Littlefield.

Freire, P. (1998a). *Pedagogy of Freedom.* Lanham, MD: Rowman and Littlefield.

Freire, P. (1998b). *Teachers as Cultural Workers: Letters to Those Who Dare to Teach.* Boulder, CO: Westview Press.

Freire, P. (1997a). "A Response." In Paulo Freire with J. Fraser et al. (eds.), *Mentoring the Mentor: A Critical Dialogue with Paulo Freire.* New York: Peter Lang, 303–29.

Freire, P. (1994). *Pedagogy of the Heart.* New York: Continuum.

Freire, P. (1997b). *Pedagogy of the Heart.* New York: Continuum.

Freire, P. (1993). *Pedagogy of the City.* New York: Continuum.

Freire, P. (1970). *Pedagogy of the Oppressed.* New York: Seabury.

Golding, P. (1998). "Global Village or Cultural Pillage." In R.W. McChesney, E.M. Wood, and J.B. Foster (eds.), *Capitalism and the Information Age.* New York: Monthly Review Press.

Gorostiaga, X. (1993). "Is the Answer in the South?" Report presented at the United Nations International Seminar on First World Ethic and Third World Economics, Sigtunn, Sweden.

Greider, W. (1997). *One World Ready or Not: The Manic Logic of Global Capitalism.* New York: Simon and Schuster.

Justice Policy Institute. 2000. *The Punishing Decade: Prison and Jail Estimates at the Millennium.* *Report.* Washington, D.C.: Justice Policy Institute.

Macedo, D. (1994). *Literacies of Power: What Americans Are Not Allowed to Know.* Boulder, CO: Westview Press.

Macedo, D. (1993). "Literacy for Stupidification: The Pedagogy of Big Lies," *Harvard Educational Review* 63, no. 2 (summer): 183–206.

Macedo, D., and A. Araujo Freire (1998). "Foreword." In P. Freire, *Teachers as Cultural Workers.* Boulder, CO: Westview Press.

McChesney, R. (1998). "The Political Economy of Global Communication." In R.W. McChesney, E.M. Wood, and J.B. Foster (eds.), *Capitalism and the Information Age.* New York: Monthly Review Press.

McLaren, P. (2000). *Che Guevara, Paulo Freire, and the Pedagogy of Revolution.* Lanham, MD: Rowman and Littlefield.

McLaren, P. (1997). *Revolutionary Multiculturalism: Pedagogies of Dissent for the New Millennium.* Boulder, CO: Westview Press.

Miles, Robert. 1993. *Racism after "Race Relations."* London: Routledge.

Molner, A. (1996). *Giving Kids the Business.* Boulder, CO: Westview Press.

Naiman, J. (1996). "Left Feminism and the Return to Class," *Monthly Review* 48, no. 2 (June) 12–28.

National Council on Crime and Delinquency. 2000. "Minority Youth and the Criminal Justice System." Report. N.C.C.D. Youth Law Center.

San Miguel, G. and R. Valencia. 1998. "From the Treaty of Guadalupe Hidalgo to Hopwood: The Education, Plight, and Struggle of Mexican Americans in the Southwest. *Harvard Educational Review* 68, no. 3 (Fall): 353–412.

Shor, I., and P. Freire (1987). *A Pedagogy for Liberation.* Westport, CT: Bergin and Garvey.

Vigil, J.D. (1997). "Learning from Gangs: The Mexican American Experience," *ERIC Digest,* no. RC020943.

Wilson, W.J. (1997). *When Work Disappears: The World of the New Urban Poor.* New York: Vintage.

Wood, E.M. (1998). "Modernity, Postmodernity, or Capitalism?" In R.W. McChesney, E.M. Wood, and J.B. Foster (eds.), *Capitalism and the Information Age.* New York: Monthly Review Press.

Wood, E.M. (1996). *Democracy against Capitalism.* Cambridge: Cambridge University Press.

NOTES

1. See also the debate that has transpired in issues of *The Monthly Review* over the last several years.

2. For more information regarding the issue of testing in public schools, contact the National Center for Fair and Open Testing in Cambridge, Massachusetts, at www.fairtest.org@aol.com or (617) 864–4810.

3. For an incisive and revealing critique of Disney's impact as popular culture, see the writings of Henry Giroux, in particular *The Mouse That Roared: Disney and the End of Innocence* (Lanham, MD: Rowman and Littlefield), 1999. Also excellent is the Media Education Foundations' video *Mickey Mouse Monopoly: Disney, Childhood, and Corporate Power* (Chyng Sun 2001), which provides a critical look at the world Disney films create in terms of race, gender, and class.

CHAPTER 8

Schooling and the Culture of Dominion

Unmasking the Ideology of Standardized Testing

Since its inception in the United States, the public school system has been seen as a method of disciplining children in the interest of producing a properly subordinate adult population. Sometimes conscious and explicit, and at other times a natural emanation from the conditions of dominance and subordinacy prevalent in the economic sphere, the theme of social control pervades educational thought and policy.

—BOWLES & GINTIS (1976)

It became considerably more clear to me that the notion of hegemony is not free floating. It is in fact tied to the state in the first place. As part of the state, education, then, must be seen as an important element...

—MICHAEL APPLE (1995)

Most Americans are probably unaware of how Washington exercises its global hegemony, since so much of this activity takes place...under comforting rubrics. Many may, as a start, find it hard to believe that our place in the world even adds up to an empire. But only when we come to see our country as both profiting from and trapped within the structures of an empire of its own making will it be possible for us to explain many elements of the world that otherwise perplex us.

—CHALMERS JOHNSON (2000)

Public education in the United States has consistently presented itself in the last century as a liberal democratizing force for the world that operates in the name of justice, freedom and excellence. However, closer examination of schooling practices reveals a culture of dominion at work—a "structure of an empire" that systematically reproduces, reinforces and sustains the hegemonic forces of social control and regulation linked to class oppression, gender inequalities and the racialization of populations. Hence it should not be surprising to discover that popular myths related to meritocracy, the rights and privilege of the elite, and the need for state consensus, have all served well to conserve an ideology that readily supports the current craze over high stakes testing in public schools today.

This rapidly growing phenomenon can be understood in connection to major changes in the socioeconomic landscape of U.S. society—changes that potentially could ignite greater class conflict and social unrest than modern history has ever known. And this condition continues to worsen for the growing numbers of working class people, given recent events associated with the global political economy that have resulted in thousands of workers being laid-off with fewer options for employment. This theme was echoed in a speech given this year at the Asia-Europe-U.S. Progressive Scholar's Forum: Globalization and Innovation of Politics in Japan by Jeff Faux (2002) of the Economic Policy Institute (EPI) in Washington D.C. In his comments, he confirmed that inequality has become worse. "In the short term, we can expect the U.S. unemployment rate...to rise.... In the long term, the U.S. economy is clearly headed for a financial crisis" (4, 8) with an account deficit of over $400 billion. Moreover, preliminary findings from "The State of Working America" (Mishel, 2002) predict that unless the economy reverses course soon, working families can look forward to high and rising unemployment that will generate wage stagnation, higher poverty rates, and rising inequality. The response of workers to the impact of this economic decline on their lives is well illustrated in a recent front page story in *The Christian Science Monitor* entitled "Labor More Militant as Economy Teeters," which reports that "the nation's economic slowdown is threatening millions of ordinary workers' paychecks and jobs" (Belsie, 2002).

Alex Molner (1996) in *Giving Kids the Business* points out that simultaneously with a depressed economy and worsening condition for workers, we find "the rhetoric about the catastrophic failure of American public schools [has] become even more feverish." Business leaders clamor for free-market solutions to educational problems, alleging that these solutions can improve education at no additional cost. What lies hidden is that these reforms "offer a public-spirited justification for introducing education to the profit motive and giving educators a healthy dose of the 'real world' in the form of competition. Most important, they keep the focus on schools and off the failure of business to promote the well-being of most of the country's citizens" (10).

In response to the pressure of business, the enterprise of education has become more and more fixated on making claims of scientific authority to carry out its instrumentalized policies in response to the academic problems faced by students from the working class and communities of color. As such, it is interesting to note the historical parallels that exist between contemporary "accountability experts" in education and the "cost-efficiency consultants" of the early part of the 20th century. Conditions that parallel these two historical eras include increasing immigration, burgeoning student enrollments in urban centers, economic decline, and overt military action overseas. Moreover, the same rhetoric of corruption and declining efficiency of public schools, so prevalent among corporate elites today, was utilized to legitimate the move by big business leaders to take control of public education in the early 1900s. At that time, elite businessmen ran for school boards and solicited the advice of efficiency experts like Frederick Taylor, in their misguided effort to make schools function like well-oiled factory machines.

The Politics of Accountability

In today's world, corporate leaders again hold the enterprise of education hostage, in exchange for support of tax hikes and budget increases. The tactics of these businessmen are closely aligned to the idea that schools should now function with the efficiency of a for-profit-business, with a chief-executive-officer type holding the reins of the district and the language and practices of schooling translated into the technical realm of accountability. Accordingly, they insist that measurable, scientifically-based objectives should be the primary impetus for making decisions, designing curricula, and articulating the pedagogical imperatives of the classroom.

Hence, business leaders advocate fervently for an increase in standardized testing. They argue that emphasis on testing ensures that 1) schools and teachers are accountable to communities, and students are accountable for their lessons,

2) quality of education is increasing as scores increase, 3) economic and academic opportunities are expanding for students that attain higher scores, and 4) schools are accountable to a patriotic curriculum. Using standardized tests as a hammer, many of these leaders tell students to be accountable for their classwork and homework, parents to be accountable for their children's performance and teachers to be accountable for their students' performance. In doing so, they effectively marginalize discussion of the real problems in education (Caputo-Pearl, 2001, 4).

In the process, the singular indicator of tests scores has achieved an overarching prominence, seriously limiting educational debates to that of numbers and categories of students to be tested. Consequently, the majority of questions welcomed and legitimated within this narrow discourse of quality and accountability uphold an uncritical adherence to standardized testing as the most effective and legitimate means for assessing academic achievement. Rather than entertaining questions regarding student abilities and overall performance, the current questions that dominate educational debates all loop back to the issue of testing and the improvement of test scores. Thus, it is not unusual for educators to primarily ponder questions such as: How soon can recent immigrant students be tested? What subjects and grade levels should be tested? What scores should be used to determine grade promotion or graduation? What degree of movement in the improvement of scores should be required to grant principal bonuses? What scores should determine teacher merit pay?

Within the current discourse of accountability, rarely is there any serious or substantive mention of academic success outside test score indicators. In this closed system of accountability, dialogue related to the very conditions under which schooling functions, its unexamined assumptions, and its effect on students is negated, as such questions are deemed irrelevant or scientifically irrational. Hence, any issue not captured by the measurement of test scores is considered simply anecdotal or, at worse, ideological prattle, justifying its dismissal as inconsequential to public policy and educational debates. And no where is this change more evident than in California, where the reform movement in support of testing and the standardization of knowledge has openly and unabashedly turned the education of working class and poor students of color into "drill and kill" exercises of teaching-to-the-test and highly scripted literacy instruction such as Open Court which is being widely used by many districts. The exceedingly prescriptive nature of these practices leaves little doubt that state testing and test-driven curricula are, directly or indirectly, linked to an academically limiting system of social control— a system that successfully sustains the reproduction of class formation within *both* public schools and the larger society.

Moreover, to ensure compliance, school funding, principal tenure and teacher incentive pay are being determined more and more by performance contracts linked to performance as measured on a single indicator—the aggregation of student standardized test scores. Hence, standardized testing is increasingly being used as the central mechanism for decisions about student learning, teacher and administrative practice, and overall school quality (Heubert & Hauser, 1999). This is exemplified by a supplementary section published in the *Rocky Mountain News* entitled *CSAP 2002: A Guide to Results of the Students Assessment Tests*. The twenty-four page supplement (of which eighteen pages consists of test scores for Colorado schools) reported "Colorado's largest-ever release of state scores…" (2E). Story headlines reveal the problems with standardized testing: "Test Scores Hit the Wall" (2E) "Schools Fare Better, Worse in DPS" (3E). "Affluent Districts Score at Top. Spotty performance to cost Jeffco $4.5 million. Tax dollars are tied to results in States largest school districts" (4E).

The consequence here is that the institutionalized locus of control over curriculum, teaching and assessment, all based upon a tightly regimented set of prescriptions, not only locates authority of educational decisions at the state level but also, as mentioned earlier, but locates the power over those decisions in the domain of business leaders. The insidious nature of this hegemonic mechanism of control is glaringly evident in a national commission report issued in the early 1990s by the Ford Foundation which estimated that nearly 130 million standardized tests were being administered to elementary and secondary students, at an estimated cost of $500 million a year (Toch,1991). This has resulted in the preponderance of testing within public schools, and the reform movement so invested in it, "that increasingly it is in terms of standardized test scores alone that the nation judges its schools and educators judge themselves" (206) .

Yet, despite its key role in the accountability reform movement, studies repeatedly show that standardized tests are flawed when used as a single measure of progress, because they fail to measure students' ability to judge, analyze, infer, interpret, or reason—namely, engage in critical thought. Standardized tests have been found even less useful in measuring student's more advanced academic knowledge. One reason for their failure is associated with the purpose behind norm-referenced tests, such as the Stanford 9 that has been widely administered in California Public Schools. These tests are designed to rank students against one another, rather than to measure students' knowledge of the material. Many of the questions "are intentionally developed so that a relatively high percentage of students will be tricked by them. This is an important method of differentiating one student from another in the rankings. Further because test scores are supposed to fall into a bell curve pattern in comparing one to the other, 50 percent of students will always be considered 'below average' or 'below middle ground" (Caputo-Pearl, 2001, 7). Other reasons associated with student failure are directly tied to questions of cultural relevancy and class biases hidden in the conceptual construction and language use of standardized tests.

If these were not enough to raise concerns, widespread testing problems related to the administration and scoring of tests are rampant. In New Mexico, 70 percent of superintendents recently reported a variety of testing errors. In Georgia, Harcourt Educational Measurement could not deliver accurate results from last spring's Stanford 9 tests in a timely fashion. In Nevada, officials reported that 736 sophomores and juniors had mistakenly been told they had failed the math portion of a test, although they had actually passed. And even states such as North Carolina "considered models of accountability are struggling to come up with reliable tests" (Jonsson, 2002, 11).

Even more disconcerting here is the manner in which the politics of standardized testing functions to silence and prevent greater public engagement within communities. When the only language of currency for the construction of educational policy is linked to accountability, this language impedes and jeopardizes the capacity for critical civic interaction among parents, communities and educators, in order to raise significant and more complex questions related to student academic success. Excluded are critiques based on democratic values, children's development, cultural differences, class privilege, and other critical questions that could potentially unveil the social and economic consequences tied to standardized testing. In the current political climate, the only conversations that are deemed meaningful are those that are linked directly to raising test scores.

In, *Contradictions of School Reform: Educational Costs of Standardized Testing*, Linda McNeil (2000) sheds light on the manner in which this insidious system of accountability is operationalized. First, the tenure for principals is replaced by 'performance contracts.' Their contract renewal, assignment, and annual bonuses are predicated on test scores results in their school—this reinforces the role of the principal as compliance officer and justifies the principal's intervention and control over the labor of teachers. Second, newspaper ratings and state rankings of schools disaggregate by race and ethnicity. Scores of all must 'improve.' "This disaggragating of scores gives the appearance that the system is sensitive to diversity and committed to improving minority education. This reporting, however, actually exacerbates...a focus on test to the exclusion of many other forms of education. Increasingly common is the substitution of commercial test-prep materials in place of traditional curricula and instructional activities for these students" (233). As a consequence, teachers are held captive to the accountability protocols set forth by the state, with virtually leave little room to generate or execute more effective criteria for assessing the academic progress of their students.

De-skilling Teachers

The requirements for standardized tests for students also sets into motion a series of state mandated curricula, all aimed at minimum skills that result from long-term pedagogical practices of social control and regulation within schools. Increasingly the curricula and tests are divorced from any serious consideration of critical forms of pedagogies or learning theories. More often than not, the development of standardized curriculum, assessment instruments, and high-stakes testing fails to consider the wealth of research and literature on teaching and learning to inform its execution. There is no question that an educational system that willingly ignores curriculum theory and child development research—not to mention the social, political and economic realities of students' lives—has the veiled organizational objective to serve as a regulatory mechanism to control teacher work and student outcomes.

Testing and teaching-to-the test serve as mechanisms to instill a teacher-proof curriculum which in many cases may include narrowly prescribed checklists for assessing teaching and student minimum skills. Undoubtedly, such regimentation makes schooling exceedingly simple for less skilled teachers. Many of these teachers are happy to teach routine lessons according to a standard sequence and format, preferring to function as deskilled laborers who do not have to do much thinking or preparation with respect to their practice. In contrast, a teacher-proof instructional approach makes it extremely uncomfortable and disturbing for those teachers who know their subjects well, who teach in ways that critically engage their students, and who want teaching to be linked to the realities of students' lives. Moreover, this "controlling, top-down" push for higher standards may actually produce a lower quality of education, precisely because the tactics constrict the means by which teachers most successfully inspire students' engagement in learning, and commitment to achieve" (Ryan and La Guardia, 1999, 46).

The standardization of the curriculum at the State level echoes the distrust of teachers by the public and legislators—a fabricated distrust that is widely used to rally sentiment and support for high-stakes testing. Consequently, standardized testing results are used to support principal efforts to hold greater power over teachers, since tests scores are deemed as a legitimate and objective way to measure teacher performance. The primary goal of the standardized curriculum then is to provide all teachers with the exact course content to which they must adhere.

Hence, any variation in the quality of student performance, according to the current logic of accountability, can be tied directly to the quality of teaching. In this way, low student scores can be justified to fire teachers without further discussion and high student scores can be used to grant merit pay to teachers for their compliance

This is an example of how a system of rewards and punishment works in schools to preserve the status quo, through a practice of using what people need or want (i.e., salary increase) as an incentive or motivation for compliance, thereby insuring teacher regulation and social control within the classroom. However, it is imperative to recognize that a such a pervasive system of rewards and punishment is not predicated on a law of nature. It reflects a particular ideology or set of assumptions that must be questioned within education, particularly in terms of dismantling social agency and reinforcing dependency on school officials. Kohn (1993), a staunch critic of the rewards and punishment system endemic to public school practices, views this system of social control and regulation as rooted in the legacy of behaviorism and scientism.

> We are a nation that prefers acting to thinking, and practice to theory, we are suspicious of intellectuals, worshipful of technology and fixated on the bottom line. We define ourselves by numbers—take home pay, percentiles (how much does your baby weigh), cholesterol counts, and standardized testing (how much does your child know. By contrast we are uneasy with intangibles and unscientific abstractions such as a sense of well-being or an intrinsic motivation to learn (9–10).

In the urgency to test students, seldom are the disempowering effects and negative impact of the testing situation itself and the removal of students from the classroom several times during the year for testing discussed. At issue here is the manner in which such practices disrupt the developmental momentum of student learning, provoke enormous unnecessary stress and tension in students, and interfere with the quality of interaction in the classroom. In many ways, the politics of testing, along with the prescribed curriculum it inspires ultimately functions to erode teacher autonomy and creativity, as well as their authority within their classrooms. In the process, teachers are socialized to become highly dependent on prepackaged materials and the authority of state sanctioned educational experts to provide the next curricular innovation.

McNeil (2000) argues that the bottom line is that the state mechanism for assessing teacher quality like proficiency testing must be cheap, quick, generalizable across all subjects and school settings and capable of being used by school-level administrators independent of their knowledge of the subjects being taught. In many case what is generated is a factory-like checklist reminiscent of the social efficiency era, reducing teaching to specific observable and thus, measurable behaviors; many having little or nothing to do with the classroom content being taught, nor the particular pedagogical needs of students. Typically, behaviors found on teacher assessment checklists can include such items as eye contact with students, having the daily objective written on the board, having a catchy opening phrase and definite closure to the lesson, and the number of times teachers vary their verbal responses to students.

A major consequence of standardized testing and teaching-to-the-test is the manner in which the emphasis of learning shifts away from intellectual activity toward the dispensing of packaged fragments of information. Meanwhile, students and teachers as subjects of classroom discourse, who bring their personal stories and life experiences to bear on their teaching and learning, are systematically silenced by the need for the class to "cover" a generic curriculum at a prescribed pace established by the state. In making the case against standardized testing, Kohn (2000) argues that

> High-stakes testing has radically altered the kind of instruction that is offered in American schools, to the point that "teaching to the test" has become a prominent part of the nation's educational landscape. Teachers often feel obliged to set aside other subjects for days, weeks, or (particularly in schools serving low-income students) even months at a time in order to devote to boosting students' test scores. Indeed, both the content and the format of instruction are affected; the test essentially *becomes* the curriculum (29).

It is significant to note that through the hegemonic process of standardized testing, teachers, as workers, have become the new scapegoats of the system. As a result of the political struggles in education rooted in the civil rights era, it became unfashionable to blame students, their parents or their culture. Teachers, whose status is located at the next lowest rung of the educational hierarchy, became the most likely suspects. State and national teacher tests, constructed upon the very same premise as those administered to their students, are now being used as a primary indicator of teacher labor, rather than the quality of their actual teaching. Such a mechanism of assessment could now more easily be used to support the notion that the problem for student failure is the fault of poor teachers.

So, once again, educational debates have shifted from the quality of teaching and the schooling process to that of "quality control"—a shift that is closely linked with conservative political efforts to dictate the agenda of public education. Inherent in this debate is a justification for taking further control of their labor away from the hands of teachers. In the process, there is no consideration for increasing classroom resources; nor provisions made for instructional materials and on-going teacher development that is linked to enhancing the quality of children's learning or teacher-parent relationships. There is little attention given to engaging communities and interest groups in a plan to rectify persistent inequalities. More clearly, there is little willingness to openly challenge the asymmetrical relations of power that result in the racialized reproduction of class formations, a strategy that must be central to efforts geared toward dismantling the educational injustices prevalent in public schools.

Schooling and the Culture of Dominion

More disturbing is the use of this system of accountability to justify the undemocratic governance of urban public schools. In many ways, one can trace how the old efficiency rhetoric was brushed off and revamped into the new accountability rhetoric and quickly seized and embraced by those mainstream educators and researchers who felt they were losing control of schooling debates to progressive multicultural educators who clamored for greater democratic participation of teachers, students, parents, and communities. The language of scientific accountability with its narrow focus on test scores was seen as a sure way to replace the messiness of "interest group" participation in schools; that is, the participation of those who had historically been excluded from debates, in the first place.

In this way, the politics of testing within public schools has historically played an insidious role in the perpetuation of underachievement among the working class and students of color. Bowles and Gintis (1976) argue that "the educational system legitimates economic inequality by providing an open, objective, and ostensibly meritocratic mechanism for assigning individuals to unequal economic positions (103)." Through the construction of testing instruments as value-free scientific tools, considered to produce objective, measurable and quantifiable data, predefined skills and knowledge have been given priority at the expense of the cultural knowledge and experience of students from economically disenfranchised communities.

As mentioned earlier, the evaluation and assessment of students (as well as teachers) then are predicated on the results of standardized tests, which are used to sort, regulate and control students. Thus, the testing of students more and more drives the curriculum and prescribes both teaching and the role of students in their learning. This prescriptive teaching hardens and intensifies the discrimination already at work in schools, as teaching of the fragmented and narrow information on the test comes to substitute for substantive curriculum in the schools of poor and minority students. This intensified discrimination and widespread pattern of substituting test-prep materials, devoid of substantive content and respect for the ways children learn, are most at work in schools where the majority of economically oppressed children attend. Hence, standardized testing has historically functioned to systematically reproduce, overtly and covertly, the conditions within schools that perpetuate a culture of elitism, privilege and exploitation.

One of the most insidious dimensions tied to the preservation of a culture of dominion within schools is tied to the unexamined philosophical assumptions and values or ideology that undergird and hence, legitimate educational policies and practices associated with standardized testing. Many of the values and assumptions at work in sustaining asymmetrical relations of power within the larger society have been engaged substantially in the work of radical educators, psychologists, sociologists, political scientists, economists and other social critics during the last century. However, given the limitation of this essay, it is impossible to provide more than a brief glance at some of the primary values and assumptions operating within the context of schooling. Nevertheless, it is must be emphasized that the interrelatedness of these assumptions often functions in concert, to successfully veil the ideological contradictions that exist between a rhetoric of democratic ideals and the undemocratic practices at work in U.S. public schools today—assumptions that teachers may seldom connect to their teaching practice but nevertheless underlie what they do within their classrooms (Kohn, 1993).

Another overarching philosophical assumption that undergirds the ideology of public schooling today is the unbridled, but veiled, acceptance of Darwinian conclusions related to the belief in the "survival of the fittest." As a consequence, substantial educational rhetoric functions to justify the existence of economic inequality, sexism, racialized notions of humanity, and good old U.S. self-promotion at the expense of the greater good. Such rhetoric is well-disguised in the false benevolence at work in the discursive justifications for standardized testing, tracking, and the competitive and instrumentalizing curricular practices found within classrooms today.

As such, "common-sense" beliefs about human nature, deeply rooted in racialized and class notions of normalcy, are actively at work in the assessment of student intellectual abilities and their potential for academic success. For example, racialized beliefs about the inferior or superior abilities and potential of particular student populations are often utilized to justify the so-called objective measurement of student knowledge and then to use these measures to justify the unequal distribution of educational resources and opportunities. Such racialized notions are at work in the disturbing 'scientific' assertion that 'race' determines academic performance made by Richard J. Herrnstein and Charles Murray (1994) in their book *The Bell Curve*. "The term 'race' serves to conceal the truth that it is not 'race' that determines academic performance; but rather, that academic performance is determined by an interplay of complex social processes, one of which is premised on the articulation of racism...to affect exclusion in the classroom and beyond"

(Darder & Torres, 1999, 181). The fact that such practices effectively work to perpetuate class interests is well-hidden by an educational rhetoric that glorifies expediency in learning, dichotomizes theory from practice, heralds the conquest of nature, and objectifies time and human experience in the name of scientifically fabricated assessment criteria.

Also at work within the culture of dominion is an overwhelming penchant for unbridled individualism, at the expense of greater collective well-being. Hence, competition among students within the context of knowledge construction is strongly reinforced and well-rewarded. Students learn very quickly to acquiesce to the wiles of competition, if they are to be deemed as material for academic success in the future. In the process, knowledge is reified and objectified in such a way that students are socialized to accept the belief that somehow knowledge actually exists objectively disconnected from the subjective realm of human experience. This is in contrast to a view of knowledge that connects its construction and evolution to the realities of the larger social milieu. The consequence is that students become convinced, particularly as they advance in the educational hierarchy of achievement, that their goal is to independently construct some "original" notion, thought, idea, theory, etc. in order to gain prominence within their chosen field. What seldom is acknowledged here are the organizational regimes of power or the hegemonic forces at work in the legitimation of knowledge and the institutional assignment of both "originality" and worthiness. It is most disturbing to note that these very qualities which are considered so essential in the education of elite students and then later, so crucial to the dictums of graduate school success, are virtually absent and almost entirely negated within the context of standardized testing within public schools.

Further, the individualistic and economist language so prevalent in the educational rhetoric of public school testing is deeply rooted in the ideological tenets of advanced capitalism. Its materialist emphasis on private property is extended to the domain of knowledge, where intellectual ideas become the property of an individual or the state. Hence, the pedagogy of the elite very early teaches students that they are the owners of their intellectual products with rights to sell or buy at their discretion. In contrast, poor and working class students are socialized to accept, accommodate and comply with knowledge deemed "truth," even when that knowledge is diametrically in opposition to their experience and their well-being. The emphasis of academic socialization then for these students is not to be creators of knowledge but consumers of specific knowledge forms as prescribed by the dominant class. No where is this prescription of knowledge for the oppressed more readily visible than in the politics of standardized testing—a prescription that is steeped in the rhetoric of scientism.

Scientism and Meritocracy

The scientific claim of accountability experts is one of the most devious and fallacious elements at work in the testing mania. An overemphasis on "hard" science and "absolute objectivity" gives rise to scientism, rather than any real science. Scientism here refers to the power and authority vested in the mechanization of intellectual work generated by specialists. As a consequence, knowledge is fragmented and instrumentalized by way of reductionist interpretations of student learning. Hence, the very claim of objectivity must be understood as steeped in the cultural assumptions or ideology of the dominant class.

Schools then operate based upon a view of the world or ideology that is clearly governed by an instrumentally technocratic rationality that glorifies a logic and method based on the natural sciences. To comply then with the scientific requirement of measuring knowledge, high stakes tests are constructed under the rubric of objective knowledge. This is knowledge that is treated as an external body of information, produced independently of human beings and independent of time and place. As such it can then be expressed in language that is technical and allegedly neutral. School knowledge then not only becomes countable and measurable, but impersonal. As such, teaching-to-the-test becomes normalized and acceptable, and testing exulted as the only truly effective and "unbiased" mechanism to measure academic success and achievement.

In the process, extensive field-based research on standardized testing that has documented its negative effects on teaching & learning, particularly to the working class and students of color, is categorically ignored. Even worse is the lasting harm that imbedded controls, the legitimization of "accountability" as the language of school policy, and the elimination of the real possibilities for wider public debates on the purpose of schooling for poor, working class, and racialized students, has on concrete educational efforts to democratize schooling practices.

Scientism also supports a carte blanche adherence to the educational practice of meritocracy—a practice that functions as one of the primary hegemonic mechanisms implicated in the inequitable achievement and advancement of students within the educational system. It constitutes a form of systemic control by which the culture of dominion is naturalized and perpetuated. Public schools persistently tout this myth to guarantee that successful participation in the educational system becomes the most visible and legitimate process by which individuals are allocated or rewarded higher status within the society at large. Through a system of merit tied to high stakes testing for example, the process of unequal privilege and entitlement is successfully smoke-screened under the guise of "fair and equal" opportunity for all students.

Through common day practices of meritocracy linked to social promotion (or demotion) and graduation, a twofold justification of the culture of dominion is upheld to justify the undemocratic distribution of wealth in this country and around the world. First, it establishes the merit of those in power as the legitimate criterion for achieved social position. And second, it persists in blaming those who fail for their underachievement (whether the blame is placed on to the teachers, the students or the parents) by implying they do not have the necessary intelligence, motivation, or drive to partake of what is freely being offered them by the educational system. In other words, if students fail it's their own damn fault!

Testing and the Politics of Schooling

Within a context of dominion, schools and educators as agents of the state are viewed as neutral and apolitical, whose sole purpose is to educate students with the necessary knowledge and skills that render them functional in and to society—in other words, to fulfill their place in the process of consumption and capitalist accumulation. Hence, ideas and practices that are in concert with dominant knowledge forms are generally perceived as neutral and acceptable, shrouding the authoritarianism of the status quo. Conversely, knowledge forms that in any substantive way might bring into question the "official" curriculum, methods or pedagogy are deemed "political" and unacceptable. To make things even more perplexing, the function of neutralizing contesting views is generally carried out simultaneously by a variety of social agents including: 1) those who knowingly support the limits and configuration of "official" authority within the fundamental order of public schools for their own personal gains; 2) those who are complicit as a consequence of insufficient knowledge and skills to contest; 3) those who protect their class interest by "playing the game" with a rhetoric of helping the oppressed; and 4) those who consent due to their overwhelming fear of authority.

Unfortunately, there are many educators and advocates from all walks of life, who confidently support the propagation of testing as a legitimate educational strategy within public schools, irrespective of the volumes that have been written linking standardized testing to cultural invasion and economic exploitation. The rallying cry of testing advocates is often tied to the question: "If we take away testing how will we have the objective criteria to demand better schools?" What is disturbing about this argument is that this myopic view fails to link an acceptance and adherence to such educational policies and practices with capitalist interests that perpetuate undemocratic life in this country and around the globe. Even more disturbing is the negative impact that such practices continue to have on students of all ages.

In the process, many well-meaning educators and advocates, who are content with playing the "race card" to rally support for their views, can actually obstruct the possibility for teachers, parents and communities to publicly question and critique those ideas, practices and events that go contrary to community self-determination and the construction of a genuinely democratic political movement in education. Many go so far as to propose that any discourse that puts into question racialized arguments in defense of testing as a good thing for students of color is somehow falling prey to white, bleeding-heart liberal tendencies. Radical efforts then to expose the long-term damage of testing to all oppressed students is rendered suspect, rather than recognizing that a concerted search for a wider range of information from which we can struggle (beyond identity politics) is crucial to dismantling the structures of capitalist domination and inequality at work in schools and society today.

What the history of civil rights struggles in the U.S. should have taught us is that our understanding of racialized practices within schools can never be separated from the reproduction of class relations. As such, practices of high-stakes testing must be understood as systematically implicated in the reproduction of racialized economic inequality and injustice. For it is precisely through the uncontested acceptance of such mechanisms of social control and regulation that students from the dominant class consistently end up at the top of the hierarchy and students from subordinate communities at the bottom—a factor that readily and unjustly fuels common-sense belief in the legitimacy of a hierarchically racialized, gendered and class stratified society.

It is no secret that in the U.S., the most politically powerful are those who retain control over the bulk of society's wealth and resources. This economic and institutional control is clearly perpetuated from generation to generation through the process of schooling. The ruling class, with its bureaucratic system of managerial officials, strives to retain control of schooling through the construction of educational public policies. As such, curriculum and pedagogical practices that support the standardization (and control) of knowledge—knowledge that functions in the interest of capitalist relations—effectively sustain the culture of dominion within schools. Moreover, through control of teacher certification and such schooling practices as curricular policies, literacy instruction, pedagogy and testing requirements tied to educational opportunities, the stratification of populations so necessary to capitalist accumulation is successfully maintained. As a consequence, even working class students and students of color learn to furiously compete for the limited "top" positions in society, rather than work to alter the social, political and economic conditions that defy the future well-being of their communities.

Testing and a Politics of Silence

Schools produce and perpetuate knowledge that serves as a silencing agent, in that it relegates legitimacy to the abstract reality developed by prescribed knowledge, rather than to the actual lived daily experiences that shape the knowledge that students bring to the classroom. Nowhere was this more evident than in the manner in which the majority of public schools responded to the events of September 11th. Here the actual experiences of students predicated upon what they were hearing and feeling about this historical moment were marginalized and suppressed. A politics of silence was the solution for a return to normalcy, with expectations that little to no discussions be held regarding this issue. And if discussions did ensue, these were to echo the language of a most superficial and vulgar patriotism, in concert with the official public discourse of the government.

As a consequence, blind flag-waving nationalism substituted for any real critical dialogue. Teachers were told that the attitude in classrooms was to be "business as usual," as students were being ushered in and out of their beginning-of-the-year standardized testing sessions. Meanwhile, administrative pressures on teachers to keep up with the prescribed curriculum and to prepare students for future testing, worked to silence the possibility for critical inquiry into the initial and subsequent events connected with the "war on terrorism." So while the practice of high stakes testing effectively contributed to an ahistorical and fragmented response to such a significant historical event in the lives of students, book sellers were rushing to develop and insert the official historical reading into traditional social studies textbooks to generate new sales. By the time the events of 9/11 and the "war on terrorism" are officially documented and taught in U.S. classrooms, the lived impact of the events will have been buried and lost for many, with only the prescribed curricula and their sanitized interpretation of the events remaining.

Last, an aspect of the culture of dominion that is seldom discussed within education but very much at work in the politics of silence is a dichotomized view of good and evil so prevalent in conservative and liberal political discourses on schooling and society. The "good" are those who conform and accept to fulfill their rightful place in the process of capitalist accumulation. From this perspective, all problems in schools and society are approached from the standpoint of how the "evil" (or deviance) may be eliminated in students, teachers, or parents. Through linking notions of evil consequences (pregnancy, drug abuse, crime, drop-outs, unemployment, etc.) to academic failure, students who fail are justifiably excluded and rendered disposable. In the testing madness, this notion has been interjected into the definition of good schools, good students, good teachers, good parents, where the level of "goodness" is determined by the measurable outcomes of standardized testing. The "good" are then all considered worthy of rewards by the state for their achievement.

This veiled moralism that unwittingly permeates educational discourse and the acceptance of high stakes testing actually socializes populations to accept uncritically the inferiority of the other and the need for corrective action, in order to assure the participation of the majority within the labor market and as rightful citizens of this nation. Hence, many unexamined assumptions that give rise to an ideology enmeshed in the nobility of "good vs. evil" shape many of the uncritical, common sense perceptions of whole populations as "evil" and in need of punishment and/or corrective action—whether the action be loss of opportunity, incarceration, or military intervention. No where is this more evident than in the demonizing "good vs evil" arguments being disseminated at this historical moment to justify the expansion of U.S. military intervention in Afghanistan and the Middle East. So whether it be the contrived political wars waged in public schools or the fabricated military wars waged overseas, it is economically dispossessed people who are most destructively affected by the practices of those who seek to retain dominion over their lives.

Hence, educators must come to understand the manner in which the hidden ideology of dominion gives rise to the politics of standardized testing and its very real and present material consequences—consequences that we must work to disrupt, if we are ever to construct any form of lasting democratic educational practice within public schools—a feat which at the moment seems much easier to define than to accomplish, given the daunting limitations we face as radical educators in the world today.

REFERENCES

Apple, A. (1995). *Education and Power,* 2nd ed. New York and London: Routledge.

Belsie, L. (2002). "Labor More Militant as Economy Teeters," *Christian Science Monitor,* August 22.

Bowles, S., and H. Gintis (1976). *Schooling in Capitalist America.* New York: Basic Books.

Caputo-Pearl, A. (2001). "Challenging High-Stakes Standardized Testing: Working to Build an Anti-Racist Progressive Social Movement in Public Education." Working Paper for Coalition for Educational Justice, Los Angeles.

Darder, A., and T. Torres (1999). "Shattering the Race Lens: Toward a Critical Theory of Racism." In R. Tai and M. Kenyatta (eds.), *Critical Ethnicity.* Lanham, MD: Rowman and Littlefield.

Faux, J. (2002). "Rethinking the Global Political Economy." Speech given at the Asia-Europe-U.S. Progressive Scholar's Forum: Globalization and Innovation of Politics, Japan, April 11–13.

Herrnstein, R., and C. Murray. *The Bell Curve: Intelligence and Class Structure in American Life.* New York: Free Press, 1994.

Heubert, J., and R. Hauser (1999). "High Stakes: Testing for Tracking, Promotion, and Graduation." Committee on Appropriate Test Use, Board on Testing and Assessment, Commission on Behavioral and Social Sciences and Education, and National Research Council, Washington, D.C.: National Academy Press.

Johnson, C. (2000). *Blowback: The Costs and Consequences of American Empire.* New York: Owl Books.

Jonsson, P. (2002). "When the Tests Fail," *Christian Science Monitor,* August 20.

Kohn, A. (2000). *The Case against Standardized Testing: Raising Score, Ruining Schools.* Portsmouth, NH: Heinemann .

Kohn, A. (1993). *Punished by Rewards.* Boston: Houghton Mifflin Company.

McNeil, L. (2000). *Contradictions of School Reform: Educational Costs of Standardized Testing.* New York: Routledge.

Mishel, L., et al. (2002). *"The State of Working America, 2002/2003" for the Economic Policy Institute.* Armonk, NY: M.E. Sharpe.

Molner, A. (1996). *Giving Kids the Business: The Commercialization of American Schools.* Boulder, CO: Westview.

Rocky Mountain News (2002). "CSAP 2000: A Guide to Results of the Student Assessment Tests." Denver, CO, August 1.

Ryan, R., and J. La Guardia (1999). "Achievement Motivation within a Pressured Society: Intrinsic and Extrinsic Motivations to Learn and the Politics of School Reform," *Advances in Motivation and Achievement,* vol. 11. Stamford, CT: JAI Press.

Toch, T. (1991). *In the Name of Excellence.* New York: Oxford University Press.

CHAPTER 9

Teaching as an Act of Love

Reflections on Paulo Freire and His
Contributions to Our Lives and Our Work

> As individuals or as peoples, by fighting for the restoration of
> [our] humanity [we] will be attempting the restoration of true
> generosity. And this fight, because of the purpose given it, will
> actually constitute an act of love. (p. 29)
> —PAULO FREIRE, *PEDAGOGY OF THE OPPRESSED* (1970)

For days, I have reflected on the writings of Paulo Freire; and with every turn of
ideas, I've been brought back to the notion of love and its manifestation in our
work and our lives. Here, let me say quickly that I am neither speaking of a liberal, romanticized, or merely feel-good notion of love that so often is mistakenly
attributed to this term nor the long-suffering and self-effacing variety associated
with traditional religious formation. Nothing could be further from the truth. If
there was anything that Freire consistently sought to defend, it was the freshness,
spontaneity, and presence embodied in what he called an "armed love—the fighting love of those convinced of the right and the duty to fight, to denounce, and to
announce" (Freire, 1998, p. 42). A love that could be lively, forceful, and inspiring,
while at the same time, critical, challenging, and insistent. As such, Freire's brand

of love stood in direct opposition to the insipid "generosity" of teachers or administrators who would blindly adhere to a system of schooling that fundamentally transgresses every principle of cultural and economic democracy.

Rather, I want to speak to the experience of love as I came to understand it through my work and friendship with Freire. I want to write about a political and radicalized form of love that is never about absolute consensus, or unconditional acceptance, or unceasing words of sweetness, or endless streams of hugs and kisses. Instead, it is a love that I experienced as unconstricted, rooted in a committed willingness to struggle persistently with purpose in our life and to intimately connect that purpose with what he called our "true vocation"—to be human.

A Commitment to Our Humanity

A humanizing education is the path through which men and women can become conscious about their presence in the world. The way they act and think when they develop all of their capacities, taking into consideration their needs, but also the needs and aspirations of others.

—FREIRE & BETTO, 1985, PP. 14–15

For Freire, a liberatory education could never be conceived without a profound commitment to our humanity. Once again, I must point out that his notion of humanity was not merely some simplistic or psychologized notion of "having positive self-esteem," but rather a deeply reflective interpretation of the dialectical relationship between our cultural existence as individuals and our political and economic existence as social beings. From Freire's perspective, if we were to solve the educational difficulties of students from oppressed communities, then educators had to look beyond the personal. We had to look for answers within the historical realm of economic, social, and political forms, so that we might better understand those forces that give rise to our humanity as it currently exists. In so many ways, his work pointed to how economic inequality and social injustice dehumanize us, distorting our capacity to love ourselves, each other, and the world. In the tradition of Antonio Gramsci before him, Freire exposed how even well-meaning teachers, through their lack of critical moral leadership, actually participate in disabling the heart, minds, and bodies of their students—an act that disconnects these students from the personal and social motivation required to transform their world and themselves.

There is no question that Freire's greatest contribution to the world was his capacity to be a loving human being. His regard for children, his concern for teachers, his work among the poor, his willingness to share openly his moments of grief, disappointment, frustration, and new love, all stand out in my mind as examples of his courage and unrelenting pursuit of a coherent and honest life. I recall our meeting in 1987, six months after the death of his first wife, Elza. Freire was in deep grief. During one of his presentations, he literally had to stop so that he could weep the tears that he had been trying to hold back all morning. For a moment, all of us present were enveloped by his grief and probably experienced one of the greatest pedagogical lessons of our life. I don't believe anyone left the conference hall that day as they had arrived. Through the courageous vulnerability of his humanity—with all its complexities and contradictions—Freire illuminated our understanding of not only what it means to be a critical educator, but what it means to live a critical life.

In the following year, I experienced another aspect of Freire's living praxis. To everyone's surprise, Freire remarried a few months later. Many were stunned by the news, and it was interesting to listen to and observe the responses of his followers in the States. Some of the same radical educators who had embraced him in his grief now questioned his personal decision to remarry so quickly after the death of Elza. Much to my surprise, the news of his marriage and his public gestures of affection and celebration of his new wife, Nita, were met with a strange sort of suspicion and fear. Despite these reverberations, Freire spoke freely of his new love and the sensations that now stirred in him. He shared his struggle with loneliness and grief and challenged us to live and love in the present—as much personally as politically.

Fear and Revolutionary Dreams

> The more you recognize your fear as a consequence of your attempt to practice your dream, the more you learn how to put into practice your dream! I never had interviews with the great revolutionaries of this century about their fears! But all of them felt fear, to the extent that all of them were very faithful to their dreams.
>
> —SHOR & FREIRE, 1987, P. 57

Challenging the conditioned fears with which our dreams of freedom are controlled and the "false consciousness" that diminishes our social agency are common themes in Freire's work. In *Pedagogy of the Oppressed* (1970), he wrote of the fear of freedom that afflicts us, a fear predicated on prescriptive relationships between those who rule and those who are expected to follow. As critical educators, he urged us to question carefully our ideological beliefs and pedagogical intentions and to take note of our own adherence to the status quo. He wanted us to recognize that every prescribed behavior represents the imposition of one human being upon another—an imposition that moves our consciousness away from what we experience in the flesh to an abstracted reality and false understanding of ourselves and our world. If we were to embrace a pedagogy of liberation, we had to prepare ourselves to replace this conditioned fear of freedom with sufficient autonomy and responsibility to struggle for an educational praxis and a way of life that could support democratic forms of economic and cultural existence.

Freire often addressed the notion of fear in his speeches and in his writings. In his eyes, fear and revolutionary dreams were unquestionably linked. The more that we were willing to struggle for an emancipatory dream, the more apt we were to know intimately the experience of fear, how to control and educate our fear, and finally, how to transform that fear into courage. Moreover, we could come to recognize our fear as a signal that we are engaged in critical opposition to the status quo and in transformative work toward the manifestation of our revolutionary dreams.

In many ways, Freire attempted to show us through his own life that facing our fears and contending with our suffering are inevitable and necessary human dimensions of our quest to make and remake history, of our quest to make a new world from our dreams. Often, he likened our movement toward greater humanity as a form of childbirth, and a painful one. This labor of love constitutes a critical process in our struggle to break the oppressor-oppressed contradiction and the conflicting beliefs that incarcerate our humanity. Freire's description of this duality is both forthright and sobering.

> The oppressed suffer from the duality which has established itself in their innermost being. They discover that without freedom they cannot exist authentically. Yet, although they desire authentic existence, they fear it. They are at one and the same time themselves and the oppressor whose consciousness they have internalized. The conflict lies in the choice between wholly themselves or being divided; between ejecting the oppressor within or not ejecting him; between human solidarity or alienation; between following prescriptions or having choices; between being spectators or actors, between acting or having the illusion of acting through the action of the oppressors; between speaking out or being silent, castrated in their power to create and re-create, in their power to transform the world. (Freire, 1970, p. 33)

Freire firmly believed that if we were to embrace a pedagogy of freedom, we had to break out of this duality. We had to come to see how the domesticating power of the dominant ideology causes teachers to become ambiguous and indecisive, even in the face of blatant injustice. Critical educators had to struggle together against a variety of punitive and threatening methods used by many administrators to instill a fear of freedom. Because if this domesticating role were not rejected, even progressive teachers could fall prey to fatalism—a condition that negates passion and destroys the capacity to dream—making them each day more politically vulnerable and less able to face the challenges before them.

Fatalism is a notion that Freire, until the end, refused to accept. At every turn, he emphatically rejected the idea that nothing could be done about the educational consequences of economic inequalities and social injustice. If the economic and political power of the ruling class denied subordinate populations the space to survive, it was not because "it should be that way" (Freire, 1997, p. 41). Instead, the asymmetrical relations of power that perpetuate fatalism among those with little power had to be challenged. This required teachers to problematize the conditions of schooling with their colleagues, students, and parents, and through a critical praxis of reflection, dialogue, and action, become capable of announcing justice. But such an announcement required a total denouncement of fatalism, which would unleash our power to push against the limits, create new spaces, and begin redefining our vision of education and society.

Capitalism as the Root of Domination

> Brutalizing the work force by subjecting them to routine procedures is part of the nature of the capitalist mode of production. And what is taking place in the reproduction of knowledge in the schools is in large part a reproduction of that mechanism.
> —FREIRE & FAUNDEZ, 1989, P. 42

The question of power is ever present in Freire's work, as is his intimacy with the struggle for democracy. At this juncture, it is vitally important that we turn to Freire's ideological beginnings—a dimension of his work that often has been negated or simply ignored by many liberals and progressives who embraced his pedagogical ideas. A quick scan of the writings cited in *Pedagogy of the Oppressed* clearly illustrates that Freire's work was unabashedly grounded in Marxist-Socialist thought. Without question, when Freire spoke of the ruling class or the oppressors, he was referring to historical class distinctions and class conflict within the structure of capitalist society—capitalism was the root of domination. As such, his theoretical analysis was fundamentally rooted in notions of class formation, particularly with respect to how the national political economy relegated the greater majority of its workers to an exploited and marginalized class. However, for Freire, the struggle against economic domination could not be waged effectively without a humanizing praxis that could both engage the complex phenomenon of class struggle and effectively foster the conditions for critical social agency among the masses.

Although heavily criticized on the left for his failure to provide a more systematic theoretical argument against capitalism, Freire's work never retreated from a critique of capitalism and a recognition of capitalist logic as the primary totalizing force in the world. This is to say that he firmly believed that the phenomenon of cultural invasion worldwide was fundamentally driven by the profit motives of capitalists. During my early years as a critical educator, I, like so many, failed to adequately comprehend and incorporate this essential dimension of Freire's work. For critical educators of color in the United States, we saw racism as the major culprit of our oppression and insisted that Freire engage this issue more substantively. Although he openly acknowledged the existence of racism, he was reticent to abandon the notion of class struggle and often warned us against losing sight of the manner in "which the class factor is hidden within both sexual and racial discrimination" (Freire, 1997, p. 86). Our dialogues with him on this issue often were lively and intense because in many ways, Freire questioned the limits of cultural nationalism and our blind faith in a politics of identity. At several different conferences, where educators of color called for separate dialogues with him, he told us that he could not understand why we insisted on dividing ourselves. With true angst, Freire explained to us: "I cannot perceive in my mind how Blacks in America can be liberated without Chicanos being liberated, or how Chicanos can be liberated without Native Americans being liberated, or Native Americans liberated without Whites being liberated" (Freire, 1987). He insisted that the struggle against oppression was a human struggle in which we had to build solidarity across our differences, if we were to change a world engulfed by capitalism. "The lack of unity among the reconcilable 'different' helps the hegemony of the antagonistic 'different'. The most important fight is against the main enemy" (Freire, 1997, p. 85). As might be expected, many of us walked away frustrated. Only recently have I come to understand the political limits of our parochial discourse.

The world economy has changed profoundly since the release of *Pedagogy of the Oppressed*, yet Freire's message remains more relevant than ever. As capital, labor, and knowledge increasingly are conceived of in global terms, the influential role of capital is expanded exponentially, and the globalization of national and local economies is changing the underlying basis of the nation-state (Carnoy, 1997), these structural changes are reflected in the theories and practices of public schooling. As a consequence, "there is now a radical separation in the curriculum between the programs that do the most concrete training for jobs and the programs that do the most critical reflection. Such job separation reduces the capacity of workers to challenge the system" (Shor & Freire, 1987, p. 47).

Moreover, as Ladislau Dowbor (1997) eloquently argues in his preface to *Pedagogy of the Heart*, we must remove the blinders and see capitalism as the generator of scarcity. We cannot afford to ignore the growing gap between the rich and the poor caused by an increasing economic polarization that belies neoliberal theories of the trickle-down effect. And despite an abundance of technological devices flooding the market place, clean rivers, clean air, clean drinking water, chemical-free food, free time, and the space for adults and children to socialize freely have diminished. "Capitalism requires that free-of-charge happiness be substituted for what can be bought and sold" (p. 26). Yet, seldom do we find with the resounding praises paid to technology a discussion of how technological revolutions have exposed the wretchedness of capitalism—millions of people dying from starvation alongside unprecedented wealth. And even more disconcerting is the deleterious impact of globalized capitalism upon the social and environmental interests of humanity—interests that seem to receive little concern next to the profit motives of transnational corporations.

Challenging Our Limitations

> In order to achieve humanization, which presupposes the elimination of dehumanizing oppression, it is absolutely necessary to surmount the limit-situations in which men [and women] are reduced to things.
>
> —FREIRE, 1970, P. 93

Although Freire's historical, regional, and class experiences were different from many of ours, his political purpose was clear and consistent. To achieve a liberatory practice, we had to challenge those conditions that limit our social agency and our capacity to intervene and transform our world. In light of this, Freire's frequent response to questions about issues that perpetuate educational injustice was to challenge us to consider the nature of the limits we were confronting and how we might transcend these limitations in order to discover that beyond these situations, and in contradiction to them, lie untested feasibilities for personal, institutional, and socioeconomic restructuring. For example, in thinking back to how many educators of color responded to Freire's insistence that we create alliances to struggle against capitalism, many of us could not break loose from our deep-rooted (and objectified) distrust of "Whites," nor could we move beyond our self-righteous justification of sectarianism. These represented two of the limit situations that prevented us from establishing the kind of democratic solidarity or unity within diversity that potentially could generate profound shifts in the political and economic systems that intensify racism. Freire knew this and yet listened attentively to our concerns and frustrations within the context of our dialogues, always with respect and a deep faith in the power of our political commitment and perseverance.

Freire deeply believed that the rebuilding of solidarity among educators was a vital and necessary radical objective because solidarity moved against the grain of "capitalism's intrinsic perversity, its anti-solidarity nature" (Freire, 1998, p. 88). Throughout his writings, Freire warned us repeatedly against sectarianism. "Sectarianism in any quarter is an obstacle to the emancipation of [human] kind" (Freire, 1970, p. 22). "While fighting for my dream, I must not become passionately closed within myself" (Freire, 1998, p. 88). In many instances, he linked our ability to create solidarity with our capacity for tolerance.

At a critical scholars' conference in Boston during the summer of 1991, I came face to face with Freire's notion of tolerance. The meetings had been quite intense, particularly with respect to the concerns of feminist scholars within the field. Rather than exemplifying dialogue, I felt the exchanges began to take on a rather virulent tone. In my frustration, I stood up and fired away at one of the presenters. Freire seemed upset with my response. The following day during my presentation, I again proceeded to critique passionately the lack of substantive commitment to the principles of dialogue and solidarity among the group, focusing my critique on issues of cultural and class differences among many of us. Freire's response to my comments that afternoon remain with me to this day. He was particularly concerned with what he judged as my lack of tolerance and beseeched me to behave with greater tolerance in the future, if I was to continue this work effectively. With great political fervor, I rejected Freire's position making the case that what we needed was to be more intolerant—of oppression and social injustice! For years, I licked my wounds over being scolded in public by Freire. But eight years later, I must confess that I recognize great wisdom in Freire's advice. Despite my undeniable political commitment, I was lacking tolerance as "revolutionary virtue—the wisdom of being able to live with what is different, so as to be able to fight the common enemy" (Freire & Faundez, 1989, p. 18).

Let us stop for a moment and recognize that just as we all face limit situations in our world and within ourselves, Freire, too, faced such issues in his private and public life. In 1964, after launching the most successful national literacy campaign Brazil had ever known, he was imprisoned and exiled by the right-wing military dictatorship that had overthrown the democratically elected government of Joao Goulart. Freire remained in exile for almost 16 years. But despite the pain and hardships he and his family experienced, Freire's work as an educator and cultural worker continued unabated. In reminiscences of those years, I recall most the sense that Freire clearly understood domination and exploitation as a worldwide phenomenon. As such, he recognized that within the political struggle for a socialist democracy, a myriad of legitimate political projects existed that, regardless of location, were unequivocally linked by their purpose and commitment to economic and cultural democracy. On a more personal level, he spoke of enduring the pain and suffering of exile, while at the same time not reducing his life to grieving alone, "I do not live only in the past. Rather, I exist in the present, where I prepare myself for the possible" (Freire, 1998, p. 67). Hence, Freire's experience of exile was as much a time of facing a multitude of fears, sorrows, and doubts within unfamiliar contexts as it was a time for remaking himself anew and restoring the dreams that had been shattered.

As Freire's work became more prominent within the United States, he also grappled with a variety of issues that both challenged and concerned him. For almost three decades, feminists across the country fiercely critiqued the sexism of his language. In some arenas, Marxist scholars criticized him brutally for his failure to provide a systematic analysis of class, capitalism, and schooling. To the dismay of many scholars, educators, and organizers of color, Freire seemed at times unwilling (or unable) to engage, with greater depth and specificity, the perverse nature of racism and its particular historical formations within the United States. Neither could he easily accept, from a historical materialist perspective, the legitimacy of the Chicano movement and its emphasis on a mythological homeland, Atzlan. Along the same lines, Freire also questioned the uncompromising resistance or refusal of many radical educators of color to assume the national identity of "American"—an act that he believed fundamentally weakened our position and limited our material struggle for social and economic justice. Beyond these issues, he also harbored serious concerns over what he perceived as the splintered nature of the critical pedagogy movement in the United States. Yet, most of these issues were seldom engaged substantively in public, but rather were the fodder of private dialogues and solitary reflections.

Given this history, it is a real tribute to Freire, that in *Pedagogy of the Heart* (or *Under the Shade of the Mango Tree*—its original title), written shortly before his death, Freire demonstrated signs of change and deepening in his thinking about many of these issues. For example, the language in the book finally reflected an inclusiveness of women when making general references, which had been missing in his earlier writings. He spoke to the issue of capitalism more boldly than ever before and considered the nature of globalization and its meaning for radical educators. He also addressed issues of diversity and racism, acknowledging openly that, "[w]e cannot reduce all prejudice to a classist explanation, but we may not overlook it in understanding the different kinds of discrimination" (p. 86). And more forcefully than ever, he spoke to the necessity of moving beyond our reconcilable differences so that we might forge an effective attack against the wiles of advanced capitalism in the world.

The Capacity to Always Begin Anew

This capacity to always begin anew, to make, to reconstruct, and to not spoil, to refuse to bureaucratize the mind, to understand and to live as a process—live to become—is something that always accompanied me throughout life. This is an indispensable quality of a good teacher.

—FREIRE, 1993, P. 98

The examples above are shared not to diminish, in any way, Freire's contribution or the memory of his work, but rather to remember him within his totality as a human being, with many of the conflicts and contradictions that confront us all, and yet with an expansive ability for sustained reflection, inquiry, and dialogue. But most important, he had an incredible capacity to reconstruct and begin always anew. For Freire, there was no question that he, others, and the world were always in a state of becoming, of transforming, and reinventing ourselves as part of our human historical process. This belief served as the foundation for his unrelenting search for freedom and his unwavering hope in the future. In the tradition of Marx, he believed that we both make and are made by our world. And as such, all human beings are the makers of history. In Freire's view, knowledge could not be divorced from historical continuity. Like us, "history is a process of being limited and conditioned by the knowledge that we produce. Nothing that we engender, live, think, and make explicit takes place outside of time and history" (Freire, 1998, p. 32). And more important, educators had to recognize that "it was when the majorities are denied their right to participate in history as subjects that they become dominated and alienated" (Freire, 1970, p. 125).

In light of this, Freire was convinced that this historical process needed to take place within schools and communities, anchored in relationships of solidarity. Freire urged critical educators to build communities of solidarity as a form of networking, to help us in problematizing the debilitating conditions of globalized economic inequality and in confronting the devastating impact of neoliberal economic and social policies on the world's population. Freire believed that teachers, students, parents, and others could reproduce skills and knowledge through networks formed around schools and adult education, youth organizations, and religious organizations that have a common democratic interest to enhance individual and collective life. More important, through praxis—the authentic union of action and reflection—these education networks could enter into the re-making of a new culture of capital, both as sites for the integration of disassociated workers and for the development of critical consciousness (or conscientizaçao), ultimately shaping the future of local and national politics, and hence, altering the nature of the global economy. Freire's notion of establishing critical networks is a particularly compelling thought considering the current political struggles in California for the protection of immigrant rights, affirmative action, and bilingual education.

In many ways, the idea of critical networks is linked directly with the struggle for democracy and an expanded notion of citizenship. Freire urged us to strive for intimacy with democracy, living actively with democratic principles and deepening them so that they could come to have real meaning in our everyday life. Inherent in this relationship with democracy was a form of citizenship that could not be obtained by chance. It represented a construction that was always in a state of becoming and required that we fight to obtain it. Further, it demanded commitment, political clarity, coherence, and decision on our part. Moreover, Freire insisted that:

> No one constructs a serious democracy, which implies radically changing the societal structures, reorienting the politics of production and development, reinventing power, doing justice to everyone, and abolishing the unjust and immoral gains of the all-powerful, without previously and simultaneously working for these democratic preferences and these ethical demands. (Freire, 1989, p. 67)

Freire also repeatedly associated the work of educators with an unwavering faith in the oppressed, who, too, were always in a state of becoming anew. "Never has there been a deeper need for progressive men and women—serious, radical, engaged in the struggle for transforming society, to give testimony of their respect for the people" (Freire, 1997, p. 84). Freire consistently identified this respect for and commitment to marginalized people as an integral ingredient to the cultivation of dialogue in the classroom. "Dialogue requires an intense faith in [others], faith in their power to make and remake, to create and recreate, faith in [their] vocation to be more fully human (which is not the privilege of an elite but the birthright of all)" (Freire, 1970, p. 79). Moreover, he insisted that true dialogue could not exist in the absence of love and humility. But for Freire, dialogue also implied a critical posture as well as a preoccupation with the meanings that students used to mediate their world. He believed it was impossible to teach without educators knowing what took place in their students' world. "They need to know the universe of their dreams, the language with which they skillfully defend themselves from the aggressiveness of their world, what they know independently of the school, and how they know it" (Freire, 1998, p. 73). Through such knowledge, teachers could support students in reflecting on their lives and making individual and collective decisions for transforming their world. As such, dialogue, through reflection and action, could never be reduced to blind action, deprived of intention and purpose.

Indispensable Qualities of Progressive Teachers

> It is impossible to teach without the courage to try a thousand times before giving up. In short, it is impossible to teach without a forged, invented, and well-thought-out capacity to love.
>
> —FREIRE, 1998, P. 3

In *Teachers as Cultural Workers*, Freire (1998) wrote Letters to Those Who Dare to Teach. Again, he brings us back to an ethics of love and challenges us to reconsider our practice in new ways and to rethink our pedagogical commitment. Freire argued that the task of a teacher, who is always learning, must be both joyful and rigorous. He firmly believed that teaching for liberation required seriousness and discipline as well as scientific, physical, and emotional preparation. Freire stressed often that teaching was a task that required a love for the very act of teaching. For only through such love could the political project of teaching possibly become transformative and liberating. For Freire, it could never be enough to teach only with critical reason. He fervently argued that we must dare to do all things with feeling, dreams, wishes, fear, doubts, and passion.

> We must dare so as never to dichotomize cognition and emotion. We must dare so that we can continue to teach for a long time under conditions that we know well: low salaries, lack of respect, and the ever-present risk of becoming prey to cynicism. We must dare to learn how to dare in order to say no to the bureaucratization of the mind to which we are exposed every day. We must dare so that we can continue to do so even when it is so much more materially advantageous to stop daring. (Freire, 1998, p. 3)

To be a progressive teacher who dares to teach requires, in Freire's eyes, a set of very particular and indispensable qualities. He believed these qualities could protect radical teachers from falling into the trappings of avant-gardism, by helping them become more conscious of their language, their use of authority in the classroom, and their teaching strategies. Through striving to develop these qualities, teachers could also come to understand that they cannot liberate anyone, but rather that they were in a strategic position to invite their students to liberate themselves, as they learned to read their world and transform their present realities.

Unlike the traditional pedagogical emphasis on specific teaching methodologies, particular classroom curricula, and the use of standardized texts and materials, Freire's indispensable qualities focus on those human values that expand a teacher's critical and emotional capacity to enter into effective learning-teaching relationships with their students. Freire begins with a humility grounded in courage, self-confidence, self-respect, and respect for others. In many ways, he believed that humility is the quality that allows us to listen beyond our differences, and as such represents a cornerstone in developing our intimacy with democracy. Freire associated humility with the dialectical ability to live an insecure security, which means a human existence that did not require absolute answers or solutions to a problem but rather that, even in the certainty of the moment, could remain open to new ways, new ideas, and new dreams. This anti-authoritarian position also works to prevent teachers from squelching expressions of resistance in their students—resistance that, in fact, is not only meaningful, but necessary to their process of empowerment. Inherent in this quality of humility also is the ability of teachers to build their capacity to express a lovingness rooted in their commitment to consistently reflect on their practice and to consider the consequences of their thoughts, words, and actions within the classroom and beyond.

In keeping with his consistent emphasis on the necessity of confronting our fears, Freire identified courage as another indispensable quality of educators. Courage here implies a virtue that is born and nourished by our consistent willingness to challenge and overcome our fears in the interest of democratic action—an action that holds both personal and social consequences. Freire believed that as teachers become clearer about their choices and political dreams, courage sustains our struggle to confront those myths, fueled by the dominant ideology, that fragment and distort our practice. Key to this process is our critical ability to both accept and control our fear.

> When we are faced with concrete fears, such as that of losing our jobs or of not being promoted, we feel the need to set certain limits to our fear. Before anything else, we begin to recognize that fear is a manifestation of our being alive. I do not hide my fears. But I must not allow my fears to immobilize me. Instead, I must control them, for it is in the very exercise of this control that my necessary courage is shared. (Freire, 1998, p. 41)

Tolerance is another of the indispensable qualities on Freire's list. Without this virtue, he contends, no authentic democratic experience can be actualized in the classroom or our own lives. But it is important to note that tolerance "does not mean acquiescing to the intolerable; it does not mean covering up disrespect;

it does not mean coddling the aggressor or disguising aggression" (Freire, 1998, p. 43). Freire adamantly stressed that tolerance is neither about playing the game, nor a civilized gesture of hypocrisy, nor a coexistence with the unbearable. Instead, the critical expression of tolerance is founded on the basic human principles of respect, discipline, dignity, and ethical responsibility.

Finally, Freire assigned decisiveness, security, the tension between patience and impatience, and the joy of living to the set of indispensable qualities. He wholeheartedly believed that the ability to make decisions, despite the possibility of rupture, is an essential strength of our work as progressive educators. He argued that teachers who lack this quality often resort to irresponsible practices of permissiveness in their teaching, a condition that is as damaging to students as the abuse of teacher authority. Further, a lack of confidence was often linked to indecision, although security (or confidence), on the other hand, stems from a sense of competence, political clarity, and ethical integrity.

The ability of teachers to practice their pedagogy within the dialectical tension of patience and impatience represented for Freire a significant leap in an educator's development. This virtue allows teachers to both feel the urgency of the difficult conditions they are facing within schools and at the same time respond with thoughtful and reflective tactics and strategies, rather than blind activism. Key to understanding this concept is recognizing the problematics of those who espouse an ethic of absolute patience on one hand, and those who manifest an uncontainable impatience on the other. Both can impair our ability to participate pedagogically in effective ways.

At no time is the ability to cultivate a dialectical understanding of the world more necessary than when we as educators are asked to live within the tension of two seemingly contradictory concepts of responses. This is to say, living an impatient patience or insecure security is predicated on our willingness and ability to grapple with the complexity and ambiguity of the present, despite a heightened level of tension we may experience. And, as such, to respond in coherence with our democratic dream, rather than to seek prescribed formulas or quick-fix recipes to alleviate the tension, potentially is a creative and liberating force in our lives. This dialectical competence also implies a verbal parsimony, which helps us to rarely lose control over our words or exceed the limits of considered, yet energetic, discourse—a quality that Freire consistently demonstrated over the years during his participation in difficult dialogues.

Freire placed great significance on our ability to live joyfully despite the multitude of external forces that constantly challenge our humanity. The indispensable quality of teaching with a joy of living personifies most the ultimate purpose in both Freire's work and life. In retrospect, I am filled with wonderful memories of Freire—the beauty of his language, the twinkle in his eyes, his thoughtful and respectful manner, the movement of his hands when he spoke, his lively enthusiasm when contemplating new ideas, and his candid expressions of love and gratitude. In his words and his deeds, Freire persistently invited teachers to fully embrace life, rather than to surrender our existence to the stifling forces of economic and social injustice.

> By completely giving myself to life rather than to death—without meaning either to deny death or to mythicize life—I can free myself to surrender to the joy of living, without having to hide the reasons for sadness in life, which prepares me to stimulate and champion joy in the school. (Freire, 1998, p. 45)

Although Freire does not explicitly speak of activism in his Letters to Those Who Dare to Teach (1998), his theoretical work was never disassociated from his activism. Moreover, he argued tirelessly for the inseparability of political consciousness and political action in our teaching and in our lives. Hence, teachers as intellectuals, cultural workers, and community activists must "aspire to become an association of truly serious and coherent people, those who work to shorten more and more the distance between what they say and what they do" (Freire, 1997, p. 83). The transformation of schools can only take place when teachers, working in solidarity, take ownership and struggle to radically change the political and economic structures of power that defile our revolutionary dreams.

> Thus I can see no alternative for educators to unity within the diversity of their interests in defending their rights. Such rights include the right to freedom in teaching, the right to speak, the right to better conditions for pedagogical work, the right to paid sabbaticals for continuing education, the right to be coherent, the right to criticize the authorities without fear of retaliation...and to not have to lie to survive. (Freire, 1998, p. 46)

REFERENCES

Carnoy, M. (1997). "Foreword." In P. Freire, *Pedagogy of the Heart*. New York: Continuum.

Dowbor, L. (1997). "Preface." In P. Freire, *Pedagogy of the Heart*. New York: Continuum.

Freire, P. (1998). *Teachers as Cultural Workers: Letters to Those Who Dare to Teach*. Boulder, CO: Westview.

Freire, P. (1997). *Pedagogy of the Heart*. New York: Continuum.

Freire, P. (1993). *Pedagogy of the City*. New York: Continuum.

Freire, P. (1987). "People of Color Caucus Dialogue." Critical Pedagogy Conference, University of California, Irvine, July.

Freire, P. (1970). *Pedagogy of the Oppressed*. New York: Seabury.

Freire, P., & Betto, F. (1985). *Essa Escola Chamada Vida*. Sao Paulo: Atica.

Freire, P., and A. Faundez (1989). *Learning to Question: A Pedagogy of Liberation*. New York: Continuum.

Macedo, D., and A. Araujo Freire (1998). "Foreword." In P. Freire, *Teachers as Cultural Workers: Letters to Those Who Dare to Teach*. Boulder, CO: Westview.

McLaren, P. (1997). "Paulo Freire's Legacy of Hope and Struggle," *Theory, Culture, and Society* 14, no. 4: 147–53.

Shor, I., and P. Freire (1987). *A Pedagogy for Liberation*. Westport, CT: Bergin and Garvey.

PART IV.
The Politics of Language

CAFE CONTEMPLATION

In a newbury street cafe
i drink my hot latte
and deliberately eavesdrop on
the scattered conversations
that compete for a place,
andean music fills the air
in a most incongruent way,
songs of indigenous people,
beautiful and melodic serve
as white noise for the crowd,
a sacred cultural form relegated
to the unnoticed and ignored,

how chic and hip this place,
they play third world flutes
to the chatter of intellectuals
who compare rimbaud with robaire
and gaugain with picasso,
critical analysis of worthy themes,
where shall we go to study abroad
italy, spain, or france,
and discussions about last night's
terrific performance piece with
only a body and a tea cup to
express the sublime of life,

the surrealism is that i sit
among these people in
the ridiculous disguise of an
accommodated indigenous woman,
here everyone sits disconnected
from the homeless man just outside
lying in a stupor on the street,
the u.s. in the middle east
tempting the wrath of armageddon,
and the 19 year old who sentenced
himself to death by resisting the cops,
i welcome the soulfulness of the

south american guitars that move
passionately to interrupt my thoughts,
now i can only feel the heart of
the indigenous spirit that created
the love which romances the air,
and while others busily chatter away,
i begin to remember who i am and
from where i have come, in spanish

—ANTONIA DARDER (1990)

CHAPTER 10

Bicultural Identity
and the Development of Voice
Twin Issues in the Struggle for Cultural
and Linguistic Democracy

> So, it you want to really hurt me, talk bad about my language.
> Ethnic identity is twin skin to linguistic identity...I am my lan-
> guage... I will no longer be made to feel ashamed of existing. I
> will have my voice...I will overcome the tradition of silence.
> —GLORIA ANZALDÚA (1987)

As suggested by the words of Gloria Anzaldúa, any struggle for cultural and linguistic democracy must center on the formation of bicultural identity and the
development of voice in students of color who attend public schools. Efforts to
address the needs of bicultural students in the United States without careful consideration of the social forces that shape the quality of the bicultural experience of
these students constitute a continued act of hostility and psychological violence.
To transform the current conditions generated by policies and practices that support cultural invasion within classrooms requires that we understand some of the
historical and political dimensions that have shaped the world as we know it today.

The notion of *biculturalism* has been discussed by sociologists, psychologists,
and educators of color (Darder, 1991; de Anda, 1984; Ramirez & Castañeda, 1974;
Rashid, 1981; Red Horse, et al., 1981; Solis, 1980; Valentine, 1971) in a variety of

ways. But the definitive thread that weaves through the fabric of these discussions posits biculturalism as a social phenomenon experienced by people of color who must survive in the midst of societal institutions that, more often than not, are defined by a cultural system of both affective and behavioral standards that are in direct conflict with those of subordinate groups.

To understand our students as cultural beings requires that we understand the manner in which social power and control function to structure the world in which we exist and how it defines our place within that world. Hence, to speak of biculturalism in the United States solely from the standpoint of an individual psychology without addressing the impact of those social, political, and economic forces that have historically sustained the cultural subordination of people of color would constitute a misleading and fraudulent act. It is impossible to ignore that every group in this country perceived outside of the English-speaking (Anglocentric) mainstream shares a history of what Iris Marion Young (1990) terms *the five faces of oppression:* marginalization, exploitation, cultural invasion, powerlessness, and violence. It is also significant to note that this has been the case even when a large majority of the members of a particular subordinate cultural group have become predominantly English speakers. In contrast to the myth, speaking English, in and of itself, has not led to an improved quality of life for the majority of Latino, African American, and Native American people.

The overt struggles by people of color to resist subordination and retain a cultural identity over assimilation to a national (homogeneous) identity have long been viewed by the mainstream as divisive and un-American. To counter such perceived ethnic and cultural divisions in the population, the conservative melting-pot ideology was combined with the liberal doctrine of individualism to fuel the Americanization movements of this century—movements that were driven as much by politically naive and well-meaning intellectuals as by politically astute intellectuals concerned primarily with preserving the dominant interests of the status quo.

One of the most pervasive impacts of these movements was the systematic erosion of the collective identity of non-English-speaking cultural and ethnic communities. In its place was substituted a national or American identity reinforced by the institutionalization of the standards and norms transmitted and reproduced by an English-speaking system of values and beliefs. This institutionalization of the English-speaking world view in the United States ensured that those already in power would not only perpetuate but maximize their control over the country's political system and economic wealth. Camouflaged by rhetoric of national unity and prosperity, "American democracy" flourished, while all other cultural and ethnic groups were systematically repressed and relegated to a subordinate status.

The systemic subordination of those cultural groups perceived as threatening to the core values of "American democracy" has been carried out primarily by implicit (or hegemonic) rather than explicit mechanisms of social control. Hence the country's institutions have championed conformity to the notion of "common values" in the face of rampant capitalism, an obsession with an ever-changing modernity, and a doctrine of rugged individualism.

This hegemonic rhetoric has been nowhere more alive and well than in the discourse of public schooling. To be a good U.S. citizen, students of color have been expected to assimilate to "American" standards and values and in so doing, discard the values of their primary culture, breaking free of all bonds to a cultural or ethnic identity. Just as schooling has been deemed apolitical and neutral by the mainstream, so too embracing values of "American democracy" has been deemed and portrayed principally as a matter of individual choice and personal freedom rather than political exigency. In both cases, the great rhetoric, of "American democracy" was flawed, for it in fact functioned to veil the social processes of power and deny the existence of an institutionalized system of subordination at work—a system that not only rigorously perpetuated the Anglocentric values inherent in the predominant colonizing culture of the United States, but also functioned to silence the majority of competing cultural definitions of humanity within the nation.

Bicultural Identity

In the midst of widespread institutional and popular practices that reinforce conformity and homogeneity, subordinate cultural groups have struggled to retain their cultural identity and find a voice in this country. When any group is forced to survive within conditions that obstruct their self-determination and require assimilation to a foreign way of life, the differing individual responses to such conditions can result in fragmentation of the group's sense of cultural integrity. Thus, it is no wonder that there would exist such extensive diversity and contradictory patterns of responses among people of color.

In *Culture and Power in the Classroom* (Darder, 1991), a framework is discussed that considers the major patterns of responses prevalent among bicultural students. In an effort to shed light on our understanding of bicultural development and identity, five primary patterns are examined. These bicultural response patterns are identified as *alienation, dualism, separatism,* and *negotiation.* Within this bicultural framework, there also are responses that might best be described within the scope of bicultural *affirmation.* These responses are less fixed than those which fall into the previous four categories mentioned. Instead, what exists here is a greater flexibility in responding to the social environment, without the necessity to abandon the reality of one's experience as a cultural human being. In considering bicultural identity, these five positions can also reflect predominant categories for determining the strength of cultural identity expressed by students of color.

In addition to students' consistent participation (or nonparticipation) in their cultural community of origin, their cultural identity and predominant bicultural responses are also influenced by their efforts to contend with the social tensions that are inherent in conditions of cultural subordination. As a consequence, students from subordinate groups must interact within societal structures that consistently produce varying levels of cultural conflict and dissonance. Their responses to the power differential and consequent inferior social status play an important role in the development of bicultural identity. For example, does a student of color primarily respond to the social tensions of cultural subordination by accommodating to domination or do they respond with resistance? In accommodating, the student may attempt to completely move away from identification with the primary culture or instead, function with two faces without engaging the conflict or contradiction in values that exists between the two worldviews. On the other hand, when students respond with resistance, they may choose to separate from the dominant culture and segregate themselves within their own primary cultural community, or they may struggle to negotiate between the dominant and subordinate structure of values in an effort to actualize some degree of social change. When students are functioning from a greater sense of affirmation with respect to their bicultural existence, their responses reflect greater flexibility and movement. This is evidenced clearly when a student's particular interaction at any given moment, more likely than not, is to emanate from a critical assessment of the actual power relations at work and, based upon their assessment, to respond accordingly. Needless to say, this type of cognitive, physical, emotional, and spiritual flexibility requires a greater sense of consciousness related to one's identity as both an individual and a social being—a consciousness that supports and nurtures both personal and collective empowerment.

The Bicultural Voice

In his writings on the nature of voice, Henry Giroux (1988) describes voice in the following terms.

> Voice refers to the principles of dialogue as they are enunciated and enacted within particular social settings. The concept of voice represents the unique instances of self-expression through which students affirm their own class, culture, racial, and gender identities. The category of voice, then refers to the means at our disposal—the discourses available to use—to make ourselves understood and listened to, and to define ourselves as active participants in the world. (p. 199)

In more specific terms, the *bicultural voice* points to a discourse that not only incorporates the world views, histories, and lived experiences of subordinate cultural groups in the United States, but also functions to rupture the historical and institutionalized silence of students of color and the beliefs and practices that support such dehumanizing forms of silence in the first place. As students of color awaken to bicultural forms of discourse through their active interaction and dialogue with one another, they come to develop a consciousness that can support their ability to (a) critically reflect upon collective and individual interactions with mainstream institutions, (b) affirm the knowledge they possess, given their particular subject position in U.S. society, (c) resist domination through explicitly challenging the implicit mechanisms of cultural subordination that dehumanize, disempower, and obstruct their democratic rights, and (d) enter into relationships of solidarity as equal participants.

From my observations of students of color over the last 12 years, it is quite apparent that there exists a strong relationship between bicultural identity, critical social consciousness, and the development and expression of the bicultural voice. For example, students of color who principally exhibit responses of cultural alienation are least likely to possess a strong primary cultural identity and critical consciousness, and hence also least likely to reflect a bicultural voice in their articulation of the world and their construction of meaning. Most of these students resist adamantly any differentiation between themselves and the dominant culture with a greater tendency to identify with the "American" culture or hold conflicting, dualistic perceptions of themselves. On the other hand, students who possess a strong primary cultural identity tend to display a greater critical understanding of social contexts and a greater proficiency for giving voice to their experiences as bicultural human beings in the United States.

Conditions That Support Bicultural Identity and Voice

Culture is an enacted phenomenon that takes place within a community context of shared meaning. Therefore, for students to fully develop their understanding of and participation in their primary culture requires consistent opportunities to engage actively with members of their cultural community. Gloria Johnson Powell's (1970) work suggests that there is a significant correlation between positive self-concept and a student's opportunity to learn and develop academically within a school setting that respects, reinforces, and enacts the child's culture. This supports the notion that students of color require people in their environment who can serve as active cultural agents, translators of the bicultural experience, and as examples of critically conscious adults with whom students can directly identify and consistently interact. Further, it has been observed that many bilingual students are more likely to give voice to their bicultural experiences when there are bilingual, bicultural adults in their classroom environments, who legitimate their perceptions, insights, and concerns, than when these adults are not present (Darder & Upshur, 1991).

In structuring classroom life to affirm and encourage the development of student voices, teachers must

> organize classroom relationships so that students can draw on and confirm those dimensions of their histories and experiences that are deeply rooted in the surrounding community...assume pedagogical responsibility for attempting to understand the relationships and forces that influence students outside the immediate context of the class room, develop curricula and pedagogical practices around those community traditions, histories, and forms of knowledge that are often ignored with the dominant school culture... create the conditions where students come together to speak, to engage in dialogue, to share their stories, and to struggle together within social relations that strengthen rather than weaken possibilities for active citizenship. (Giroux, 1988, pp. 199–201)

Herein lies the foundation for creating the conditions for a culturally democratic critical education environment where students of color may come to know themselves and the world in relation to their own conditions, rather than based upon contrived notions of life that are often completely foreign to their own existence. The bicultural voice is awakened through a critical process of dialogue and reflection within the context of the classroom, when students find opportunities to reflect together on their common lived experiences, their personal perceptions of the bicultural process, and their common responses to issues of cultural domination, alienation, resistance, negotiation, and affirmation.

In summary, students of color require teachers in their environments who understand the dynamics of cultural subordination and the impact that this has upon students, their families, and their cultural communities. These students also need critically conscious teachers who come from their own cultural communities, who can speak and instruct them in their native language, who can serve as translators of the bicultural experience, and who can reinforce an identity grounded in the cultural integrity of their own people. Students of color also require classroom relationships that make explicit social injustice and that reinforce their inalienable rights to participate and have a voice within and outside of the classroom environment. Further, students of color require participatory approaches and curricular materials that will assist them in discovering themselves as historical beings and empowered subjects in the world.

Critical Pedagogy and the Education
of Bicultural Students

To attempt a brief discussion of critical pedagogy is in itself a difficult task, for there is always the danger of oversimplification and reductionism—both completely contrary to its very foundations. So what is necessary to emphasize here is that critical pedagogy is not a technique, model, or recipe for educational practice. Instead, it represents a set of guiding principles for the enactment of an emancipatory classroom culture—principles that are intimately linked to an emancipatory paradigm, or way of thinking, about human beings, culture, knowledge, social power, and the world. To understand education in this way means to deinstrumentalize the practice of teaching and infuse it with the possibilities of passion and creativity informed by the vibrant critical presence of both teachers and students.

To support an educational environment that can sustain the complexity and diversity of such a reality requires educators who are theoretically well grounded in principles of democratic schooling—principles that can shape classroom practices and relationships that will nurture and cultivate the development of bicultural identity and voice among students from subordinate language communities.

The following provides a general introduction to the major principles that constitute the theoretical foundations of critical pedagogy. More specifically, this includes brief discussions related to cultural politics, economics, the historicity of knowledge, dialectical theory, ideology, hegemony, resistance, praxis, dialogue, and the notion of *conscientizaçao*. Within the various dimensions of these theoretical foundations are found important key concepts that can contribute effectively to the education of bicultural students.

Cultural Politics

The fundamental commitment of critical educators is to empower the powerless and transform those conditions that perpetuate human injustice and inequity (McLaren, 1989). This purpose is inextricably linked to the fulfillment of what Paulo Freire (1970) defines as our *vocation*—to be truly humanized social agents in the world. Hence, a major function of critical pedagogy is to critique, expose, and challenge the manner in which schools impact upon the political and cultural life of students. Teachers must recognize how schools unite knowledge and power and how through this function they can work to influence or thwart the formation of critically thinking and socially active individuals.

Unlike traditional perspectives of education that claim to be neutral and apolitical, critical pedagogy views all education as intimately linked to ideologies shaped by power, politics, history, and culture. Given this view, schooling functions as a terrain of ongoing struggle over what will be accepted as legitimate knowledge and culture. In accordance, critical pedagogy addresses the notion of cultural politics by both legitimizing and challenging cultural experiences that encompass the histories and social realities that shape the forms and boundaries that give meaning to students' lives (Darder, 1991).

Economics

Critical education theory contends that, contrary to the traditional view, schools actually work against the interest of those students who are most needy in society. The role of competing economic interests of the marketplace in the production of knowledge and the structural relationships and policies that shape public schools are recognized as significant factors, particularly in the education of disenfranchised students. From the standpoint of economics, public schools serve to position select groups within asymmetrical power relations that serve to replicate the existing values and privileges of the dominant culture. It is this uncontested relationship between school and society that critical pedagogy seeks to challenge, unmasking traditional claims that education provides equal opportunity and equal access to all students, irrespective of race, class, and gender.

Historicity of Knowledge

Critical pedagogy embraces the view that all knowledge is created within a historical context, and it is this historical context that gives it life and meaning. This notion of the historicity of knowledge requires that schools be understood within the boundaries of not only their social practice but also their historical realities. Along the same lines, students and the knowledge they bring into the classroom must be understood as historical. And as such, opportunities must be created that permit students to discover

> [T]hat there is no historical reality which is not human. There is no history without men [and women)...there is only history of men [and women]. It is when the majorities are denied their right to participate in history as subjects that they become dominated and alienated. (Freire, 1970, p. 125)

This historical view of knowledge also challenges traditional emphasis on historical continuities and historical development. Instead, there is a mode of analysis that stresses the breaks, discontinuities, conflicts, differences, and tensions in history, all which serve in bringing to light the centrality of human agency as it presently exists, as well as the possibilities for change (Giroux, 1983).

Dialectical Theory

In opposition to traditional theories of education that serve to reinforce certainty, conformity, and technical control of knowledge and power, critical pedagogy embraces a dialectical view of knowledge that functions to unmask the connections between objective knowledge and the cultural norms, values, and standards of the dominant society. Within the dialectical perspective, all analysis begins first and foremost with human existence and the contradictions and disjunctions that both shape and make problematic its meaning. Peter McLaren (1988) explains critical pedagogy as beginning

> with the premise that men and women are essentially unfree and inhabit a world rife with contradictions and asymmetries of power and privilege. The critical educator endorses theories that are, first and foremost, dialectical: that is, theories which recognize the problems of society as more than simply isolated events of individuals or deficiencies in the social structure. Rather, these problems are part of the interactive context between the individual and society. (p. 166)

The purpose here is to assist students to engage the world with its complexity and fullness in order to reveal the possibilities of new ways of constructing thought and action beyond the original state. It seeks to nourish the dynamic interactive elements rather than to support the formation of dichotomies and polarizations. Hence, this supports a view of humans and nature that is relational, an objectivity and subjectivity that are interconnected, and a theory and practice that are coexistent. Efforts to negate such relations eventually lead to the distortion and fragmentation of knowledge and to practices that dehumanize and objectify human life.

Dialectical thought brings to the surface the power of human activity and human knowledge as both a product and force in the shaping of our world in the interest of domination or liberation. Hence, the process of dialectical critique is informed by an emancipatory interest in social change. In this way, critical pedagogy addresses two primary concerns: 1) the linking of social experiences with the development of critical modes that can interrogate such experiences and reveal both their strengths and weaknesses; and 2) the presentation of a mode of practice fashioned in new critical thought and aimed at reclaiming the conditions of self-determined existence.

Ideology

Ideology can best be understood as the framework of thought that is used in society to give order and meaning to the social and political world in which we live (Hall, 1981). Ideology resides within the deep embedded psychological structures of the personality and manifests itself in the inner histories and experiences that give rise to questions of subjectivity as they are constructed by individual needs, drives, and passions, as well as the changing conditions and social foundations of society. In addition, ideology also provides the means by which we structure and shape our critique of the world, ourselves, and one another.

As a pedagogical tool, ideology can be used to interrogate and unmask the contradictions that exist between the dominant culture of the school and the lived experiences and knowledge that students use to mediate the reality of school life. Ideology can also provide teachers with the necessary context to examine how their own views about knowledge, human nature, values, and society are mediated through the common sense assumptions they use to structure classroom experiences. In this way it can serve as a starting point for asking questions that will help them to evaluate critically their practice and to better recognize how the dominant culture becomes embedded in the hidden curriculum—curriculum that is informed by ideological views that silence students and structurally reproduce the dominant society's assumptions and practices.

Hegemony

Hegemony refers to a process of social control that is carried out through the moral and intellectual leadership of a dominant society over subordinate groups (Gramsci, 1971). Critical pedagogy incorporates this notion of hegemony in order to demystify the asymmetrical power relations and social arrangement that sustain the dominant culture. Further, hegemony points to the powerful connection that exists between politics, culture, ideology, and pedagogy. As such, teachers are challenged to recognize their responsibility to critique and attempt to transform those classroom conditions tied to hegemonic practices that perpetuate the oppression of subordinate groups. This process must be ongoing, for hegemony must be fought for constantly within the mainstream in order to maintain the status quo. Each time a radical form is considered to be a threat to the integrity of the status quo, this form is usually appropriated, stripped of its transformative intent, and reified into a palatable form of popular culture for mass consumption (i.e., Cinco de Mayo, Malcolm X, rap music, etc.). This process of social control has been used in the U.S. to undermine the efforts of emancipatory political projects. Yet, understanding how hegemony functions in society provides educators with the basis for understanding not only how the seeds of domination are produced and perpetuated, but how they can be overcome through resistance, critique, and social action.

Resistance

Critical pedagogy incorporates a theory of resistance in order to better understand the complex reasons why many students from subordinate groups consistently fail in the educational system. It accepts the notion that all people have the capacity and ability to produce knowledge and to resist domination. But how they resist is clearly influenced and limited by the conditions in which they have been forced to survive.

A theory of resistance functions to uncover the degree to which student oppositional behavior is driven by their need to struggle against elements of dehumanization or participation in the perpetuation of their own oppression. As in other areas, the notion of emancipatory interests serves as the central point to determining when oppositional behavior reflects a moment of resistance.

Praxis: The Union of Theory and Practice

From a dialectical view of knowledge emerges the notion that theory and practice are inextricably linked. In keeping with this view, all theory is considered with respect to the practical intent of transforming inequity. Unlike the external determinism, pragmatism, and technical application of theory so prevalent in traditional educational discourses, praxis is conceived as self-creating and self-generating free human activity. All human activity is perceived as consisting of action and reflection, or praxis, and as praxis, all human activity requires theory to illuminate it and provide a better understanding of our world as we find it and as it might be. Hence within critical pedagogy, all theorizing and truth claims are subject to critique, a process that constitutes analysis and questions mediated through dialogue and democratic relations of power (Giroux, 1983).

Freire (1985) strongly supports this relationship between theory and practice within the educational process. He argues that a true praxis is impossible in the undialectical vacuum driven by the splitting apart of theory and practice. For within the context of such a dichotomy, both theory and practice lose their power to transform reality. Cut off from practice, theory becomes *simple verbalism*. Separated from theory, practice is nothing but *blind activism*. Given this perspective, teachers cannot be prepared for classroom life by simply exposing them to canned curriculum and a variety of prescribed instructional methods. Instead, teachers must participate in developing their critical understanding of theory and practice, so they may be prepared to function in the classroom as creative, dynamic, and spontaneous educators who recognize that knowledge production is shaped and influenced by the intersubjective responses between students and teacher, students and students, and their shared responses to the living texts that emerge.

Dialogue and Conscientizaçao

The principle of dialogue is one of the most significant aspects of critical pedagogy. It speaks to an emancipatory educational process that is above all committed to the empowerment of students through challenging the dominant educational discourse and illuminating the right and freedom of students to become subjects of their world. Dialogue constitutes an educational strategy that centers upon the development of critical social consciousness or what Freire (1970) terms *conscientizaçao.*

Within the process of a critical pedagogical approach, dialogue and analysis serve as the foundation for purposeful reflection and action. It is this educational strategy that supports a problem-posing approach to education: an approach in which the relationship of students to teacher is, without question, dialogical— students learn from the teacher; teachers learn from the students. Here, the actual lived experiences cannot be ignored or relegated to the periphery. They must be incorporated in exploring the existing conditions in order to better understand how these came to be and how these might be different.

Conscientizaçao is the process by which students, as empowered subjects, achieve a deepening awareness of the social realities that shape their lives and discover their own capacities to recreate or transform them. This constitutes a recurrent, regenerating, and powerful process of human interaction that is used for constant clarification of the hidden dimensions, as students continue to move into the world and enter into dialogue anew.

Questions Informed by Critical Educational Principles

One of the ways in which we can get a better grasp of critical pedagogy and how it can assist us in creating the conditions for cultural and linguistic democracy within schools is to identify some questions that are directly informed by critical educational principles. More importantly, these questions can be used to assess existing educational conditions and practices, and their impact on bicultural students. But taking this concept one step further, the responses elicited by these questions can guide us in transforming our daily practice within the classroom. A few of the questions to consider include:

- Does the curriculum reflect the cognitive, motivational, and relational styles of the student population?
- Who is involved in the development of curriculum and the selection of materials?

- Are the everyday lives and community realities of the students integrated into the daily life of the classroom? If so how is this done?
- Are there consistent and ongoing opportunities for bicultural students to engage together in dialogue that centers upon their own experiences and daily lives? If so, what are some examples of this practice?
- Are there adults in the classroom environment who are able to consistently engage students in their native tongue and who address students' issues related to both their primary cultural and bicultural experiences?
- Are there sufficient opportunities for students to engage with their personal cultural histories and to develop their consciousness with respect to their subject position in the United States? If so, what are some examples?
- Are parents and community members involved in the students' educational process and school governance? If so, in what ways does this take place and what roles do they play?
- Are classroom relations and curricular activities designed to stimulate and nurture the ongoing development of cultural identity, voice, participation, solidarity, and individual and collective empowerment? If so, give some examples.
- Does the teacher make explicit relations of power at work in the classroom, school, community, and society, with respect to the students lives? If so, give examples of how this is done.
- Does the teacher struggle with students of color to overcome limiting and debilitating forms of resistance, while at the same time supporting resistance to cultural subordination and human injustice? If so, how is this undertaken?
- Does the teacher understand the relationship between theory and practice? If so, how is this apparent in the manner in which the teacher perceives her (his) role, relates to students of color, their parents and community, defines student expectations, creates and establishes new curriculum, acknowledges personal limitations, and perceives the production of knowledge and the development of literacy, and bilingual proficiency.

Many of the questions posited here would not be asked within traditional educational environments where knowledge is perceived, neutral and education resembles what Freire (1970) describes as a *banking system*—namely, a system where students are passive objects who come to school in order to be filled with the knowledge of the teacher. Even more frustrating is the persistent failure of traditional education to acknowledge the importance of cultural identity, the primary language, and the bicultural experience of students of color who live in conditions shaped by social, political, and economic marginalization. Instead of making explicit the power relations and elitist interests that structure institutional life within schools in the United States, these remain veiled in the guise of adopted standard curricula. The hidden values of the standard curricula support and encourage assimilation, along with neoconservative notions of multiculturalism that perpetuate cultural and language domination with their inherent subordination of identity, critical consciousness, and voice—carried out, in part, by the best intentioned and well-meaning teachers and educational leaders of our time.

REFERENCES

Anzaldúa, G. (1987). *Borderlands/La Frontera: The New Mestizo.* San Francisco: Spinsters/Aunt Lute Press.

Darder, A. (1991). *Culture and Power in the Classroom.* New York: Bergin and Garvey.

Darder, A., and C. Upshur (1991). *What Do Latino Children Need to Succeed in School? A Study of Boston Public Schools.* Boston: Mauricio Gaston Institute for Latino Community Development and Public Policy.

de Anda, D. (1984). "Bicultural Socialization: Factors Affecting the Minority Experience," *Social Work* no. 29:2; 101–7.

Freire, P. (1985). *The Politics of Education.* Westport, CT: Bergin and Garvey.

Freire, P. (1970). *Pedagogy of the Oppressed.* New York: Seabury.

Giroux, H. (1988). *Teachers as Intellectuals.* Westport, CT: Bergin and Garvey.

Giroux, H. (1983). *Theory and Resistance in Education.* Westport, CT: Bergin and Garvey.

Gramsci, A. (1971). *Selections from the Prison Notebooks.* New York: International.

Hall, S. (1981). "Cultural Studies: Two Paradigms." In T. Bennett et al. (eds.), *Culture, Ideology, and Social Process.* London: Batsford Academic and Educational.

McLaren, P. (1989). *Life in Schools: An Introduction to Critical Pedagogy in the Foundations of Education.* New York: Longman.

Powell, G. (1970). *Black Monday's Children.* New York: Appleton, Century, Crofts.

Ramirez, M., and A. Castafieda (1974). *Cultural Democracy: Bicognitive Development and Education.* New York: Academic Press.

Rashid, H. (1981). "Early Childhood Education as a Cultural Transition for African-American Children," *Educational Research Quarterly* 6:3; 55–63.

Red Horse, J.G., et al. (1981). "Family Behavior of Urban American Indians." In R. Dana (ed.), *Human Services for Cultural Minorities.* Baltimore: University Park Press (55–63).

Solis, A. (1980). "Theory of Biculturality," *Calmecac se Aztlan en Los* 2:1; 36–41.

Valentine, C. (1971). "Deficit, Difference, and Bicultural Models of Afro-American Behavior," *Harvard Educational* Review 41:2; 137–57.

Young, I.M. (1990). *Justice and the Politics of Difference.* Princeton, NJ: Princeton University Press.

CHAPTER 11

"Mami, What Did Nana Say?"

Public Schooling and the Politics
of Linguistic Genocide

> Language is a form of human praxis inscribed by the historical,
> political and economic conditions in which human beings...must
> survive.
>
> —J.L. AMARIGLIO, S.A. RESNICK, AND R.W. WOLFF[1]

The title of this essay was inspired by some rather painful moments when my children were young. As a single mom, isolated from family, living in poverty, working two jobs and trying to go to school, my tendency was to speak to my children in English, with an occasional Spanish word thrown in here and there. It was more an economy of words and attention than a lack of desire for my children to speak Spanish. Still, it was difficult for them to communicate with their Nana Chuy and their Grandpa Rudy, who spoke only Spanish. It was not unusual for them to ask repeatedly, "What is Nana saying?" I remember, in those moments, how my stomach would churn and I would feel that I was such a bad mother because it was so difficult for me to teach my children Spanish, given the conditions in which we were struggling to survive.

As I began to work within the Latino community, I discovered that this was not an unusual phenomenon among second-generation Latino parents. Many of them also grappled with this issue, particularly when they did not have family around to speak to the children consistently in Spanish. In the absence of active and ever-present familial linguistic support, working parents struggle with the preservation of the primary language in their children. As is often the case, parents are generally blamed for this loss, even by folks in their own community, and they internalize the loss of the language in their children as solely a failure on their part. Seldom are the structural conditions that perpetuate linguistic inequalities (historically witnessed also in the loss of a whole host of European languages) engaged and linked to racialized class inequalities at work in public schools and other social institutions.

Language and Schooling

> With all its complexity, the language policy of the United States revealed an overarching monolingualism.
>
> —BERNARD SPOLSKY[2]

It is impossible to contemplate the process of democratic schooling outside the realm of language policies and their relationship to our formation as literate human beings. From the most personal to the most theoretical, the question of language raises both profound and difficult questions that must be thoughtfully considered and critically engaged. In our efforts to seriously interrogate literacy development, issues of language rights and their relationship to culture, identity, class, and citizenship must remain ever at the forefront of our inquiry. Yet, no matter where such a discussion begins or where it leads, what cannot be denied is the political nature of language and, in particular, its powerful influence in structuring the lives of language minority populations.

Linguistic inequalities and their relationship to schooling must be central concerns for educators who profess a commitment to both critical literacy and a democratic society. In saying this, I wish to suggest that the development of literacy is as much a cultural, political, and economic concern as it is an academic one. For these reasons, neither academic issues of language nor the politics of literacy can be fully understood outside of their historical relationship to colonization, national power, class struggle, and the ideologies that sustain mainstream educational policies and practices, often at the expense of linguistic minorities.

It is significant to note that although the right to become literate in students' language of origin and the dominant language of the society in which they reside represents a key tenet of linguistic rights around the globe, this precept has often been ignored. For example, in the United States, with first the passage of Proposition 227 in California and later the institutionalization of No Child Left Behind, fundamental attention to linguistic rights has taken a back seat to so-called accountability measures. These accountability measures, which more often than not promote a teach-to-the-test curriculum—particularly in low-income schools where the large majority of English-language learners attend—place a greater emphasis on high-stakes test scores than on the critical literacy skills that will enhance democratic participation and social empowerment.

In response, critical educators have challenged the misguided notion that elevated test scores automatically translate into highly literate and critically conscious students. Contrary to the rhetoric of No Child Left Behind advocates, high-stakes testing is neither the panacea for improving literacy and academic achievement among English-language learners nor working-class students in general. Instead, it represents a significant step backward in educational policy and practice—a situation that should particularly concern administrators, teachers, parents, and education activists within all low-income communities. In fact, the success of Proposition 227 or the English for the Children campaign in California (and in its revised formulation in states like Massachusetts and Arizona) represents the tip of the iceberg in neoliberal efforts to "turn back the clock" on linguistic rights. This is a disingenuous effort by conservatives to preserve structures of inequality and social exclusion in the United States, in the name of national unity and economic imperatives.

Ironically, it is as a direct consequence of U.S. foreign economic policies in Latin America and other parts of the globe that many immigrants have been forced to flee from regional wars and growing poverty. U.S. foreign trade agreements, such as GATT and NAFTA, have generated a decline in living standards both in this country and abroad. In the last decade, thousands of jobs have disappeared as factories have closed down shop and exported jobs to cheap labor markets around the world. The outcome of geopolitical economic crisis in Latin America has been particularly visible in California, which has historically served as a port of entry for a large percentage of Spanish-speaking immigrants.

Nearly 50 percent of the 40 million Latinos residing in California today are foreign born. In Los Angeles County alone, more than 4.2 million are Latino. And although the largest percentage is from Mexico, there is a growing number of immigrants from other Latin American countries, including El Salvador, Nicaragua, and Argentina. Latino and Asian populations are expected to experience the greatest growth, more than doubling their numbers by 2040. Meanwhile, population projections estimate that by the year 2020 Latinos will become the largest ethnic group in the state. This echoes national projections that "minority" residents will very soon become the majority of the population in most large urban centers, a reality that is already a fact in many large U.S. cities today. Moreover, the 2000 census documented an astonishing increase in Latino immigrants in the Deep South, showing Latino population increases of nearly 300 percent in North Carolina, Arkansas, Georgia, and Tennessee.

Yet, despite the growing diversity in languages in communities across the nation, public schools seldom link the importance of primary languages (other than English) to the notion of public good. Even in the presence of large linguistic communities other than English—such as the large Chicano/Mexican communities in the Southwest, indigenous-language communities on Native American reservations, large Chinese- and Japanese-speaking communities of northern California and New York, the French-speaking Cajun communities of Louisiana, the large Puerto Rican communities in Chicago and on the East Coast, and the growing Middle Eastern and African populations in such states as Washington and Oklahoma—the dominant culture of institutions has remained monolingually English speaking. Even with volumes written asserting the academic benefits of an additive approach to second-language acquisition, little has changed today with respect to the repressive politics of language rights in the United States.

Language as Public Good

Language is perhaps the quintessential public good.
—MICHAEL H. GOLDHABER[3]

In the popular meaning, the notion of the public good is generally tied with anything that concerns or affects a community of people. In the same vein, common good describes a specific "good" that is shared and beneficial for all (or most) members of a given community. The term *public good* is often used to refer to goods where it is not possible to exclude individuals from the goods' consumption. Language is considered a public good, since, technically, it is not considered possible to prevent people from speaking it, devoid of coercive measures.

Language, then, is a significant public good, for without the free flow of words, indeed there can be no public. Language does not derive its meanings through the private will of an individual speaker, but publicly, language is a communal phenomenon tied to shared linguistic rituals of sound and gestures. As Wittgenstein argues, a purely private language is impossible, meaningless.[4] Language requires acceptance and adoption by a community in continual public interchange. If language, then, is to retain its central value as a public medium of expression and communication, we cannot permit initiatives and reforms that subject any language to communal restrictions or legal restraint or threats of such restraint. In efforts to advocate for language rights, a clear rule is that all languages must be under minimal public constraint. However, over recent years, educational policies and corporate entities have moved more aggressively toward linguistic restrictions and constraints, with respect to the propagation of minority languages, in an effort to protect monolingualism as an imperative of the nation-state.

Thus, to reestablish minority languages as a public good, minority-language advocates must work to resist and counter institutional policies and practices to control and suppress their communal use. The most effective manner in which to accomplish this is to create and utilize a variety of public venues for acquisition, free use, and continued development—all considered effective in retaining the language use of subordinate languages. Hence, this points to the aggressive opposition to bilingual education, minority-language media, and general public use of Spanish by xenophobic nativists who adhere to the dominance of English. Stephen May[5] engages such oppositional perspectives and discusses the "temptation by English-only advocates to sanitize history" by ignoring the historical diversity of languages in America and the elimination of minority languages. Instead, conservative pundits assert the historical inevitability of the dominance of English, while turning a blind eye to restrictive language policies deliberately constructed, systematically imposed, and openly sanctioned by educational and other public institutions.

For example, historically, teachers were explicitly and in no uncertain terms told by principals that they were to speak English (only) when conversing with bilingual students and their parents. When I was a child in the 1950s, I was repeatedly humiliated, shamed, and punished for speaking Spanish in the classroom or even on the playground. The message that we, as bicultural children, received was very clear: Spanish is forbidden. Many educators today are quick to dismiss such horror stories as ancient history. But incidences of shaming and punishment for not adhering to an English-only rule of schools and employers persist today. In December 2005, the *Washington Post* ran a story entitled "Spanish at School Translates to Suspension."[6] The story focused on Zach Rubio, a sixteen-year-old boy suspended from a public high school for having a brief hallway exchange with another boy in Spanish. The teacher explained in her discipline referral that "This is not the first time we have [asked] Zach and others to not speak Spanish at school," as if the student's persistent practice of speaking his primary language were a reasonable cause for suspension or expulsion.

Language and the State

> Language conflicts...represent more than contending philosophies of assimilation and pluralism, disagreements about the rights and responsibilities of citizens or debates over the true meaning of "Americanism." Ultimately language politics are determined by material interests—that is, struggles for social and economic supremacy, which normally lurk beneath the surface of the public debate.
>
> —J. CRAWFORD[7]

On January 21, 1974, U.S. Supreme Court Justice William O. Douglas issued the historic decision that made *Lau v. Nichols* the major legal precedent regarding the educational rights of language minorities. However, the ruling was not based on constitutionality, but rather was grounded in the statute provided by Title VI of the Civil Rights Act of 1964. The court deemed that Chinese-speaking minority children in San Francisco received fewer benefits from the school system, which denied them a meaningful opportunity to participate in the educational programs of the district. The court held the district responsible for the children's "language deficiency" in failing to meet the language needs of these children. This ruling opened a new era in federal civil rights enforcement. The era was a time of a strong welfare state. Despite inequalities, there still remained a sense that the government, indeed, had a responsibility to protect the civil rights of the disenfranchised and assist in meeting the needs of those less fortunate.

Fast forward to the late 1980s and what we find is a deepening neoliberal, conservative force within the nation. The political economy of the capitalist state advanced its neoliberal solutions, which carefully constructed a conservative ethos of social justice and human rights. Reified notions of justice, devoid of history, context, or conditions, prevailed. This perspective categorically ignored the historical and contemporary disparities in material conditions and reintroduced more blatantly a victim-blaming ideology. Meanwhile, economic frustrations and insecurities of workers and small producers were on the rise; real incomes had been suffering a downward trajectory since 1973 with decreasing assistance of the government to contend with their plight. These conditions intensified throughout the

1990s, when again real wages of workers dropped dramatically, even as corporate profits boomed.

With the dismantling of the welfare state, the liberal idea that the state should care for the needy was supplanted by neoconservative notions of social justice. With unbridled fervor and shameless disregard of the masses, neoconservatives and liberals alike busily channeled massive expenditures toward the military and prison industrial complex, while poverty worsened across the nation. Meanwhile, a similar dynamic was at work in the international arena of globalization, where Keynesian-inspired policies were systematically displaced by the neoconservative philanthropic policies of the International Monetary Fund and the World Bank—wreaking havoc in third world nations, all in the name of progress and modernization.

In the midst of national anxieties provoked by the rapidly changing political and economic landscape, xenophobic attitudes began to resurface publicly in the political imagination. These reactions were crystallized by public figures like Patrick Buchanan and his "take back" America rhetoric.[8] New "middle-class" anxieties about the declining quality of life, overcrowding, crime, rootlessness, and incivility, all of which find a scapegoat in our growing multiculturalism,[9] exacerbated and morphed into reactionary anti-immigrant sentiments at almost every level of society. Accordingly, conservative forces went into a frenzy attacking public policies and practices that promoted cultural or linguistic diversity. In 1998, US English released an ad that read, "Deprive a child of an education. Handicap a young life outside the classroom. Restrict social mobility. If it came at the hand of a parent it would be called child abuse. At the hand of our schools...it's called 'bilingual education.'"[10]

During an aggressive economic restructuring in the 1980s and increasing immigration from Latin America, English-only activism seemed to have come out of nowhere, with an in-your-face racism that many thought had ended with the civil rights movement of the 1960s. Previously no one had warned that the nation's dominant language was endangered by the encroachment of other tongues— creeping bilingualism—or that it needed "legal protection" in the United States. Suddenly there were legislative campaigns to give English official status, an idea never proposed at the federal level before 1981—to restrict the public use of minority languages. In concert with the rhetoric of the campaign, Official English measures have been adopted by twenty-three states.

In 1996, for the first time, Congress voted on and the House of Representatives approved a bill designating English as the federal government's sole language of official business. Coincidentally, it was in the same year that the campaign for Proposition 227 was initiated, which ushered in the gradual but steady demise of bilingual education in California public schools. Since the *Lau v. Nichols* decision, bilingual education in the state had enjoyed some legitimacy and attention, within the context of both state and national educational public policy arenas. The success of Proposition 227 systematically stripped away the right of bilingual communities to claim bilingual instruction as an educational right protected by law—a right that had been so painfully earned during the civil rights era. As a consequence, minority-language students found themselves immersed in English-only classes, while bilingual education advocates struggled to retain a limited foothold on bilingual education in public schools. In California, Governor Schwarzenegger vetoed a bill authorizing various academic subjects to be tested in Spanish in the state's public schools. Efforts to prevent teachers from offering parents bilingual waivers and to roadblock the recertification of the bilingual teaching credential were not only part of a nationwide campaign for English-only policies and practices within public schools but also an increasing anti-immigrant sentiment that still prevails, as is witnessed by the recent legislative action in Arizona to both sanitize the curriculum of ethnic studies and dismantle bilingual education.

Regardless of the immense potential for rich linguistic diversity that exists in the United States, an assimilative linguistic imperative predominates. And although minority-language rights enjoyed a moment of vogue, the movement to support language rights proved to be short lived and terribly insufficient in nature—perhaps teaching us that any radical educational struggle, without a grounded political movement, is limited in transformative possibility. Hence, seldom was the deep-rooted racism or class privilege associated with dominant-language policies and practices effectively unveiled—policies and practices that not only violate the principles of language as a public good but ultimately support linguistic genocide in this country and around the globe.

Linguistic Genocide

> All nation-states, whatever their political ideology, have persecuted minorities in the past and many continue to do so today. Many immigrants to the U.S. were "indoctrinated" to think that their languages and cultures were inferior and therefore had to be abandoned for the sake of being American. Widespread assimilationist policies are generally ignored, since there is an assumption that assimilation is voluntary and uncoerced.
>
> —D. NETTLE AND S. ROMAINE[11]

Statistics on academic achievement point to the persistent practice of the United States, as a modern nation-state, to blatantly racialize language-minority populations within our borders—particularly when such actions are judged by the dominant class to be in the interest of national security or economic well-being. More often than not, the move to obtain cultural and class dominion over a nation's diverse population has rendered minority-language speakers problematic to capitalist accumulation. To ensure that the "other" was (and is) kept in line with the system of production, a variety of racialized institutional policies and practices have been implemented during the nation's history—policies and practices that have led to the widespread deportation, assimilation, incarceration, and even genocide of minority populations.

Tove Skutnabb-Kangas,[12] a leading international biodiversity and linguistic rights advocate, argues that the majority of language communities over the last hundred years have become victims of linguistic genocide—that is, where the language is killed rather than the person. Without question, she associates this genocide with the destruction of potential competition for political and economic power, in order to eliminate any claims to nation-state rights among indigenous and minority populations. This view provides a hint to the linguistic genocide associated with the plight of African Americans who were separated from their families and forced into slave labor; the Diné who were stripped of much of their land, their children arbitrarily removed to English-speaking boarding schools; and Mexican, Puerto Rican, and Chinese workers who were exploited for cheap labor and subjected to substandard housing and schooling. Similar mechanisms of language loss are at work today in public schools where students are systematically ushered into English-only environments, not only preventing them from learning their primary language, but socializing them into an inadequate educational process that does little to promote their cultural and material empowerment.

Given the pressure and strain of surviving such conditions, many students have now lost much of their linguistic connection to their ancestral culture. Again, key to this discussion is the manner in which racism, manifested through linguistic genocide, is intricately linked to political economic power, control of natural resources, and the subordination of those inferiorized as the "other" within U.S. society. As job opportunities decline, policing of the barrios, anti-immigrant sentiments, and English-only campaigns intensify, tightening the very controls that were loosened at an earlier time when the need for cheap, unskilled labor existed. This intensification is fueled by the debates of conservative political gatekeepers who allege that undocumented immigrants take jobs away from citizens, lower property values, threaten law and order, consume education and welfare resources, and, now, constitute a national security risk.

Current anti-immigrant sentiments and efforts to thwart bilingualism are every bit as politically vicious as they were in the earlier decades of the twentieth century—fueled by similar political alliances and the xenophobic nativist rhetoric of conservative policymakers and big business. Specific conditions that parallel both these historical eras include increasing immigration, burgeoning student enrollments in urban centers, economic decline, and overt military spending overseas. Assimilative policies and practices developed then continue to shape the hidden barriers that stall the implementation of language rights and critical literacy reform efforts today.

Critical Literacy as a Moral Imperative

There is no unity between school and life, and so there is no automatic unity between instruction and education. In the school, the nexus between instruction and education can only be realized by the living work of the teacher.

—A. GRAMSCI[13]

Critical literacy is intricately tied to the living work of the classroom teacher. This is so because literacy and ideology are linked by the very relationships that sustain material inequality and exclusionary social forces within schools and society. More simply put, ideology shapes the legitimation of knowledge within schools and underlies the hidden curriculum of literacy instruction. This constitutes an important factor, as we consider the values and beliefs of classroom teachers and the educational formation that they have received in teacher education programs.

Unfortunately, despite the increasing diversity of the U.S. population, many of the traditional homogenizing pedagogical notions persist. These notions essentially incorporate, on the one hand, the belief that cultural and class differences are a malady that must be remedied or stomped out in order for students from subordinate populations to achieve academically. On the other hand, students who are considered to be the "other" are deemed intellectually suspect, unable to accommodate to academic expectations. As a consequence, there are few curricular materials for literacy instruction that fundamentally respect the cultural and class values and beliefs that students bring to the classroom. Instead, teacher perceptions of English-language learners and other students considered outside the mainstream, along with the pedagogical materials they employ, often function to perpetuate notions of deficit and structures of inequality—despite their well-meaning efforts.

If teachers, then, are to engage effectively in the literacy instruction of English-language learners, they must be prepared to examine their personal views and perspectives related to how minority students use language, their accents, and their variant speech patterns. But this alone is not enough. Beyond individual reflection, teachers must also become cognizant of the ideological dimensions that underscore the curriculum and educational processes that are most often promoted in schools for the teaching of language and literacy skills. They must learn to decode the racialized, gendered, class, homophobic, and other oppressive meanings that are encoded in curricular materials that appear neutral and benign yet carry real consequences of social exclusion.

It is also important that teachers understand the manner in which ideology has a profound impact on educational policies and curricular decisions made by federal, state, and local policymakers. Ideology, with its unexamined assumptions, functions as an interpretive lens to both determine and sustain relations of power as well as the distribution of authority, resources, and opportunities within schools. As such, ideology is central to the material subordination of working-class populations, including minority-language communities. In this respect, linguistic and cultural formations represent significant material forces that are meaningful in light of the racialized conditions of inequality faced by oppressed populations.

If teachers are to become effective in their classroom literacy efforts, they must rigorously interrogate the consequences of literacy policies and practices in the lives of the students they teach. The unwillingness of many teachers to step outside the familiar terrain of mainstream literacy instruction converts them into just another problem that students must contend with in the course of their public school education. To counter this phenomenon, teachers must embrace, as part of their living work, a willingness to question critically the consequences of their literacy practice. They must interrogate the consequences of the curriculum they are implementing and pursue with students and their parents possible alternatives that can function to create opportunities for "getting real" about the literacy development needs of English-language learners. "Getting real" here also means that teachers recognize cultural, cognitive, and linguistic differences as central to a dynamic and stimulating educational environment and an authentic democratic body politic. In addition, teachers must take note that differences in culture and cognition are also tied to class differences and alternative strategies for survival, within the context of a society that is not only highly diverse but economically unjust.

In order for teachers to contend successfully with the differences in problem-solving and communication styles that their students bring to the classroom, they must work to create a living classroom experience of democracy, where oppressive structures can be courageously challenged and transformed. Unfortunately, the failure to engage with the realities of students' lives results in an educational process that is abstracted and disconnected. This ultimately functions to further alienate English-language learners not only from their relationship with their teachers, but from their ability to participate actively in the knowledge construction necessary to become empowered and literate human beings.

In making a case for a critical literacy instruction that engages student experience as a central component does not mean that this is where the educational process ends—for this is actually the beginning. Critical literacy constitutes an approach where the intimacy of learning established between teachers and students opens the field for examining and reexamining together their particular and shared views about the world. In this way, they learn to affirm, question, resist, challenge, and transform their views, through an experience of knowledge construction grounded in a democratic process of participation, voice, and action in their everyday lives.

When teachers utilize a critical approach to literacy development that integrates issues associated with culture, language, and class, they are better able to infuse vitality into the emancipatory dynamics of their teaching. By so doing, English-language learners are challenged to consider in meaningful ways the experiences and perceptions that shape their cultural histories and class realities. This is tied to assisting students to explore the manner in which they ascribe meaning to their everyday lives and how they construct what they perceive as knowledge and truth. Literacy here becomes more than just simply a functional process of learning to read and write. Instead it becomes an opportunity for students to not only learn about themselves and their histories in ways that are meaningful and in concert with the struggles they face each day but also become critically literate about the manner in which power and privilege operate. They learn through their personal engagement with texts and the world how, why, by whom, and for whom knowledge is constructed. This speaks to a literacy development that fosters the confidence of students to openly question, think creatively, become inventive, and hence, more expansively explore and name their world.

Inherent in a critical approach to literacy development is also the expectation that reflection, dialogue, and action—namely praxis—within the classroom will also function as the foundation for establishing school involvement among the parents of English-language learners. Through an emphasis on critique, dialogue, and conscientization, a critical pedagogical approach to literacy supports a problem-posing pedagogy in which the relationship of students to teachers and teachers to parents is, unquestionably, dialogical in nature. Within the context of critical dialogue, there must exist an implicit faith in the capacity of teachers, students, and parents to participate collaboratively in the process of schooling, with each having something to contribute and gain through their participation. It is through meaningful interactions and the establishment of working collectively for the benefit of students that teachers and parents construct intimate relationships of solidarity and school community coherence.

Lastly, ethics, civic responsibility, and literacy as a moral imperative must also be significant features of how teachers comprehend the significance of critical literacy, particularly in the lives of disenfranchised students who must constantly resist the oppressive structures and practices that defile their dreams. Whether to affirm, resist, or transform their lives, English-language learners must develop the skills for voice and participation—skills that can be garnered only through their development as ethical and moral subjects of history. It is for this reason that Paulo Freire[14] repeatedly insisted that ethics had to occupy an increasingly significant role in our pedagogy and our scholarship. To critical educators of literacy committed to democratic principles of everyday life, ethics must be understood as a political and pedagogical question that in the final analysis constitutes a moral one. For without morality, education becomes an instrument of oppression. Here, we must not mistake morality for moralism. Instead, being moral is to explore deeply the texture and quality of human behavior, ideas, and practices in the living—which cannot be done by abstracting our students from their social surrounding, from their culture, from their language, or from their histories of survival. This requires instead that we interweave the pedagogical with the moral and political, where literacy development recognizes that "ethics is about excelling at being human, and nobody can do this in isolation."[15]

Along the same vein, the pernicious legacy of racisms—the multiplicity of ideologies, policies, and practices that result in the racialization of populations and the destruction of linguistic rights—must be understood in the context of everyday struggles and the formation of student identities. Here, identities are often conditioned by a capitalist-inspired language curriculum, fueled by fabricated consumer sensibilities of gendered, racialized, homophobic, and nationalist patriotic notions of "the good life." Moreover, it is this core ideological process that sustains the ravages of globalization and that must be challenged and dismantled if poverty and human suffering are to be eradicated.

In light of this, critical educators must come to terms with the fact that injustice "is not an unfortunate aberration of capitalism, but an inescapable outcome and an essential condition of its successful economic functioning. Capitalism is—and this is surely as clear today as it ever was—a social system based on class and competition."[16] Capitalism functions as a globalized system, which requires as its prerequisite the deep impoverishment and exclusion of three quarters of the world's population. Given this reality, it is unfortunate that so many theories and practices of literacy development function conveniently to deaden and annul opposition to the capitalist order, while existing social controls are conserved even in the wake of increasing impoverishment and incarceration. Meanwhile, the marketplace continues to move people away from few, modest needs to the creation of many false needs, through the use of advertising and the belief that consumption equals happiness.[17] Oftentimes, these beliefs are carefully hidden behind the assimilative notions and ideas that masquerade as literacy education in the United States.

Capitalism disembodies and alienates our daily existence within the larger society and within classroom life. As the consciousness of teachers and students becomes more and more abstracted, they become more and more detached from their material bodies. For this reason, it is absolutely imperative that critical educators acknowledge that the origin of emancipatory possibility and human solidarity resides in our bodies. And as such, language constitutes the vehicle by which the body's needs, wants, desires, fears, joys, aspirations, and hopes are expressed. Given the relationship of the body to a student's linguistic faculties, critical literacy development cannot effectively take place in the absence of the body's full participation. This is only possible when students' linguistic experiences, within the classroom and the larger society, are understood as integral to their humanity and their liberation as full citizens of the world.

ENDNOTES

1 J.L. Amariglio, S.A. Resnick, and R.W. Wolff, "Class, Power, and Culture," in C. Nelson and L. Grossberg (eds.), *Marxism and the Interpretation of Culture* (Chicago: University of Illinois Press, 1988).

2 B. Spolsky, "Language Policy," Proceedings of the 4th International Symposium on Bilingualism (Somerville, MA: Cascadilla Press, 2005).

3 M.H. Goldhaber, "Language as a Public Good Under Threat: The Private Ownership of Brand Names."(1999)http://www.well.com/~mgoldh/Language_as_Public_Good.html

4 S. Kripeke, *Wittgenstein on Rules and Private Language* (Cambridge: Harvard University Press, 1982).

5 S. May, "Language Rights: Implications for Liberal Political Theory," in W. Kymlicka and A. Pattern (eds.), *Language Rights and Political Theory* (London: Oxford University Press, 2003), 129–31.

6 T.R. Reid, "Spanish at School Translates to Suspension," *Washington Post*; December 9, 2005.

7 J. Crawford, *At War with Diversity: U.S. Language Policy in an Age of Anxiety* (129–131) Clevedon, UK: Multilingual Matters, 2000).

8   See: http://buchanan.org/blog/1992-republican-national-convention-speech-148.

9   J. Fishman, *Reversing Language Shift: Theoretical and Empirical Foundations of Assistance to Threatened Minority Languages* (Clevedon, UK: Multilingual Matters, 1991).

10 S. May, "The Politics of Homogeneity: A Critical Exploration of the Anti-bilingual Education Movement," *Proceedings of the 4th International Symposium on Bilingualism* (Somerville, MA: Cascadilla Press, 2005), 1561.

11 D. Nettle and S. Romaine, *Vanishing Voices: The Extinction of the World's Languages* (London: Oxford University Press, 2002, 19.

12 T. Skutnabb-Kangas, *Linguistic Genocide in Education—or Worldwide Diversity and Human Rights?* (Mahwah, NJ: Lawrence Erlbaum Associates, 2000).

13 A. Gramsci, *Selections from The Prison Notebooks* (New York: International Publishers, 1971), 35.

14 P. Freire, *Pedagogy of the City* (New York: Continuum, 1971), *Pedagogy of Hope* (New York: Continuum, 1996), and *Teachers as Cultural Workers* (Boulder, CO: Westview, 1998).

15 T. Eagleton, *After Theory* (New York: Basic Books, 2003), 142.

16 S. Gindin, S. (2002). "Anti-Capitalism and Social Justice," *Monthly Review* 53, no. 9 (2002): 3.

17 R.A. Brosio, *A Radical Critique of Capitalist Education* (New York: Peter Lang, 1994).

CHAPTER 12

The Politics of Restrictive Language Policies

A Postcolonial Analysis of Language and Schooling

With Miren Uriarte

[A]ny meaningful analysis of the post-colonial situation in society requires an interpretation of the historically situated material, political, and cultural circumstances out of which policies of language use are produced.

—THEMBA MOYO (2009)

Central to the history of colonization has been the use of restrictive language policies to ensure the exclusion of racialized populations from full participation within the economic and political landscape of the nation-state. Hence, understanding the educational barriers of exclusion, along with the academic impact that such language policies produce, are the central questions that strike at the heart of this postcolonial analysis. More specifically, we examine the manner in which restrictive language policies were implemented over a four-year period within the public schools of Boston, Massachusetts, following the passage of Referendum Question 2 in 2002, a mandate to repeal the use of transitional bilingual education in favor of immersion programs. This story is particularly poignant in that Massachusetts was the first state in the nation to officially enact, in 1971, a transitional bilingual program to meet the needs of the state's growing Spanish-speaking student population. But that was the era of civil rights, when a myriad of educational efforts to address the long-standing historical inequalities faced by children in communities of color were being moved forward by civil rights activists everywhere.

Today, however, it seems that previously held goals of educational equality and social concern for the most disenfranchised have fallen by the wayside, displaced by conservative solutions that assert the practicality and superiority of restrictive language policies in schools. Instead, neoliberal priorities have forcefully taken precedence over the goal of equality, despite educational rhetoric about the need to "narrow achievement gaps." Accordingly, business agendas and corporatist approaches prevailed, creating strong pressures for accountability structures and measures that have often trumped sound educational practices. Complex testing schemes bind the work of teaching and learning, while punitive practices tied to high-stakes testing create inordinately stressful environments for both students and teachers. This is further exacerbated by privatizing initiatives that invite charter schools to compete with declining public educational funds. Similarly, accountability practices single out underperforming students and schools, which could result in positive outcomes were material and pedagogical resources mobilized to address the needs, but instead such measures are being enacted precisely at the same time as the capacity of districts and schools to respond to the needs of English-language learners has become ever more limited.

Over the last two decades, Massachusetts, as is true across the nation, has experienced a rapid increase in immigration, and with it an increasing enrollment of speakers of languages other than English in its public schools. This phenomenon is now at work in most major urban centers but also has become increasingly an issue for large suburban and rural areas as well. The underlying cause of this unprecedented demographic shift is unquestionably the result of economic conditions that have given rise to job instabilities, not only in the United States but globally. An examination of restrictive language policies and their implementation within the Boston schools serves as an excellent site of inquiry, in that it mimics many of the same conditions currently at work in the schooling of English learners across the nation.

Anchoring our "interpretation [within] the historically material, political, and cultural circumstances out of which policies of language use are produced," as Themba Moyo suggests, is particularly salient here, given that the majority of English learners in Boston are from populations whose personal histories are deeply marked by the impact of colonization—Puerto Rico, the Dominican Republic, Haiti, and Cape Verde, just to name a few. Hence, our analysis of the politics of language and schooling is enhanced by a postcolonial reading, which provides us the analytical specificities to make sense of restrictive language policies across the larger national landscape, given the impact of these policies on the lives of (post)colonized students from impoverished working-class communities.

Our effort here is to engage concerns tied to language and inequalities front and center, shattering any illusions that languages other than English in the United States are genuinely welcomed and cultivated in public schools. Nothing could be further from the truth. Even in the light of research that specifically speaks to the cognitive advantages of bilingualism in sharpening intelligence and the capacity to engage more expansively within the world,[1] education in the United States has been and continues to be firmly grounded upon chauvinistic traditions of linguistic domination upheld by the colonizers who "culturally invaded," to use Paulo Freire's (1970) words, the Western hemisphere. Hence, just as colonial formations of slavery, land dispossession, and wealth extraction were enacted upon racialized subjects worldwide to ensure dominion, so were restrictive language practices that, in many cases, resulted in linguistic genocide and cultural erosion (Darder and Torres 2004; Skatnubb-Kangas 2000; Freire and Macedo 1987).

Furthermore, restrictive language policies can formidably be traced to political economic exigencies of the nation-state that seek to safeguard the control of its working populations in order to ensure the quasi-stability of its ever-increasing low-wage service sector—a labor market that requires a growing sector to be minimally educated. In fact, Jean Anyon (2005) asserts that "most job openings in the next ten years will not require either sophisticated skills or a college degree. Seventy-five percent of new and projected jobs will be low paying. Most will require on-the-job training only, and will not require college; most will be in service and retail, where poverty zone wages are the norm" (370). Simultaneously, more and more manufacturing and technical jobs continue to be outsourced to cheap centers of a now-global workforce, increasing competition for access to the shrinking elite workforce of the knowledge economy, which is simply unable to absorb the growing population of U.S. workers—the largest number now coming from historically racialized communities.

This infusion of material conditions is significant to our analysis in that, generally speaking, many advocates for bilingual education programs over the years have discussed questions of language and schooling in provincial or romanticized cultural terms, without linking the imperatives of culture, language, and identity to questions of collective sustainability, social agency, and class struggle. This is to say, there has been a failure to consider the education of English learners and their language rights with greater analytical depth, despite the manner in which workers are positioned within the U.S. political economy. Yet, it is only through such discussions that we can begin to get at the core assumptions at work in the construction of educational language policies that impede the academic success of English learners in U.S. schools—who, contrary to public opinion, are overwhelmingly U.S. citizens and not exclusively undocumented immigrants, as the media and nativists would have us believe. Hence, we argue that current restrictive language policies for English-language learners must be critically interrogated in relationship to not only high school dropout rates, poor academic performance, or college attrition rates but also the long-term consequences associated with lack of educational attainment. Typically, these consequences include housing segregation and labor (non)participation patterns, rising incarceration rates, and growing conditions of poverty—all intimately linked to the social arrangements responsible for the reproduction of racism and gross class inequalities.

Inseparability of Racism and Class Inequalities

> Language conflicts...represent more than contending philosophies of assimilation and pluralism, disagreements about the rights and responsibilities of citizens or debates over the true meaning of "Americanism." Ultimately language politics are determined by material interests—that is, struggles for social and economic supremacy, which normally lurk beneath the surface of the public debate.
>
> —J. CRAWFORD (2000, 10)

Racism as an inherently political strategy of exclusion, domination, and exploitation cannot be extricated from its economic imperative, whether discussing questions of academic achievement or larger concerns tied to labor opportunities. Segregation, for example, as an outcome of racialization and class reproduction, is firmly entrenched within the wider systematic necessity of a capitalist mode of production—which supports policies and practices within schools and the labor market that sustain the skewed economic interests of capital.

As such, inequalities resulting from restrictive language policies generally operate in sync with structures that perpetuate school segregation. Studies conducted in the last decade by the Civil Rights Project (Orfield 1999, 2001; Orfield and Lee 2007) found that although progress toward school desegregation peaked in the late 1980s, as the court concluded that the goals of *Brown v. Board of Education* had been largely achieved, 15 years later the trend has moved in the opposite direction (Orfield 1999). Questions of segregation, therefore, still remain salient factors, particularly for working-class Latino populations—now dubbed "the new face of segregation"—given that Latino students find themselves even more segregated today than their African American counterparts. This increase in Latino segregation has been particularly marked in western states, where more than 80 percent of Latino students attend segregated schools, compared with 42 percent in 1968 (Dobbs 2004). In the Northeast, 78 percent of Latino students attend schools with over 50 percent minority student population, and 46 percent attend schools with over 90 percent minority population (Orfield 1999). Similar patterns are quickly emerging in the South, where Latino population increases have been reported to exceed 300 percent in North Carolina, Arkansas, Georgia, and Tennessee. Thus, it should not be surprising to learn that 90 percent of neighborhood schools where English-language learners and children of color—most of whom are, in fact, citizens—attend are all located in areas of concentrated poverty. Moreover, students of color who are English-language learners are eleven times more likely to live in areas of concentrated poverty than students of all ethnicities who attend predominantly "white" schools.

It is also significant to note that socioeconomic conditions that are clear producers of gross racialized inequalities, such as lack of job security; insufficient income(s) to care for one's family; dwindling youth employment; the demise of "middle-class" union jobs; lack of health care; expanding poverty; and increasing incarceration of working-class men and women of color are seldom raised as key factors in discussions of language and schooling. Yet, such conditions of political and economic disenfranchisement ensure greater incidence of residential segregation as well, which has been found to be a significant factor in the English-language development of children from language-minority communities. This is so, in that English learners, who are taught exclusively within English-only classrooms, are more likely to struggle with a home-school linguistic transition process that expects them to isolate and compartmentalize their language usage in ways that have been found to disrupt not only English-language development but academic achievement patterns (Genesee et al. 2006; Cummins 2000; Crawford 2000; Valenzuela 1999). Consequently, recent reports belie notions that sheltered English instruction will radically improve student performance. In fact, studies show no considerable improvement in rates of English acquisition (Thomas and Collier 2002). Moreover, what cannot be overlooked here is the loss of bilingual programs, which once afforded English-language learners the opportunity to study academic content in their primary language, while learning English (Genesee et al., 2006; Suarez-Orozco and Suarez-Orozco 2001; Portes and Rumbaut 2001; Tollefson 2004; Cummins 2000; Skatnubb-Kangas 2000).

Complaints of cost have also been used by conservative forces to rally popular opposition to appropriate bilingual education programs for English-language learners. Yet, absent from these discussions are the trillions of dollars being poured yearly into military spending, while public welfare concerns are redefined by neo-liberal interests in such ways that essentially abdicate the State of its responsibility to adequately educate all children attending U.S. schools, including English learn-ers. Instead, a sink-or-swim philosophy tied to the ethos of free market enterprise has overwhelmingly penetrated the policy-making arena of educational language policies. As such, one-year English immersion programs have become the pre-ferred mainstream intervention, despite overwhelming evidence collected over the last four decades that challenges the folly of an expedited English-only approach and exposes the negative academic consequences to the academic formation of English learners, save for the small number who succeed and are then paraded as the exceptions in racialized populations stereotypically perceived as less intel-ligent, less communicative, and less psychologically able to contend with main-stream expectations of schooling (Darder and Torres 2004).

Here, we want to note that although state laws may call for only a one-year immersion program for language support, most English-language learners must remain in these programs a longer period of time. This is not surprising, in that studies consistently indicate that students require six years to learn English pro-ficiently, even under conditions that provide them "cognitively complex curri-cula that develop thinking skills, through both their first and second languages" (Collier and Thomas 2010). However, both the use of English immersion strate-gies and the overwhelming intent of districts to mainstream these students quickly lead to conditions where English learners are not offered sufficient subject content in either their mother tongue or English, yet are expected to perform adequately on tests that do not account for these debilitating academic conditions.

Even more disconcerting is the lack of adequate training and preparation that mainstream educators, including school psychologists, receive in the areas of appropriate teaching strategies and language assessment protocols for English-language learners. This, unfortunately, perpetuates false beliefs—again, despite research to the contrary—that teachers and allied personnel do not require any additional preparation to teach or assess English-language learners, given that innately "intelligent" children will surely excel no matter what type of educational program is offered them. Such fallacious conservative arguments allow school dis-tricts, if they choose, to relinquish any responsibility to provide professional devel-opment to mainstream educators, who are inexperienced in teaching or assessing English-language learners. One of the most striking consequences of this lack of knowledge is the statistically significant number of English-language learn-ers, compared to their English-proficient counterparts, who are referred to spe-cial education programs for questionable intelligence, communicative disorders, and developmental delays (English Language Learners Sub committee 2009). Of course, given restrictive language policies implemented in most school districts and the lack of preparation in teacher education programs, classroom teachers alone cannot be held responsible for this unfortunate institutional deficiency.

All this said, it is striking to note that in the last two decades, as well-paying jobs in the United States began to disappear in the wake of the globalizing agenda of neoliberal interests and its shock doctrine economics, exclusionary restrictive language policies, along with mean-spirited anti-immigrant debates, have surged. As a consequence, deep racialized resentments have been generated by job scarcity and subsequent competition across working-class and immigrant populations. Moreover, this misdirected resentment has been capitalized on by conservative forces not only to garner support from English-speaking working-class populations for English-only policies but also to confuse parents of English-language learners into believing that English-only instruction is in the best interest of their children. Even more disturbing is the manner in which victim-blaming rhetoric, aimed at English-language learners and other students from racialized communities who fail to succeed in public schools has been repeatedly used to obscure the deepening structures of economic inequality inherent in U.S. capitalism.

Moreover, contradictory class-based attitudes are widespread with respect to bilingualism in the United States. For example, while elite private schools place an increasing emphasis on the development of bilingual language skills for "global citizenship," and wealthy transnational corporations send high-ranking employees to Latin America, China, or other countries to learn a second language so they can compete more readily within the global marketplace, English-language learners in U.S. public schools—who most readily could develop bilingual skills—are being forced into English-only programs. Similarly, affluent public schools offer gifted language programs in Spanish, French, or Chinese, while these opportunities are almost nonexistent in low-income schools, where most English-language learners attend and where little effort is placed on expanding knowledge of their primary languages. Hence, access to genuine bilingual development and the cultural and global advantages it affords is a prerogative only of students from affluent classes. As such, racism and class inequalities fully converge in contradictory ways to perpetuate linguistic racialization.

The Process of Linguistic Racialization

The cultural imperialism of the last century relegated the language of the colonized to a peripheral role by excluding it from

institutions such as the education system—at issue are the role
and status of language & its people.

—PAUL SPOOLEY (1993)

In light of a colonial history of language imposition, a postcolonial lens is useful
in forging an analysis of restrictive language policies and their impact on English-
language learners, in that it historicizes conditions of language loss beyond that of
individual choice or the practical inducement of English for academic and labor
success. Moreover, views of language as "purely mechanical devices" (Nieto 2007)
or solely signifiers of national allegiance can be de-centered as we engage with the
powerful reality that language, political power, and economics are all inextricably
tied to the ideological formations of the nation-state, and, as such, language functions as a fundamental human resource for the construction of meaning and the
establishment of relationships within both the private and the public spheres. "In
fact, the human being cannot exist without communicating; eliminating the possibility of communication from the human spirit entails removing its humanity"
(Nieto 2007).

This is precisely the experience of many English-language learners when they
enter a classroom where the supremacy of English functions not only against their
academic well-being but against their democratic participation as well. Upon
entering the English-only classroom, English-language learners are rendered
voiceless in a foreign sound system and cultural milieu that does not afford them
a place for self-expression or self-determination. And often, even when these students learn English, stereotypical perceptions of deficiency persist, which deny
them meaningful opportunities to participate that English proficient students
readily enjoy in the process of their learning, considered critical to effective academic formation. Without these opportunities, the ability of English-language
learners to succeed in school is overwhelmingly compromised, as they struggle
not only to learn the grade-level content but also grapple with traversing limited
language comprehension in a context that affords them little, if any, language support (Freire and Macedo 1987; Darder 2002; Valenzuela 1999).

Hence, it is no wonder that language constitutes such a deeply contested
terrain of struggle in the education of English-language learners. Instructional
language is, thus, implicated in significant ways when considering the future possibilities and limitations students will experience not only in the classroom but
also out in the world. Similarly, community conditions that infuse life, meaning,
and belonging to individual and collective life are important factors in their academic achievement as well, given that education, economics, political voice, and
democratic participation are significant to minority-language community empow-

erment. This is to say that when important human conditions shaped by a long-standing history of oppression and marginalization are ignored, disregarded, or maligned within schools, the political empowerment and well-being of English-language learners and their families are also negatively affected (Olivos 2006; Darder 2002, 1991). This process can, unfortunately, leave language-minority communities at the mercy of a hegemonic process that prevents them from naming their world and, hence, from participating in significant educational language policy debates and decisions that will impact their children's destiny.

As a consequence, English-language learners, who enter the classroom with a primary language other than English, as mentioned earlier, are often (mis) assessed too quickly as intellectually deficient or developmentally delayed, as a consequence of assessment measures that do not take into account the dissonance experienced by otherwise intellectually capable children entering into a new language context. Unfortunately, the linguistic forms of racialization at work in the schooling of English-language learners, or what Angela Valenzuela (1999) terms "subtractive schooling," disrupt the ability of both educators and policy makers to see beyond their shrouded projections of inferiority—a phenomenon that stifles the ability to recognize, assess, and employ the strengths and capacities these students already possess.

Thus, unexamined racialized perceptions of English-language learners often, unwittingly, render teachers blind to those cognitive resources that would normally provide the logical foundation for the new linguistic experience of learning English. Accordingly, the inability of mainstream teachers to engage the knowledge and skills that English-language learners bring to the classroom is a key barrier to academic success, as is the absence of the primary language as the medium of instruction, which not only discourages the use of minority languages in the United States but also disrupts the successful academic formation of marginalized students, who are further rendered vulnerable by restrictive language policies and practices.

In many ways, we can understand the task at hand, even today, to be one that requires us to decolonize our minds from debilitating beliefs that persistently racialize English-language learners, quickly judging them in need of remediation yet unworthy of the expenditure of additional resources. In the logic of Race to the Top (RTT) and its predecessor, No Child Left Behind (NCLB), the goal of education is to create the global competitive edge that can ensure domination of the world's political economy—at the expense of children from the most vulnerable populations. As such, expenditures of educational resources are liberally being directed toward science, technology, engineering, and mathematics (STEM) in the government's frenzied attempt to meet its overarching goal. In the world of high-stakes accountability, STEM initiatives are pronounced the grand scheme for progress and global supremacy, while questions of democratic life have been almost entirely eclipsed.

In accordance, linguistic racialization here is implicated as part of a larger and more complex system of economic and political oppression that positions English-language learners and their families as disposable, second-class citizens (Darder and Torres 2004). This encompasses a process of racialization that often distorts the ability to see working-class minority-language communities in the United States as worthy of full educational rights. The consequence is the perpetuation of a culture of failure and educational neglect that relegates these communities to a politically invisible netherland—aided by the politics of the labor market, ill representations of the media, and the increasing incarceration of poor working-class men and women of color (Gilmore 2006).

Linguistic racialization within schools is further exacerbated by what Phillipson (2008) argues are the deleterious socioeconomic and cultural effects of the colonial language and the failure of elected leaders to implement a consistently democratic language policy. Indifference to the negative consequences of English-only instruction is particularly debilitating for working-class students who enter school as predominantly Spanish speakers. Unfortunately, as already discussed earlier, the failure of schools to engage the material conditions that these students and their families navigate daily circumvents accurate assessment and the development of public language policies and educational practices to support their effective academic development. And, despite the fact that Latino students can comprise 50 to 90 percent of the total student population in many districts, there has been a stubborn unwillingness to critically engage the manner in which the language needs of these children may differ. This is often reflected in the manner in which educators are trained to understand and contend, if at all, with the needs of Spanish-speaking children as only individuals, rather than as being within a larger collective history of colonization, often taking place *within* their own lands. This is particularly the case for Puerto Ricans in the Northeast and Chicanos in the Southwest, both groups whose racialized histories are indelibly fused with the African Diaspora and indigenous populations through processes often referred to as "miscegenation" and "mestizaje" (Anzaldúa 1987; Rodriguez 2000; Valle and Torres 2000).

Central to this history is a Spanish-speaking population that overwhelmingly comprises the largest minority group in the United States. Los Angeles, for example, is second only to Mexico City as the city with the largest number of Spanish speakers. Other large Spanish-speaking populations are found in cities like New York, Miami, and Chicago, with Boston's Latino population having grown swiftly in the last two decades. This is to argue that the educational needs and politics of language conservation in these instances warrant greater collective reconsideration and community participation, given that "Spanish speakers represent 75% of the nation's English learners" (Collier and Thomas 2010) and in Boston, a full 25 percent of the student population are now considered English learners (Uriarte et al. 2010).

Yet, whenever there are efforts to engage more substantively with the significance of this phenomenon in the schooling of English learners, policy makers and district officials quickly retort that there are over a hundred languages spoken in many of these districts, and ask how teachers can be expected to realistically meet the language needs of all these children. Rather than simply devolve into classically individualistic views of English-learner students or essentialize all English learners into one neat population, it is imperative that the larger communal questions tied to language conservation and dual-language issues be recognized as quite a different affair, when considering the language needs of children who reside within very large language communities that existed in North America even prior to the official establishment of the United States as a nation-state.

Hence, theories and assessment of language needs, as well as educational policy considerations tied to language of instruction, must contend with this significant linguistic history, along with its pedagogical meaning for cultivating community empowerment and democratic participation—both processes that are, unfortunately, at odds with powerful nativist interests in the United States today. As a consequence, mean-spirited public debates have ensued, resulting in two decades of initiatives and referendums that have worked to simultaneously eliminate language rights, immigrant rights, and worker rights in states like California and Arizona. As would be expected, these political debates have led to increased policing of the U.S.-Mexico border, arguments against "political correctness," and a politically disabling national culture that seems to have lost its former ties to the long-held democratic principle of social justice for all.

Nativist Preoccupations

There is no room in this country for hyphenated Americanism.
—THEODORE ROOSEVELT (1915)

We have argued here that educational language issues associated with English learners must be understood within historical and material conditions that inextricably link racism and class inequalities in powerful ways. Yet, this view, now more than ever, has become contentious ground, in that it goes countercurrent to both conservative and neoliberal ideologies that support English-only policies, individual rights over collective rights, exclusive nation-state allegiance, unified national identity, and schools as economic engines for the advancement of the U.S. free market economy—all touted as the only guarantees for the progress and prosperity of the nation. These, of course, are at the heart of the many arguments launched against bilingual education and, most recently, against high school ethnic studies programs in Arizona, where the state passed legislation opposing courses that focused on teaching the history of U.S. minority groups. Proponents of such policies claim that programs such as bilingual education and ethnic studies promote divisiveness and weaken the fabric of national identity.

In concert with colonial roots, there has been a long history of nativist attitudes, policies, and practices in the United States. In the late 1700s, refugees from France and Ireland prompted the passage of the Alien and Sedition Acts. Then again in the mid-1800s, another wave of immigration from Europe caused contentious political debate. In the early 1900s, protests against Chinese workers intensified and led to the passage of the Chinese Exclusion Act. Then the Gentlemen's Agreement aimed to control Japanese populations. During much of the twentieth century, schools in the southwest were driven by a strong assimilative Americanization curriculum that segregated Mexican children, with the expressed intent to civilize them to an American identity (Sanchez 1951). In the civil rights era, many efforts were launched to ameliorate the impact of racialization processes at work in the schooling of African American and other children of color. The political and legal challenges to racism in U.S. schools ultimately led to the successful ruling in *Brown v. Board of Education*, which opened the door for a multitude of educational efforts, giving rise to both the multicultural education and bilingual education movements.

In the last two decades, many of the gains of the civil rights era have been successfully eroded by nativist forces. A strong conservative wave in California led to the successful passage of anti-immigrant (Proposition 209) and anti-bilingual (Proposition 227) initiatives in the state. These conservative campaigns led to the dismantling of the *Lau v. Nichols* decision, which guaranteed the rights of bilingual children to be educated in their primary language. Following the 1998 passage of Proposition 227 (or "English for the Children") in California, Arizona immediately followed suit. Then in 2002, the voters of Massachusetts overwhelmingly approved Question 2, a similar initiative that ended transitional bilingual education for English learners. In each of these cases, bilingual programs that utilized the primary language as the medium of instruction were replaced by one year of sheltered English instruction.

As a consequence, educational issues rooted in the cultural and linguistic needs of minority-language students now find little room for discussion, leaving minority-language rights advocates to weather serious political attacks. In the process, conservative anti-immigrant supporters seek to extinguish the strength and vitality of Spanish-speaking communities. The growing Spanish-speaking immigrant population, in particular, along with its culture and language, is deemed a threat to the integrity of the nation. These xenophobic attitudes expressed by the English-only movement are also heard in the vociferous anti-immigrant attacks of the newly formed ultra-right, populist Tea Party, and in the nativist discourse of many conservative public intellectuals, political figures, and media broadcasters. Bilingual education, ethnic studies, and, especially, Latino immigration are all blamed for not only a crisis in national identity and the economic decline but a growing national security risk, which they insist is leading the nation into insurmountable political and economic turmoil.

From the standpoint of nativist groups, anti-immigrant sentiments and English-only proposals are justified on the grounds that Spanish-speaking immigrants are an expense to the government; isolated within their own communities; refuse to learn English; steal jobs from native citizens; disrupt patriotic ideals; are a burden to social services; overpopulate; and are a growing threat to the stability of "American culture." These claims underscore fierce opposition to bilingualism in schools, ignoring the truth that most English-language learners are either legal residents or American citizens. Moreover, despite the fact that English is clearly the top contending hegemonic language of globalization, nativist organizations such as U.S. English "believe that English is threatened by other languages in the U.S., mainly Spanish. This organization advocated for the implementation of different language policies to secure that English is threatened no more as the common language in the United States" (Nieto 2007, 236).

Hence, nativists often scapegoat Latino populations (immigrant or not) and are content to sacrifice the language needs of Spanish-speaking children in order to conserve the economic and political interests of elites who have consistently bankrolled both anti-immigrant and anti-bilingual campaigns across the country (Gandara 2000; Crawford 1992). Restrictive language policies in public schools are clearly marked by a larger set of conservative and neoliberal goals associated with protecting White Anglo-Saxon Protestant dominance, in which the supremacy of English has become a significant political battleground.

The Impact of Restrictive Language Policies on English Learners: A Boston Study

[Restrictive language] policies and educational practices are *always* situated in relation to wider issues of power, access, opportunity, inequality, and, at times, discrimination and disadvantage.
— STEPHEN MAY AND NANCY HORNBERGER (2008)

As might be expected, political goals tied to the conservation of English as the official language of schooling for all children in the United States have seldom reaped positive consequences for language-minority children and their communities, who are forced to navigate the negative outcomes of English immersion strategies. Such strategies forsake the linguistic strength of the primary language, and in its place resurrect former assimilative assumptions and practices of the pre-civil rights era, namely "that children learn English best by being immersed in an English-only classroom environment" (Uriarte et al. 2010). Yet, despite little empirical evidence to support this contention, many school districts across the country have switched in the last decade from more comprehensive bilingual approaches to the use of sheltered English immersion programs as the preferred mode of language support.

At this juncture, it is worth noting that a variety of leading language researchers in the field, including James Crawford (2004), Jim Cummins (2000), Wayne Thomas and Virginia Collier (2002), and Stephen Krashen (2003) argue that the mainstreaming of English-language learners into English-only classrooms blatantly disregards ongoing research that repeatedly illustrates the importance of an additive approach, rather than one that subtracts the students' primary language from their academic learning experience. Moreover, an English immersion mandate is generally based upon purely instrumentalized and fragmented notions of language, divorced of language as a human right and the significance of culture, identity, and community interaction to the effective development of both the first and second languages (Skutnabb-Kangas 2000).

Rather than accelerate English acquisition, the subtraction of native language development deprives children of the numerous benefits conferred by bilingualism. While affirming the importance of English language acquisition, most recent studies on effective models of immigrant adaptation point to the importance of children retaining the ability to function in their original culture, even as they attain a new one. Portes and Rumbaut (2001) refer to this ability to manage both cultures as "selective acculturation," the most advantageous way for children to undergo an adaptive integration into the new context. In this framework, children are typically fluent in both languages, minimizing intergenerational conflict and preserving parental rights over their children. "Dissonant acculturation" emerges when there is a loss or a rupture with the culture of origin, including limited bilingualism or the loss of the primary language, thereby rupturing family ties and causing intergenerational conflict (Portes and Rumbaut 2001, 52, 145). This process has been positively associated with all significant indicators of high school academic performance—including math and reading levels, as well as overall grade point average (Portes and Rumbaut 2001).

This knowledge, however, did not make much of a difference as the "English for the Children" campaign, liberally financed by California's conservative businessman Ron Unz, made its way through the Massachusetts electorate in the fall of 2002. Similar referenda sponsored by the right-wing organization U.S. English Only had been successful in California (Proposition 227 in 1998) and in Arizona (Proposition 203 in 2000). Following this lead, Massachusetts's Question 2 was passed overwhelmingly by 68 percent of the voters. The referendum, similar to its predecessors, stipulated that "with limited exceptions, all public school children must be taught English by being taught all subjects in English and being placed in English language classrooms," replacing both transitional and maintenance bilingual programs that had been available to English-language learners with sheltered English immersion programs.[2]

From afar, Massachusetts was an unlikely candidate for this change, being a state that historically prided itself on its liberal and innovative approaches to social policy, including education. But perhaps the most jarring aspect of this shift in political direction was the fact that Massachusetts had led the nation in 1971, when the state legislature mandated transitional bilingual education for English-language learners. Hence, it is not surprising that, once U.S. English Only forces began taking Question 2 to the streets, many teachers were vocal in their opposition to the measure, as were immigrant and language-minority communities. But most educational leaders, although they seemed to understand that this was not a sound educational initiative, remained silent.

The Context of Language Restrictive Policies in Massachusetts

Unlikely as it may seem, the roots of this dramatic change were actually not too far under the surface. For one, the 1971 legislative mandate for bilingual education resulted from the lack of implementation of the 1967 Bilingual Education Amendment to Title VII of the Elementary and Secondary Education Act of 1965, which instituted federal commitment to the implementation of bilingual education. By 1970, little headway had been made in the establishment of bilingual programs. In Boston, for example, despite documentation of the lack of matriculation of Puerto Rican children,[3] the Boston Public Schools insisted that there was no evidence of need. This forced the community to prove a need existed. And this the community did, obligating the School Committee to begin funding limited bilingual programs, until 1971, when the state legislature finally mandated bilingual programs for all English-language learners and assigned community organizations the responsibility for their implementation.

It was the Latino community's direct participation in the education of their children that led to a strong preference for maintenance bilingual education. With this model, students were assisted to maintain and develop in the capacity to use their first language, even as they acquired English as a second. However, there was strong resistance at that time to the implementation of maintenance programs by those who advocated for immersion, as a recipe for quick assimilation for the city's new (im)migrants. Transitional bilingual education, as legislated in 1971, represented a compromise between these two poles—and, as a likely result, neither side was satisfied with the outcome, as Latino parents and community leaders continued to advocate for more comprehensive bilingual programs, while conservative proponents of immersion pushed in the opposite direction. Nevertheless, school districts developed a wide array of approaches ranging from programs that emphasized the use of the native language to those that minimized it. Moreover, as new immigrant groups arrived, new language programs were offered.

For thirty years this remained Massachusetts's framework for the implementation of bilingual education; however, throughout most of this period, bilingual programs largely languished. For example, in Boston, with the largest number of English-language learners, the well-documented process of desegregation of the Boston Public Schools coincided and largely submerged the implementation of bilingual programs. Nevertheless, parents organized in the Master Parent Advisory Council (MasterPAC) were ardent advocates for district bilingual accountability. They negotiated a voluntary Lau Compliance Plan with the Boston School Committee in 1979, to comply with the U.S. Office of Civil Rights' Lau Remedies, which followed the Supreme Court's ruling in *Lau v. Nichols* in 1974 (Boston Public Schools 1999, 14), and then amended this plan in 1981, 1985, and 1992. Parents also sued the district successfully to obtain equitable services for bilingual students (Boston Public Schools 1999, 13). This consistently strong advocacy on the part of parents was the bane of superintendents, leading one to complain that the district was nurturing the organization of parents so that they could, in turn, sue the district (Tung et al. 2009).

Bilingual programs in Boston and elsewhere in the state evolved in the shadow of parents' activism, with strong support from teachers and others directly involved in their development. Advocates demonstrated many successes, including the involvement of most districts with more than twenty students requiring language support; the development of new programs to support the education of students of dozens of languages; and the development of exemplary dual-language programs. But in spite of these successes, there was no consistent documentation or evaluation of the progress of English language acquisition for English-language learners, despite the fact that districts reported this information to the Massachusetts Department of Education on a yearly basis (DeJong et al. 2005, 597–98), and, as a consequence, bilingual programs lingered, largely from state neglect.

Two additional factors greatly influenced the outcome of this story. The first is the state's shift to a high-stakes environment, as part of the implementation of its 1993 Educational Reform initiative. At the onset, this broad initiative increased spending in education and distributed funding more equitably between urban and suburban districts, offering new resources to the education of language-minority students. The initiative proposed higher standards for all students and schools and new curriculum standards and requirements in core academic areas, which were to guide the development of local curricula, increase time-on-task for students, and tighten standards for new teacher certification and teacher education, as well as retraining established teachers, including special training in multicultural education and teaching strategies for English-language learners. This all seemed a welcome step toward alleviating the devastating results of the cultural clash between minority students and the mostly white teaching force. The reform also introduced measures to hold districts accountable for identifying students, schools, and districts in need of assistance, in an effort to guarantee improved school performance. Alongside, multiple measures of student achievement were to be integrated into the process of aligning local curricula to the statewide "frameworks," as a way of establishing student competence in those areas (Uriarte 2002).

No group stood to gain more from these proposed changes than Latinos, whose children had the lowest levels of achievement of any group in the commonwealth.[4] Latino enrollment in the state's public schools, which had been growing for three decades, had skyrocketed, particularly, in urban districts. At the time, more than 66,000 Latino children were enrolled in Massachusetts schools, a 20 percent increase in just five years. In Boston, for example, 20 percent of the students were Latinos, and in the suburbs of Lawrence and Holyoke, they made up almost 70 percent of students enrolled (MDOE 1992). As far back as 1976, reports by Latino community agencies and state task forces pointed to high grade retention and high school dropout rates. In 1986, the Education Task Force of the Massachusetts Commission on Hispanic Affairs, a commission sponsored by the Massachusetts legislature, concluded that "the Massachusetts public education system is failing to carry out its mission and its responsibility to the Hispanic community" (Massachusetts Commission on Hispanic Affairs 1986, 5). In the opinion of the task force, this was due to underfunding of school systems where Latino students predominated, as well as the absence of culturally sensitive curricula and classroom practices. In 1989 and 1990, protests reached a crescendo in a series of contentious meetings with the leadership of the Boston Public Schools, when it was reported that the annual Latino dropout rate had reached 30 percent in some Boston high schools, forcing the city to recognize its failure in educating Latino students.[5] Hence, when the Massachusetts legislature passed the Educational Reform Law in 1993, many Latinos supported the initiative.

But conditions changed swiftly as the political leadership of the state moved to the right. Under great pressure from the business sector, the composition of the State Board of Education changed, as did the orientation of the reforms. Most notable and controversial was the board's decision to adopt a series of standardized tests, administered in several grades, as the primary measure of student achievement; and to require that students pass the tenth-grade version of the standardized test in order to graduate from high school. With the Massachusetts Comprehensive Assessment System (MCAS), Massachusetts began the implementation of high-stakes testing as the sole measure for graduation.[6]

The implementation of this tenth-grade graduation requirement had a devastating effect on the graduation rate of Latino students. In the first two years of its implementation, more than half of Latino tenth graders taking the Math and English Language Arts (ELA) tests failed one or both exams, and therefore did not graduate from high school (Uriarte and Lavan 2006). In cities like Lawrence and Holyoke, the failure rates reached more than 70 percent. By 2008, 23 percent of Latino students were still failing either in Math, ELA, or both and therefore did not graduate from high school (Uriarte and Agusti 2009). Although this appears to show improvement, the data are called into question by a high dropout rate among Latino students, a rate that has remained almost 30 percent for more than a decade. Hence, those students taking the MCAS test in grade ten excludes the most vulnerable Latino students, most of whom now drop out prior to the tenth grade. Consequently, high dropout rates and the high-stakes environment has resulted in Latinos attaining the lowest graduation rates in the state. This consistent failure by schools to deliver a minimum level of education has had devastating effects on the lives of Latino students and on their communities.

The context for the shift in the focus of the state's educational reform is in concert with the earlier analysis of recent transformations in the political economy of public education in the United States. The competitive advantage of Massachusetts, vis à vis other states, centers on the education of its workforce as the state reinvents its economic base to stay at the forefront of innovation. Massachusetts, the "poster child" of the knowledge economy, with its plethora of high-ranking educational institutions, has an economy that is in its fourth transformation since the 1950s—from manufacturing to high-technology manufacturing, to software and finance, to biotechnology and life sciences—with each change requiring a workforce with higher levels of education. These industries represent a growing but limited number of jobs. Supporting this economy is a vast array of service employment that has less stringent educational requirements (although in Massachusetts, some service employment still demands a significant level of education) and is increasingly becoming a niche for Black, Latino, and immigrant workers (Sum et al. 2006; Borges-Méndez et al. 2008). As would be expected, Latinos, because of their poor level of educational attainment, do not fare well in this economy. Among all groups, Latinos have the highest proportion working in the service sector, with 52 percent of Latinos employed in service occupations compared to 40 percent of the general population. Moreover, Latinos occupy the lower-wage niches of this sector, and, although their participation in the labor force is high (many working more than one job), the median income of Latino households is only 48 percent of that of the general population. Latinos have the highest poverty rate of all groups in Massachusetts (Borges-Méndez et al. 2006; Uriarte et al. 2006).

Meanwhile, the state remains committed to its neoliberal reform agenda, in great measure because in the eyes of most educational policy leaders the strategy of high standards and strong accountability is considered a success, given that Massachusetts has shown the highest performance of all states for National Assessment of Educational Progress (NAEP) for close to a decade. What is not so readily disclosed is that Massachusetts also ranks among the five states with the widest "gap" in achievement between white and Latino students in both NAEP Math and Reading (NAEP, n.d.). This achievement gap particularly affects students from racialized working-class communities, but, according to a 2010 report from the Massachusetts Board of Elementary and Secondary Education's Proficiency Gap Task Force, the widest gap is between English-language learners and English-proficient students (Proficiency Gap Task Force 2010).

The other factor that influenced the success of the referendum was the reemergence of anti-immigrant sentiments in the state. Although Massachusetts does not have an immigrant population that is comparable to that of southern or western states, there had been rapid growth of the immigrant population in the previous three decades and a not so subtle change in the origin of these immigrants. Historically, Massachusetts had been a port of entry for immigrants from Canada and Europe, and the state is home to large populations of French Canadians, Portuguese, Irish, Italians, and Greeks. At the start of the twentieth century, about 30 percent of the population of the state was foreign born, a proportion that declined steadily until it reached less than 9 percent in 1970. But between 1970 and 2000, the immigrant population in the state began to rise again, reaching almost 13 percent. By 2000, the composition of immigrants had changed, and instead of the largely Canadian and European stock of the earlier era 65 percent of the state's foreign born hailed from Latin America (30 percent), Asia (25 percent), and Africa (7 percent) (Sum and Fogg 1999).

Despite these changes, the state continued to support social programs for immigrants, even in light of federal restrictions by the 1996 Personal Responsibility and Work Opportunity Reconciliation Act (PRWORA). However, anti-immigrant sentiments flared following September 11, radically shifting attitudes in the state. Researchers who polled voters during the November 2002 election concluded that the approval of the referendum against bilingual education reflected a reemergence of negative attitudes toward immigrants, due to their increasing population. Capetillo-Ponce and Kramer (2006) also found a general lack of information among voters about bilingual education and the implications of the proposed changes. Furthermore, they argue that, in the absence of objective information, voters were easily swayed by other factors. Looming large among these was the belief that high levels of immigration were tolerable only as long as "the newcomers pay their own way, don't get special breaks (such as bilingual education), and assimilate at a relatively rapid rate" (17). As such, nativist arguments anchored in traditional assimilationist notions and bolstered by neoliberal imperatives led Massachusetts voters to undo thirty years of educational practice, radically changing the educational conditions of English-language learners across the state.

The Impact of Question 2

In the academic year 2002–2003, the year Question 2 was approved by Massachusetts voters, 141,408 students enrolled in Massachusetts public schools were native speakers of a language other than English, representing over 14 percent of all Massachusetts public school enrollments, and of these, 51,622 were designated as of limited English proficiency (LEP), or 5.2 percent of all enrollments (MDOE 2003). The referendum became law as Chapter 386 of the Acts of 2002 in December and was implemented across the state in the fall of 2003, replacing a wide-ranging set of bilingual programs with Sheltered English Immersion (SEI). Unlike transitional bilingual education, which relied on the English learners' own language to facilitate the learning of academic subjects as they mastered English, the SEI model is based on the concept that the English language is acquired quickly (within one year) and relies on the use of simple English in the classroom to impart academic content. For this reason, the law has the goal that English-language learners be in SEI programs for no longer than one year and then transition into mainstream classrooms, as discussed earlier. Parents can seek to "waive" the placement of their children in SEI programs and request to have their children placed in General Education or in a limited number of available bilingual education programs.

The changes instituted by the new law had broad implications for the education of English-language learners. It prohibited the use of the native language in instruction, favoring the placement of students from various language backgrounds in the same classroom to force the use of English as the sole language for communication. The law stipulates that students can be provided some nominal assistance in their first language, but this is seldom available or implemented. The use of instructional materials and books in the primary language of English-language learners is prohibited—a fact that was interpreted by some districts in ways that led to the disappearance of all books in languages other than English. The organization of programs changed, with many districts interpreting this not only as the end to bilingual instruction but as the "end of programs" for English learners. There is evidence that the implementation of the changes required by Question 2 varied substantially across the state (DeJong et al. 2005) and that the professional development of teachers, overall, fell woefully behind the need (The Rennie Center for Education Research and Policy, 2007), resulting in many English-language learners being placed in classrooms with teachers who were not adequately prepared to teach them.

Yet, despite the grave implications of this policy change and the number of children affected, the state has yet to conduct a thorough evaluation of the impact of the law. Immigrant communities and education advocates confused about the implementation of the law and aware of the soaring incidence of high school dropout rates among English-language learners finally forced the first assessments of the law's impact, focused first in Boston and then across the state (Tung et al. 2009; Uriarte et al. 2009; Uriarte and Karp 2009; English Language Learners Sub committee 2009). Below we summarize the key findings of these initial assessments:

1. Increasing enrollments. The enrollment of English-language learners increased 27 percent statewide since 2001 (Uriarte and Karp 2009).

Boston has the highest number of English-language learners enrolled in the state's public schools (Tung et al. 2009).

2. Gross misassessments. Although the state showed growth in enrollments, some districts experienced sharp declines. In Boston, for example, both the identification of students of limited English proficiency and their participation in programs for English-language learners declined significantly, due to problems with assessment and the information provided to parents about the choices of programs for their children. The problems with gross misassessment were consistent and increasing through time, so that by 2009 almost half of the English-language learners requiring services were not receiving them. This disregard for the needs of vulnerable children prompted a review by the U.S. Department of Justice and the Office of Civil Rights of the U.S. Department of Education, which is ongoing (Vaznis 2009).

3. Overenrollment in special education. The overenrollment of students of limited English proficiency in special education (SPED) programs is, of course, tied to mistakes in assessment of students. Between 2004 and 2009, the statewide assignment of English-language learners to SPED programs increased from 12.7 percent to 16.0 percent and, in some Massachusetts districts, reached 40 percent (in Holyoke) and 30 percent (in Springfield) in 2009 (Uriarte and Karp 2009; English Language Learners Sub committee 2009, 10). The sharp differences among the districts suggest that determinations of the need for SPED programs may have resulted from judgments made by district staff with varying levels of professional competence in determining appropriate placements. Informal reports suggest that in some districts assessments are conducted by monolingual English-speaking staff through the use of translators or by professionals who are not qualified to assess and evaluate English-language learners for special education needs. This is particularly problematic, given that the assessment of disability relies heavily on direct communication between the child and the examiner, which may explain why the three high-incidence disabilities among English-language learners are communications, intellectual disabilities, and developmental delays—all sensitive to the efficacy of this communication (English Language Learners Sub committee 2009).

4. Problems with the measurement and reporting of performance. Most reported measurements of achievement for English-language learners do not take into account that they are the result of the aggregation of the performance of children at various levels of language proficiency. The

measurement in itself projects an expectation that students at all levels of English proficiency should perform comparably to English-proficient students on standardized tests in English, when, in fact, this should only be expected of students who have reached the highest levels of English proficiency. For example, in Massachusetts, the pass rates for the English Language Arts test of the Massachusetts Comprehensive Assessment System (MCAS) of English-proficient students and all English-language learners show wide disparities (over 30 percentage points) between the groups, a disparity that is expected, given that it includes children at very low levels of English-language proficiency. However, when the English Language Learners Sub-Committee of the Proficiency Gap Task Force of the Board of Elementary and Secondary Education disaggregated the outcomes of English-language learners by level of language proficiency, one conclusion from their 2009 report was particularly striking. Although, as expected, the lowest pass rates were among the students with the lowest levels of English proficiency, English-language learners who had attained the highest levels of English proficiency actually outperformed English-proficient students in Massachusetts. Hence, the narrative of failure that shadows these students throughout their schooling is largely a result of the way districts measure and report their performance.

5. Premature imposition of testing regimen. The problem in Massachusetts, then, is not that English-language learners are not capable of scoring well on the MCAS, but rather that they are prematurely thrown into the accountability regimen, before they have been taught English well enough to do so. English-language learners are tested after just one year in Massachusetts schools, even though it is well known that it is highly unlikely that these students will attain the level of English-language performance required to pass the MCAS in only one year. In fact, only a relatively low proportion of English-language learners at all grade levels had attained full English proficiency, even after five years in Massachusetts schools (MDESE 2009, 6). Hence, this imposition of testing regimens, with full knowledge that these students are unable to perform adequately, inserts them into a "meant to fail" situation that represents an educational injustice and a deleterious environment for the academic development of these children.

6. Academic content taught in English. Recent studies using random assignment of students have found that students in both sheltered English immersion and transitional bilingual programs show similar advances in learning to read English (Zeher 2010). At issue is the time the process of

language acquisition takes under both models and the impact of each to academic content. This is certainly the quandary facing Massachusetts educators. Due to changes in instruction mandated by Question 2, all academic content must be taught in English, including all books and materials. Given that it takes several years for students, particularly older students, to attain the level of proficiency in English that would allow them to obtain grade-level understanding of academic content taught only in English, this represents a major concern. As would be expected, for eighth and tenth graders, large gaps exist between English-proficient students and those at the highest levels of language performance (English Language Learners Sub committee 2009). This is surely tied to the "watering down" of the curriculum of English-language learners, which is inevitable under conditions where students are forced to learn in a language they do not fully comprehend. The gaps between these two groups in science—a content dependent on language for its delivery—are even more salient, reaching a more than 30-point difference among eighth-grade students (English Language Learners Sub committee 2009). The lower levels of performance in Math and Science, even for students at the highest levels of language proficiency, indicate both that students with newly acquired English-language skills may not have enough command of the language to access academic content and that this content may not have been successfully delivered through the scaffolding of content, as required in sheltered English immersion instruction. And although the logical conclusion would be that these students should be provided content in their own language as they learn English, by law school systems cannot provide this instruction in the student's primary language. The restrictive language policies that are today law in Massachusetts bind teachers, schools, and districts to the implementation of educational practices that set students up to fail, leaving them defenseless against the difficult material struggles that they are likely to face as they enter adulthood.

7. Academic disengagement and a rise in dropout rates. Sheltered English immersion, even when taught well by teachers who are professionally trained to deliver it, scaffolds the academic content to match the level of English proficiency of the students. This means that English-language learners entering a Massachusetts school in ninth grade and with an English proficiency at level 1 or 2 are receiving academic content at a very basic level. This not only leads to lower levels of achievement but also to students disengaging from school altogether and dropping out. Perhaps the most salient effect of the change from transitional bilingual education

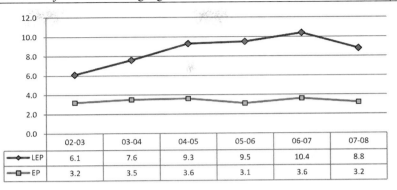

	02-03	03-04	04-05	05-06	06-07	07-08
LEP	6.1	7.6	9.3	9.5	10.4	8.8
EP	3.2	3.5	3.6	3.1	3.6	3.2

FIGURE 1: Annual High School Dropout Rate. EP and LEP. MA, 2003–2008

Source: Data provided by MDESE to the Gastón Institute, University of Massachusetts, Boston, on 5/20/09

to sheltered English immersion has been the rise in the dropout rates for English-language learners, while the dropout rates for English-proficient students remains relatively stable. The trend for both groups in the five years following the implementation of Question 2 is shown in figure 1.

Analysis of dropout data from specific districts supports the findings of the state trends and adds some important dimensions. Studies of outcomes for Boston English-language learners, for example, show that their annual high school dropout rate nearly doubled from 2003 to 2006 (6.3 percent to 12.1 percent). It is also noteworthy that students in transitional bilingual programs for the year 2002–2003 showed a dropout rate lower than that of native English speakers (8.7 percent for native speakers versus 6.3 percent for those in ELL programs). However, by 2006 the dropout rate for English-language learners (at 12.1 percent) had surpassed that of native speakers (at 11.7 percent) (Tung et al. 2009). The Boston data show the effect of the dismantling of bilingual education programs, which in many cases provided a nurturing environment for students and promoted their academic engagement.

8. Lack of teacher and school preparedness. Evidence of both the lack of preparedness of students emerging from sheltered English immersion programs and the failure of general education high schools to welcome these students comes from Worcester. Data compiled by the subcommittee on English-language learners show that the highest dropout rate (67 percent in 2009) is found among students at the higher levels of English profi-

ciency, that is, those English-language learners transitioning into general education programs. The lack of an engaging curriculum at the students' grade and intellectual level (not just their level of English proficiency), together with the scant preparation of these students to address content in general education high schools, are critical factors affecting their disengagement once they transition. The unchallenging and/or inhospitable environment created by teachers and schools unprepared to address the needs of these students is of major concern, given that lower levels of educational attainment are more likely to ensure that English-language learners will have a poorer quality of life than their educated peers—and, hence, fewer opportunities for full democratic participation in the larger society.

Conclusion

Democracy is severely limited when people cannot use their own languages.

—NETTLE AND ROMAINE (2000)

In this chapter we have provided a postcolonial discussion of language and schooling as it pertains to English-language learners, followed by the story of the impact of language-restrictive policies in the state of Massachusetts, which expelled the use of primary-language instruction in the schooling of English-language learners and replaced it with sheltered English immersion programs. The Massachusetts case well illustrates and echoes, through an examination of the historical context and discussion of empirical data, the most salient points of the preceding theoretical analysis. One significant question that remains, of course, is in what ways parents of English-language learners and their communities will grapple with the negative impact of restrictive language policies upon their children, particularly with respect to questions of democratic participation and their efforts to transform the negative material conditions that shape their lives. This is a particularly salient point given that Latinos, for example, despite their huge numbers in many regions, still contend with political invisibility and lack of decision-making power within mainstream educational institutions.

Yet, despite many of the problems at work in Boston, what cannot be overlooked is that it was principally Latino parents and community leaders who historically placed pressure upon the Boston school district and the state of Massachusetts to be responsive to the needs of their children; it was parents and community advocates who demanded transparency in assessing the effects of the implementation of the restrictive language policies mandated by Question 2. As such, the social agency enacted by Latino parents and community leaders was directly responsible for challenging violations of the educational rights of their children and, with that, review of Boston schools by both the Department of Justice and the Department of Education's Office for Civil Rights. This is, by no means, a powerless community of victims. Nevertheless, we are well aware that in the current political climate, public institutions seem more and more immune to community advocacy efforts, as neoliberal agendas function, wittingly or unwittingly, to perpetuate a culture of failure and educational neglect. Unfortunately, these conditions often render community efforts not only less effective, but far more difficult to sustain.

There is no question that "for many Latinos in Massachusetts, the vote on Question 2 was probably an uneasy introduction to the American political system, especially if they understood the vote for English-only as an assault on their language and parental rights" (Capetillo-Ponce 2003). Hence, all this speaks to the need for greater consolidation of community strength and the importance of cultivating greater knowledge of educational institutions and the political processes tied to policy decisions that impact the schooling of language-minority children. We know that in Boston, as in other parts of the nation, community political efforts that utilized the powers of federal intervention and the protections still afforded by civil rights laws were successful in creating new avenues for reform and in democratizing the education of English-language learners (Beck and Allexsaht-Snider 2002).

However, given current neoliberal policy restraints, where only a small number of English-language learners are receiving the educational preparation they require to academically succeed, we are left with a daunting task: to struggle together, as political allies, educators, parents, and members of language-minority communities, in an effort to, once again, transform racialized inequalities connected to restrictive language policies in U.S. public schools. This discussion truly reminds us, as Edward Said and other postcolonial theorists have so rightly insisted, that *democracy is never guaranteed.* It is a contested political field of social relations, which requires us to return, time and time again, to the struggle for social justice and self-determination. It signifies *a revolution in the living,* rather than an objective and absolute utopia to which we will someday arrive.

REFERENCES

Anyon, J. (2005). "The Political Economy of Race, Urban Education, and Educational Policy." In C. McCarthy et al. (eds.), *Race, Identity, and Representation in Education* (2nd ed.). New York: Routledge.

Anzaldúa, G. (1987). *Borderlands La Frontera: The New Mestiza.* San Francisco: Aunt Lute Books.

Beck, S.A., and M. Allexsaht-Snider (2002). "Recent Language Minority Education Policy in Georgia: Appropriation, Assimilation, and Americanization." In S. Wortham et al. (eds), *Education in the New Latino Diaspora: Policy and the Politics of Identity.* Westport, CT: Ablex Publishing.

Borges-Méndez, R., J. Jennings, D. Haig-Friedman, M. Hutson, and T. Eliot Roberts (2008, May). *Immigrant Workers in the Massachusetts Health Care Industry.* Malden, MA: Immigrant Learning Center.

Borges-Méndez, R., N. Lavan, and C. Jones (2006, August). *Latinos in Massachusetts: Selected Economic Indicators.* Boston: University of Massachusetts Boston, Gaston Institute.

Boston Public Schools (1999, January). *The Bilingual Education Task Force, Report to the Boston School Committee.* Boston: Boston Public Schools.

Boston Public Schools (1989, May). *Brief Report on Dropout Statistics for Hispanic Students in the Boston Public Schools: Focus on High Schools and Neighborhoods,* exhibit 2, Office of Research and Development. Boston: Boston Public Schools.

Boston Public Schools (1989a, May). *Hispanic Dropout Program,* Office of Equal Opportunity, Boston, MA.

Capetillo-Ponce, J. (2003). *The Vote on Bilingual Education and Latino Identity in Massachusetts.* Boston, MA: Mauricio Gaston Institute for Latino Community Development and Public Policy.

Capetillo-Ponce, J., and R. Kramer (2006). "Politics, Ethnicity, and Bilingual Education in Massachusetts," in A. Torres (ed.), *Latinos in New England.* Philadelphia: Temple University Press.

Collier, V. P., and W. P. Thomas (2010). "Helping Your English Learners in Spite of No Child Left Behind," in *Teachers College Record* (March 11). Available at: http://www.tcrecord.org, ID Number: 15937. Accessed: 5/11/2010.

Collier, V.P., and W.P. Thomas (2009). *Educating English Learners for a Transformed World.* Albuquerque: Dual Language Education of New Mexico/Fuente Press.

Commonwealth of Massachusetts, Secretary of State (n.d.). *Question 2: Law Proposed by Initiative Petition: English Language Education in Public Schools. Information for Voters, The 2002 Ballot Questions.* Available at: http://www.sec.state.ma.us/ele/ele02/elebq02/bq022.htm. Accessed: 6/11/2010.

Crawford, J. (2004). *Educating English Learners: Language Diversity in the Classroom.* Los Angeles, CA: Bicultural Education Services, INC.

Crawford, J. (2000). *At War with Diversity: U.S. Language Policy in an Age of Anxiety.* Clevedon, UK: Multilingual Matters.

Crawford, J. (ed.) (1992). *Language Loyalties: A Source Book on the Official English Controversy.* Chicago, IL: University of Chicago Press.

Cummins, J. (2000). *Language, Power, and Pedagogy.* Clevedon, UK: Multilingual Matters.

Darder, A. (2002). *Reinventing Paulo Freire: A Pedagogy of Love.* Boulder, CO: Westview Press.

Darder, A. (1991). *Culture and Power in the Classroom.* Westport, CT: Bergin and Garvey.

Darder, A., and R.D. Torres (2004). *After Race: Racism after Multiculturalism.* New York: New York University Press.

DeJong, E., M. Gort, and C. Cobb (2005). "Bilingual Education within the Context of English-Only Policies: Three Districts' Response to Question 2 in Massachusetts," *Educational Policy* 19, no. 4: 595–620.

Dobbs, M. (2004). "U.S. Segregation Now at '69 Level: Study Shows 15 Year Decline; Hispanics Less Integrated than African Americans," *Washington Post* (January 18): A10.

English Language Learners Subcommittee (2009, December). *Halting the Race to the Bottom: Urgent Interventions for the Improvement of the Education of English-language learners in Massachusetts and Selected Districts.* Final Report to the Massachusetts Board of Elementary and Secondary Education's Committee on the Proficiency Gap. Available at: http://www.massmabe.org/Portals/0/2009_HaltingRace percent20Full.pdf.

Freire, P. (1993). *Education for Critical Consciousness.* New York: Continuum.

Freire, P. (1970). *Pedagogy of the Oppressed.* New York: Continuum.

Freire, P., and D. Macedo (1987). *Literacy: Reading the Word and the World.* New York: Routledge.

Gandara, P. (2000). "In the Aftermath of the Storm: English Learners in the Post 227 Era," *Bilingual Research Journal* 24, nos. 1 and 2 (winter and spring): 1–13.

Genesee, F. (ed.) (1999). *Program Alternatives for Linguistically Diverse Students.* Washington, D.C.: U.S. Department of Education, Center for Research on Education, Diversity, and Excellence.

Genesee, F., K. Lindholm-Leary, W.M. Saunders, and D. Christian (2006). *Educating English-Language Learners: A Synthesis of Research Evidence.* New York: Cambridge University Press.

Gilmore, R. (2006). *The Golden Gulag.* Los Angeles: University of California Press.

Hispanic Office of Planning and Evaluation (1978, December). *Puerto Ricans in Boston: Current Conditions in Education and Employment.* Boston: Hispanic Office of Planning and Evaluation.

Krashen, S. (2003). *Explorations in Language Acquisition and Use.* Portsmouth, NH: Heinemann.

Massachusetts Commission on Hispanic Affairs (1986). *Report of the Education Task Force.* Boston: Massachusetts Statehouse.

Massachusetts Department of Education (MDOE) (2003, August). "Questions and Answers Regarding Chapter 71a: English Language Education in Public Schools." Available at: www.doe.mass.edu/ell/chapter71A_faq.pdf.

Massachusetts Department of Education (MDOE) (1992, October). "School District Profiles." Available at: http://www.doe.mass.edu/pic.www/profmain.htm.

Massachusetts Department of Elementary and Secondary Education (MDESE) (2009). "Massachusetts English Proficiency Assessment (MEPA) Statewide Results: Spring 2009," 6. Available at: http://www.doe.mass.edu/mcas/mepa/2009/results/09state.pdf.

May, S., and N. Hornberger (2008). *Language Policy and Political Issues in Education: Encyclopedia of Language and Education*, Vol. 1. (New York: Springer Publishing Company.

Moyo, T. (2009). *Linguistic Diversity and Development: The Language Question and Social Justice in Southern Africa.* Urbana, IL: Forum on Public Policy.

National Assessment of Educational Progress (NAEP) (n.d.). "State Comparisons." National Center for Education Statistics, U.S. Department of Education. Available at: http://nces.ed.gov/nationsreportcard/nde/statecomp/.

Nettle, D., and S. Romaine (2000). *Vanishing Voices: The Extinction of the World's Languages.* London: Oxford University Press.

Nieto, S. (2009). *Culture, Language and Teaching: Critical Perspective.* New York: Routledge.

Nieto, D.G. (2007). "The Emperor's New Words: Language and Colonization in Human Architecture," *Journal of the Sociology of Self Knowledge* (summer): 231–37.

Olivos, E. (2006). *The Power of Parents: A Critical Perspective of Parent Involvement in Schools.* New York: Peter Lang.

Orfield, G. (2001). *Schools More Separate: Consequences of a Decade of Resegregation.* Report of the Harvard Civil Rights Project. Boston: Harvard University Press.

Orfield, G. (1999). "New Study Finds Increasing Segregation." Civil Rights Project, Harvard Graduate School of Education (June 8).

Orfield, G., and C. Lee (2007). *Historical Reversals, Accelerating Resegregation, and the Need for New Integration Strategies.* Report of the Civil Rights Project/Proyecto Derechos Civiles. Los Angeles: University of California Press.

Phillipson, R.P. (2008). *Rights to Language: Equity, Power, and Education.* New York: Routledge.

Portes, A., and R. Rumbaut (2001). *Legacies: The Story of the Immigrant Second Generation.* Berkeley and Los Angeles: University of California Press.

Proficiency Gap Task Force (2010). *A Roadmap to Closing the Proficiency Gap.* Massachusetts Board of Elementary and Secondary Education (report presented at the meeting of the MBESE), May 24.

Ramanathan, V., and B. Morgan (2007). "TESOL and Policy Enactments: Perspectives from Practice," *TESOL Quarterly* 41, no. 3 (September).

Rennie Center for Education, Research and Policy (2007). Seeking Effective Policies and Practices for English Language Learners. Cambridge, MA. See: http://renniecenter.issuelab.org/research/listing/seeking_effective_policies_and_practices_for_english_language_learners

Ribadeniera, D. (1989) "Wilson, Hispanics Agree on School Plan," *Boston Globe*, November 19, 45.

Rodriguez, C. (2000). *Changing Race: Latinos, the Census, and the History of Ethnicity.* New York: New York University Press.

Sanchez, G. (1951). *Concerning Segregation of Spanish-Speaking Children in the Public Schools.* Austin, TX: Inter-American Occasional Papers.

Skutnabb-Kangas, T. (2000). *Linguistic Genocide in Education—or Worldwide Diversity and Human Rights?* Mahwah, NJ: Lawrence Erlbaum.

Spooley, P. (1993). *Racism and Ethnicity.* Aukland, NZ: Oxford University Press.

Suarez-Orozco, C., and M. Suarez-Orozco (2001). *Children of Immigration*. Cambridge, MA: Harvard University Press.

Sum, A., and N. Fogg (1999). *The Changing Workforce: Immigrants and the New Economy of Massachusetts*. Boston: MassINC and Citizens Bank. Available at: http://www.massinc.org/ handler.cfm?type=2andtarget=ChangingWorkforce/index.html.

Sum, A., I. Khatiwada, S. Palma, and P. Tobar (2006, October). *Immigration's Impact on the Workforce Research Brief*. Boston, MA: Commonwealth Corporation.

Task Force of Children out of School (1969). *The Way We Go to School*. Boston: Massachusetts Advocates for Children.

Thomas, W.P., and V.P. Collier (2002). *A National Study of School Effectiveness for Language Minority Students' Long-Term Academic Achievement*. Santa Cruz, CA: Center for Research on Education, Diversity, and Excellence.

Tollefson, J.W. (2004). *Medium of Instruction Policies: Which Agenda? Whose Agenda?* Mahwah, NJ: Lawrence Erlbaum.

Tung, R., M. Uriarte, V. Diez, N. Lavan, N. Agusti, F. Karp, and T. Meschede (2009). *English Learners in Boston Public Schools: Enrollment, Engagement, and Academic Outcomes, AY2003–AY2006: Final Report*. Boston: Mauricio Gastón Institute for Latino Community Development and Public Policy, University of Massachusetts. Available at: http://www.gaston.umb.edu/articles/2009 percent20Final percent20ELL percent20Report_online.pdf.

Uriarte, M. (2002). "The High Stakes of High Stakes Testing." In Z. Beykont (ed.), *The Power of Culture: Teaching across Language Differences*. Cambridge, MA: Harvard Education Publishing Group.

Uriarte, M., and N. Agusti (2009, May). *Latino Students in Massachusetts Public Schools: 2009 Status Report*. Prepared for the Governor's Latino-American Advisory Commission.

Uriarte, M., and L. Chavez (2000). *Latino Students and the Massachusetts Public Schools*. Boston: Mauricio Gastón Institute for Latino Community Development and Public Policy, for Dropout Rates through the 1990s.

Uriarte, M., P. Granberry, and M. Halloran (2006). "Immigration Status, Employment, and Eligibility for Public Benefits among Latin American Immigrants in Massachusetts." In Andrés Torres (ed.), *Latinos in New England*. Philadelphia: Temple University Press.

Uriarte, M., and F. Karp (2009, October). *English-Language Learners in Massachusetts: Trends in Enrollments and Outcomes*. Boston: Mauricio Gastón Institute for Latino Community Development and Public Policy, University of Massachusetts. Available at: http://www.gaston.umb.edu/UserFiles/09ELLsinMA percent20brief.pdf.

Uriarte, M., and N. Lavan (2006, September). *Trends in Enrollments and Outcomes for Latino Children in Massachusetts Public Schools*. Boston: Mauricio Gastón Institute for Latino Community Development and Public Policy, University of Massachusetts.

Uriarte, M., N. Lavan, N. Agusti, M. Kala, F. Karp, P. Kiang, L. Lo, R. Tung, and X. Villari (2009). *English Learners in Boston Public Schools: Enrollment, Engagement, and Academic Outcomes of Native Speakers of Cape Verdean Creole, Chinese Dialects, Haitian Creole, Spanish, and Vietnamese*. Boston: Mauricio Gastón Institute for Latino Community Development and Public Policy,

University of Massachusetts. Available at: http://www.gaston.umb.edu/articles/2009 percent-20Language percent20Groups percent20Report_online.pdf.

Uriarte, M., R. Tung, N. Lavan, and V. Diez (2010). "Impact of Restrictive Language Policies on Engagement and Academic Achievement of Boston Public School Students in Programs for English Learners." In P. Gandara and M. Hopkins (eds.), *Forbidden Language*. New York: Columbia University Teachers College Press.

Valenzuela, A. (1999). *Subtractive Schooling: U.S. Mexico Youth and the Politics of Caring*. New York: State University of New York Press.

Valle, V., and R.D. Torres (2000). *Latino Metropolis*. Minneapolis: University of Minnesota Press.

Vaznis, J. (2009, August 26). "U.S. Inspects Boston's Language Instruction," *Boston Globe*, A1.

Wheelock. A. (1990). *The Status of Latino Students in Massachusetts Public Schools: Direction for Policy Research in the 1990s*. Boston: Mauricio Gastón Institute for Latino Community Development and Public Policy, University of Massachusetts.

Zeher, M.A. (2010, April 9). "Bilingual Ed., Immersion Found to Work Equally Well," *Edweek*. Available at: http://www.edweek.org/ew/articles/2010/04/09/29bilingual_ep.h29.html.

ENDNOTES

1. BBC News, "Research to Find Effects in Brain of Bilingualism," reports on the research of Virginia Gathercole at Bangor University, who is exploring the benefits of being bilingual. She stated in the article, "The very act of being able to speak, listen, and think in two languages and of using two languages on a daily basis appears to sharpen people's abilities to pay close attention to aspects of tasks relevant to good performance."

2. Following the protest of parents and education advocates, two-way bilingual programs were retained.

3. Hubie Jones, then director of the Roxbury Multiservice Center and chairperson of the Task Force of Children out of School, years later would explain that in *The Way We Go to School*, a 1969 report of children not in school, "we estimated that there may have been 10,000 kids not attending school who had a right to do so because of the exclusionary policies and practices, primarily practices, of the school system. The largest group of those people that we estimated were Latinos." At that time, the vast majority of Latinos in Boston were Puerto Rican.

4. See Hispanic Office of Planning and Evaluation (1978), for attendance, dropout, and retention rates in the late 1970s; Wheelock (1990) for dropout and truancy rates through the 1980s; and Uriarte and Chavez (2000) for dropout rates through the 1990s.

5. Boston Public Schools (1989 and 1989a) and Ribadeniera (1989, 45).

6. For a full description of the initial impact of high-stakes testing on Latino students, see Uriarte (2002) and Uriarte and Chavez (2000).

PART V.
Latino Studies

THE UNEXPECTED REAPPEARANCE
OF DON QUIXOTE

I step into a cold
and snowy Boston morning
to meet my bus; inside,
a toothless old man
loudly sings a long
forgotten venceremos song
from the Spanish civil war.

The faces of the passengers
are all tightly drawn,
some in fear,
some in disdain,
some in an effort
to maintain safely hidden
in their closed interiors.

As I wiggle into place,
he yells out to me
across the crowded bus
"Eres puertorriqueña?"
I contemplate for a split second
whether to enter into his world,
I look into his eyes and step in,
"Si." I shake my head and smile,
"Bueno mija estas para ti."

He closes his eyes for a moment
in a fitful effort to retrieve
a melody from the cobwebs
of his rusty rememberances,
and then begins to play
a perfect rendition of
"en mi viejo san juan,"
on a kazoo.

The old familiar tune
warms my heart and brings
a smile to my face and to
the other boricuas who, now
cannot resist to smile, as well.

It is in this unexpected
moment of delight that we,
the lost children of la perla,
experience community produced
by an old shabby fellow who
for all intents and purposes
would be diagnosed a raving lunatic.

His song ends as he moves
to get off the crowded bus,
instinctively, i clap
and say "bravo maestro!"
he smiles, bows, and affirms
the courage of my spirit
("tu si tienes valor"),
as he steps gallantly out
into the cold world,
once more.

CHAPTER 13

Problematizing the Notion
of Puerto Ricans as "Underclass"

A Step toward a Decolonizing Study of Poverty

> Whereas the perceived problems of groups cannot be ignored, neither can the interest groups that define their membership and deviance.... Once a concept is incorporated in general perceptions and becomes a guide for program development, it is almost impossible to eradicate. Social scientists, who are often active members of the labeling professions, may...exhibit insensitivity to political consequences. The result of their giving the intellectual's imprimatur to a concept is often the creation of a convenient terminology that unwittingly reinforces existing stereotypes and prejudices.
>
> —STAFFORD AND LADNER (1990, P. 140)

For those of us who have grown up as members of a subordinate culture and class in the United States, the words of Stafford and Ladner strike deep chords. Many of us are quite conscious of the effects that social science language and practices have had on our own lives. An effect that is often not dispelled by our own professional socialization into the social sciences. As a consequence, I am intimately linked to the following discussion in two very significant ways.

The first link is my birth. I am a Puerto Rican woman who was born, grew up, and lived through my early adulthood in conditions that are currently described by social scientists as "underclass." And even today as I write this article as a scholar and researcher, I am acutely conscious of the many stored memories of suffering, humiliation, and despair experienced by my family as a result of poverty.

The second link is an incident that I experienced with my students at a Community Fellows seminar.[1] A young social science researcher was invited to present his work on the current trends in the labor market and its impact on communities of color. Repeatedly, he used the term "underclass" to refer to those who live in poverty. Each time he spoke the term, the room grew increasingly tense and the silent resistance of the participants became quite noticeable. Finally, several of the students who could no longer contain their distress stated that they did not appreciate having the people in their communities referred to as underclass and that the term was demeaning and degrading to their human dignity.

The researcher, a well-meaning White, middle-class male, who considers himself very politically conscious, became quite confused by the anger of the group. And despite the student objections, he could not stop using the term. It was as if the term "underclass" had become tenaciously embedded and intertwined into the linguistic structure that represented his thoughts. Even after several efforts by the group to bridge the gap for him, his comments inadvertently expressed suspiciousness as to the validity of the group's response. This caused him to become even more abstracted and encapsulated in the content of his presentation and hopelessly distanced from any possibility of dialogue with the group.

Hence, it is from the context of these two separate but related experiences that I will briefly discuss the problems inherent in the notion of Puerto Ricans as "underclass" and some beginning steps towards a decolonizing study of poverty.[2]

Underclass: Its Origins, Meaning, and Usage

Although there are a variety of ways in which the term "underclass" was used in the past, the most recent meaning emerged out of Gunnar Myrdal's (1962) text, *The Challenge to Affluence*, where he described an "underclass" that was cut off from society. He described the group as lacking the necessary education, skills and personality traits required to integrate successfully into the modern economy. Myrdal's definition focused primarily on economics. Douglas Glasgow (1981) provided the earliest of the underclass formulations in the 1980s. He proposed that the underclass emerged from a combination of institutional racism and structural changes in the economy that produced and reinforced a cycle of poverty in the Black community.

As a result of the work of social scientists such as these, the use of the term "underclass" has spread like wildfire during the past two decades. So much so, that it is now readily used by economists, political scientists, social scientists, and policymakers to refer to a group of people perceived as untouchable. And despite the claims of scholars such as Glasgow (1981) who deny that the term connotes "moral or ethical unworthiness" (p. 8), the term has, in fact, conveyed pejorative images of human beings as underlings, deficient, inferior, disadvantaged, and deprived.

From a historical context, it is significant to note that most of the descriptive categories used in reference to people who live in poverty have been derived primarily from research pertaining to the African American community. Yet much of the contemporary poverty metaphors in the social sciences can be readily traced to Oscar Lewis's (1963, 1968) "culture of poverty" arguments based on his study of Puerto Ricans and ghetto life. Prior to this time, those who lived in poverty were generally referred to as the poor by the well-meaning and as paupers or rabble by others not so empathetic to the plight of those who lived in impoverished conditions.

I believe that it is also of particular interest to note that social science christenings of the poor with such terms as the "culturally deprived," "disadvantaged," and later the "underclass" just happened to coincide with a historical period when communities of color were most actively involved in group struggles for self-determination. The introduction of such terminology in reference to communities of color at such a critical emancipatory period in their history leaves one open to speculate about the underlying motivations that may have informed the introduction of such terms in the first place.

It is also significant to mention that the contemporary use of the term "underclass" has come into vogue at a time when a major attitude of retrenchment is taking place with respect to questions of cultural diversity in the academy. Presently, a debate that is quickly gaining ground, and to a certain extent is supported by the work of William Wilson (1978), is shaped around questions related to the significance of race as a legitimate research category in the study of poverty. The underclass metaphor conveniently permits social science researchers to return to the politically disguised language of universalism by disengaging with subordinate cultural questions in their studies.

Although the term "underclass" may be considered to have a variety of meanings, there currently exists enough agreement in the social sciences to prompt the United States Accounting Office to issue a staff study entitled "The

Urban Underclass: Disturbing Problems Demanding Attention" (U.S. General Accounting Office, 1990). To one extent or another, this study has accepted the primary characteristics described in much of the current literature on the underclass (i.e., Auletta, 1982; Danziger & Gottshalk, 1987; Ellwood, 1988; Glasgow, 1981; Jencks, 1988; Kasurda, 1983; Lemann, 1986; Mincey, Sawhill, & Wolf, 1990; Murray, 1984; Ricketts & Sawhill, 1988; and Wilson, 1987). More specifically, the document assigns the following characteristics to the underclass (U.S. General Accounting Office, 1990, p. 1):

- They are permanently without connection to the legitimate labor force.
- The women in the group are likely to be persistently poor, to experience prolonged welfare dependency, and to experience high rates of out-of-wedlock births, often starting in their teen years.
- The children in the group are likely to be persistently poor and to experience high drop-out rates.
- Some people in the group exhibit disproportionately high rates of criminal behavior; others experience high rates of criminal victimization.

Further, it states that "those discussing the underclass are usually referring to people who are concentrated in urban neighborhoods and who are predominantly black and Hispanic" (p. 1).

Puerto Ricans as Underclass

To engage in a discussion of a subordinate culture in the United States without examining the historical events that have shaped the group's presence in this country is to ignore the historicity of common day experiences and hence, to be in danger of perpetuating group misrepresentations. Social science misrepresentations inadvertently arise as a consequence of decontextualizing the realities of people's lives by thrusting them carelessly into the realm of universalism and ahistorical analysis. Such has been the experience of African Americans, Native Americans, Puerto Ricans, Chicanos, Mexicanos, Japanese, Chinese, and other people of color in the United States.

To better understand the Puerto Rican reality in the United States requires an understanding of two significant conditions—colonization and immigration. These two social forces have contributed greatly to the realities faced by Puerto Rican people in this country today. On one hand, Puerto Ricans have been forced to accept foreign political conquest and economic control of their native land, along with the cultural domination inherent in a colonized existence. On the other hand, they have had to contend with the forces of racial and economic discrimination and the pressure of assimilation as colonized immigrants in the United States (Blauner, 1987).

The majority of Puerto Rican immigrants landed in New York City, where even today, the largest population of Puerto Ricans living off the island reside. Most arrived with a limited knowledge of English, few skills, and very few financial resources. As a consequence, Puerto Rican communities were established wherever extended familial survival strategies could be established and the national cultural identity affirmed. In many cities, community based organizations were created during the late 1960s and early 1970s in efforts to struggle for Puerto Rican political rights and self-determination through participation in local politics as well as state and national efforts to impact public policy.

But despite poverty programs that have resulted in modest socioeconomic gains for other communities of color, Puerto Ricans today are the most economically depressed group in the United States, with a poverty rate that has remained unchanged in the last decade. In New York City alone, over 45% of all Puerto Rican families live in poverty. In 1987, the median family income for Puerto Ricans was less than half of Whites (Center on Budget and Policy Priorities, 1988). In addition, studies indicate that the number of Puerto Rican students dropping out of high school has increased as has the number of female-headed households.

This highly vulnerable status is coupled with labor statistics that show lower rates for Puerto Ricans' labor participation than for any other group, with those employed working fewer hours on the average (Borjas, 1985). It is this picture of not only persistent but increasing economic disenfranchisement that has caused some researchers to foster "considerable speculation that Puerto Ricans have become part of the urban underclass" (Tienda, 1989, p. 105).

But despite the speculation of social scientists such as Marta Tienda (1989) about the Puerto Rican population, the term "underclass" has been widely criticized by Puerto Rican researchers (Bonilla, 1989; Hernandez, 1990; Torres, & Rodriguez, 1991). Here I would like to turn to the critique of Torres and Rodriguez (1991). Specific research areas addressed in their critique include the use of inadequate data, inadequate models, and the inaccessibility of the indigenous factor. In the first area, they point to the dearth of specific data on Puerto Ricans and problems with conclusions based on data derived from labor market studies concerning African Americans and Mexican Americans. The second area specifically critiques the use of statistical models for labor research that do not fit Puerto Ricans. Torres and Rodriguez (1991) explain that:

> Key differentiating factors may be at work, which have not been effectively incorporated into the models thus far developed. These include: the multiracial character of the Puerto Rican population and the difficulties this presents vis a vis the racial dichotomy in U.S.

society; the status of Puerto Ricans as colonial immigrants; the influence of long-term structural regional change on Puerto Rican communities; the excessively high levels of urbanization and the impact of housing abandonment in areas of high Puerto Rican concentration. In addition, these models fail to capture the positive effect of a functional dual migration.

Third, Torres and Rodriguez (1991) address the problem related to the inaccessibility of understanding the indigenous factors that constitute the cultural values and social practices at the heart of the Puerto Rican community. They also argue against ignoring prior studies. An act that permits researchers to make, for example, frivolous claims about "a new poverty" and to ignore that it is, in fact, "the same poverty that originated in the 50s; it is a continuation of the same trend; it has just been given a new appearance and a new name (i.e., 'underclass')" (Torres & Rodriguez, 1991). Instead, they call for research that "builds on the historically unique and multifaceted reality of the group" which incorporates indigenous input. More specifically, Torres and Rodriguez (1991) further warn against the consequences of omitting the "indigenous factor." Here, they explain that this increases the possibility of producing research that "may be seen as alien to the self-defined needs of the community."

On the specific use of the term "underclass," Torres and Rodriguez (1991) examine several points. One of these specifically relates to methodological disputes over measurement and causality. Also of concern is the impact of the term with respect to the Puerto Rican community as a whole. They emphasize that "it is disparaging and stigmatizing; this makes it both offensive and impractical." From the pragmatic side, they question "who is and who is not a member of the underclass?" And last, Torres and Rodriguez criticize the indiscriminate manner in which the term is being used in the literature. They specifically cite Tienda's (1989) article entitled "Puerto Ricans and the Underclass Debate."

> It is of interest to note that the article refers to what is a prevailing conception in many circles: That is, not that there is a growing sector within the Puerto Rican community which evidences a persisting disadvantage, but rather that the whole group is becoming an underclass. (Torres & Rodriguez, 1991).

The Colonizing Impact of Social Science Language

In a variety of ways, the Torres and Rodriguez critique makes inference to what is essentially the potential colonizing impact of social science language on the Puerto Rican community. In this particular case, the focus in on the use of the underclass concept to describe a human phenomenon that on one hand is extremely complex and distant from most researchers, and on the other hand instills a fear of disorientation and loss of control that could result from the mere thought of confronting the unpredictable nature of the group in the concrete. This dilemma intensifies the potential for projections and distortions that can function to distance the researcher from the people being discussed. Often the mechanism by which one distances oneself from unacceptable conditions or human affliction is to formulate language that permits one to more rationally engage with realities of an unknown and highly feared situation.

Hence, social science language can serve the purpose of constructing artificial boundaries in order to make physical phenomena controllable to the mind of the researcher. It is through this process by which social scientists create terms for human conditions they wish to control. In this way, a categorical term functions to facilitate the ability to refer to a specific condition, quantify the condition, identify particular aspects of the condition, see the condition with respect to cause, set goals with respect to it, and even believe that the condition is understood. Unfortunately, it is often this scientifically sanctioned process of masking reality that can inadvertently "lead to human degradation" (Lakoff & Johnson, 1980, p. 236).

Paulo Freire (in Shor & Freire, 1987) addresses the standardization of language and social science constructs from the standpoint of "political and ideological foundation." A major concern is centered on the action of those in a society who use their position of power to assign meaning, determine values, set criteria, and standardize phenomena.[3]

> The question of power is there, enveloping our idioms and the problem of language even though we don't always perceive this power....The dominant class has the power to establish its language [and values] as the standard. (Shor & Freire, 1987, p. 149)

At issue here is the question of who is doing the naming? In a culture that places great value on the notion of absolute truths such as that which generally gives structure to social science research, the people who impose their language on subordinate groups also have the power to define that which is considered "absolute and objective" truth in the society-at-large.

In their reference to the "politics of definition," Stafford and Ladner (1990) note that language plays "a critical role not only in the analysis of social problems but in the determination of power relationships" between groups in society (p. 143). Given the manner in which this operates, it is clear to see how language can function in the interest of social empowerment or in the interest of social domination. One of the most significant ways in which this occurs is where language is used to highlight properties of injustice or to shift our attention away from these properties.[4]

The colonizing influence of terms such as "the underclass" on the members of a particular subordinate group cannot be ignored. In many instances, when a group is labeled, the members of such a group learn to perceive themselves as persons who deserve the label and, hence, come to act accordingly. Herbert Gans (1990) in his critique of the underclass concept speaks to the danger of its widespread legitimation on those who live in poverty:

> Insofar as poor people keep up with the labels the rest of society sticks on them, they are aware of the latest ones. We do not all know the "street level" consequences of stigmatizing labels, but they cannot be good. One of the likely, and most dangerous, consequences of labels is that they can become self-fulfilling prophecies. People who are described as members of the underclass may begin to feel that they are members of such a class and are therefore unworthy in a new way. At the least, they now have to fight against yet another threat to their self-respect, not to mention another reason to feel that the society would just soon have them disappear, (p. 274)

In an effort to summarize the colonizing impact of the underclass concept, it is useful to refer to Gans's (1990) discussion on "deconstructing the underclass." In his work, Gans lists 10 dangers inherent in the use of the underclass concept for naming the reality of people who live in poverty. These include:

1. Its unusual power as a "buzz word"
2. Its use as "a racial code word that subtly hides anti-black and anti-Hispanic feeling"
3. Its "flexible character" that allows wider and wider use for more and more people
4. Its use as a "synthesizing notion" that permits the lumping together and labeling of different people
5. The term's interference with antipoverty policy and other kinds of planning
6. The persuasive capacity of the underclass concept to serve as a reified definition of groups that can lead to moralistic victim-blaming notions
7. The manner in which the underclass has been analyzed in terms of neighborhoods or regions
8. The "concentration and isolation" hypothesis
9. The term itself "sidesteps" issues of poverty
10. The danger of inventing new unnecessary words which further marginalize subordinate groups

Finally, it is worth noting that a number of social scientists have addressed the colonizing impact of social science language on subordinate cultural groups (Bosmajian, 1990; Fanon, 1967; Freire, 1970; Freire & Macedo, 1986; Memmi, 1965; O'Neill, 1985). In particular, their work speaks to the tragic consequences of social science language with respect to the ways in which it often functions to silence and perpetuate the alienation of those groups who are perceived as deviant and, hence, excludes them from a social process where they can name their own experiences and actively participate in changing the conditions in which they live.

Toward a Decolonizing Social Science Study of Poverty

Kenwyn Smith (1990) asserts that "when we notice that our social institutions are driven by the larger political contexts in which they are embedded, we are forced to acknowledge that the content of our research and the methods we use are likewise subject to the prevailing political forces" (p. 121). As such, social science researchers must acknowledge the colonizing impact of traditional social science research language and methodology—a language and methodology which have often perpetuated elitist, authoritarian, fragmented, and hence, disempowering notions of poverty.

In efforts to overcome such a legacy, any social scientist who authentically seeks to participate on behalf of those who live in poverty must, first and foremost, enter into a relationship with the people. As a consequence of ignoring many of the issues discussed above, traditional social science has failed to function as a tool for empowerment and transformation in the lives of those who live in poverty. Instead, it has served to sustain the interests of a few, at the expense of the many. There is no place where this is more evident than in the outcome of thirty years of compensatory education, social welfare reform, and "war on poverty" programs— programs that were born of paternalistic notions of poverty or abstract liberal notions of generosity sustained by traditional forms of poverty research. Freire (1970) addresses the failure of such programs in the following manner:

> The task implies that...leaders do not go to the people in order to bring them a message of "salvation," but in order to know through dialogue with them their objective situation and their awareness of that situation—the various levels of perception of themselves and of the world in which they exist. One cannot expect positive results from an educational or... action program which fails to respect the particular view of the world held by the people. Such a program constitutes cultural invasion, good intentions notwithstanding (p. 84).

What is clear from what we have seen in the past is that social scientists need a different vision of the world if we are to truly comprehend the nature of poverty in this country. This vision must incorporate a perception of human beings as having the capacity to overcome those social forces that function to dehumanize and disempower them. It is a vision that must define all human beings within the context of the social, political, economic, and historical forces at work in their lives—a view of human beings that refuses to separate them from nature or to decontextualize them from the reality of the power relationships that give shape to their world. And clearly it is a vision that supports the notion that people must actively participate in the process of their emancipation from those adverse social conditions that threaten their self-determination.

If we are to move toward a praxis of decolonization as researchers, we must be willing to embrace dialogical principles—that is, critical principles that position us to move contextually in communion with communities, rather than in opposition to their right to control their lives. In such an approach we are called to use our knowledge, resources, and influence to unmask those conditions and social forces that strip people of their humanity and perpetuate their suffering.

From the standpoint of overcoming forms of linguistic colonization, it requires that we examine carefully, in both theory and practice, the manner in which particular terms such as "underclass" work to perpetuate the social oppression of particular groups and to sustain the interest of the dominant culture. More specifically, this requires that such a term as "underclass" be problematized through a dialogical exercise in which the social reality is deconstructed, in order to fully unveil the overdetermination of the word by the structures of power that have imposed it upon the people.

John O'Neill (1985) describes a "praxis of conscientization" as an alternative approach to social science research. It is an approach that begins and ends with those who are the subjects of the study. That is, the participants are actively involved in the planning and development of the study, the collection of data, the final analysis of the information gathered, and the development of a set of recommendations for action. This suggests a form of study that carries a vision of empowerment through returning to the people what truly belongs to them. Inherent in this approach is not an attempt to learn about the people but to come to know with them the reality that challenges them and through this process to discover those actions that will function to transform the conditions that limit their lives.

As it might be evident even by this brief description of a dialogical research approach, the process requires time and cannot be accomplished simply through the quasi-involvement of the researchers nor solely quantifiable data. It is a form of research grounded in relationships that can move all the participants of a study through those critical steps that truly permit us to actively learn from one another, in order that we might transform our world together.

Quantitative descriptions coupled with disembodied terminology will only function to deepen the colonizing structures that permeate the lives of all people. Let us instead work toward participatory social science research efforts that can begin to answer honestly the many long-standing questions of poverty. It is this kind of research that we need in the Puerto Rican community.

REFERENCES

Auletta, K. (1982). *The Underclass.* New York: Random House.

Blauner, R. (1987). "Colonized and Immigrant Minorities." In R. Takaki (ed.), *From Different Shores.* New York: Oxford University Press (149–60).

Bonilla, F. (1989). *Breaking out of the Cycle of Poverty.* Washington, D.C.: National Puerto Rican Coalition.

Borjas, G. (1985). "Public Spending for the Poor: Trends, Prospects, and Economic Limits." In S. Danziger and D. Weinberg (eds.), *Fighting Poverty: What Works and What Doesn't.* Cambridge, MA: Harvard University Press (151–64).

Bosmajian, J. (1990). *The Language of Oppression.* Lanham, MD: University Press of America.

Center on Budget and Policy Priorities. (1988). *Shortchange: Recent Developments in Hispanic Poverty, Income, and Employment.* Washington, D.C.

Danziger, S., and P. Gottshalk (1987). "Earning Inequality: The Spatial Concentration of Poverty and the Underclass," *American Economic Review* 77:2; 211–15.

Ellwood, D. (1988). *Poor Support.* New York: Basic Books.

Fanon, F. (1967). *Black Skin, White Masks.* New York: Grove Press.

Freire, P. (1970). *Pedagogy of the Oppressed.* New York: Seabury Press.

Freire, P., and D. Macedo (1986). *Literacy: Reading the Word and the World.* South Hadley, MA: Bergin and Garvey.

Gans, H. (1990). "Deconstructing the Underclass: The Term's Dangers as a Planning Concept," *Journal of the American Planning Association* 56:3; 271–77.

Glasgow, D. (1981). *The Black Underclass.* New York: Vintage.

Hernandez, J. (1990). "Latino Alternatives to the Underclass Concept," *Latino Studies Journal* 1: 95–105.

Jencks, C. (1988, June 13). "Deadly Neighborhoods," *New Republic,* 23–32.

Kasurda, J. (1983). "Caught in the Web of Change," *Society* 21: 41–47.

Lakoff, G., and M. Johnson (1980). *Metaphors We Live by.* Chicago: University of Chicago Press.

Lemann, N. (1986, June). "The Origins of the Underclass," *Atlantic Monthly,* 54–68.

Lewis, D. (1968). *La Vida: A Puerto Rican Family in the Culture of Poverty in San Juan and New York.* London: Panther Books.

Lewis, D. (1963). "The Culture of Poverty," *Scientific American* 215: 19–25.

Memmi, A. (1965). *The Colonizer and the Colonized.* Boston: Beacon Press.

Mincey, R., I. Sawhill, and D. Wolf (1990). "The Underclass: Definition and Measurement," *Science* 248: 450–52.

Murray, C. (1984). *Losing Ground: American Social Policy, 1950–1980.* New York: Basic Books.

Myrdal, G. (1962). *The Challenge to Affluence.* New York: Pantheon.

O'Neill, J. (1985). "Decolonization and the Ideal Speech Community: Some Issues in the Theory and Practice of Communicative Competence." In J. Forrester (ed.), *Critical Theory and Public Life.* Cambridge, MA: M.I.T. Press (57–76).

Ricketts, E., and I. Sawhill (1988). "Defining and Measuring the Underclass," *Journal of Policy Analysis and Measurement* 7: 316–25.

Shor, I., and P. Freire (1987). *A Pedagogy for Liberation.* Westport, CT: Bergin and Garvey.

Smith, K. (1990). "Notes from the Epistemological Corner: The Role of Projection in the Creation of Social Science," *Journal of Applied Behavioral Science* 26: 119–27.

Stafford, W.W., and J. Ladner (1990). "Political Dimensions of the Underclass Concept." In H. Gans (ed.), *Sociology in America.* Newbury Park, CA: Sage (138–55).

Tienda, M. (1989). "Puerto Ricans and the Underclass Debate: Evidence for Structural Explanations of the Labor Market Performance," *Annals of the American Academy of Political and Social Science* 501: 105–19.

Torres, A., and C. Rodriguez (1991). "Latino Policy: Problems, Debates, and Prescriptions." In E. Melendez, C. Rodriguez, and B. Barry Figueroa (eds.), *Hispanics in the Labor Force.* New York: Plenum.

U.S. General Accounting Office (1990). "The Urban Underclass: Disturbing Problems Demanding Attention" (GAO/HRD-90-52). Annapolis, MD: U.S. General Accounting Office.

Wilson, W.J. (1987). *The Truly Disadvantaged: The Inner City, the Underclass, and Public Policy.* Chicago: University of Chicago Press.

Wilson, W.J. (1978). *The Declining Significance of Race: Blacks and Changing American Institutions.* Chicago: University of Chicago Press.

Zinn, M.B. (1989). "Family, Race, and Poverty in the Eighties," *Signs: Journal of Women in Culture and Society* 14: 856–74.

ENDNOTES

1. The Community Fellows Program, established by Mel King in 1971, is a unique community development program of the Massachusetts Institute of Technology's Department of Urban Studies and Planning. The program brings together community based people of color from major cities in the country who are specifically grappling with issues related to youth who live in poverty. Many of the Fellows were actually born and raised in the same communities in which they live and work.

2. A similar discussion can be waged for other terms such as "culturally deprived," "disadvantaged," "minority," and even the now common label of "Hispanic," which emerged into being as a governmentally assigned classification in the 1970s. It is particularly important to keep in mind that these all represent terms that emerged outside of the context of the communities or groups for which they are currently still used.

3. As with the use of the term "underclass," the "feminization of poverty" concept also serves as a means of perpetuating middle class societal norms in order to dominate the lives and self-image of women, rather than to engage directly with the realities faced by women who parent children alone (Zinn, 1989). In both instances, the process constitutes an abuse of power that is executed through research language and methods that decontextualize or compartmentalize the experience of those who live in poverty.

4. This brings the discussion back to the earlier concern regarding the current use of the term "underclass" as a deliberate or inadvertent shift away from engaging with questions of race as legitimate social science category in the study of impoverished communities. It is impossible for social science researchers to fully comprehend the realities that exist in the lives of Puerto Ricans or any other subordinate cultural group that lives in poverty without a willingness to engage critically with the intersection of race, class, and gender in the study of poverty. The complexity of these relationships cannot be addressed through research language and methods that artificially reduce or simplify what constitutes a complex entanglement of social, political, and economic relations of power.

CHAPTER 14

Radicalizing the Immigrant Debate in the United States

A Call for Open Borders and Global Human Rights

> For what was once hailed as a human right is now opposed as an economic liability. Our governments are trapped in a morally warped and ideologically unsustainable paradigm. They applaud the free movement of capital; while they abhor the free movement of labor.
>
> —HUMAN RIGHTS WATCH[1]

The United States border with Mexico constitutes one of the most bloody and contentious geopolitical arenas in the world. Since its inception in 1848, increasing violence and conflict, varying in nature according to political and economic pressures, have plagued the border.[2] In the last decade, active campaigns of Human Rights Watch http://www.hrw.org or the militarization of the border by both official border patrol agents and border vigilantes have prevailed. Many of the names of some of these campaigns—*Operation Rio Grande* at the Brownsville-Matamoros border, *Operation Hold the Line* at the El Paso-Juarez border, and *Operation Gatekeepers* and the *Minuteman Project* at the San Diego-Tijuana border—attest to the war-like mentality.[3]

In the midst of this intensification of border security, there are now an estimated 12,000,000 undocumented immigrants in the U.S. Of those unable to enter successfully, 3000 have died in the last five years. The unsolved murders of almost 400 young *maquiladora* workers in the border cities of Juarez and Chihuahua are considered by some to be directly linked to the on-going contested border politics of the region. Over a thousand would-be immigrants are deported or detained each month—a number that actually tripled in the last year, despite the raging national debate on immigration. The U.S. Citizenship and Immigration Services (USCIS) under the auspices of the Department of Homeland Security, has in custody more than 15,000 detainees in detention centers and jails across the country.

The same anti-immigrant sentiments that have historically fueled U.S.-Mexico border conflicts are also brewing in Washington today, where the contentious debate on U.S. immigration reform threatens to become the most important national issue of the 2008 presidential campaign. Over the last year, Congress Democrats and Republicans have debated furiously over the best approach to address the issue of "illegal immigration." In May 2007, the debate resulted in the introduction of numerous measures to intensify enforcement of anti-immigrant policies, including a "compromise bill" touted to ease the path toward legalization for many immigrants. However, immigrant rights groups vehemently protested the proposed legislation, which is expected to turn as many as 12 million immigrants into "guest workers" and dissolve family reunification laws, creating greater hardship for undocumented immigrant families.

Such policies and practices surrounding immigration blatantly reflect an ideologically unsustainable paradigm. Thus, I wish to argue for the need to transform the U.S. immigration debate from one that primarily demonizes and criminalizes Mexicans as violent smugglers of drugs and people to one that forthrightly focuses on the underlying forces of capital that thwart global sustainability. Hence, this chapter seeks to link issues of local concern with the historical phenomena of migration and capital. By doing so, local immigration debates can more effectively create the political space for discussing questions of education, youth unemployment, labor abuses, housing shortages, transportation needs, police abuses, and social tensions related to immigrant communities, beyond nativist notions that position immigrants as *the problem* to be solved.

This, of course, does not mean that we should be blind to the particular problems faced daily by immigrants or the difficulties experienced by those living in previously homogeneous communities who are unprepared to negotiate the local conditions that result from U.S. economic folly abroad. So yes, local communities must work together with new immigrant residents to address the class conflicts associated with immigrant life and labor in the United States. There is a need to jettison stereotypical attitudes and ignorance of immigrant populations. It requires negotiating differences in culture, aesthetics, uses of space, and tolerance for more intimate living arrangements. In addition, class issues, camouflaged behind a discourse of racialization, must be weeded out and transformed.

The realities of the changing economy in many cities and rural communities must be renegotiated. Downtown areas that once were abandoned have taken on new life in the presence of immigrant residents. New enclaves of immigrants have developed and new businesses inspired by immigrant consumer patterns have begun to be frequented by the larger community. Often these factors stimulate tremendous economic revitalization in blighted communities but are generally ignored or even maligned in mainstream immigration debates.

But other factors are also ignored. For example, with almost 12 million undocumented people in the United States, how can we, by any stretch of the imagination, speak about immigration as an aberration? Instead what seems clear here is that immigration is a necessity of the system. It results from the policies and practices tied to the current political economy—including the culture of business and government—and the economic imperatives of the nation-state. We must speak to what exists in this country as an exploitive de facto guest worker system, integral to the U.S. wage-labor system. And as de facto guest workers, undocumented immigrants labor without equal rights, labor without representation, subsist on meager wages, suffer medical neglect, are consistently subjected to oppressive institutional conditions, and are denied *carte blanche* the recognition of the important economic role they play in this society. Meanwhile, the differences in the conditions between men and women immigrants are generally overlooked, while the emotional needs of families living in exile don't even make it on the radar screen.

Yet immigrants from Mexico, Latin America, and the Caribbean continue to make the arduous journey northward seeking a better quality of life for themselves and their families. Their trek northward is the most logical response to the global structures of inequality. They move from geographical regions where wealth concentrations are low to the empire of capital—the USA—where concentrations of capital are high and density is still low by many world standards. They move to the region of the world that has the highest consumption rate of all industrialized nations. Hence, what cannot be denied is that the decision to emigrate is overwhelmingly one of economics.[4]

Nevertheless, the aspiration for survival and a better quality of life—oftentimes cited by immigration advocates and neoconservative alike—is not the root cause of immigration. For people have been on the move since the beginning of time and had it not been for this phenomenon, with its economic imperatives and the dispossession of lands from Native American nations, the U.S. would not exist today. Thus, the politics of immigration has always been tied to the prevailing politics of capital accumulation. For example, since 2001 the U.S. has effectively capitalized on the tragedy of September 11[5] to exacerbate hostilities against those perceived as outsiders and step up the regulation and monitoring of the movement of people on U.S. territory. Moreover, conflicting and contradictory national efforts, which "on one hand, advocate for the open and unrestricted movement of commerce, trade, finance capital, technology and ideas; and on the other, [install] deeply isolationist policies to restrict the movement of people and workers across its borders"[6] function to intensify the anti-immigrant debate. As the Iraq situation has become more and more volatile, the media's anti-immigrant fervor has been heightened, obscuring more important reasons for the current economic instability.[7]

Yet, despite the intensification of anti-immigrant backlash, millions of immigrants and their supporters took to the streets during the Spring of 2006 to effectively protest against the Sensenbrenner bill.[8] Key provisions of this broad-reaching legislation call for the building of 700 miles of walls and fences along the U.S.-Mexico border; the mandatory federal custody of "illegal aliens" detained by local authorities; and mandatory employer verification of legal status of workers through electronic means. In addition, the bill criminalizes as a felony anyone remaining in the United States without proper documentation as well as those who provide assistance to undocumented immigrants.

During the summer of 2006, the action of Elvira Arrellano became an important symbol of immigrant resistance against the inhumanity of both federal and local anti-immigrant policies and practices. Arrellano, seeking to resist her deportation, took refuge in a Chicago church so she could remain in the country with her seven-year-old son, Saul, who is a U.S. citizen. Her action powerfully defied the powers of the INS and Homeland Security combined. Her courageous act of resistance helped to put a human face on national immigration debates. In fact, in November 2006, Arrellano's son, Saul, addressed the Mexican Congress, pleading for help in stopping the deportation of his mother. As a result, the Mexican government passed a resolution against deportations, appealing to humanitarian principles of family cohesion. Yet despite this action, the Mexican government is equally responsible for the reasons that Mexican citizens find little recourse for their lives than to resort to an existence as undocumented immigrants.

Challenging Nativism in the Face of Poverty

People hunger for modernity and they gamble. Knowing full
well that the odds are stacked against them...they move...if they
sense there is even a small chance of advancement and a new life.

—MIKE DAVIS [9]

A long history of impoverished people on the move calls into question nativist
condemnations of neoconservatives like Samuel P. Huntington who bemoan the
cultural wars and the *clash of civilization*. He argues:

> The persistent inflow of Hispanic immigrants threatens to divide the United States into
> two peoples, two cultures, and two languages. Unlike past immigrants groups, Mexican
> and other Latinos have not assimilated into mainstream U.S. culture, forming instead
> their own political and linguistic enclaves—from Los Angeles to Miami—and rejecting
> the Anglo protestant values that built the American dream. The United States ignores
> this challenge at its peril. [10]

In this alarmist attack of Latino immigration, Huntington invokes racialized
images of despicably deficient Latino immigrants who defy democratic values, are
responsible for lowering U.S. wages, harbor contempt for U.S. culture, and stub-
bornly insist on retaining their culture and language. The danger of such ruthless
anti-immigrant rhetoric is that it functions to not only distort the relevance of necessary debates but unfortunately also makes its way into the arena of public policy,
where restrictive immigration policies in the name of sustainability camouflage a
deeply entrenched egoistic defense of privilege. [11]

This was most recently apparent when the City Council of Farmers Branch, a
town located just north of Dallas, Texas, unanimously approved some of the most
daunting anti-immigrant measures in the nation by first in November 2006, requiring all property owners and employers to report illegal immigrants; then, again, in
May 2007 passing the first ordinance in the nation barring undocumented immigrants from renting apartments. [12] The Farmers Branch proposal followed similar
legislation passed in Escondido, California and Hazleton, Pennsylvania to fine
property owners who rent to illegal immigrants, deny business permits to companies that employ or do business with undocumented workers, and require tenants
to register and pay for rental permits. [13]

Almost as problematic are the rhetorical responses of some Latino officials
and national publications—responses that lacked the depth of analysis to counter the obstructive vitriolic of anti-immigrant backlash. Typical responses of such
publications as *Hispanic Business*, for example, assert that "The majority of immigrants arrive in the United States in search of the *American Dream*." [14] In con-

cert, the publication has gone to great lengths to showcase the entrepreneurial qualities of Latino immigrants, along with their contribution to the economy.[15] Unfortunately these responses to the anti-immigrant backlash degenerate into superficial and defensive posturing, which fails to interrogate the political economy of migration and its roots in imperialism.

Hence, Mexican migration must be traced historically to imperial rule in the last century, a dynamic that predates the "globalization" debate. Implicit here is a critique of contemporary notions of globalization, such as Thomas Friedman's[16] celebration of globalization in The World Is Flat or Michael Hardt and Antonio Negri's[17] argument in Empire that classical imperialism has disappeared and along with it both powers of the nation-state and the working class. Both these views fail to prove out in today's world and steer observers away from the salient question that must be asked: What is the underlying structural root of increasing immigration?

Both Friedman and Hardt and Negri's arguments seem to dismiss or ignore the implications of the movement of people and their relationship to the accumulation of wealth, on one hand, and the global dispossession of large populations, on the other. For example, the conditions of northward migration are intimately linked to the participation of ruling elites in countries such as Mexico, which has a long historical connection to U.S. imperial polices and practices. For over a century, the Mexican government and capitalist's interests have partnered with the U.S. in pursuit of their own self-interests, while neglecting the needs of the majority of the Mexican people. For example,

> ...in 1991, the Salinas government passed a reform law that both permitted and encouraged privatization of the *ejido* lands. Since the *ejido* provided the basis for collective security among indigenous groups, the government was, in effect, divesting itself of its responsibilities to maintain the basis for that security. This was moreover, one item within a general package of privatization moves under Salinas which dismantled social security protections in general and which had predictable and dramatic impacts upon income and wealth distribution.[18]

Hence it should be no surprise that many indigenous communities in opposition to these reforms joined the Zapatista rebellion in January 1994 against the Mexican government, on the very day that the NAFTA agreement went into enforcement.

However, again it must be repeated that even these contributing factors predate the contemporary globalization debate and entail a long history of U.S. capital relations with members of the Mexican ruling class, via the nation-state apparatus, irrespective of which party has been in office. Hence, immigration reforms must take into account the trends of migration tied to U.S. economic and political interests in the southern hemisphere and the need for cheap labor to carry out dispossessing strategies of accumulation.

Another distortion in the current debate is that immigrants live at the margins of our nation's economy. Nothing is further from the truth. In fact, immigrants are strategically integrated into the U.S. class-wage system and exploited as cheap labor. To ignore the implications of this reality is to be duped by the ruse that somehow immigrants are extraneous to the class-wage system when they are undeniably integral to sustaining its vitality.

Moreover, it is seldom noted that Huntington's lamentations—including Latino immigrant concentration in particular areas, their cultural and linguistic influence on social formations, and their impact on the economy—are the result of the very neoliberal policies he has advanced. Global neoliberal policies have led to a widening gap worldwide between the rich and the poor, resulting in unbridled migration to this country, not only immigrants from Latin America.

Also often ignored are the actual hardships of migration and the fact that most people would much prefer to remain in their own countries, on their own land, in familiar surroundings, providing their children and families a decent quality of life. When this possibility becomes more and more difficult, in the wake of neoliberal accumulation by dispossession, people are left little choice than to endure the hardships of staying or risk the hardships of leaving for a potentially better life. Immigrants repeatedly mourn leaving their families behind and living a life of exile in order to ensure economic subsistence. Yet, U.S. ethnocentrism, with its smug arrogance, is often at work in the criminalization of immigrants, preventing the empire's pampered citizens from understanding life beyond material comforts.

Meanwhile, it is the increasingly unfettered movement of capital, which helps create the poverty that prompts economic migration from the so-called "developing" countries. Structural adjustment programs, imposed on countries by the International Monetary Fund and the World Bank in return for loans, generally lead to cuts in health, education and welfare spending and mass privatization, with people pushed out of their exploitable lands to serve the interests of capital. To illustrate the enormous impact of these policies on the world's disenfranchised population, consider the following facts and statistics on poverty:[19]

- half the world—nearly 3 billion people—live on less than two dollars a day
- the GNP (Gross Domestic Product) of the poorest 48 nations (25% of the world's countries) is less than the wealth of the world's three richest people combined
- less than 1% of what the world spent every year on weapons was needed to put every child into school by the year 2000, but it did not happen

- the wealthiest nation on earth (U.S.) has the widest gap between the rich and poor of any industrialized nation
- 20% of the population in the wealthiest countries consumes 86 percent of the world's goods
- A few hundred millionaires now own as much wealth as the world's 2.5 billion people
- Approximately 790 million people in the developing world are still chronically undernourished
- A mere 12% of the world's population uses 85% of water resources
- 1.7 million children will die this year alone due to poverty

Hence, anti-immigration reform policies must be challenged in ways that both expose and disrupt institutional practices anchored in neoliberal orthodoxy—draconian reforms that result in great metropolises of capital, expanding an economics of poverty that gives rise to *global slums*.[20] And the building of a 700-mile border wall between the U.S. and Mexico[21] will certainly not ameliorate these conditions. For a border wall cannot contain the political mendacity, exploitive labor practices, and shameful poverty tied to the unchecked excesses of capital and efforts to safeguard capitalism from impending crisis. On another note, we cannot ignore that these are the same interests that proclaim the virtues of accountability, yet wash their hands of responsibility for the forced migration created by unrelenting policies of accumulation.

Global immigration today is inextricably tied to a historical context in which the internationalization of capital does not work to dismantle the nation-state but rather is legitimated through its apparatus. Instead of causing the demise of the working class, this mechanism has solidified class divisions by placing greater power in the hands of the state to regulate (or deregulate) the affairs of capital while, simultaneously, utilizing the media and other cultural and technological means of ideological control to undermine the powers of mass protest along with the movement of people—whether that is by control of migration patterns or the mass incarceration of impoverished populations.

Immigration and the New Imperialism

A never-ending accumulation of property must be based on a never-ending accumulation of power.

—HANNAH ARENDT[22]

The difficulty in addressing the question of immigration in the U.S. is sifting throughall the sources of misinformation and constantly shifting rhetoric. Moreover there is a need to counter the *othering* of immigrants as "evil," criminals, or demons who are wickedly threatening the well-being and stability—or sustainability—of the *American Dream*. To do this requires that that we understand that increasing immigration is not rooted in the wayward individual aspirations of *illegal immigrants*. Instead, as David Harvey argues in *The New Imperialism*, it is rooted in the:

> uneven geographical conditions that arise out of the uneven patterning of natural resource endowments and locational advantages, but, more importantly, are produced by the uneven ways in which wealth and power themselves become highly concentrated in certain places by virtue of a symmetrical exchange relations.[23]

Moreover, for the U.S. to maintain its political dominance and its relentless strategies of capital accumulation, it has extended its military, political, and economic power (most notably in Iraq) to the point that the dangers of overreach are undeniable. Today's so-called "immigration problems" constitute only the tip of the iceberg of the enormous global chaos being created by ruthless forces of capital excess. Current efforts to control or "liquidate" immigrants, then, must be tied to the overreaching of U.S. power worldwide. Hence, the threat to this nation is not increasing immigration but rather the destructive impact of "accumulation by dispossession."[24] This refers to the wide range of processes by which the United States has made major economic gains through:

> ...the commodification and privatization of land and the forceful expulsion of peasant populations; the conversion of various forms of property rights (common, collective, state, etc.) into exclusive private property rights; the suppression of rights to the commons; the commodification of labour power and the suppression of alternative (indigenous) forms of production and consumption; colonial, neo-colonial, and imperial processes of appropriation of assets (including natural resources) [such as water and air]; the monetization of exchange and taxation, particularly of land; the slave trade; and usury, the national debt, and ultimately the credit system as radical means of accumulation.[25]

Such forms of accumulation worldwide have been carried out with little regard to the destructive outcome of neoliberal policies and practices on impoverished populations. Moreover, the elimination of regulatory statutes designed to protect labor and the environment from degradation must also be seen as a loss of human rights. And the reversion of hard won common property (i.e., state pensions, health insurance, etc.) to the private domain constitutes one of the most flagrant policies of dispossession to come out of neoliberal orthodoxy.

Unfortunately, the rogue nature of such economic imperialism is not new to the United States, despite the culture of denial that has prevailed among a large portion of the U.S. population. In fact, Harvey argues that the United States "has a history of ruthlessness that belies its attachment to its constitution and the rule of law."[26] More specifically he cites:

> McCarthyism, the murder or incarceration of Black Panther leaders, the internment of Japanese in the Second World War, surveillance and infiltration of opposition groups of all kinds, and now a certain preparedness to overthrow the Bill of Rights by passing the Patriot and Homeland Security Acts. It has been even more significantly ruthless abroad in sponsoring coups in Iran, Iraq, Guatemala, Chile, and Vietnam (to name a few) in which untold thousands died. It has supported state terrorism throughout the world wherever it has been convenient. CIA and Special Forces units operate in innumerable countries. Study of this record has led many to paint a portrait of the US as the greatest "rogue state" on earth.[27]

Xenophobic neoconservative rhetoric blatantly accuses immigrants of 1) being a drain to the economy, 2) being the cause of mass unemployment, and 3) threatening the course of "sustainable development." Yet the real culprit is the internationalization of capital with its neoliberal solutions. For example, capitalists use technological changes and speculative investment to induce unemployment, thus creating an industrial reserve army of unemployed workers. Rather than immigrants, it is this deliberate creation of unemployment that has exerted a downward pressure on wage rates, thereby creating new opportunities for profitable deployment of capital. This exploitive process of capital accumulation at the expense of workers has been responsible for stagnant and declining real wages over the last 15 years. In fact, it must be noted that this form of *othering* of both immigrants and unemployed workers has been necessary to the stabilization of capitalism.

Meanwhile, the liberalization of the market has served to produce greater levels of social and economic inequality. Within this dynamic, the "predatory" rhetoric of immigration serves to effectively camouflage capitalism's predatory practices, which have created the impetus for increasing immigration to the centers of concentrated wealth in the United States—whether that be their movement to global cities or promising rural communities. Moreover, it cannot be left unsaid that "the State, with its monopoly of violence and definitions of legality plays a crucial role in both backing and promoting"[28] the predatory rhetoric of immigration.

So, the so-called "problems of immigrants" must be linked to the over-extension of political economic power abroad, which results in "chronic insecurity at home."[29] In response, Harvey argues, the middle classes took to the defense of territory, nation, and tradition, mobilizing the territorial logic of power to shield themselves against the alienating forces of neoliberal capitalism. The racism and nationalism that had once bound nation-state and empire together re-emerged among the working class, and blaming the problems on immigrants became a convenient diversion for elite interests. As a consequence, exclusionary identity politics based on race, ethnicity, and religion again flourished.[30]

Moreover, the inflammatory rhetoric toward immigrants, with its focus on building a border wall, works to effectively camouflage the current vulnerability of the U.S. economy, by deflecting attention from burgeoning corporate debt, U.S. dependence on foreign investment inflow to cover foreign debts, and the increasing devaluation of the U.S. dollar. Furthermore, blaming immigrants for the social and economic ills puts window-dressing on the vast drain created by the turn to a permanent war economy—a desperate attempt by U.S. interests to conserve political and economic dominance worldwide.

The Rhetoric of Population Control

From Nazi-era eugenics to forced sterilizations, the population [control] framework is indelibly linked to colonial paternalism.
—ADAM WERBACH[31]

Many anti-immigration debates are firmly anchored in a discourse of human overpopulation.[32] Leading anti-immigrant policy institutes, including *NumbersUSA* and *Center for Immigration Studies*, wield arguments about the negative impact of immigrants on community sustainability and resource depletion. The environmental wing of anti-immigrant forces, which emerged from the zero-population movement of the 1960s and 1970s, includes members of such organizations as *Environment-Population Balance, Carrying Capacity Network*, and *Negative Population Growth*. These organizations point to immigration as the most incorrigible factor in U.S. population growth.[33]

Public figures such as former governor of Colorado, Richard Lamm, co-author of *The Immigration Time Bomb: The Fragmenting of America*,[34] suggest that "uncontrolled immigration" will put the United States in peril if strict measures to curb immigration are not enforced. Meanwhile, anti-immigrant zero-population advocates contend that the current population of the Earth, now over six billion, is simply too many people for our planet to sustain at current consumption levels. However, this challenge for sustainability is distributed unevenly, given the fact that the so-called first world consumes over 86% of the world's resources. But rather than move toward changing consumption and redistribution patterns, a campaign to stop population growth is their major concern. Hence, it is not surprising that aggressive population control efforts in disenfranchised communities have led to human rights violations—violations directly linked to the involuntary sterilization of Puerto Rican, African American, and Mexican immigrant women in the U.S.

Xenophobic attitudes linked to population growth are also used as rationales for the establishment and enforcement of anti-immigrant public policies. Here, the principal cause for poverty in the world is attributed to the reproductive function of poor and immigrant women; a phenomenon I refer to as "the politics of colonized wombs."[35] That is, the cause of social and economic ills among immigrants becomes defined as a question of reproductive control. The racialization and sexism inherent in this biologically determinist view of the problem also preclude, unfortunately, an examination of the predatory nature of capitalism as enumerated earlier.

More recently, for example, the reactionary reproductive rhetoric of immigration took a new spin. On November 14, 2006, a Missouri Republican-led panel on immigration asserted that abortion is partly to blame for increasing immigration, because it has caused a shortage of American workers. According to David Lieb:[36]

> The report from the House Special Committee on Immigration Reform says that liberal social welfare policies have discouraged Americans from working and have encouraged immigrants to cross the border illegally.

> The statements about abortion and welfare policies, along with a recommendation to abolish income taxes in favor of sales taxes, were inserted into the immigration report by Rep. Edgar G.H. Emery (R), the panel's chairman...who equates abortion to murder.

> [Emery asserted that] "We hear a lot of arguments today that the reason that we can't get serious about our borders is that we are desperate for all these workers," he said. "You don't have to think too long. If you kill 44 million of your potential workers, it's not too surprising we would be desperate for workers."

> "Suggestions for how to stop illegal hiring varied without any simple solution," the report states. "The lack of traditional work ethic, combined with the effects of 30 years of abortion and expanding liberal social welfare policies have produced a shortage of workers and a lack of incentive for those who can work."

What is clear here is 1) pro-life neoconservatives are primarily concerned with life that looks like them, while calling for population control of immigrants; and 2), the long historical tradition to blame women's reproduction for the ills of the world is still alive and kicking. The misogyny of the latter view seems to trump the plethora of research and United Nations reports[37] that repeatedly argue that the most important factor in reducing population increase around the world is the improvement to quality of life and economic well-being of impoverished communities. Incidentally, it is also considered the quickest road to full citizenship and democratic participation in the political affairs of any society.

Open Borders: A Radical Possibility

In all, the irrepressibility of movement seems a powerful argument against state efforts to suppress it.

—ALAN DOWTY[38]

The radical possibility of open borders is in concert with a United Nations proclamation that "the right to leave or stay [is] nothing less than a right of personal self-determination."[39] Moreover, given the current struggles of millions of people on the move having to contend with the hostility of border enforcement and anti-immigrant views, the right to remain or return constitutes one of the major problems faced by immigrant populations. Coercive migration policies, as we are currently witnessing in the United States, place immigrant population often in harm's way.

Yet what cannot be denied is that whether in indigenous contexts around the world or the ancient civilizations of Greece and Egypt, the freedom of movement has always been seen as a natural right and a universal aspiration. In Greece, for example, the Delphi priests regarded the right of unrestricted movement as one of the four freedoms that distinguished liberty from slavery.[40] Moreover, the insuppressible nature of human movement alone seems to fly in the face of current coercive efforts to control immigration.

In the current hostile climate of border policy debates, the issue of immigration (entering the country) also becomes an issue of emigration (leaving the country). Often temporary undocumented immigrant workers are prevented from leaving given the hostile border conditions, which would require them to make another dangerous and costly journey back into the United States. Or, should they be detained at the border, this can mean the revocation of ten years of all legal rights to visit with the threat of incarceration should one be caught attempting to cross the border during the time period. As a consequence, many workers become stuck in the United States and are forced to remain permanently, rather than solely during periods of seasonal work.

Increased surveillance and the building of a 700-mile wall at the border will only exacerbate the problems that they portend to solve. Along these lines, an *Albuquerque Tribune* editorial argued that "History has shown that border fences and walls, from the Berlin Wall to the Great Wall of China, have done little to improve relations or security between nations. That is best done not by building walls but by building trust and respect through diplomacy, economic development and common labor, environmental and social agreements."[41]

Stephen Castles contends that "barriers to mobility contradict the powerful forces which are leading toward greater economic and cultural interchange."[42] Rather than shut people out, the United States should adopt the same policy for the movement of people that it adopts for the movement of capital. Instead of archaic policing methods at the border that intensify animosities and violence, the United States should open up the borders and move toward greater economic integration with Mexico and Latin America. Such a move could potentially open opportunities to pursue investment policies that support the democratization of the economy by way of cooperative economic ventures rooted in the material and social needs of all people, rather than the narrow accumulative pursuits of transnational corporations.

Instead of blaming immigrants for the difficulties communities encounter in creating sustainable development, let's point the finger where it belongs: at the ruthless neoliberal policies of privatization that have pillaged and plundered the world's resources. The historical record speaks volumes and we don't have to look very far for examples. The devastating impact of NAFTA in Mexico and the Caribbean alone (and more recently CAFTA in Central America[43]), where wages have fallen and people have less access than ever to the goods they produced, is a stark example. On the agricultural front, the subsequent lowering of import barriers allowed the entrance of extremely cheap imports from the highly subsidized agribusiness in the United States, driving down the prices of produce to a level that small, local agricultural producers could not rival. People who found themselves close to starvation, as a result, were forced to leave their lands and join the ranks of unemployed workers in large urban cities. This pattern of dispossession has been repeated among rural populations worldwide. And although some neoliberal analysts might point to a few exceptions of job creation or the increased flow of certain goods to support the legitimacy of their claims, the historical record belies their hypocrisy.

Hence, despite neoconservative alarmist rhetoric to the contrary, some of the potential benefits of open borders might include:

- the democratization of border culture
- the increasing possibility of economic justice through mutual efforts to meet the material needs of all people
- the growth of opportunities for a more equitable distribution of wealth and increasing reciprocity of natural resources
- a more tension-free atmosphere for cultural exchange
- an expanding interaction and flow of ideas across the border
- a decrease in the social tensions and animosities reinforced by rigid "closed border" beliefs and practices

- increasing responsiveness to the welfare of both U.S. and Mexican citizens
- Stopping all punitive actions sanctioned against immigrants and their families
- ending the border abuse of immigrants and would-be immigrants
- dismantling the exploitive underground economy of border-crossing
- releasing all those who are currently incarcerated for crossing the border without documents
- and finally, creating a global citizenship that both respects cultural sovereignty and yet functions in concert with global human rights

Globalizing Human Rights

Of all human rights failures today, those in economic and social areas are by far the larger numbers and are the most widespread across the world.

—HUMAN RIGHTS WATCH[44]

Given widespread human rights failures in both economic and social arenas, what we need at this historical juncture are coherent counterhegemonic strategies to interrupt international imperialist practices that have precipitated forced immigration to the centers of concentrated wealth. We need an ethics of sustainable development that functions at the local level, in concert with the global struggle for emancipation from the devastating impacts of the new imperialism with its dispossession of three-quarters of the world's population. Such a politics must be firmly grounded in both a critical analysis of the political economy of migration and the aggressive efforts towards globalizing human rights. If we were to begin with an understanding that the freedom of movement constitutes a fundamental human right, then the integration of a globalizing human rights agenda, within debates on immigration policy and reform, can be understood as a most reasonable and logical conclusion.

In 2003, the Immigrant Workers Freedom Rides campaign made four central demands that must be integrated into any globalizing human rights agenda. These include 1) legalization and a "road to citizenship"; 2) family reunification; 3) immigrant's rights in the workplace; and 4) civil rights and civil liberties for all.[45] Thus if we were to take these four demands, we can begin to craft a preliminary global agenda of human rights for immigrants around the world. The sense that all human beings should be acknowledged as legitimate and legal subjects, irrespective of where they reside, goes without saying. Moreover, citizenship must be redefined within a global context, opening the road to the creation of societies that function in the interest of the collective global good, rather than in the interests of a few.

The issue of family reunification dramatically exposes the manner in which current neoconservative immigration policies betray the so-called *family values* of their architects. It seems that family values in this context are only legitimate if they are about white, Christian, U.S. citizens. However, globalizing the right of family reunification can serve to shift the dynamics of political and economic abuses suffered by immigrants worldwide.

Globalizing worker rights for all workers, irrespective of national documentation, is a central concern that cannot be overlooked. Policies and practices that stop labor abuses of immigrant workers, as with all workers, must be forthrightly addressed within a human rights agenda. The failure to address labor issues in connection to immigrant populations is an egregious offense that places state officials in complicity with the injustice of unfair and dangerous labor practices, which dehumanize and strip workers of their dignity.

Lastly, the struggle for civil rights and civil liberties must be a central tenet of a globalizing human rights agenda. In a time when we are witnessing our civil liberties quickly eroding, political debates on immigration must be inextricably linked to the unveiling of neoliberal policies and practices, and their subsequent impact on civil liberties of undocumented populations in the United States.

Closing the border cannot solve the problems attributed to immigration. The flow of immigrants is the expression of a long set of political economic arrangements that have created huge economic needs and conditions that provoke movement to the empire. To transform these conditions requires a major disruption of neoliberal policies and practices that reproduce savage inequalities along with despicable forms of human rights violations that guarantee their preservation. To counter this dehumanizing trend also calls for a bold and aggressive move toward a fundamental political commitment and solidarity with those who are weary and dispossessed by the ravages of capital. It embodies nothing less than an uncompromising commitment to become citizens of the world and join in the dismantling of neoliberal abuses that not only threaten all our lives but the very sustainability of the planet.

ENDNOTES

1. Human Rights Watch; see: http://www.hrw.org.
2. R. Delgadillo Hernández (2000). "Violence, Subalternity, and El Corrido along the U.S.-Mexico Border," *Berkeley McNair Research Journal* 8 (winter).

3. L. Siu Hin (1998). "Violence, Killing, Life, and Rape on the U.S.-Mexico Border: Can a Conscience Human Being Ignore the Facts?" Human Rights Watch (June); available at: http://www.change-links.org/ Violence.html.

4. See S. Castles (2000), *International Migration at the Beginning of the Twenty-first Century: Global Trends and Issues for UNESCO* (Oxford: Blackwell Publishers), for a discussion of definitions and causes of migration.

5. On September 11, 2001, the twin towers of the World Trade Center in New York City were destroyed when two passenger airliners were hijacked and diverted to crash into each tower. The September 11 attacks generated xenophobic and anti-immigrant violence in some U.S. communities.

6. See S. Sassen (1998), "The de factoTransnationalizing Immigration Policy" in C. Joppke (ed.) *Challenge to the Nation State* (New York: Oxford Press) for an insightful discussion on globalization, immigration, and the role of the state.

7. A. Darder and R. Torres (2004), *After Race: Racism after Multiculturalism* (New York: New York University Press).

8. The Border Protection, Anti-terrorism, and Illegal Immigration Control Act of 2005 (H.R. 4437) or the Sensenbrenner bill—after its sponsor, Wisconsin Republican, Jim Sensenbrenner—was passed by the House of Representatives and contains the following provisions, among others (see: http://thomas.loc.gov/cgi-bin/bdquery/z?d109:h.r.04437):

    *   Requires up to 700 miles (1120 km) of fence along the U.S.-Mexican border at points with the highest number of illegal border crossings. (House Amendment 648, authored by Duncan Hunter (R-CA52).

    *   Requires the federal government to take custody of undocumented aliens detained by local authorities. This would end the practice of "catch and release," where federal officials sometimes instruct local law enforcement to release detained undocumented aliens because resources to prosecute them are not available. It also reimburses local agencies in the twenty-nine counties along the border for costs related to detaining undocumented aliens. (Section 607)

    *   Mandates employers to verify workers' legal status through electronic means, phased in over several years. Also requires reports to be sent to Congress one and two years after implementation to ensure that it is being used. (Title VII)

    *   Eliminates the Diversity Immigrant Visa (also known as Green Card Lottery) program. (House Amendment 650, authored by Bob Goodlatte)

    *   Prohibits grants to federal, state, or local government agencies that enact or maintain a sanctuary policy. (House Amendment 659, authored by Thomas Tancredo; withdrawn 12/16/2005 by unanimous consent)

    *   Incorporates satellite communications among immigration enforcement officials. (House Amendment 638, authored by John Carter)

    *   Requires all U.S. Border Patrol uniforms to be made in the United States to avoid forgeries. (House Amendment 641, authored by Rick Renzi)

    *   Institutes a timeline for deployment of US-VISIT to all land-based checkpoints. (House Amendment 642, authored by Michael N. Castle)

- Requires the Department of Homeland Security (DHS) to report to Congress on the number of Other Than Mexicans (OTMs) apprehended and deported and the number of those from states that sponsor terrorism. (Section 401)
- Formalizes congressional condemnation of rapes by smugglers along the border and urges Mexico to take immediate action to prevent them. (House Amendment 647, authored by Ginny Brown-Waite)
- Requires all undocumented aliens, before being deported, to pay a fine of $3,000 if they agree to leave voluntarily but do not adhere to the terms of their agreement. The grace period for voluntary departure is shortened to sixty days.
- Requires DHS to conduct a study on the potential for border fencing on the U.S.-Canada border.
- Sets the minimum sentence for fraudulent documents at ten years, fines, or both, with tougher sentencing in cases of aiding drug trafficking and terrorism.
- Establishes a Fraudulent Documents Center within DHS.
- Increases penalties for aggravated felonies and various frauds, including marriage fraud and document fraud.
- Establishes an eighteen-month deadline for DHS to control the border, with a progress report due one year after enactment of the legislation.
- Requires criminal record check, terrorist watch list clearance, and fraudulent document checks for any illegal immigrant before being granted legal immigration status.
- Reimburses states for aiding in immigration enforcement.
- Causes housing of a removed alien to become a felony and sets the minimum prison sentence to three years.
- Allows deportation of any undocumented alien convicted of driving under the influence (DUI).
- Adds human trafficking and human smuggling to the money-laundering statute.
- Increases penalties for employing undocumented workers to $7,500 for first-time offenses, $15,000 for second offenses, and $40,000 for all subsequent offenses.
- Prohibits accepting immigrants from any country that delays or refuses to accept its citizens who are deported from the United States. (Section 404)

9. Mike Davis in *Planet of Slums* from an interview with *Socialist Worker*, June 24, 2006; available at: http://www.socialistworker.co.uk/article.php?article_id=9073.

10. S.P. Huntington (2004). "The Hispanic Challenge" (Foreign Policy); see: www.foreignpolicy.com.

11. I. Ropke (2006). "Migration and Sustainability—Compatibility or Contradictory," *Science Direct: Ecological Economics* (March 7).

12. See J. Lane (2006), "Unbridled Anti-immigrant Racism in Texas," available at: www.pww.org/article/view/10161; and S. Sandoval (May 13, 2007), "FB Immigration Law Wins Easily," *Dallas News*, available at: http://www.dallasnews.com/sharedcontent/dws/news/politics/local/stories/051307dnmetfarmersbranch.621241fe.html.

13. In several cases where challenges have been brought against local ordinances, the courts have found that the cities had over-reached when trying to pass a law that is preempted by federal immigration laws and agreed to temporarily block their implementation. Nearly twenty of the

laws that have passed have been tabled or defeated. In December 2006, the city of Escondido, California, agreed to a permanent injunction against enforcement of its anti-immigrant ordinance. See: http://www.aclu.org/immigrants/discrim/29164prs20070322.html.

14. See: "Immigrants Gain Power," *Hispanic Business*, May 30, 2006.

15. See: "Immigrants Are Behind One Quarter of Startups," *Hispanic Business*, November 15, 2006.

16. T.L. Friedman (2005). *The World Is Flat: A Brief History of the Twenty-first Century* (New York: Farrar, Straus, and Giroux).

17. M. Hardt and A. Negri (2001), *Empire* (Cambridge, MA: Harvard University Press).

18. D. Harvey (2005), *The New Imperialism* (New York: Oxford University Press), 160.

19. See: A. Shah, "Causes of Poverty." http://www.globalissues.org/TradeRelated/Facts.asp.

20. See: M. Davis (2006), *Planet of Slums* (New York, Verso).

21. A House bill, passed on a 239-182 vote, includes a proposal to build seven hundred miles of additional fence through parts of California, Arizona, New Mexico, and Texas at a potential estimated cost that could reach as high as $7 billion. The government will also enlist military and local law enforcement to help stop illegal entrants. See J. Reno, "Is U.S.-Mexcio Border Wall a Good Idea? Border Expert David Shirk Discusses Controversial Border Fence Legislation," *Newsweek*, October 12, 2006.

22. H. Arendt (1968), *Imperialism* (New York: Harcourt Brace Jovanovich), 23.

23. Harvey, *The New Imperialism*, 32.

24. See Harvey's discussion of accumulation through dispossession and the issues of chronic insecurity in *The New Imperialism*.

25. Harvey, *The New Imperialism*, 145.

26. Ibid., 28.

27. Ibid., 38.

28. Ibid., 145.

29. Ibid., 188

30. Ibid.

31. A. Werbach (2005), "The End of the Population Movement," *American Prospect* (October); available at: http://findarticles.com/p/articles/mi_hb3463/is_200510/ai_n18248157>.

32. See: C. Hayes, "Round Population Numbers Fuel the Immigration Scare," *The Nation*, October 24, 2006.

33. See: T. Barry, "Immigration Debate: Politics, Ideologies of Anti-Immigration Forces," for International Relations Center: America's Program (June 17, 2005); available at: www.americas.irc-online.org/am/652.

34. R. Lamm and G. Imhoff (1985), *The Immigration Time Bomb: The Fragmenting of America* (New York: Dutton).

35. A. Darder (forthcoming), *Forging a Puerto Rican Feminism: The Poetics of Consciousness and Embodied History* (New York and London: Routledge).

36. See: report by David A. Lieb, Associated Press, Tuesday, November 14, 2006.

37. See: Ropke, "Migration and Sustainability," 191–94; United Nations (2001), "Population, Gender, and Development: A Concise Report," ST/ESA/SER.A/193; and P. Pinstrup-Andersen and R. Pandya-Lorch (eds.) (2001), "The Unfinished Agenda: Perspectives on Overcoming Hunger, Poverty, and Environmental Degradation," International Food Policy Research Institute, Washington, D.C.

38. A. Dowty (1987), *Closed Borders: The Contemporary Assualt on Freedom of Movement* (New Haven, CT, and London: Yale University Press), 13.

39. Ibid., 4.

40. Ibid., 11.

41. "The Border Wall: Who Will Build It?"; available at: www.pww.org/article/articleprint/10093.

42. Castles, *International Migration*, 279.

43. See: "Coalition Mourns One Year of CAFTA; Calls for Trade with Justice" and other articles on the negative impact of the Central American Free Trade Agreement at www.stopcafta.org.

44. Human Rights Watch: http://www.hrw.org.

45. See: "The Immigrant Workers Freedom Ride," *Free Press Journal* (2003); available at: www. freepress.org/departments.php/display/20/2003/182/1/23. Also see: "Voices of the Immigrant Workers Freedom Rides," *New York Amsterdam News*, October 9–15, 2003. For more organizational information on the Immigrant Workers Freedom Rides, also see: www.iwfr.org/.

CHAPTER 15

Mapping Latino Studies

Critical Reflections on Class and Social Theory

With Rodolfo D. Torres

When you say "America" you refer to the territory stretching between the icecaps of the two poles. So to hell with your barriers and frontier guards!

—(DIEGO RIVERA)[1]

The conservative climate befalling universities across the United States raises serious concerns for the future of Latino Studies. This is particularly true where university discourse, victim to its own political retrenchment, wrongly concludes that questions of culture, race, diversity and multiculturalism were sufficiently attended to in the post-civil rights era. Correspondingly, as the multicultural or diversity rhetoric wanes in the marketplace of ideas, raising dollars emerges as the top priority for universities nationwide—a feat accomplished primarily by adjusting faculty scholarship and research agendas to coincide with the priorities and mandates of the corporate world. In the main, many academic departments and university policy centers or "think tanks" are almost entirely dependent on corporate monies, advance research priorities and policy "solutions" which, in the final analysis, are commensurate with the needs of capital. The impact of such measures is, unfortunately, to render most Latino Studies scholars virtually invisible, stifling our efforts to influence the course of public policy or political direction toward greater democratic and participatory solutions.

The social project of Latino Studies has been deemed intellectually suspect, as original analysis and innovative research and teaching approaches are sharply eclipsed by a revamped emphasis on traditional pedagogy and positivist scientific methods. Here we are referring to reductionistic, instrumentalized, and fragmented methods of research and teaching that, historically, have been most responsible for promoting intellectual parochialism (i.e., teacher-centered lecture format or the dominance of psychology paradigms in education). Critical comparative studies and collaborative interdisciplinary efforts to construct a full-bodied knowledge of Latino life and thought are thus often discouraged by those who continue to privilege the narrow rationality of quantitative enthusiasts.

As a consequence, Latino studies scholarship within the humanities, for example, can seldom forge a solid relationship with the social sciences, nor can either field readily establish a foothold within the "hard" sciences of physics, mathematics or the "applied" disciplines. Hence, despite recent seismic paradigm shifts that have challenged positivist claims regarding a single, fixed truth or scientific recourse to grand narratives, there still exists a real need to break down the strictures of discipline-specific knowledge construction. To accomplish this, we argue that Latino Studies needs to move more vigorously toward what Bob Jessop and Ngai-Ling Sum (2001) term a post-disciplinary approach to our teaching and research in the field.

This is not to suggest that we reject the wealth of information that can be gleaned from well-designed quantitative studies. Rather, our concern is linked to the preferential and exclusive legitimacy frequently assigned to the use of quantitative methods. When taken solely on their own merit, the latter fail to render the complexity of the racialized cultural experience and cannot provide the analytical richness required to transform our scholarship into a truly emancipatory political project. In contrast, Latino Studies scholarship needs to be independent, critical, and infused with what C.W. Mills (2002) terms "sociological imagination"—a pedagogical and investigative discourse that provides us with an agenda of policies and practices that can assist Latino Studies scholars to map out the possibilities for economic democracy and social justice, particularly in the face of neo-liberal excess and scientism.

Critical Scholarship

What we choose to emphasize in this complex history will determine our lives.

—(HOWARD ZINN)[2]

Our discussion of Latino Studies is forthrightly directed toward promoting critical
scholarship—scholarly work carried out with the expressed intent of challenging
the current nature of economic inequality and social oppression. This approach
is particularly significant to how we participate in the construction of knowledge
in our classrooms and as public intellectuals out in the world. As such, a critical
Latino Studies program must begin with a clear vision of our work and its relationship to the world. This is no easy task, given that Latino Studies is not monolithic and that we all work within the contested terrain of both multidisciplinary
expectations and community exigencies. Nevertheless, what allows us to struggle
together across our differences is the fact that social justice and economic democracy are central to the political project that first inspired the scholarly formation
of the field. With this as our starting point, there are several issues that need to
be consistently revisited in the course of Latino Studies research. In the spirit of
W.E.B. Du Bois, we need to "return to the basics"—history, political economy, and
public policy—in our efforts to effectively challenge racism and class inequality
within education. Greater focus must be placed on comparative work in the field
(i.e., studies which compare different marginalized groups or studies which compare the US Latino experience with that of the populations in Latin American
countries). In doing so, we can develop not only knowledge of how we are similar,
but also of how we are different. This knowledge can help build a robust field of
Latino Studies that is usefully complex and needfully inclusive. A key criticism of
Latino Studies to date is that much of the research within the field is "fuzzy" and
overly concerned with texts. In response, we need to move beyond merely descriptive, anecdotal accounts of Latino life in the United States if we are to provide
greater analytical specificity and rigor to our construction of theories that examine the dynamics of exploitation and domination.[3]

Currently, there are a variety of theoretical debates influencing both research
and pedagogy within Latino Studies. It is important for us to be consistently cognizant and engaged in these debates. For example, feminist theories are vital to our
knowledge of Latinas and their location within our communities and the larger
social context. This is particularly significant for understanding how Latinas move
across contested terrain to give meaning to their racialized, gendered identities.
The work on Latino masculinities seeks to provide a more complex understand-

ing of Latino men, their identities, and subjectivities, in an effort to disrupt commonly held assumptions that make homogenous and reify the experience of Latino males within US contexts. Postmodern theories, with their emphasis on fragmentation and difference, the rupture of meta-narratives, and engagement with identity politics have also had an influence on how issues of culture and identity are approached within the classroom and community. In contending with questions of "race," Latino critical race theory, or LatCrit (Crenshaw et al., 1995; Delgado, 1995; Wing, 1997; Guinier and Torres, 2002) has left its mark in the field. Using this approach, legal scholars whose work represents theoretically diverse perspectives ascribe primary explanatory power to the concept of "race." Similarly, post-colonial theories have contributed to our understanding of human agency, the politics of location, and the struggle for decolonization—all key concepts in understanding the complexity of Latino lives in the US.

At the same time that Latino Studies is experiencing something of a renaissance within the academy, there has been a renewed intellectual and political interest in historical materialism. Unlike Latino Studies scholars who impertinently deride Marxist methodology as unfashionable and obsolete, we welcome its renewal. In the past, the retreat from political economy and class within African American and Latino Studies scholarship was stirred by a response to the narrowness of reductionist economic arguments. And rightly so, for many of the early Marxist scholars tended to focus on class, without rigorous attention paid to questions of racism, sexism, or heterosexism. However, today we dispute post-Marxist claims that classical Marxism hinders engagement with important issues of racialized identities and inequalities. Instead, we contend that it is not a feat of economic reductionism to treat with analytical specificity the notion of class as a relationship and as a means for examining inequalities of power and wealth. Nor is it reductive to understand how class relations of power lead us to organize our work and political involvement in particular ways; or guide our practical consideration as to the strategies we use to struggle for workers' rights, housing, education, immigration, and health care. Instead, such forms of analysis engage class as intrinsic to all social relations, and thus, view all social arrangements as configured, dialectically, within the context of contemporary capitalist social formations.

As Latino Studies scholars strive to make sense of the current political economy operating locally and globally, theories of globalization also surface in discussions of late capitalism and the rapid movement and exploitation of labor, resources, as well as the economic and political power wielded by multinational corporations.[4] However, these arguments have generated considerable debate among many progressives, educators and theorists. While there are those who have incorporated theories of globalization in their critiques of contemporary social problems, others argue that it is just the same old capitalism working as usual—the same old capitalism that must be fiercely challenged.[5] This latter view seeks to reintroduce a class analysis to the construction of social theory and public policy and, by so doing, make central a critique of capitalism.

Ellen Meiksins Wood (1994) explains succinctly what it means to challenge capitalism. "Addressing capitalism means considering it as a historically specific system of social relations, a social form with its own logic and its own laws of motion…the imperatives of competition, profit maximization, "productivity," "growth," and "flexibility" with all their social and ideological consequences" (28). Wood clearly calls for scholarship that engages with how power is tied to external conditions; the social impact of changing modes of production upon workers; the political economy and the ways it structures the social conditions of institutions and community life to impact on class formations; the increasing significance of class; and the specificity of capitalism as a totalizing system of social and political domination and exploitation. In concert with this view, we argue that to ignore this dimension has far-reaching political implications for the future, particularly during a time of dramatic demographic shift.

The Changing Demographics

> Official celebratory pronouncements…hardly conceal diffused
> anxieties about the impending impact of projected demographic
> changes in the Latino population of the United States.
> —RENATO ROSALDO (1993)

In January 2003, the US Census Bureau estimated the Latino population to be 37 million, constituting 13% of the total population. With these new numbers, Latinos have the dubious distinction of being the nation's largest minority group, surpassing African Americans with an estimated population of 36.2 million. To make sense of the current conditions, we must remain attentive to the impact of such changes in the regions where large Latino populations reside and what these changes mean to the local, national, and international political economy. For example, it is impossible to ignore what many are calling the "browning" or "Latinization" of vast metropolitan areas in the US. This phenomenon is vividly exemplified in the current population of Los Angeles County, where, of the 9.8 million residents, over 4.2 million are Latinos.

Population projections claim that by the year 2005, "minority" residents are expected to become the majority in most large urban centers. Already, today, in densely populated neighborhoods of Los Angeles, New York, Chicago, Dallas and Miami, Latino residents comprise the majority. In fact, according to Jorge Mariscal (2003), this phenomenon is even beginning to occur in the deep South where "Latino immigrants have moved in large numbers into the old Confederacy." Indeed, within the past decade, the national census documented a dramatic increase in the Latino population of North Carolina (393.9%), Arkansas (323.3%), Georgia (299.6%), and Tennessee (278.2%).

Important to understanding the evolving public needs of these cities is recognizing the migratory patterns that give shape to the shifting landscape of many working class Latino neighborhoods. For example, more than 50% of all Latinos in California are foreign born, over 700,000 who have their origins in Central America. The significance of this statistic cannot be downplayed, since many have come to California in response to regional wars and impoverishment spurred on by historical and contemporary US economic policies in Latin America. The growing number of diverse Latino immigrants poses a positive challenge to our scholarship and pedagogy, pushing against the grain of traditionally defined notions of Latino identities—from the more obvious political concerns related to how we label Latino populations to the more complex issues of redefining ideas of citizenship (Oboler, 1995).

We maintain that complex ideas such as citizenship need to be contested concepts, precisely because they are interrelated with wider cultural and social issues of racialized class identities. Such issues have often been sidelined or neglected by research and practices anchored in Latino identity politics. This is particularly the case when there is failure to engage the complexity of histories, cultures, and regional economies that inform the construction of diverse Latino identities. This is well illustrated by many US-born and immigrant Latinos, who not only identify with indigenous or mestizo roots, but who identify themselves as Afro-Latinos. This complexity was clearly evident in the 2000 Census, where Latinos were asked to claim a particular "racial origin." "Some of the nation's 35 million Latinos scribbled in the margins that they were Aztec or Mayan. A fraction said they were Indian. Nearly 48% described themselves as white, and 2% as black. Fully 42% said they were 'some other race'" (Fears, 2002: A1). Accounts such as this clearly point to the need for careful analytical attention to be paid to racialized constructions of identities in these times of major demographic shifts, changing class formations, and new forms of global dislocation. Minimally, they serve to explain why one-size-fits-all responses to Latino education, citizenship and well-being within the US will always be insufficient.

The Limits of Identity Politics

We work with raced identities on already reified ground. In the context of domination, raced identities are imposed and internalized, then renegotiated and reproduced. From artificial to natural, we court a hard-to-perceive social logic that reproduces the very conditions we strain to overcome.

—JON CRUZ (1996)

Over the last three decades, there has been an overwhelming tendency among Latino Studies scholars to focus on notions of "race" in ways that draw directly on the intellectual and political tradition of many African American scholars. The use of "race" among Chicano scholars of the 1960s can be linked to academic acts of resistance to the term "ethnicity," and theories of assimilation, which were generally applied to immigrant populations of European descent. In efforts to distance Chicano history from this concept and link it to a theory of internal colonialism, cultural imperialism, and racism, Chicanos were discussed as a colonized "racial" group in much the same manner that many radical theorists positioned African Americans within the US political economy. As such, association of the term "race" with power, resistance, and self-determination has veiled the problematics of "race" as a social construct. Protected by the force of cultural nationalist rhetoric, "race" as an analytical term has remained a "paper tiger"—seemingly powerful in discourse matters but ineffectual as an analytical metaphor, incapable of moving us away from the pervasive notion of "race" as an innate determinant of behavior.

Consequently, much of the past literature on Latino populations, with its emphasis on such issues as "racial inequality," "racial segregation," "racial identity," "racial consciousness" has utilized the construct of "race" as a central category of analysis for interpreting the social conditions of inequality and marginalization. In turn, this literature has reinforced a racialized politics of identity and representation, with its problematic emphasis on "racial" identity as the overwhelming impulse for political action (Darder and Torres, 1999).

Given this legacy, it is not surprising to discover that the theories, practices, and policies that have informed social science analysis of racialized populations today are overwhelmingly rooted in a politics of identity—an approach that is founded on parochial notions of "race" and representation, which ignore the imperatives of capitalist accumulation and the existence of class divisions within Latino communities. The folly of this position is critiqued by Wood (1994) when she exposes the limitations of a politics of identity which fails to contend with the fact that capitalism is the most totalizing system of social relations the world has ever known. Yet despite this fact, in much of the work on Latino, African American, Native American, and Asian populations, a systematic analysis of class and a critique of capitalism are often conspicuously absent. And even when class is mentioned, the emphasis is primarily on an undifferentiated plurality of identity politics or an "intersection of oppressions," which, unfortunately, ignores the overwhelming tendency of capitalism to homogenize rather than to diversify human experience.

This practice is particularly disturbing since no matter where one travels in the world, there is no question that racism as an ideology is integral to the process of capital accumulation. The failure of Latino Studies scholars to confront this dimension in their analysis of contemporary society as a racialized phenomenon or to continue treating class as merely one of a multiplicity of (equally valid) perspectives, which may or may not "intersect" with the process of racialization, is a serious shortcoming.[6] In addressing this issue, we must recognize that identity politics, which generally glosses over class differences and/or ignores class contradictions, has often been used by even radical scholars and activists within African American, Latino, and other racialized communities in efforts to build strong political bases that distinguish Latino Studies from other fields of inquiry. Here, constructions of "race" are objectified and mediated as truth to ignite political support, divorced from the realities of class struggle.

Hence, if we are to effectively challenge the horrendous economic impact of globalization on racialized and other marginalized communities, we must recognize that a politics of identity is grossly inept and unsuited for building and sustaining collective political movements for social justice and economic democracy. Instead what we need is fundamentally to reframe the very terrain that gives life to our political understanding of what it means to struggle against widening class differentiation and ever-increasing racialized inequality.

Class Matters

One of the main reasons for studying class structure is because of its importance in explaining other elements of class analysis, especially class formation, class consciousness and class struggle.

—ERIK OLIN WRIGHT (1997)

Central to our comprehension of pedagogy and research in Latino Studies is our ability to engage class not as an identity or a phenomenon equal to other forms of oppression but rather as relations of power that encompass social processes that reproduce structural inequality. From this standpoint then, we can consider how the relationship between culture, class, power, and ideology impacts the construction of knowledge; how we might move toward dismantling the structures of racialized inequality which persist in society today, as opposed to reform efforts; and how we contend with political efforts to completely dismantle the remnants of progressive health, education, and welfare policies.

The collapse of the Soviet Union in the 1980s in conjunction with the shift toward post-modern paradigms of knowledge and theoretical orientations resulted in a retreat from class analysis. As mentioned earlier, Latino Studies was no exception. Hence, we are well aware that to reassert the importance of class analysis in our discussion of Latino Studies scholarship may be viewed by some as a return to an outdated theoretical paradigm. However, Marxist theory has always been a site of conflicting and competing perspectives. Moreover, our concern with the question of class analysis is far beyond simple ideological contestation. For us, class is tied intrinsically to material conditions within society and how we understand the manner in which relations of production and asymmetrical structures of power are at work in very concrete ways within the daily life of Latino populations.

For example, there is no doubt that large numbers of African American, Latino, and Native American workers fail to ever find long-term or substantial employment in the labor market. In fact, Latino and other racialized minorities are disproportionately represented in low-income jobs and state unemployment rolls. Moreover, an inter-relationship clearly exists between Latin American migration to the United States and exclusionary processes which ensure that the ranks of the small entrepreneur include Latino immigrants who sustain a complex of financial and cultural ties with their countries of origin. These are but two simple examples that speak to the significance of class, in the structural conditions and social realities that impact Latino communities today.

A class analysis must also be central to our efforts to better understand Latino communities and issues of education; otherwise, we risk reinscribing existing inequities pertaining to educational attainment and achievement opportunities. For example, the digital divide within the US is no longer concerned primarily with describing inequitable physical access to computers at school for certain marginalized, low-income groups. Instead, it is increasingly used to describe inequitable differences in the quality of new technology use in schools (Cuban, 2001) . As we move from living and working in an industrial to a "postindustrial" society, there remain fundamental questions still to be answered concerning the "proper" relationships among education, work and new technologies. These include: Which groups have the most ready access to effective uses of new technologies in schools, and why? What is (or what should be) the emancipatory role of technology within schools, colleges and universities (i.e., distance learning, flexible course offerings, small and large-scale activism, and access to vital information)? What are the consequences of technology-rich education in relation to Latino students' social and academic development—particularly when these students have historically had far less access to new technologies than their White or Asian counterparts (Tornatzky et al., 2002)? What social and moral values does technology-driven education cultivate, and what might this mean for Latino students currently enrolled in US public schools in terms of current and future conceptions of and practices associated with "being a good citizen"?

To engage such questions effectively requires that we recognize that class and "race" are concepts of a different sociological order. Class and "race" do not occupy the same analytical space and, thus, cannot constitute explanatory alternatives to each other. Class is a material space, even within the mainstream definition that links the concept to occupation, income status, and educational attainment—all of which, in turn, reflect the materiality of class, though not with any analytical specificity. Hence, the significance of class can be rigorously considered only through an approach that recognizes the social relations of production as germane to any social justice or emancipatory political project.

By posing critical questions that interrogate the power relations that condition and structure the nature and extent of exploitation across classes, Latino Studies scholars can unveil the internal organization and social relations at work between contending classes. In the final analysis, the relationship between appropriators and producers rests on the relative strength of classes and the manner in which these are thrust into the political arena of class struggle (Wood, 2000). True to this view, we challenge the post-Marxist dismissal of class as an analytical category. Instead, we reaffirm class analysis in Latino Studies research and pedagogy as essential in the face of staggering economic inequality.

Inequality in the "New Economy"

We are all living through an unprecedented situation marked by dramatic new developments, including not only the New Economy boom and bust, but also an unheard of polarization of wealth...a phenomenon of capital accumulation and crisis—hence class struggle.

—MONTHLY REVIEW[7] (EDS., 2001)

The growing gap between the rich and the poor is one of the most compelling issues of the United States, particularly when we consider the overwhelming concentration of wealth and income that remains in the hands of a few. In spite of this, it is commonplace for educators to consider questions of pedagogy in the absence of fundamental social questions related to economic inequality. Yet, we cannot gain a better understanding of what is driving many of the difficulties Latinos are facing in this country today without addressing the changing nature of the capitalist economy. By grounding our work in material concerns, we are intellectually and politically motivated to consider, at the very least, such questions as: Who is working? And who is not? Who is gaining economic ground? And, who is losing ground?

It is imperative that Latino Studies scholars investigate more seriously changing conditions of labor and the consequences of "globalization." In so doing, we must recognize that there is considerable theoretical debate over how best to describe the changing nature of work and the direction of the modern capitalist economy. Competing opinions abound as to the extent and meaning of these changes, and whether they represent a new kind of epochal shift in the basic logic of capitalist accumulation. Once again, the city of Los Angeles can provide a worthy illustration as to why we raise this particular issue.

As a consequence of the de-industrialization of Los Angeles, thousands of workers have experienced, first hand, what it means to see work disappear and to contend with the accompanying structural conditions that have created deep-seated class divisions in the region. As a direct outcome, Los Angeles unemployment was higher at the end of the century, than it was in 1969 (Scott and Soja, 1996). Similarly, it is these conditions that have had a perilous effect on the city's diverse populations. It is not surprising then to discover that the 1992 uprising in South Central Los Angeles, contrary to portrayal by the media and many academics, resulted largely from high rates of joblessness, rather than issues of "race relations" between Blacks and Whites. In fact, over 60% of those arrested were Latinos. By characterizing this event as a crisis in "race relations"—first, between Blacks and Koreans; then between Blacks and Latinos; and finally, back to Blacks and Whites—the media both avoided and prevented any substantive inquiry into the structural economic problems of the city and region. Moreover, the interpretation of the riots as a "race relations" problem failed to take into account the drastic shifts in demographic patterns which have created new dynamics of class and racialized relations in Los Angeles (Valle and Torres, 2000).

This perspective is further sustained by an analysis of the problems inherent in contemporary capitalist restructuring. The reindustrialization of large urban centers with light manufacturing, for example, represents an urban development strategy that is partly responsible for stagnant wages, given the abundance of surplus labor owed to increasing rates of unemployment and cheap immigrant labor. Undoubtedly, this has contributed to further economic decline of many working class neighborhoods in the large and densely populated inner cities. Similarly, the closing of heavy manufacturing production plants (such as automotive and aerospace factories) across the nation has had a deleterious effect on Latino and African American workers, in particular. Such closures, along with the negative repercussions of NAFTA on workers, have contributed to the phenomenon discussed openly even by the Right—the dismantling of the middle class and the increasing polarization of wealth. In addition, the economic instability of many working class Latino communities has been further exacerbated by the replacement of union labor by non-union labor and the reduction of benefits and real wages over the last decade (Darder and Torres, 1997).

Although these conditions are tremendously detrimental to the quality of life for Latino populations in the US, we believe it is important for Latino Studies scholars to also take note of positive grassroots efforts to strike back against the ravages of deepening economic inequality. For example, recent neighborhood efforts in Latino communities have resulted in the introduction and passage of Living Wage ordinances. Latino youth involved with *Californians for Justice* have been instrumental in the *Schools not Prisons* community organizing campaign for democratic schooling. Such community-wide efforts represent a significant and tangible possibility for the implementation of structural reforms at the local level—efforts that can only be successful when structural inequalities are intricately linked with the process of racialization.

From "Race" to Racialization

For three hundred years black Americans insisted that "race" was no usefully distinguishing factor in human relationships. During those same three centuries every academic discipline...insisted that "race" was the determining factor in human development.
—TONI MORRISON (1989)

Everywhere we look, policy pundits, journalist, and academics alike, all continue to work within categories of "race" as though there is unanimity regarding their analytical value. Like all other components of what Antonio Gramsci called common sense, much of the everyday usage of "race" is uncritical. This phenomenon, of course, is no different within the context of Latino populations. Yet, some would argue that there exists more fluidity in the manner in which Latinos relate to the issue of "race" than is the case with other racialized groups. This is said to be reflected in the various terms used to describe a person through the significa- tion of his or her skin color (i.e., mestizo, morena, trigueno, mulata, etc.). However, this fluidity—albeit a legacy of Spanish colonization and carefully constructed social and exclusionary hierarchies of status—does not find a home within US bureaucratic structures. It is not unusual to find that dark-skinned Latino immi- grants from Brazil, Colombia, Panama, and other Latin American countries are surprised to learn that they are categorized as black within the context of the US racialized gaze.

Hence, there are those who might conclude that "race matters in Latin America, but it matters differently" (Fears, 2002; Al). This may well be related to the historical fact that, until recently, questions of class have foregrounded most liberatory struggles, despite the obvious fact that racism has long been at work in all Latin American countries. In the simplest terms, this is reflected by the typi- cally light-skinned phenotypical characteristics of the elite class, as compared with the generally darker-skinned features of most members from poor and working class populations. So, although the notion of race may be engaged differently by Latino immigrants, there is no question that their perceptions are, nevertheless, linked to the particular processes of racialization inherent in the histories of Latin American conquest and slavery.

In these times, we would be hard pressed to find scholars who would sub- scribe openly to the use of "race" as a determinant of any specific social phe- nomenon associated with inherent genetic characteristics. Even the American Anthropological Association in 1997 issued a recommendation that the US gov- ernment scrap the term "race" on official forms, since it held no scientific justifica- tion in human biology. More recently, human genome research supports the fact that "race" has no biological foundation. However, such events have done little to challenge or erase such disturbing "scientific" assertions as those made by Richard Herrnstein and Charles Murray (1994) in their book, *The Bell Curve*.

It is within the historical and contemporary contexts of such scholarship that differences in skin color are signified as marks suggesting the existence of different "races." As a consequence, a primary response among many progressive activists and scholars, when we call for the elimination of "race" as an analytical category, is to reel off accusations of a "color-blind" discourse. This is not what we are argu- ing. What we do argue is that the fixation on skin color is a product of significa- tion, rather than a product of some "truth" concerning some essential relationship between skin color and inherent abilities. This is to argue that people identify skin color as marking or symbolizing other phenomena in a variety of social contexts in which other significations occur. As a consequence, when social practices include and exclude people in light of the signification of skin color, collective identities are produced and social inequalities are structured (Miles and Torres, 1996).

"Racialization" is the term we give to the use of "race" in structuring social relations. More specifically, Robert Miles (1982, 1989, 1993) in his book *Racism* defines this process of racialization as "those instances where social relations between people have been structured by the signification of human biological characteristics in such a way as to define and construct differentiated social collectivities…the concept therefore refers to a process of categorization, a representational process of defining an Other (usually, but not exclusively) somatically" (75). Hence, to interpret more lucidly the conditions faced by Latino populations requires us to move beyond the idea of "race" to an understanding of racialization and its impact on class formations. To continue using the concept of "race" as an analytic term is to affix and essentialize skin color characteristics in relation to certain groups, in a way that elides the processes involved in the social construction of "race." The former holds no hope of change or reform (i.e., skin color is something to be "worked around"); while the latter concept is far more dynamic, in that it offers chinks and possibilities for challenging categories that serve to undermine the agency of many marginalized groups. As such, this summons a bold analytical transition from the language of "race" to recognizing the centrality of racism and the process of racialization in our understanding of exclusionary practices that give rise to structural inequalities.

Central to this discussion is also the manner in which social theories of racism are predominantly anchored in the black-white paradigm of "race relations," which severely limits our efforts in Latino Studies to speak to the complexity of Latino racialization. One of the most limiting aspects of the black-white framework is its tendency to obstruct or camouflage the need to examine particular histories and contextual dimensions that give rise to different forms of racisms around the globe. The subsequent conflation of racialized relations into a black-white paradigm has often functioned to render Latino populations invisible or to a "second-class oppression" status. This has prevented Latino Studies scholars from engaging with significant differences among Latino populations and from delving more fully into comparative histories of racism and how these are linked to class inequalities.

If we are then to theoretically grasp the complexity of contemporary Latino life, the racialized language of "black" and "white" must be dispensed with and replaced by a new conceptual language rooted in but not determined by, the political economy of labor migration, and capitalist social and class relations.[8] Mariscal (2003) alludes to this need with respect to Latino immigrant workers in the deep

South, where demographic changes reflect the historical nature of the racialization process. "They have little knowledge of the struggles for equal rights and the history of anti-Mexican racism in the Southwest. As they enter a culture based on black/white relations, these workers are unaware of regional histories, past labor struggles and the persistence of long-standing 'southern values.' In effect, they walk into a black/white universe like virtual aliens from another planet." Further, he reminds us that the recent media coverage of the Trent Lott affair reveals that the discussion of race in this country "is still firmly grounded in a narrow and anti-quated black/white reality."

Toward a Critical Theory of Racism

The idea of "race" has profound meanings in the everyday world, but these have no scientific credibility and I can therefore find no reason why those who write in the Marxist tradition should wish to legitimise an ideological notion by elevating it to a central analytical position.

—ROBERT MILES (1984)

Recent structural changes in the US political economy and the increasing diversity within Latino communities have made the issue of racism more complex than ever before. But rather than occupying a central position, these historical socio-economic changes have served merely as a backdrop to the contemporary theoretical debates on the meaning of "race" and representation in the US today, debates that, more often than not, are founded on deeply psychologized or abstracted notions of racialized differences and conflicts. This constitutes a significant point of contention, generating many questions yet to be answered regarding the continued use of the idea of race in theorizing the Latino life condition. What does it mean to utilize "race," in light of the growing complexities we are facing, within both social and political arenas? What are the strengths and limitations of a "race-centered" politics? How is racism structured within the context of advanced capitalist relations of power?

Such inquiry into the analytical utility of "race" in Latino Studies scholarship is, by no means, meant to negate the worthiness of on-going work on racialized inequalities or obstruct the struggle against racism or deny that "race" is a social construction. Rather, it represents an effort to seek greater analytical clarity in how we make sense of cultural, historical and political differences. Moreover, there remains a need to expose critically, and with greater specificity, the manner in which the ideology of racism produces notions of "race," as opposed to the popular belief that the existence of "races" produces racism.

This highlights the need for Latino Studies scholars to interrogate with greater analytical depth the terms we use and the concepts we commonly uphold. For example, it is not uncommon to find the interchangeable use of "race" and "culture" in discussions of Chicanos, Puerto Ricans, and other Latino populations. It is significant to note, for instance, that instead of linking the notion of culture to class relations which emerge at the point of production (or social relations of production), most scholars link culture to the notion of "race"—a concept associated with phenotypical traits but now linked to the notion of social construction, shared histories, and narratives associated with the racialized category of Latino.

Meanwhile, the habitual practice of framing social relations as "race relations" continues to obscure material conditions of inequality. This is exemplified by educational theories that assign significance to "racial" characteristics, rather than attributing student responses to school conditions, historically shaped by structural inequalities that determine the context in which students must achieve. This unfortunate absence of class analysis veils the real reasons why so many Latino, African American, and other racialized students fare poorly on standardized tests, are over-represented in remedial programs, and continue to drop out of high schools and universities at alarming rates. As a consequence, educational solutions are often derived from distorted perceptions of the problem and lead to misguided policies and practices.

The previous example points to the manner in which racialized constructs of culture can obscure the reality that class is intrinsic to all social arrangements—including racism. To conceal this fact makes it more difficult to address effectively the motivating forces for the construction of particular social arrangements, whether these be marked by physical, geographical or ideological signifiers. Hence, an interrogation of the use of "race" is tremendously important within Latino Studies, given that nothing occurs without implicating the material conditions that shape how individuals and groups locate themselves within the context of the larger society (Torres and Darder, 2004).

Yet, we recognize that mere efforts to undo and eliminate the idea of "race" as an analytical category in our scholarship are insufficient to remove its use from the popular imagination and the discourse of everyday life. Moreover, in a country like the United States, filled with historical examples of exploitation, violence and murderous acts justified by both popular opinions and scientific ideas of "race," it is next to impossible to convince people that "race" does not exist as a "natural" category. So in Colette Guillaumin's (1995; 107) words "let us be clear about this. The idea of race is a technical means, a machine for committing murder. And its effectiveness is not in doubt." But "races" do not exist. What exists is the tenacious and unrelenting idea of "race" that fuels racism throughout the world.

Hence, the future struggle against the ravages of racism and capitalism must at long last contend with the reality that there are no "races" and therefore no "race relations." In light of this view, we call for a critical reconceptualization of racism with which to analyze the historical and contemporary social experiences and institutional realities faced by Latino communities and other racialized populations. Insofar as such a concept, whether employed in social investigation or political struggle, reveals patterns of discrimination and resulting inequalities, it also helps us to grapple more specifically with those actions that must be taken to dismantle the structural inequalities we encounter in our everyday lives. Such a critical theory of racism represents a bold and forthright move to challenge commonsense notions of "race" that often lead to profound forms of essentialism and ahistorical perceptions of oppression. Moreover, these notions make it nearly impossible to dismantle the external material structures of exploitation and domination that sustain racialized inequalities within the body politic of the capitalist state.

The Nature of the Capitalist State

A theory of the state is always a theory of society and of the distribution of power in that society.

—RALPH MILIBAND (1969)

The nature of the capitalist State is another important issue so often ignored in the bulk of Latino Studies scholarship. Yet, this is a serious omission when we consider current material conditions of contemporary society. During the last decade alone, the State has been seized on the one hand by neoliberal capitalist interests of the likes of Bill Gates; and on the other, by the politicians—whether they be weak-willed Democrats the likes of Clinton or reactionary Republicans like George W. Bush. As a consequence, State policies, which have ushered in significant welfare cutbacks, corporate corruption, the war in Afghanistan, "homeland security," and now the war on Iraq, have also fueled the anti-intellectual fervor of the popular media. Meanwhile, news reports of the atrocities of US oil companies in Nigeria, the unabashed sale of obsolete US weapons to impoverished developing nations, and the role of the United States in the creation of instability and unrest in the Middle East remain almost nonexistent in world reports on the evening news.

With the unbridled ferment and advancement of capital, the safety net of the Welfare State is quickly being eroded. As conservative interests flagrantly channel massive expenditures towards the military and prison industrial complex, support for health, education, and housing for the poor continues to wane in comparison. The recent projections for California's budget reflect this unfortunate trend in the distribution of public expenditures. The yearly allocation for state prisons was the only line-item in the budget to increase for 2004. In addition, popular conservative campaigns over the last 20 years have also done their part to destroy the power of unions, abolish immigrant rights, privatize education and health services, eradicate affirmative action, and dismantle bilingual education.

How then do we come to understand the nature and impact of such State policies and campaigns upon Latino populations? To best respond, we argue that we must recast our scholarship and pedagogy in more rigorous analytical ways, so that we might better understand how State policies and practices have historically functioned to reproduce inequalities. Although, for the most part, this critical analysis of the capitalist State and its class structure remains conspicuously absent in much of the research in Latino Studies, one notable exception is the neo-Marxist inspired work of Mario Barrera (1979). In his seminal volume, *Race and Class in the Southwest*, Barrera provided a formidable class analysis of racialized class inequality and the positioning of the capitalist State in Chicano economic history.

What we are suggesting here is that the nature of the State be fully interrogated as a site of conflict and counter-hegemonic struggle. As such, questions that must be engaged include: What is the role of the capitalist State in the reproduction of inequality? To what extent are racialized relations a sphere of action autonomous from State-structured economic relations? In what ways are class, gender, and racialized relations structured by policies of the State? How do class, gender and racialized relations structure each other? Hence, we argue that research on the accumulation and legitimation needs of the capitalist State (Jessop, 2003) can provide needed clarity in understanding Latino conditions of racialized class inequality. Such research can also point to the kinds of public policies that can function to restructure conditions of social and economic exploitation in a liberal capitalist democracy.

Critical Policy Studies

The Promise of the social sciences is to bring reason to bear on human affairs.

—C. WRIGHT MILLS (2002)

More than ever, there is a need to consider issues of pedagogy and research in Latino Studies with respect to public policy and the conditions of everyday life. It is disheartening to find that Latino Studies scholars often ignore, in both their teaching and research, the particulars of public policy and its impact on communities. And when policy is engaged, there is often a lack of specificity and rigor in their theoretical understanding of what constitutes public policy. To address both these concerns requires us to shift toward both a social theory and community-informed public policy discourse, and away from the limits of traditional quantitative policy interventions that have historically been highly technical and grounded in normative political science—a perspective typically anchored in either statistical or descriptively anecdotal approaches to frame public policy debates.

In response to traditional policy approaches, there are those in the field of Latino Studies who advance the human capital model in public policy recommendations as a solution to structural inequalities. However, this model of analysis provides only a narrow view of production and an even more limited understanding of social reproduction in the political economy. Hence, left to its own device, the human capital model can inadvertently lead to victim-blaming interpretations in which Latinos are ultimately held responsible for institutional failures to provide adequate schooling, job opportunities and optimal health care within Latino communities.

Instead, we would argue that critical policy approaches to class/structural analysis provide greater possibilities for comprehending and transforming the social and economic inequalities faced by Latinos today. From this perspective, income inequalities result from the normal operation of the capitalist economy. That is, income inequality is a structural aspect of the capitalist economy and does not derive from individual differences in skills and competencies. More importantly, class is defined within the social relations of production, giving it a central role in mediating income inequalities in US society.

For years, the hope of social change was founded on possibilities of litigation to correct social wrongs. But today, the terrain of social change is shifting as the role of litigation for social change seems to be declining and the role of public policy, increasing. This is particularly evident in states like California, where the initiative process seems to have run amok,[9] and litigation is too slow a process to counter the wave of right wing corporate interests that dominate the political scene—especially within the context of education. Thus, 50 years after the monumental victory in *Brown vs. The Board of Education*, it is strikingly evident that the traditional approach to framing public policy is insufficient to address effectively racialized, gendered, and class inequalities.

Moreover, constructing public policy formulated on political sound-bytes tied merely to number crunching or limited personalized accounts has failed to provide Latino scholars and activists with the necessary mechanisms to dismantle the pervasive structures of inequalities. There is a dire need then to engage not only with the technical dimensions of public policy (i.e., initiatives, referendums, and the ballot box), but also with its conceptual ideological apparatus. This requires us to question more deeply the philosophical dimensions and political interests that undergird public policy discourse. It also demands that our work focus on "the things people see everyday, around issues that touch people's daily lives, like health and work, the environment and housing, and the education of their children" (Marable, 1998).

For these reasons, we insist that our work must not stay hidden within the safety of the classroom nor remain invisible and excluded within the realm of policy discourse. We need a proactive approach to public policy within the field of Latino Studies—an approach that advances empirically rich and theoretically bold policy alternatives. Through combining our pedagogy, research and activism, Latino Studies scholars can begin to draw up alternative city, state, and federal budgets that target health, education and welfare spending. In so doing, our scholarship can be used widely to help lay out alternative strategies that support the practice of anti-corporate and democratic social action. Such efforts are not meant to serve primarily the interests of policy makers and government agencies but rather to support independent and critical research in Latino Studies that scrutinizes policy in relation to its actual consequences for equality, social justice and economic democracy.

In these times of political unrest and economic uncertainty, we need our scholarship to be tied to a moral imperative of policy and social reconstruction. Public policy initiatives that are grounded in social movements and the changing class realities of Latino communities are urgently needed. However, such a daunting task cannot be accomplished without working together to build coalitions (Valle and Torres, 2000). In practice, this requires that we become more creative about how we utilize both institutional and community resources. In addition, it requires that we work to acknowledge the existence of racialized class divisions within our communities, in order to advance and support greater democratic participation within the context of public policy debates.

All this is to argue that we must work to participate more openly in the arena of public policy, in order to challenge the policy pundits and political sycophants who exploit and repress community political development. In an age where urban legends, public relations schemes, and manufactured perceptions can often yield greater currency than the facts, there is a real need for critical scholars in Latino

Studies to speak truth to power. This implies a willingness to use our academic pursuits in ways that publicly expose the corrupt corporate politics of urban development, the contradictions of labor leadership, the racialized policies and practices of public education, the inhumanity of the prison industrial complex, the atrocities of war, and other obstructions to democratic life.

In a world that is becoming fiercely polarized, Latino Studies scholars must use their influence to establish and participate in policy forums that support cross-dialogues among people in labor, education, community organizing, religion, health care, and public office. Here again, the community must serve as an indispensable site for the construction of knowledge and political action, upon which to anchor our theoretical endeavors to actual events and conditions we find in the world. By connecting our teaching practice and research to a larger social democratic project, the classroom becomes a workplace for both professors and students. In so doing, we can expand our influence in the field in ways that can effectively contribute to our struggle against racism and economic injustice, while we infuse our pedagogy and scholarship with individual passion, political commitment, and sociological imagination.

REFERENCES

Barrera, Mario. 1979. *Race and Class in the Southwest*. Notre Dame, IN: Notre Dame Press.

Crenshaw, Kimberle, Neil Gotanda, Gary Peller, and Kendal Thomas, eds. 1995. *Critical Race Theory: The Key Writings That Formed the Movement*. New York: The New Press.

Cruz, Jon. 1996. From Farce to Tragedy: Reflections in the Reification of Race at Century's End. In *Mapping Multiculturalism*, eds. Allen Gordon and Christopher Newfield, 29. Minnesota: University of Minnesota Press.

Cuban, Larry. 2001. *Oversold and Underused: Computers in Classroom*. Cambridge, MA: Harvard University Press.

Darder, Antonia, and Rodolfo D. Torres. 1997. *The Latino Studies Reader: Culture, Politics and Society*. Boston, MA: Blackwell.

Darder, Antonia, and Rodolfo D. Torres. 1999. Shattering the "Race" Lens: Toward a Critical Theory of Racism. In *Critical Ethnicity: Countering the Waves of Identity Politics*, eds. Robert Tai and Mary Kenyatta, 173-192. New York: Roman and Littlefield.

Davis, Mike. 2001. *Magical Urbanism: Latinos Reinvent the US City*. New York and London: Verso Books.

Delgado, Richard, (ed) 1995. *Critical Race Theory: The Cutting Edge*, Philadelphia, Temple University Press.

Editors, The New Economy: Myth and Reality. 2001. *Monthly Review* 52, (11): 15.

Fears, Darryl. 2002. People of Color Who Never Felt They Were Black: Racial Labels Surprises Many Latino Immigrants. *Washington Post*, December 26, Al.

Gilroy, Paul. 2000. *Against Race: Imaging Political Culture Beyond the Colorline*. Boston: Harvard University Press.

Guillaumin, Colette. 1995. *Racism, Sexism, Power and Ideology*. London: Routledge.

Guinier, Lani, and Gerald Torres. 2002. The Miner's Canary: Enlisting Race, Resisting Power, Transforming Democracy. New York: Harvard University Press.

Herrnstein, Richard J., and Charles Murray. 1994. *The Bell Curve: Intelligence and Class Structure in American Life*. New York: The New Press.

Jessop, B. 2003. *The Future of the Capitalist State*. UK: Polity.

Jessop, Bob, and Ngai-Ling Sum. 2001. Pre-disciplinary and Post-disciplinary Perspectives. *New Political Economy* 6, (1): 89–101.

Loeb, Paul. 1999. *Soul of a Citizen: Living with Conviction in Changing Times*. New York: St. Martin's Press.

Marable, Manning. 1998. Being Left: A Humane Society is Possible Through Struggle. *Z Magazine* interview with Manning Marable. www.znet.org.

Mariscal, Jorge. 2003. A Chicano Looks at the Trent Lott Affair. *La Prensa San Diego*, January 3.

Miles, Robert. 1982. *Racism and Migrant Labor*. London: Routledge.

Miles, Robert. 1989. *Racism*. London: Routledge.

Miles, Robert. 1984. Marxism versus the Sociology of "Race Relations"? Ethnic and Racial Studies, 7, (2): 232.

Miles, Robert. 1993. *Racism After "Race Relations."* London: Routledge.

Miles, Robert, and Rodolfo D. Torres. 1996. Does "Race" Matter? Transatlantic Perspectives on *Racism after "Race Relations."* In *Re-situating Identities: The Politics of Race, Ethnicity, and Culture*, eds. Vered Amit-Talai and Caroline Knowles. Ontario, Canada: Broadview Press.

Miliband, Ralph. 1969. *The State in Capitalist Society*. New York: Basic Books.

Mills, C. Wright. 2002. *The Sociological Imagination*. London: Oxford University Press.

Morrison, Toni. 1989. Unspeakable Things Unspoken: The Afro-American Presence in American Literature. *Michigan Quarterly Review* 28: 3.

Oboler, Suzanne. 1995. *Ethnic Labels, Latino Lives: Identity and the Politics of (Re)Presentation in the United States*. Minneapolis: University of Minnesota Press.

Pardo, Mary. 1990. Mexican American Women Grassroots Community Activist: "Mothers of East Los Angeles." *Frontiers* xi: 1–7.

Rosaldo, Renato. 1993. *Culture and Truth: The Remaking of Social Analysis*. Boston: Beacon Press.

Scott, Allen, and Edward Soja. 1996. *The City: Los Angeles and Urban Theory and the End of the Twentieth Century*. Berkeley, CA: University of California Press.

Tornatzky, Louis, Elsa Macias and Sara Jones. 2002. *Latinos and Information Technology: The Promise and the Challenge*. Claremont, CA: The Tomas Rivera Policy Institute.

Torres, Rodolfo D., and Antonia Darder. 2004. *After Race: Essays on Racism, Class and Inequality*. New York: New York University Press.

Valle, Victor, and Rodolfo D. Torres. 2000. *Latino Metropolis*. Minnesota: University of Minnesota Press.

Wing, Adrien Katherine, ed. 1997. *Critical Race Feminism*: A Reader. New York: New York University Press.

Wood, Ellen Meiksins. 2000. *Democracy Against Capitalism: Renewing Historical Materialism*. New York: Cambridge University Press.

Wood, Ellen Meiksins. 1994. Identity Crisis. In *These Times*, June 28–29.

Wright, Erik Olin. 1997. *Class Counts: Comparative Studies in Class Analysis*. New York: Cambridge University Press.

NOTES

1. Cited in Davis (2001)

2. Cited in Loeb (1999)

3. A good example is found in the work of Mary Pardo (1990) with the "Mothers of East L.A.," where she provides both a class and gender critique of women workers.

4. For an excellent review of contemporary debates on globalization see David Held & Anthony McGrew, *Globalization/Anti-Globalization*, Polity (2002).

5. In the last decade, *Monthly Review* has published some of the most incisive critiques and formidable interrogations into the globalization debate. Some of these authors included Ellen Meiksins Wood, Harry Magdoff, Frances Fox Piven, Robert McChesney, Peter Meiksins, Bill Tabb, and Istvan Meszaros.

6. One of the most significant theoretical contributions made during the post-civil rights era regarding questions of racialized identities was formulated by radical feminists of color who rendered the most sophisticated articulations of the intersectionality argument, with its often cited mantra of "race, class and gender."

7. See "The New Economy: Myth and Reality" by the *Monthly Review* editors (2001), Vol 52, No. 11, April 2001.

8. The groundbreaking work of Robert Miles has strongly influenced our views on the question of "race." See *Racism and Migrant Labor*, (1982); *Racism* (1989); and *Racism After "Race Relations"* (1993). We would also like to note that Paul Gilroy, an early critic of Miles, recently has advanced in his new book, *Against Race: Imaging Political Culture Beyond the Colorline* (2000), a similar position.

9. During the 1990s, the initiative process (once envisioned as a legislative vehicle for the masses) became co-opted as an effective tool for neoliberal interests in California. Several conservative initiatives were successfully passed by voters including Proposition 227, which called for the elimination of bilingual education in public schools; Proposition 187 which called for the elimination of health, education, and welfare benefits to undocumented immigrants; and Proposition 209, which called for the elimination of race as a determinant of educational admission to state colleges and universities.

PART VI.
Pedagogy of the Body

THE GREAT MOTHER WAILS

The Earth extends her arms to us;
Revealing through her nature the
changing condition of our existence.

She bends and twists,
Deflecting the swords of
Our foolishness,
Our arrogance,
Our gluttony,
Our deceit.

Unbridled by red alerts or amber
   warnings,
Her ire gives rise to monsoon winds,
Jarring us from the stupor of
Our academic impunity;
Our disjointed convolutions,
Our empty promises; our
black and white dreams.

Filled with unruly discontent,
we yearn to dominate her mysteries;
reducing her to microscopic dust,
we spit upon her sacredness,
tempting the fury of her seas.

We spill our unholy wars
upon her belly's tender flesh,
blazing dislocated corpses,
ignite her agony and grief.

Still, in love with her creations,
she warns of our complacency
to cataclysmic devastation,
rooted in the alienation of
our disconnection
our rejection,
our oppression,
our scorn.

And still, we spin ungodly
tantrums of injustice
against her love,
against ourselves,
against one another.
When will we remove blindfolds
    from our eyes?
When will we stretch our arms—to her?
When will the cruelty of our
Hatred cease; teaching us to
abandon the impositions of
patriarchy and greed?

Oh! that we might together renew
Our communion with the earth,
She, the cradle of humanity;
She, the nourishment of our seeds;
She, the beauty of the song within;
She, the wailing that precedes.

—ANTONIA DARDER (2008)

CHAPTER 16

It's Not Nice to Fool Mother Nature

Eco-Pedagogy in the Pursuit of Justice[1]

It is urgent that we assume the duty of fighting for the fundamental ethical principles, like respect for the life of human beings, the
life of animals, the life of birds, the life of rivers and forests....
Ecology takes on fundamental importance....It has to be present in any radical, critical, liberationist educational practice. For
this reason, it seems to me a lamentable contradiction to engage
in progressive, revolutionary discourse and have a practice that
negates life.

—PAULO FREIRE (2004, 37)

When first preparing for this presentation,[2] I remembered a 1970s TV ad for
Chiffon margarine that claimed to be as good as butter. The ad ended with Mother
Nature's retort, "It's not nice to fool Mother Nature!" Yet, the truth is that U.S.
capitalist culture has an arrogant obsession to fool Mother Nature, whether it is
by stripping her coal and petroleum resources or fabricating indigestible nuclear
waste products or wholesale neglect of fragile levees in need of repair. Cataclysmic
disasters, such as Hurricane Katrina, are unfortunate testimonies to the danger of

ignoring the warnings of the earth. But more unfortunate, as Naomi Klein (2007) documents in her book *The Shock Doctrine*, is the manner in which so-called natural disasters are capitalized on by unscrupulous and ruthless capitalists who see no problem with turning a huge profit off the backs of oppressed populations—whether they be victims of weather disasters, catastrophic illnesses, or the over 1 million inmates incarcerated for nonviolent crimes in the United States.

I also could not help but be reminded about the ways in which the revolutionary intent of multicultural education has taken a terrible beating after forty years. Suddenly, "diversity" is used to speak of any and all differences, trivializing culture and weakening our claims to linguistic and ceremonial rights and our sovereignty as distinct cultures of this nation. Accordingly, multicultural education, as are the historical struggles of people of color in this country, is often seen as simply a worn-out educational fad from the civil rights era, a fad now passé. The new proof that will be now be used to claim the irrelevance of this work, of course, is the ascendance of Barack Obama, a Black man, to the presidency of the United States. What these cynics fail to understand is that the work is only now truly beginning!

Moreover, their shortsightedness dishonors the contemporary suffering of poor and working-class African American, Latino, Native American, Asian American, and other racialized communities. Not to mention the fact that Obama's election to the presidency is a reality not because he is Black, but because he offered the nation an alternative to the wretched abuses of power by the Bush administration. But rather than placing a central focus on both Obama's strengths and the challenges he'll face as the executive statesperson of the nation, the mainstream political discourse of the presidential campaign became highly racialized—a proof, in itself, that the United States has yet to overcome the racism that distorts the capacity of its citizens to move beyond apologia when it comes to the color of one's skin. Moreover, those who have shouldered the contradictions of a racialized world know only too well of the wholesale dismissal of our struggles and our claims to equal voice in the future of this country—land that rightly belonged to the native people of this hemisphere if it belonged to anyone at all.

The incessant search by news commentaries for Obama's ability to appear or not appear assimilated and homogenized at times dominated much of the discussion. In fact, it brought many folks real comfort to feel that Obama's white maternal roots rendered him beyond Afro-centric concerns and that "racelessness" was central to his personality. Again, this belies any notion that we are done with the conversation about racism and other forms of social exclusions.

Confronting Unsustainability

Liberation in our genocidal times is, first and foremost, the freedom to stay alive.

—VANDANA SHIVA (2005, 185)

In her book *Earth Democracy*, Vandana Shiva adamantly calls us to "shift our worldview from one dominated by markets and military, monocultures and mechanistic
reductionism, to the peaceful co-creation and co-evolution of diverse beings, connected through the common bonds of life." She argues that this shift in paradigm
is necessary if we are to remove the blinders of capitalism and colonialist expan-
sions and imagine new possibilities for life on the planet. In order that we, as educators, might enter more fully into such a shift in paradigm, we must be willing to
contend forthrightly with the ecological devastation currently at work, through a
lens that acknowledges the political economy as inextricably linked to all forms of
oppressive practices, including those that devastate a potential for sustained life on
the planet. Along with such a foundation for an eco-pedagogy, we are summoned
politically to work in pursuit of cultural and linguistic democracy, indigenous sovereignty, and human rights—all significant to reestablishing a formidable relationship with the earth and one another. Such an ethos of education can only be rooted
in our integral knowledge and acceptance of ourselves as physical, emotional,
intellectual, and spiritual beings. Within the context of an ecologically rooted epis-
temology, our organic relationship with the earth is intimately tied to our struggles
for cultural self-determination, environmental sustainability, and social justice.

Everywhere we look, we are bombarded with signs of political systems and
social structures that propel us toward unsustainability and extinction. At this
very moment, the planet faces some of the most horrendous examples of the devastation of natural resources ever to be experienced in the history of humankind.
Hurricane Katrina and a variety of other cataclysmic "natural disasters" in the last
decade have sung the environmental hymns of planetary imbalance and reckless
ecological practices gone awry.

The devastation that has resulted locally and globally is heavily marked by
an increasing concentration of wealth within the U.S. oligarchy and its agents of
capital. In addition, we see the growing loss of livelihood among working people everywhere; the gross inequalities in education; the absence of decent health
care; an unprecedented number of people living behind bars; trillions spent on
fabricated wars fundamentally tied to the control and domination of the earth's
resources; and all this financed through the systematic destruction of safety nets
for the poor, while neoliberal policies abundantly line the pockets of the wealthy.
And this comes at the expense of the most vulnerable populations, while simul-

taneously huge financial institutions vie for the pork-barrel rewards of corporate welfare to the tune of $700 billion dollars. Hence, one of the most resounding principles of a multicultural education must be anchored to an uncompromising commitment to economic democracy, along with ecological sustainability.

Unfortunately, the Western ethos of mastery and supremacy over nature has, to our detriment, supported the unrelenting expansion of capitalism and its unparalleled domination over all aspects of human life. In the process, it has broken our sense of interconnection, in the name of an egotistical individualism run amok. This is the contemporary worldview that has been unmercifully imparted within the hidden curriculum of schools and universities. As a consequence, irrespective of any liberal democratic rhetoric that insists "we are all created equal," racism, patriarchy, technocracy, and the economic piracy of globalization—once known, rightly, as imperialism—have led to the unprecedented ecological exploitation and devastation of societies in the last century, creating conditions that threaten real peril if we do not reverse its course.

Yet, despite the importance of this process to the survival of the planet and the manner that an ethos of ecological sustainability should earnestly underscore all the major decisions we make in our lives, seldom are questions of ecological concern made central to the discourse of pedagogical preparation or mainstream multicultural debates. Perhaps it is exactly this historical "missing link" in the curriculum that is most responsible for an uncritical and inhumane response to the suffering of human beings under regimes of genocide, slavery, and colonialism. In truth, a deeper view exposes a legacy that persists today in the shrouded values and attitudes of educators from the dominant class and culture who expect the oppressed to adhere to the cultural domination of the powerful elite.

Often this veiled expectation translates into a need for those with power and privilege to obsessively seek some specific identification with the "other," in order that they might deem those viewed as "different" worthy of their love, empathy, and respect. In many corners, this is what is meant by multicultural education— essentially a conservative education project that on the one hand seeks to find in the "other" only that with which the mainstream can readily identify, while on the other hand seeking to erase everything that has no relevance to mainstream U.S. life. What is truly unconscionable about this process is that if satisfactory identification with the humanity of the "other" cannot be found, then racialized institutional policies and practices render the "untouchables" as problematic to the political project of capitalist democracy and, hence, unworthy and disposable.

It is precisely such a worldview that participates in the extinction of whole species or thinks nothing of the destruction of cultures and languages outside of a "first world" tongue classification. Rapidly our biodiversity is slipping away, despite scientific findings that clearly warn of the loss of hardiness and vitality of human life, as a direct consequence of assimilation and homogenization. It is truly ironic that in a world that obsessively denies its participation in the oppression of life and simultaneously embraces all sorts of confounded rhetoric about multiculturalism or diversity we find ourselves more and more pressured into a "safe" essentialized world of sameness and homogenized familiarity. There are examples of this everywhere we look, but nowhere is the oppression of it felt more than in the lives of youth, who are still far more organically present to the genuine diversity of life.

The consequence here, of course, is the manner in which the repression of the body is manifested with capitalist fervor to commodify as quickly as possible its design on the new generation. Schools are some of the most complicit institutions in the repression of the body and thus also the repression of our emotional nature, our sexual energies, our intellectual passions, and the spiritual capacities that open us to communion with both one another and the natural world.

Here, I wish to argue that the paradigm and values that shape our connection or disconnection to nature, or the earth, also intermingle in the design of contemporary classroom life. These are most visible in the manner in which teachers allow or disallow the bodies of their students to be fully present and alive. Given, then, the significance of the body in the construction of knowledge and the impact of repression on this process, we must fully contend with what it means to decolonize the flesh within the context of a revolutionary multicultural education.

The Body and the Construction of Knowledge

> I know with my entire body, with feelings, with passion and also with reason. It is my entire body that socially knows. I cannot, in the name of exactness and rigor, negate my body, my emotions and my feelings.
>
> —PAULO FREIRE (1997)

As evidenced by this quotation, Paulo Freire often referenced the body in his effort to consider the integral needs of students within the classroom (Darder 2002). I argue that this is so because if we, as teachers, are to struggle in our classroom toward an emancipatory vision of life, then we too must know our own bodies, respect the myriad feelings and sensations that are central to one's capacity to know the world, and embrace the multiplicity of ways in which human beings express their particular sensibilities and understandings of life. This is precisely in concert with Freire's recognition of the illusive belief that intellectual exactness could somehow free us of the messy sensations of being a flesh-and-blood human being.

Yet, despite the role of the body in the process of knowing, notions of students as embodied and integral human beings seldom receives the attention it so fully merits in teacher education or multicultural discussions of classroom praxis. Missing even in multicultural discussions of pedagogy is a more complex understanding of our humanity and the significance of the body to the intellectual formations and cultural predispositions at work in the process of human development and the behavior of students. Generally speaking, such discussions have been left to educators whose tendency has been to overemphasize the role of subjectivity or fall into an over-psychologizing of the self. No matter how well meaning, this highly individualistic reading often fails to address the material conditions and issues of power and privilege at work in shaping the lives of historically disenfranchised students and their communities.

The reticence in education to engage issues of the body has also been tied to scholarly tendencies to ignore the material conditions of public schooling that shape classroom life. This historical absence of the body has been so because "bringing the body into critical discussion is readily considered potentially disruptive and subversive" (Levy 2000, 82) to the rigid and authoritarian social order of schooling. Grounded in such a worldview, many educators assume that teaching and learning are solely cognitive functions and, as such, teachers need not concern themselves with the physical nature of their students unless one is deemed "inappropriate," at which time officials or psychologists are summoned to evaluate and hopefully "fix the problem."

To support students in becoming *full subjects of history*, Freire often urged teachers to grapple with the fact that their students construct knowledge through the multitude of collective interactions of their bodies with the world and with nature. Similarly, in thinking about this question of the body, Amanda Sinclair (1999) reminds us that

> ...the immediate impact of a person's body on another is profound. A great deal happens before a person opens their mouth. Emotions are aroused, judgments are made. Comfort or discomfort levels are established well in advance of verbal communication. We unconsciously or consciously register and make judgments about stature and voice. Bodies elicit feelings of excitement and admiration, attraction and desire, envy and distaste.[3]

The material conditions and histories of students are made visible by their bodies. Their histories of survival are witnessed in their skin, their teeth, their hair, their gestures, their speech, and even the movement of their arms and legs. In a multitude of ways, our "bodies are maps of power and identity" (Haraway 1990, 2), as is the earth herself. It is for this reason that teachers must work to engage students' physical realities more substantively, in an effort to forge an emancipatory pedagogy that thrives in everyday life. It is not enough to rely on abstract learning processes, in which only the analysis of words is privileged in the construction of knowledge, as if the body had no place in the construction and reading of text.[4] Such an educational process of estrangement functions to alienate and isolate students from the natural world around them, from themselves, and from one another, disrupting their potential for both intimacy and solidarity.

In contrast, an eco-pedagogy that sustains life and creativity is firmly grounded in a material understanding of our human existence, as a starting place for classroom practice and our struggle to reinvent the world. Freire (1993) again posits this as vital to our teaching: "We learn things about the world by acting and changing the world around us. It is [in] this process of change, of transforming the material world from which we emerged, [where] creation of the cultural and historical world takes place. This transformation of the world [is] done by us, while it makes and remakes us" (108).

However, there is nothing automatic or "natural" about social change and transformation. Nor is it a process that can rely solely on calculating logic or cold rationality, given the manner in which the body's sentient forces overwhelmingly shape human experiences and emotional responses to social structures—long before we become fully conscious of our egocentric preoccupations. Struggles within multicultural education, then, in the name of social justice, must hold steadfast the fullness of our human existence if we are to truly craft a decolonizing practice of multicultural education.

In our efforts to understand the process of schooling, teaching and learning must also be acknowledged as human labor, that which takes place within our bodies. This also requires that we incorporate, consciously or unconsciously, the totality of who we and our students are, in and out of the classroom. This corporal phenomenon is always at work, whether acknowledged or not, as we strive to make sense of the material conditions and social relations of power in schools—relations that, more times than not, demand that our mind split off from our body. This frequently occurs through an unexamined curricular assumption that racialized and marginalized people should gladly surrender our bodies to an assimilative educational process—a colonizing process that requires us to abandon the wisdom of our bodies in exchange for meritorious recognition. In *Teaching to Transgress*, bell hooks (1994) describes this colonizing phenomenon in the following way:

> I have always been acutely aware of the presence of my body in those settings that, in fact, invite us to invest so deeply in a mind/body split so that, in a sense, you're almost always at odds with the existing structure, whether you are a black woman student or professor. But if you want to remain, you've got, in a sense, to remember yourself—because to remember

yourself is to see yourself always as a body in a system that has not become accustomed to your presence or to your physicality (135).

Through such an awareness of presence, multicultural educators who remember themselves can build a practice of education in which students are asked to confront themselves and each other not as disconnected strangers but rather as fully embodied human beings, from the moment they enter the classroom. In this way, a critical praxis of the body seeks to contend in the flesh with the embodied histories of the disenfranchised, as teachers and students work together to disrupt the social and material forces that perpetuate conditions of marginalization, domination, and exploitation.

Freire (1993) speaks of the body as indispensable to the process of learning. "The body moves, acts, rememorizes, the struggle for its liberation; the body, in sum, desires, points out, announces, protests, curves itself, rises, designs and remakes the world...and its importance has to do with a certain sensualism...contained by the body" (87). But it is precisely this sensualism, with its revolutionary potential to nurture self-determination and the empowerment of disenfranchised students as both individuals and social beings, that is systematically stripped away from the educational process of public schooling. Most teachers "already well-versed in maintaining a grey world of unsexy knowing...are well placed to take up the challenge" (McWilliam 2000, 29) of policing expressions of passion, excitement, and physicality within the classroom, particularly when working with youth.

Conservative ideologies of social control—historically linked to Puritanical views of the body as evil, sensual pleasure as sinful, and passions as corrupting to the sanctity of the spirit—continue to be reflected in the narrow, rule-based pedagogical policies and practices of public schooling. The sensuality of the body is discouraged through the prominent practice of immobilizing students within hard chairs and desks[5] that contain and restrict their contact with one another and the environment around them. Viviane Laroy (2000) contends that

> The body is not usually granted a lot of space in our educational system; it is nothing more than what allows us to remain seated for hours and to move from one classroom to another and to meet the requirements...90% of the time spent in schools is typically in a state of immobility. Learning is reduced to an airborne exchange of knowledge between different minds: the knowledge in the teacher's mind is transmitted to the learners, defined as minds able to receive new knowledge, or not (1).

Laroy correctly argues that this tradition of fettered bodies is anchored in three paradigmatic figures: Socrates, Christianity, and Pavlov's dog. In the classical tradition, the sensual body is quickly subordinated to the mind, while ideas are privileged over the senses (Seidel 1964). In an Anglo-centric Christianity, the separation between the body and the soul constitutes an essential pedagogical concern, in preserving purity of thought. In the Pavlovian model, the body is transformed into an instrumentalized object to be manipulated and controlled through external stimulus in the process of learning.

Such views of teaching and learning ultimately lead to pedagogical practices that do emotional and psychological violence through their erasure of the body and the annihilation of the flesh. Accordingly, inequalities are reproduced by classed, racialized, gendered, homophobic, normative-abled perceptions and distortions of male and female bodies—perceptions and distortions embodied within the pedagogy of even the most well-meaning teachers.

Consequently, students from communities where the body—with all its senses and spontaneities—is given greater primacy in the act of knowing and being are often coerced into sacrificing their knowledge of the body's sensuality, creativity, and vitality in favor of an atomized, analytical, and instrumental logic of being. In light of this tendency, revolutionary multicultural educators need "to reflect on what bodies we give 'permission' to in our classrooms and the extent to which we let those bodies speak" (Kazan 2005, 394) or move freely. Such reflections may prove, for example, significant to explaining the overwhelming tendency of teachers and school officials to label African American and Chicano boys as hyperactive or as having an attention deficit when they find it difficult to comply with classroom expectations of forced immobility that is placed upon them. This is so, particularly, within classrooms where there is an inadequate presence of cultural and linguistic democracy, leaving these students little familiarity from which to build their evolving understanding of the world. The long-term physiological and psychological response to such an essential pedagogical absence is, in fact, increased agitation and stress for the student.

Intrusions of the Body

The corporeal, physical and sexual realms are unwelcome intrusions.
—SUSIE O'BRIEN (2000, 46)

In considering the role of the body, Susie O'Brien (2000) posits that in the everyday world of the classroom the physical and sexual dimensions of the body are considered an intrusion on the sanctimony of intellectual pursuit. This systematic disembodiment of students in the process of learning begins early in their academic formation. Despite child development theories that assert that human beings are sexual beings even before birth, sexuality as an ever-present phenomenon is systematically repressed and denied within the four walls of the classroom.

This is the case even at puberty, when adolescent bodies are particularly sensitive to the heightened and confusing sensations driven by *normal* pubescent changes in hormonal activity. Yet seldom do teachers—many of whom are not particularly comfortable with their own bodies or sexuality—critically engage questions of the body and sexuality, beyond the often repeated cliché of "raging hormones" to signify teenage sexuality, which is usually followed by a freakish laugh.

Meanwhile, students are not only pedagogically abandoned at an often vulnerable and critical moment in their lives, but also left at the mercy of the media and corporate pirates[6] that very deliberately and systematically prey upon the confusing field of powerful bodily sensations, emotions, and stirrings of youth. Henry Giroux (1998), an acerbic critic of the consuming mayhem of predatory corporate practices on children and youth, argues,

> In the slick world of advertising, teenage bodies are sought after for the exchange value they generate in marketing an adolescent sexuality that offers a marginal exoticism and ample pleasures for the largely male consumer. Commodification reifies and fixates the complexity of youth and the range of possible identities they might assume while simultaneously exploiting them as fodder for the logic of the market (39).

Often frightened by their own corporal ambivalence and the physical liveliness of youthful bodies, educational policy makers institute practices that coerce teachers into silence, rigidly limiting and even outlawing discussions of one of the most significant aspects of our humanity—our sexuality. The message is clear: everyone, but especially youth, is expected to check their sexuality (along with all other aspects of their lived histories) at the door prior to entering. And despite the difficulties and hardships that such silence portends for many students—isolation and increasing rates of suicide among many gay youth, for example—schools, much like churches, act as moral leaders, policing and repressing the body's participation in public life. A prime national example of this phenomenon was the dismissal of the former U.S. Surgeon General, Joyce Elders, an African American woman, who had the guts to speak publicly in favor of educating youth about being responsible for their sexuality, including issues related to contraception, the use of condoms, and masturbation. When hearing that Dr. Elders had been asked for her resignation, I couldn't help wondering if those officials who condemned her, including religious leaders, had actually never pleasured their own body. So threatening was her transgression of silence that few were willing to stand up publicly in support of her courage to be honest, mature, and down-to-earth real about the need of young people to be conscious and informed about their sexuality.

This minimalist attitude of U.S. schools in the area of human sexuality can be contrasted with the approach in other parts of the world, where straightforward facts about "the birds and bees" are considered a pedagogical imperative.

In Sweden, for example, compulsory sex education has been in place since 1956, given their recognition of sex as a natural human act and the frank acknowledgment that most people become sexually active before they are twenty. Toward this end, students learn at an early age about their sexuality, reinforcing a more open and positive view of sex and the body. Curriculum begins at age six with anatomy, and from age twelve on the topics are geared more toward developing tools for taking responsibility for their sexual lives. The outcome is that Sweden's rate of teen pregnancy and sexually transmitted diseases is among the lowest in the world.[7]

The issue of teen pregnancy also illustrates how schooling practices and policies associated with the body are inextricably tied to gendered ideologies of power and control. Sinclair reminds us that schools, like most institutions, are only able to "assimilate women's bodies so long as they conform to a neutral or desexualized form."[8] Young teen mothers violate this norm by "drawing attention to their femaleness, their sexuality, and difference from the male norm."[9] Hence, teen pregnancy is addressed by "excommunicating" and exiling young expectant mothers from the school campus to an alternative location—often silenced and unseen—while young fathers are left virtually untouched by the same system, to proceed with life as usual.

Missing, even in the university, is the willingness to contend with the sexuality of students in the process of their academic formation, despite the fact that "intense desires are played out in the university classroom" (O'Brien 2000, 49). In keeping with the mind-body split, educators readily ignore the manner in which learning is both visceral and sensual. Consequently, the severing of the body's desires and sensations from the construction of knowledge interferes dramatically with students' capacity for self-knowledge; this dynamic of silence is further intensified for transsexual and gender-nonconforming students. Similarly, such practices also thwart our knowledge of the "other," rendering us alienated and estranged from human suffering caused by oppression predicated on class, gender, ethnicity, sexuality, skin-color, physical-ableness, or spirituality (Shapiro 1999; Soelle 1975). In fact, Spender (1995) argues that the absence of pedagogical engagement with the body seriously inhibits the development of empathy and respect for the "other."

Thus it should be no surprise to learn that many traditional curricular policies and practices that reinforce abstract, fragmented, and decontextualized theories of teaching and learning seldom function in the interest of oppressed populations. Instead, disenfranchised students are objectified, alienated, and domesticated into passive roles, through the threat of marginalization or expulsion. As such, schools discourage us all from thinking about ourselves as bodies (Kazan 2005). This not only interferes with student achievement but also silences innate intelligence, sabotages social agency, and disrupts the evolution of political consciousness. This is blatantly visible when the emotional and physical nature of students is diminished or ignored in an overriding effort to obtain their obedience and conformity.

Teachers, whose bodies are similarly restricted, alienated, and domesticated by their workplace, are often under enormous pressure to follow strict policies and procedures for classroom conduct. In many cases, they are similarly expected to dispense prepackaged curriculum instead of employing more creative and critical approaches grounded in the actual needs of students. Given the impact of disembodied practices, teachers generally experience an uphill battle in meeting standardized mandates, which systematically extricate students' bodies from the equation of learning. Nowhere is this more apparent than in low-income schools across the nation, where teaching-to-the-test fronts as the "rigorous" and "scientific" curriculum of choice.

Along with teaching-to-the-test, there exists what Katherine Hayles (1999) terms "incorporated knowledge"—that is, notions of gender, sexuality, and racialized identities that are "deeply sedimented into the body and…highly resistant to change" (205). This constitutes knowledge that is generally beyond the reach of conscious view, given its habitual and ritualized nature. Its outcomes include repressive educational policies and practices that marginalize the knowledge and languages of oppressed populations, infantilize adult students, criminalize youth of color, and render suspicious any ideas or uses of the body perceived as existing outside the narrow mainstream view of normalcy. Similarly, this supports the transmission of disembodied knowledge, summarily cut off from students' lived histories and the environments in which they must struggle to survive.

Surrendering to Justice and Beauty

A critical [eco-pedagogy] involves the ability to articulate the myriad of ways in which cultures and societies unfold and develop ideological political systems and social structures that tend either towards ecological sustainability and biodiversity or unsustainability and extinction.

—RICHARD KAHN (2008, 553)

What all this heralds, then, is the need for a more complex understanding of human diversity and its multitude of legitimate expressions, beyond those made available by the academic dictates of power and capital. Here again, issues of social justice and human rights within the context of schooling cannot be addressed outside of the political economy and the myriad ways in which it orchestrates a politics of hate and fear in the name of progress and democracy. This is to say that without a deep willingness to interrogate the manner in which educational policies and the practice of teachers as moral leaders support the inhumanity of capitalism in this country and abroad it is impossible to build a new ecological paradigm of teaching that supports all human life as precious and worthy of love and respect.

Critical ecologist and educator Richard Kahn has forcefully argued the importance of an eco-pedagogy in our work with diverse populations, arguing that the majority of the social and political problems facing us today are fundamentally rooted in hierarchical relations founded on competition, paternalism, arrogance, elitism, absolutism, violence, and greed. Such attitudes are predicated upon an ahistorical and uncritical view of life that enables the powerful to abdicate their collective responsibility to democratic ideals of social justice while superimposing a technocratic and instrumental rationality that commodifies and instrumentalizes all human existence. Through such a perspective, the purpose of education is to educate students to identify as consumers and exploiters of the earth, rather than to seek a life that exits in harmony and communion with all of nature, including our own bodies.

Through a systematic web of hierarchal meritocratic relationships, neoliberal education has functioned to sustain a political economy of oppression, both locally and globally. And it is precisely these values that have served to warp the promise of cultural and linguistic democracy and a diversity of knowledge in this country, by repetitive and unimaginative curricula and fetishized methods, even in the field of multicultural education. Hence, it is no surprise that education for oppressed populations has generally functioned to immobilize and disable the cultural brilliance of our innate intelligence, while the heirs of the elite are provided mobility in their bodies, a wide variety of content and opportunity, as well as consistent access to every state-of-the-art technology available.

Our work in the field of multicultural education must begin to incorporate an understanding of social justice, the politics of peace, and environmental priorities as central to the struggle to overcome oppression. As educators, activists, and human kin, we must turn to the wisdom of our own communities, in serious and sustained ways, in order to work toward the abandonment of colonizing values and practices that denigrate our bodies and disable our capacities to sustain life. Similarly, a clear message must be sent to those who express a commitment to multicultural education that if they are to grapple with the wretched inequalities of public schooling, they must link their efforts to a larger emancipatory vision of everyday life.

Moreover, contending effectively with issues of class privilege, racism, sexism, homophobia, disablism, and all other forms of inequalities necessitates a life-affirming ecological praxis. This encompasses a firm refusal to adhere to artificial disconnections that falsely separate political and economic dynamics that shape the local, global, regional, rural, urban, and so on and, instead, challenge forthrightly static views of humanity and the planet—views that inadvertently serve the commodifying interests of capital and its penchant to divide and conquer, through paternalistic and pretentious discourses of authority and expertise. In contrast, what a critical eco-pedagogy for social justice must encompass are philosophical principles that are at home with ambiguity and dissonance as an ever-present social phenomenon, where human differences are both commonplace and valued for their necessary and creative potential in the making of a truly democratic, just, and peaceful world.

In an effort to move beyond the orthodoxy of consumerism, careerism, and corporate profiteering, multicultural educators committed to a critical eco-pedagogy must courageously pose a new paradigm for living a transformative critical pedagogy—one that encompasses the power of human emotions; honors the ritual of cultural ways of being; respects universal human rights; cherishes simplicity, peace, and care for all life; and embraces a planetary consciousness rooted in the integrative coexistence with all our fellow species on the earth. More important, a critical eco-pedagogy of justice points toward a reenvisioning of our work as revolutionary educators committed to ending oppression in all its manifestations, while embracing with love and respect all life on the planet.

Vandana Shiva ends her book *Earth Democracy* by writing, "Imperialism has always had global reach. Today's movements must have a planetary reach and a planetary embrace. We have just begun to tap our potential for transformation and liberation. This is not the end of history, but another beginning (185–86)." Similarly, Murray Bookchin, in *The Ecology of Freedom*, explains the need for our reconnection with nature:

> Humanity has passed through a long history of one-sidedness and of a social condition that has always contained the potential of destruction, despite its creative achievements in technology. The great project of our time must be to open the other eye: to see all-sidedly and wholly, to heal and transcend the cleavage between humanity and nature that came with early wisdom (107).

Echoed in these words can be found indigenous wisdom that reminds us to be mindful of the earth and all our actions, for our words and our deeds will be felt unto seven generations. Through such an organic ethics of connection, educators can embrace a more deeply communal understanding of life—an understanding that supports our relationship with the earth, our loved ones, our students, and one another with the strength and courage to be steadfast and true to the beauty of justice. It is precisely with this spirit in mind that I hold in my heart the words of the great Sufi poet Rumi[10] who wrote:

When we've totally surrendered to that beauty,
We'll become a mighty kindness.[10]

REFERENCES

Bookchin, M. (2005). *The Ecology of Freedom: The Emergence and Dissolution of Hierarchy.* Oakland, CA: AK Press.

Darder, A. (2002). *Reinventing Paulo Freire: A Pedagogy of Love.* Boulder, CO: Westview.

Freire, P. (2004). *Pedagogy of Indignation.* Boulder, CO: Paradigm.

Freire, P. (1997). *Pedagogy of the Heart.* New York: Contiuum.

Freire, P. (1993). *Pedagogy of the City.* New York: Continuum.

Giroux, H. (1998). Teenage Sexuality, Body Politics, and the Pedagogy of Display. In J.S. Epstein. *Youth Culture: Identity in a Postmodern World.* New York: Wiley-Blackwell.

Haraway, D. (1990). A Manifesto for Cyborgs. In L. Nicholson (Ed.), *Feminism/Postmodernism* (pp.190-233). New York, Routledge.

Hayles, K. (1999). *How We Become Posthuman: Virtual Bodies in Cybernetics, Literature, and Informatics.* Chicago: University of Chicago Press.

hooks, b. (1994). *Teaching to Transgress.* New York: Routledge.

Kahn, R. (2008). "Toward Eco-pedagogy: Weaving a Broad-Based Pedagogy of Liberation for Animals, Nature, and the Oppressed People of the Earth." In A. Darder, M. Baltodano, and R.D. Torres, *The Critical Pedagogy Reader.* New York: Routledge.

Kazan, T. (2005). "Dancing Bodies in the Classroom: Toward an Embodied Pedagogy," *Pedagogy* 5, no. 3: 379–408.

Klein, N. (2007). *The Shock Doctrine: The Rise of Disaster Capitalism.* New York: Metropolitan Books.

Laroy, V. (2000). "The Body in a Pedagogy of Being," *Humanizing Language Teaching* 4, no. 6. Available at: www.hltmag.co.uk/nov02/martnov021.rtf.

Levy, B. (2000). "Pedagogy: Incomplete, Unrequited." In C. O'Farrell, D. Meadmore, E. McWilliam, and C. Symes (eds.), *Taught Bodies.* New York: Peter Lang, 81–90.

McWilliam, E. (2000). "Stuck in the Missionary Position." In C. O'Farrell, D. Meadmore, E. McWilliam, and C. Symes (eds.), *Taught Bodies.* New York: Peter Lang.

O'Brien, S. (2000). "The Lecherous Professor." In C. O'Farrell, D. Meadmore, E. McWilliam, and C. Symes (eds.), *Taught Bodies.* New York: Peter Lang.

Rukeyser, M. (1996). *The Life of Poetry.* Ashfield, MA: Paris Press.

Seidel, G. (1964). *Martin Heidegger and the Pre-Socratics.* Lincoln: University of Nebraska Press.

Shapiro, S. (1999). *Pedagogy and the Politics of the Body: A Critical Praxis.* New York: Garland Publishing.

Shiva, V. (2005). *Earth Democracy: Justice, Sustainability, and Peace.* Boston, MA: South End Press.

Sinclair, A. (1999). *Working Paper: Body and Pedagogy.* Available at: http://www.mbs.edu/index.cfm?objectid=951E3441-123F-AoD8-42535588B213E90B.

Soelle, D. (1975). *Suffering.* Philadelphia: Fortress Press.

Spender, D. (1995). *Nattering on the Net: Women, Power and Cyborspace.* Melbourne: Spinifex.

NOTES

1. Versions of this essay appeared in A. Darder, "Decolonizing the Flesh: The Body, Pedagogy, and Inequality" in R. Sintos Colinos (ed.), *Postcolonial Challenge of Education* (New York: Routledge), 217–213; and A. Darder (2010), "Schooling Bodies: Critical Pedagogy and Urban Youth," in S. Steinberg (ed.), *19 Questions: Teaching in the City* (New York: Peter Lang).

2. This paper was presented at the National Association of Multicultural Educators on November 13, 2008.

3. See A. Sinclair, *Body and Pedagogy,* available at: http://www.mbs.edu/index.cfm?objectid=951E3441-123F-AoD8-42535588B213E90B (3).

4. For an interesting dialogue between Giovanni Fusetti and Suzy Willson regarding this question and others related to *The Pedagogy of the Poetic Body,* see: http://www.giovannifusetti.com/public/file/Poetic.body.pdf.

5. Linda Perlstein, in "Rethinking the School Desk," argues that in addition to the terribly uncomfortable desks that children are forced to sit in most of the day, "School systems give short shrift to the physical needs of their students in other ways—they use school buses without seatbelts, send backpacks home filled with weighty textbooks, cut gym class to the bone, run jocks through sometimes life-threatening football drills, and serve junk food as part of the federal nutrition program." Read more: http://www.slate.com/id/2269307/.

6. See the *Frontline* episode, "Merchants of Cool," by Douglas Rushkoff, for an incisive report on the creators and marketers of popular culture for teenagers.

7. See "Straight Facts about the Birds and Bees," *U.S. News and World Report* 142, no. 11 (March/April 2007).

8. A. Sinclair, op. cit., 5.

9. Ibid.

10. Stanza from "A Zero-Circle," in *Say I Am You: Rumi.* Translated by J. Moyne and C. Barks. Athens, GA: Windrush.

CHAPTER 17

Unfettered Bodies
Forging an Emancipatory Pedagogy of the Flesh

> Estranged labor...estranges humanity from its own body, as it does the external, natural world, as it does...[our] mental existence...[our] human existence.
>
> —KARL MARX (1844)

> A theory of the flesh means one where the physical realities of our lives—our skin color, the land or concrete we grew up on, our sexual longings—all fuse to create a politic born out of necessity.
>
> —CHERRIE MORAGA AND GLORIA ANZALDÚA (1981)

The human body constitutes primacy in all material relationships. Without the materiality of the body, all notions of teaching and learning are reduced to mere abstractions that attempt to situate the mind as an independent agent, absent of both individual and collective emotions, sensations, yearnings, fears, and joys. It is the body that provides the medium for our existence as subjects of history and politically empowered agents of change. But, as Peter McLaren (1999) reminds us, "bodies are also the primary means by which capitalism does its job" (xiii). We are molded and shaped by the structures, policies, and practices of domination and exclusion that violently insert our bodies into the alienating morass of an intensified global division of labor.

In *Pedagogy and the Politics of the Body*, Sherry Shapiro (1999), similar to other feminist educational theorists before her, contends that "any approach committed to human liberation must seriously address the body as a site for both oppression and liberation" (18). Yet seldom are the significance and central role of the body in the process of teaching and leaning made central to discussions of emancipatory pedagogy. As a consequence, educational efforts to reinvent the social and material conditions within classrooms are often devoid of close consideration of the significance of the flesh in mediating conditions of schooling. That is, unless the discussion turns to "classroom management"—a convenient euphemism in the service of both regulating and controlling student corporeality.

Meanwhile, the classroom exists as an arena of estranged labor where abstract knowledge and its construction are objectified, along with the students who are expected to acquiesce to its alienating function, limiting rationality, and technocratic instrumentalism. Hence, the production of knowledge is neither engaged nor presented as a historical and collective process, occurring within the context of the flesh and all its sensual capacities for experiencing and responding to the world. Instead, as Christopher Beckey (2000) argues in *Wicked Bodies*, "the flesh, the material aspect of the body, is seen as a hindrance which must be overcome, negated, and transcended" (71), as if it were not involved in our actions at all, beyond the nuisance of its daily care and containment.

Students as Integral Beings[1]

> I know with my entire body, with feelings, with passion and also with reason.
>
> —PAULO FREIRE (1997, 30)

Even in the writings of progressive educators, the notion of engaging students as embodied and integral human beings has received limited attention in discussions of life in schools. And when such discussions are raised, they often are either shaped by concerns of deviance or notions that privilege individuality and subjectivity discourse at the expense of critical development and collective consciousness. Moreover, the lack of criticality of discourse on the body even among progressive educators may be tied to historical tendencies on the left to place far greater importance on material analysis of societal structures and the political apparatus of the state, rather than the materiality of embodied relationships of the everyday. Hence, this absence of pedagogical and political attention to the flesh has inadvertently worked to sideline affective and relational concerns of estranged bodies—bodies that must endure, resist, and struggle to become free from the social and material entanglements of a society that imprisons them, both ideologically and corporally.

As teachers we cannot deny that the body is enormously significant to the development of students' critical capacities. Yet often missing in discussions of critical praxis is an axial understanding of our humanity and the significance of the body to both critical intellectual formation and political consciousness. Instead, the rubrics of traditional pedagogy assume a posture of teaching and learning as solely cognitive acts. Thus, to bring the body into plain sight is equivalent to opening Pandora's box, intruding and disrupting accepted mechanisms of power and control in the subordination of disenfranchised students (Levy 2000). Teachers are expected to simply concern themselves with the affective responses of students, when they comport themselves "inappropriately," at which time either psychologists or police officers can be summoned to contend with the momentary disruption of the "problem" student.

Yet we cannot deny that all learning, as well as teaching, happens through responses and interactions of the body with texts, others, and the world. And these interactions tied to learning can often be experienced as exciting, painful, frustrating, and joyful. Freire (1998) often referred to these very human responses when he considered the process of studying. For Freire, "Studying is a demanding occupation, in the process of which we will encounter pain, pleasure, victory, defeat, doubt and happiness" (78)—all affective and physical responses of the body.

Thus, to become *full subjects of history* requires teachers to grapple with the fact that our intellect, as cognitive function, is but one function of our humanity, which develops within the multitude of collective interactions with the world. As such, this requires our willingness to engage with students' bodies more substantively, in our efforts to forge a revolutionary practice of education. It is not enough, then, to teach and learn solely as an abstract cognitive process, where the analysis of words and texts are considered paramount to the construction of knowledge. Such an educational process of estrangement functions well to alienate students from "nature…the inorganic body of humanity" (Marx 1844), and, thus, from their own bodies and those of others. Moreover, as Snaza and Lensmire (2006) remind us, "At the level of classroom or school, it seems that we should always be extremely worried about the conditions of production (and not just response to already-produced texts). Progressive and critical critiques of schooling vary, certainly, but one way or another they all point to students being rendered objects of the control of powerful others" (12).

Hence, teachers and students must labor in the flesh, investing themselves materially, within their praxis and their struggle to reinvent the world. This is vital to a critical pedagogy of the body, given that "we learn things about the world by acting and changing the world around us" (Freire 1993, 108). And true to the Marxist axiom, this process of learning is intimately aligned simultaneously to a larger process of making history, where we, as subjects of history, change and are changed by the world. Yet, as Chris Shilling (2003) so accurately argues, "social change does not happen automatically...nor does it occur simply as a result of purely intellectually-motivated actions. Instead, student experiences of, and responses to, social structures are shaped significantly by their sensory and sensual selves." (210)

Teaching and Learning in the Flesh

And your very flesh may be a great poem.
—WALT WHITMAN[2]

The process of teaching and learning must then be acknowledged as a process of human labor—constitutive labor in association with the intricacies of our material being. For racialized subjects, such labor also emerges from our efforts to make sense of the repressive material conditions and social relations of power that shape the limitations and possibilities inherent in our histories of survival. Only through such an understanding of schooling can teachers construct a revolutionary practice of education, where students are asked neither to deny the wisdom of their bodies nor to estrange themselves from one another in the name of academic competition and debilitating practices of meritocracy. In contrast, a critical pedagogy of the body begins with acknowledging students as fully embodied subjects of their own existence, from the moment they enter our classrooms. To do so, critical educators must be prepared to contend, in the flesh, with the embodied histories of the disenfranchised *and* the social and material forces that impact their own labor as teachers committed to a democratic praxis.

Freire's (1993) allegiance to the body and its centrality is well accented in his notions of liberatory pedagogy. He argued for the indisputability of the body within the process of teaching and learning and pointed to the sensualism contained in the body—a sensualism that is inseparable from "rigorous acts of knowing the world" and our passionate ability to know as human beings. Freire's perspective undoubtedly echoes aspects of Herbert Marcuse's (1987) thesis in *Eros and Civilization*. Here, Marcuse boldly argues for a widening of our experience of the body through embracing a *polymorphous sensuality*—a sensuality more in line with our human capacity to exist as freely empowered subjects of history.

Not surprisingly, it is precisely this passionate sensual freedom with which we produce revolutionary thought and action that are held hostage by deeply fractured, objectified, and instrumentalized curricula administered to disenfranchised student populations. In the process, conscious, sensual bodies that could potentially defy the perversities of bourgeois capitalism are systematically disabled and conditioned to normalize the ravages of the neoliberal state. Hence, it is not surprising that this phenomenon of fettered bodies, anchored in the Western classical tradition of the mind-body split, prevails in the logic of U.S. public schooling.

Yet in spite of major institutional efforts to control the body's desires, pleasures, and mobility within the classroom, students seldom surrender their bodies completely or readily acquiesce to authoritarian practices—practices in which they themselves provide the impetus for resistance, especially in those students whose dynamic histories are excluded within mainstream education (Shapiro 1999). Instead, many of them engage in the construction of their own cultural forms of resistance that may or may not always function in their best interest. More often than not these expressions of student resistance are enacted through counterculture alterations of the body—be they clothing, hairstyle, posturing, manner of walking, way of speaking, the piercing and tattooing of the body. These represent not only acts of resistance but alternative ways of experiencing and knowing the world, generally perceived by officials as both transgressive and disruptive to the social order. Moreover, such views of students are exacerbated by what Henry Giroux (1998) contends is a "new form of representational politics [that] has emerged in media culture fueled by degrading visual depictions of youth as criminal, sexually decadent, drug crazed, and illiterate. In short, youth are viewed as a growing threat to the public order." This is a deeply troubling gaze, one that unfortunately is reflected internationally by corporate media portrayals of poor, working-class, racialized youth.

Teachers, whose bodies are similarly restricted, alienated, and domesticated by their workplace, are under enormous pressure to follow strict policies and procedures for classroom conduct, while being expected to dispense prepackaged curricula instead of employing more creative and critical approaches grounded in the actual needs of students. Given the impact of disembodied practices, teachers generally experience an uphill battle in meeting standardized mandates, which systematically extricate students' bodies from the equation of their learning. Nowhere is this more apparent than in low-income schools across the nation where teaching-to-the-test has become the curriculum of choice, even at colleges and universities.

As a consequence, many teachers, consciously or unconsciously, reproduce a variety of authoritarian classroom practices—in the name of classroom management—in efforts to maintain physical control of their students. Teachers who struggle in this repressive climate to implement more liberating strategies are often forced to become masters of deception—saying what the principal or district office wishes to hear, while doing behind closed doors what they believe is in concert with a more democratic vision of education. Unfortunately, having to shoulder the hidden physical stress of such duplicity can drive some of the most effective teachers away from their chosen vocation, irrespective of their political commitment. The experience of alienation that this engenders often becomes intolerable. Others, who begin to sense defeat, in frustration adopt more authoritarian approaches to manipulate and coerce *cooperation*, while justifying their means in the name of helping students succeed academically. What cannot be overlooked here is the manner in which authoritarian practices are designed not only to "blindfold students and lead them to a domesticated future" (Freire 1970, 79) but also to alienate and estrange teachers from their labor as well. Concerned with the need to restore greater freedom, joy, and creativity in their classrooms, Freire (1998) urged teachers to reject this domesticating role within their classrooms "by demythologizing the authoritarianism of teaching packages and their administration in the intimacy of their world, which is also the world of their students" (9).

A critical praxis of the body is also salient to rethinking university education, where there seems to be little pedagogical tolerance for the emotional needs of adult learners. Lifton (1990) argues, "Somewhere in the intellectual history of the West there developed the wrongheaded idea that mind and heart are antagonists, that scholarship must be divested of emotion, that spiritual journeys must avoid intellectual concerns" (Lifton 1990, 29). This tradition sets an expectation, for example, that professors and students should compartmentalize themselves within the classroom, without any serious concern for the fact that university education is often associated with moments of major life transitions. It is a time when students are being asked to make major commitments and material investments in the direction of very uncertain futures. Simultaneously, students are expected to carry out their studies and research as objective, impartial observers, even when the object of their study is intimately linked to conditions of human suffering.

Freire (1993) argues that traditional academic expectations of the university affirm "that feelings corrupt research and its findings, the fear of intuition, the categorical negation of emotion and passion, the belief in technicism, [which] ends in convincing many that, the more neutral we are in our actions, the more objective and efficient we will be" (106) in the construction of knowing. Hence, graduate students, in particular, are slowly but surely socialized to labor as uncritical, descriptive, "neutral" scholars, dispassionate and disembodied in their intellectual formulations of the world. This results in scholarship conceived through a deeply *estranged* way of knowing, where "values are restricted to a scientific definition" and knowledge becomes the property of something separated from human emotions, feeling, and connection" (Shapiro 1999, 40). The sad and unfortunate consequence here is that such knowledge seldom leads students to grapple with moral questions or actions that might fundamentally challenge the social and material relations that sustain human suffering in the first place. As Shapiro (1999) argues, "abstraction and exclusion break down relational understanding and bleed history dry, leaving the scars of separation" (39).

Principles for a Pedagogy of the Body

The body marks a crucial juncture where we can begin to make sense of the connections between the individual and the culture, the mind and the body, the rational and the sensual.

—SHERRY SHAPIRO (1999, 81)

As our consciousness becomes more abstracted, we become more detached from our bodies. One could say that a hidden function of public schooling is to initiate and incorporate poor and working-class students and students of color into social and material conditions of labor that normalize their alienation and detachment from the body. Such function is absolutely necessary for social control and the extraction of surplus labor, given that the body is the medium through which we wage political struggle and through which we transform our historical conditions as individuals and social beings (Eagleton 2003). Hence, the perception of students as integral human beings is paramount to both questions of ethics and the development of critical consciousness. All aspects of our humanity and, thus, our pedagogical needs are ever present and active; all aspects of our humanity are integral to the process of teaching and learning. To perceive students in terms of only the mind or only one way of knowing translates into an objectifying and debilitating experience for students, despite the intellectual and cultural strengths they bring to their education.

Students must therefore be acknowledged, respected, and treated as worthy and respected co-creators of knowledge within the classroom. The degree to which this is possible is linked to both the political consciousness and skill of teachers to be fully present, to negotiate power in the process of learning *with* their students, and to establish meaningful interactions in the classroom community. Such a horizontal view of student-teacher relationships goes hand in hand with obliterating the myth that an impersonal and emotionally distant approach to engaging students is professionally and pedagogically justifiable or correct. Hence, this view of pedagogical relationships unquestionably counters misguided beliefs among elitist mentors, who brutalize their students with acts of humiliation, as well as cultivate self-doubt, insisting that such pedagogical dynamics actually engender respect and rigorous scholarship. What we often find is a reproduction of pedagogical brutality in their mentees, who, having survived the hazing of privilege, now feel equally special and entitled to begin the cycle anew. They defend dehumanizing pedagogical relations of power as they become the new gatekeepers of their disciplines. This condition is especially devastating to observe in students from oppressed communities who, "earning" entry into the elite group, embrace their standing as a sign of "empowerment."

At issue is the reproduction of veiled class distinctions that educators enact in the classroom and in the "real world." Ira Shor and Paulo Freire (1986) insist that

> What we do in the classroom is not an isolated moment separate from the "real world." It is entirely connected to the real world and it is the real world which places both powers and limits on any critical course. Because the world is in the classroom, whatever transformation we provoke has a conditioning effect outside our small space. But the outside has a conditioning effect on the space also, interfering with our ability to build a critical culture separate from the dominant mass culture (26).

Nathan Snaza and Timothy Lensmire (2006) likewise argue that "we must cease to think of our lives separate from the operations of capital.... School *and* society is a false dichotomy: school *is* society" (15, emphasis in original).

Accordingly, critical principles that support a pedagogy of the body oblige educators to be cognizant of the larger social, political, and economic conditions that shape their lives and the lives of their students. In brief, the following provides an initial summary of important pedagogical considerations associated with classroom interventions that can assist in decolonizing the body.

- Teachers engage the emotional and physical responses and experiences of students. These responses and experiences are recognized as meaningful indicators of strengths, limitations, and possibilities that students bring to the process of their intellectual formation and social consciousness.
- Knowledge is understood as a historical and collective process emanating from the body's relationship to self, others, and the world. The body, as also inscribed by history, is seen as primary in the construction of knowledge and the development of moral thought.
- The mind and its cognitive capacities are understood as but one important medium for the construction of knowledge. Hence, students are seen as integral human beings whose minds, bodies, hearts, and spirits are implicated in the process of teaching and learning. Our pedagogical practices

must seek to reach into students' innermost affective and psychic centers if we are committed to a pedagogy of solidarity and emancipation.

- The knowledge derived from the body's interactions with the world constitutes a significant dimension of a critical educational praxis. As such, classroom and community relationships, materials, and activities reflect this knowledge, through the integration of a cultural and linguistic democracy that is in sync with students and their communities.

- Teaching and learning are understood as, together, a process of human labor that is tied to the material conditions and social relations of power that shape classroom life. Hence, the question of power and uses of authority are consistently interrogated with students, parents, colleagues, and the community.

- Knowledge construction is understood as a communal and collective historical phenomenon that takes place continuously, within and outside of school. To privilege school knowledge and ignore the knowledge and power of lived experiences limit students' social agency and diminishes important opportunities for active participation in the process of their intellectual and political formation.

- Teachers create meaningful interactions and activities in classrooms and communities that support and encourage students to grapple honestly with the tensions of differences in worldviews, whether these are linked to class, race, gender, sexuality, ability, or culture, and the consequences of these inequalities.

- The knowledge that teachers have of their own bodies, including their sexuality, is an important aspect of their ability to effectively interact with and competently educate diverse student populations.

- Acts of resistance connected to the body signal meaningful alternative ways of knowing and relating to the world. Opportunities are created for students to reflect, affirm, and challenge the meaning of these acts of resistance in their lives and the lives of their communities.

- Opportunities are created in classrooms and communities that permit students to control the physical conditions under which they labor as students, including the legitimate definition and execution of knowledge construction, aesthetics, politics, fashion, voice, participation, and decision making.

These principles for a critical praxis of the body are linked to a decolonizing project of the body, which can potentially free students and teachers from educational and social constraints that repress the development of voice, disrupt democratic participation, and thwart the self-determination of disenfranchised populations. Educators too must work in community with students, parents, colleagues, and the larger community to challenge conditions of labor in schools that render them passive and domesticate their dreams.

Emancipating the Fettered Body

> The body is also directly involved in a political field; power relations have an immediate hold upon it; they invest it, mark it, train it, torture it, force it to carry out tasks, to perform ceremonies, to emit signs.
>
> —MICHEL FOUCAULT (1995, 259)

There is no question that we live in a society of the incarcerated body, the schooled body, the enslaved body, the embattled body, the surgically altered body, the starved body, the abused body, the worn, and the torn body. Everywhere the "scars of separation" are evident. Cherríe Moraga (2009)[3] speaks of these scars as internalized bodily stories, "the story of conquest and the story of colonization or the story of indigenous enslavement or the story of all of the forced displacement, all of this, these are things that we carry in our bodies." As such, racism and all other of forms of social exclusion, exploitation, and domination cannot be fully interrogated nor understood if such inquiry is alienated from the social and material conditions that normalize and perpetuate the mass violation of living bodies. As Marx so rightly notes, as our consciousness becomes more and more abstracted, we become more and more detached from our material realities and their consequences to our bodies. One could say that a hidden function of schooling is, indeed, to initiate and incorporate poor, working-class, and racialized students into social and material conditions of labor that normalize their alienation and detachment from the body. This function is absolutely necessary for social control and the extraction of surplus labor, given that the body is the medium through which we wage political struggle and through which we transform our historical conditions.

In *After Theory*, Terry Eagleton (2003) reflects on questions of the body both ethically and politically. He reminds us that "it is the material body that we share most significantly with the rest of our species. And although needs, desires, and suffering are considered to be culturally determined, our material bodies are such that they are, in principle, completely capable of feeling compassion" (198) for all others, when released from ideologies and commonsense notions that render us strangers to one another. The alienation of capitalist relations blinds us to this fact, since it is precisely upon this capacity for shared subjectivity and sense of kinship that moral values are founded, that emancipatory knowledge is constructed, and that a practice of human solidarity is established.

Forging a new vision, then, is about bringing us all back home to our bodies in a world where every aspect of our daily life—birth, death, marriage, family, school, work, leisure, parenthood, sexuality, spirituality, and even entertainment—has been not only colonized[4] but commodified. Hence, we struggle to exist, as Donald Lowe (1995) argues, in "a world where all aspects of our lives, the environment we live in, and everything in between, have become means, or signifiers of exchange value" (15). With the rapid and constant changing needs of late capitalism, this hegemony of exchange practices renders the freedom and sensuality of our bodies more problematic—unless, of course, our bodies become addicted to the pleasures of a perverse sensuality predicated on consumerism.

Under such a regime of power our bodies are left numb, alienated and fragmented, often leaving us defenseless and at the mercy of capital. Meanwhile, the marketplace tricks us into believing that consumption equals happiness. As our consciousness becomes more hardened and estranged from nature, we become more detached from our organic existence, while becoming more and more dependent on fabricated illusions, devoid of human groundedness and communal roots. The consequence is a deep sense of personal and collective dissatisfaction generated by a marketplace that cannot satisfy the human needs of the body—needs that can only be met through relationships that break the alienation and isolation so prevalent in our lives today (Brosio 1994).

As such, it is absolutely imperative that in forging a new emancipatory vision of liberation, we acknowledge that the origin of emancipatory action and human solidarity resides squarely in the body. Eagleton (2003) states poignantly that "it is the moral, fragile, suffering, ecstatic, needy, dependent, desirous, and compassionate body which furnishes the basis for all moral thought" (198). And so, it is moral thought that places our collective bodies back into history and into the political discourse. Moreover, it is the absence of a truly democratic moral language and practice of the body that stifles our capacity for social struggle today. For example, many teachers across the country bemoan, justifiably so, the conditions created by high-stakes testing and other accountability measures that negatively impact their lives as teachers and the lives of their students. Yet there has been a failure among educators to communicate a clear and coherent emancipatory moral message to challenge the shallow moralism of the Bush administration's educational panacea—No Child Left Behind.[5] In response, there are those who would argue that this is a direct result of teachers' alienated complicity with the structure of educational inequality and the contradictions inherent in their lack of grounded politics within a highly charged political arena.

Efforts to forge a new vision of the body within schools and society require the development of a moral political language that can safeguard the dignity and integrity of all human differences intrinsic to a pluralistic nation. Again, Eagleton (2003) reminds us that this entails a language that is uncompromisingly anchored in the needs of the body. For without our bodies to enact the principles we embrace, any notion of an emancipatory democracy is meaningless. This idea extends beyond the notion of student *voices*; genuine democracy is about the body's interaction with the social and material world as well, in ways that nurture meaningful and transformative participation. A critical pedagogy of the body exists, then, as a practice in which human beings interact individually and collectively as equally empowered subjects in order to contribute to the world the best of what we have to offer. Such a practice must be embodied within a field of fluid human actions and interactions, the place from which we construct all culture.

Shapiro (1999) argues that all "human beings produce their lives collectively" (65). Hence, any critical praxis of the body must engage oppression as "the starting point for the explanation of human history. This then becomes a materialist liberation, where explanations cannot be limited to any one oppression, or leave untouched any part of reality, any domain of knowledge, any aspect of the world" (65). All forms of social and material oppression block, disrupt, and corrupt the fluid participation of oppressed bodies within the world, reifying exclusionary human relations in the interest of economic imperatives, without regard for the destruction to bodies left behind.

"Capital must always develop at the expense of all bodies" (Lowe 1995, 175). And nowhere is this better illustrated than in the horrifying fiasco of the war in Iraq. Thousands of mutilated bodies of men, women, and children have been written off as simply "very sad" but necessary casualties in the struggle for, in the words of Arundhati Roy (2004), "Democracy, the modern world's holy cow." And all these dead bodies are just the bitter medicine we must swallow for freedom, according to the moralism (or better yet immorality) of both the Bush and Blair administrations and their neoconservative supporters.

When human needs such as safety, food, shelter, clothing, livelihood, health care, education, and the necessary intimacy of a community are not met, bodies are violated. And, oftentimes, violated bodies easily gravitate to whatever can provide a quick fix to ease the pain and isolation of an alienated existence—no matter how extremist that ideology might seem to those comfortably situated in the lap of comfort and privilege.

Again, all this calls to mind to mind the urgent need for a pedagogy of the body founded upon "resisting capital's marginalization of us as mere means" (Lowe 1995, 176), aligned with a counterhegemonic practice that redefines and reinscribes an emancipatory political vision to our reading of both local and world events. To do this effectively, we must subvert the presumed individualism and transcendence of academic formation, while living a politics of the body that not only provides alternative interpretations of the world but alternative ways of collectively enacting a politics of resistance and transformation in the everyday.

To provide a concrete example of how such a vision might guide our political understanding and responses to historical events, I want to turn for a moment to Hurricane Katrina, one of the most devastating weather disasters in U.S. history. In the wake of Katrina, the mainstream media were sorrowfully inept in providing substantive reporting of the disaster, particularly in the first weeks. In the paparazzi of disaster reporting, the media focused on private property over human lives. In the drone of endless television reporting, the major theme became the looting of stores. Few reports ventured into the historical impoverishment and environmental neglect of New Orleans, a city some called a third world within the first world. Myopic Mardi Gras illusions of the French Quarter became the salve for the wounds of despair suffered by the impoverished and disenfranchised of New Orleans. The slowness of federal response to the needs of poor, weak, aged, and colored bodies struggling to survive the devastation spoke volumes to the disposability and lack of significance given to the poor in the age of capital.

Five years before Katrina hit, an environmental study warned of the possibilities of such a disaster in the Gulf of Mexico due to the weakening of the levees and the forces of global warming. To this date there has been little critical engagement with the unrelenting interests of capital that have contaminated the global environment to such a degree that it is now considered a likely cause of cataclysmic disasters around the world, causing environmental experts to fear that Katrina is just the tip of the iceberg. This wholesale neglect of the environment, our body-planet, is directly tied to capitalism's penchant for disembodiment, centralization, mega-scale enterprises, and anonymity, at whatever the cost, if it turns a profit.

And while much of the U.S. population remained drugged by the evangelizing rhetoric of the right, the ingredients for violence have been steadily fomenting—directing us on a crash course. There will be no need to gaze in disbelief at the televised reports of youth rioting on the streets of Paris, London, Los Angeles, or Chicago. We will need only step outside our own suburbs and watch our estranged youth expose the hypocrisy and sham that is our democracy. This is a democracy that, unfortunately, has evolved from a disembodied rationality and false moralism of privilege, through which the wiles of globalization have moved unfettered—bringing with it environmental devastation, social unrest, wars, and genocide.

A critical pedagogy of the body rejects globalization's allegiance to an instrumental rationality as the lowest common denominator of progress. Instead, as Wendell Berry (2002) contends, we must embrace the impulse toward interconnection. This entails affection for our home place, the local topography, the local memories, and the local creatures. A social movement grounded on a critical pedagogy of the body can assist us to counter estrangement, dismemberment, and disfigurement. Such a movement recognizes that our environmental problems, for example, have causes that are not only political and economic but human-made. And, as such, we cannot solve our problems only with "environmental protections laws." Human issues of survival must be solved, ultimately, by correcting the way we use our home places and local landscapes, how we design our communal public spaces and our most intimate relationships. Opposition to all forms of colonialism is implicated in our efforts to regain the fullness of bodily capacities. Hence, one of the central principles is clearly that landscapes should not be appropriated by people who do not live in them and share their fate. There is no question that if this principle had been at work, perhaps the story in New Orleans—a city that has always been exploited because of its port capacity—would have looked very different today.

Love as an Emancipatory Principle

> Understanding that love [is] the antithesis of the will to dominate and subjugate, we allow that longing to know love, to love one another, to radicalize us politically.
> —BELL HOOKS (1996, 265)

In grounding our struggle within such an incisive critique of capitalism, we open the possibility for building a collective resistance that will re-center our practice "by up-ending the opposition between capital accumulation and bodily needs. [So that] in the very process of attempting to change the world, we change ourselves and others" (Lowe 1995, 176). With this in mind, an emancipatory pedagogy of the body seeks to create the social and material conditions that can give rise to the organic expression of our humanity, through principles inherent in *teaching as an act of love* (Darder 2002; Freire 1997, 1998).

Love as an emancipatory and revolutionary principle compels us to become part of a new, decolonizing and embodied culture that cultivates human connection, intimacy, trust, and honesty, from the body out into the world. "With love we affirm and are affirmed. In the sociopolitical struggle against death from hunger, disease, exploitation, war, destruction of the earth, and against hopelessness, there is a great and growing need for our capacity to become 'body-full' with love" (Shapiro 1999, 99).

Love, in this context, also means to comprehend that the moral and the material are inseparably linked. And, as such, our politics must recognize love as an essential ingredient of a just society. Love as a political principle motivates the struggle to create mutually life-enhancing opportunities for all people. It is a love that is grounded in the mutuality and interdependence of our human existence. This is a love nurtured by the act of relationship itself. It cultivates relationships across our differences, without undue fear. Such an emancipatory love allows us to realize our nature, in a way that allows others to do so as well. Inherent in such a love is the understanding that we are never at liberty to be violent, authoritarian, or exploitive (Eagleton 2003).

In accordance, Freire repeatedly argued that ethics is a significant place of departure, for both our private and public lives.[6] Here, ethics constitutes a political question, which in the final analysis is also a moral one. For without morality our politics becomes an instrument of oppression. But morality here should not be confused with moralism. Eagleton (2003) argues that to be moral entails exploring the texture and quality of our sensations, ideas, and practices—a process that teachers and students cannot surely accomplish by abstracting life from our social surroundings, from our cultures, or from our histories of survival. This requires us, as educators, to bring together the moral and political, the particular and universal, acknowledging through both our teaching and our daily lives that nothing can survive in isolation.

Moreover, Lowe (1995) links political resistance to the question of ethics and collective action:

> The politics of resistance is intrinsically an ethical issue. Ethical concepts do not reside within a text. The deconstruction of a text yields no ethical answer. The concept of ethics has to do with personal choice and conduct; in other words practice. It has to do with reflexive intention and social, human responsibility....There is no "we" constituted prior to social [action] (176).

So it is through collective action waged in our bodies that consciousness is born. Through our actions with students, colleagues, comrades we can struggle together, not only for the shifting of consciousness, but for the transformation of real material conditions. This requires our participation in the actual settings in which we live and work. What good does it do for us to run around the world as professing activists or radical scholars and, yet, fail to infuse ourselves in the very struggles that are taking place beneath our noses, in the universities and communities in which we live? To not act in the immediacy of our workplace and lived environment places us in danger of living out abstracted lives, devoid of grief or other empathetic feelings that visible forms of oppression, in particular, are meant to stir in the healthy human soul.

There is no doubt that great moral courage is required to stand up against educational policies and practices that betray oppressed communities, rendering them disposable. To transform such conditions within schools and society, we need a revolutionary pedagogy solidly committed to the unfettering of the body, through embracing the liberation of our humanity as sensual, thinking, knowing, and feeling subjects of history. This entails rewriting the body into our understanding of critical praxis, by calling forth the establishment of new conditions for academic formation. Classroom conditions that begin with the primacy of the body carry radical possibilities for reconnecting students more deeply to their development as fully integral human beings. Most important, the body "is the material foundation upon which the desire for human liberation and social transformation rest" (Shapiro 1999, 100). And, thus, it is only in our bodies that we can ultimately enact a revolutionary love—a love grounded in shared human kinship, political self-determination, and economic justice.

REFERENCES

Beckey, C. (2000). "Wicked Bodies: Toward a Critical Pedagogy of Corporeal Differences for Performance." In C. O'Farrell, D. Meadmore, E. McWilliam, and C. Symes (eds.), *Taught Bodies*. New York: Peter Lang (57–80).

Berry, W. (2002). "Two Minds," *The Progressive* (November): 21–29.

Brosio, R. (1994). *A Radical Democratic Critique of Capitalist Education*. New York: Peter Lang.

Darder, A. (2002). *Reinventing Paulo Freire: A Pedagogy of Love*. Boulder, CO: Westview.

Eagleton, T. (2003). *After Theory*. New York: Basic Books.

Foucault, M. (1995). *Discipline and Punish*. New York: Vintage.

Freire, P. (1998) *Teachers as Cultural Workers*. Boulder, CO: Westview.

Freire, P. (1997). *Pedagogy of the Heart*. New York: Contiuum.

Freire, P. (1995). *Pedagogy of Hope*. New York: Continuum.

Freire, P. (1993). *Pedagogy of the City*. New York: Continuum.

Freire, P. (1970). *Pedagogy of the Oppressed*. New York: Seabury.

Giroux, H. (1998). "Teenage Sexuality, Body Politics, and the Pedagogy of Display." In J. Epstein (ed.), *Youth, Youth Culture, and Identity*. Malden, MA: Basil Blackwell (24–55). Article available at: http://www.gseis.ucla.edu/courses/ed253a/Giroux/Giroux3.html.

hooks, b. (1996). *Killing Rage: Ending Racism.* New York: Macmillan.

Lefebvre, H. (1971). *Everyday Life in the Modern World.* London: Penguin.

Levy, B. (2000). "Pedagogy: Incomplete, Unrequited." In C. O'Farrell, D. Meadmore, E. McWilliam, and C. Symes (eds,), *Taught Bodies.* New York: Peter Lang (81–90).

Lifton, R. (1990). "The Genocidal Mentality," *Tikkun* 5, no. 3: 29–32 and 97–98.

Lowe, D. (1995). *The Body in Later Capitalist USA.* Durham, NC, and London: Duke University Press.

Marcuse, H. (1987). *Eros and Civilization,* 2nd ed. London: Routledge.

Marx, K. (1844). *The Alienation of Labor.* In *Economic and Philosophic Manuscripts of 1844.* Available at: www.wsu.edu:8080/~dee/MODERN/ALIEN.HTM#NT2.

McLaren, P. (1999). "Foreword." In S. Shapiro, *Pedagogy and the Politics of the Body: A Critical Praxis.* New York: Garland Publishing.

Moraga, C. and G. Anzaldúa (1981). *This Bridge Called My Back.* Latham, NY: Kitchen Table Press.

Roy, A. (2004). *Instant-Mix Imperial Democracy and Come September.* Oakland, CA: AK Press. See: http://www.informationclearinghouse.info/article3441.htm

Shapiro, S. (1999). *Pedagogy and the Politics of the Body: A Critical Praxis.* New York: Garland Publishing.

Shilling, C. (2003). *The Body and Social Theory.* Thousand Oaks, CA: Sage Publications.

Shor, I., and P. Freire. (1986). *A Pedagogy for Liberation.* South Hadley, MA: Bergin and Garvey.

Snaza, N., and T. Lensmire. (2006). "Abandon Voice? Pedagogy, the Body, and Late Capitalism," *InterActions: UCLA Journal of Education and Information Studies* 2, no. 2: 1–23.

NOTES

1. This essay expands on the idea of "students as integral beings" first presented in chapter 3 of A. Darder (2004), *Reinventing Paulo Freire: A Pedagogy of Love* (Boulder, CO: Westview).

2. From *Walt Whitman: Selected Poems, 1855–1882,* 2nd ed., Walt Whitmen and G. Schmidgall (ed.) (London: Stonewall Inn Editions, 2000), 6.

3. From an interview with Cherrie Moraga on *Liberacion!,* WEFT 90.1 FM, "The Politics of LGBT Life" (2009), available at: http://www.radioliberacion.org/.

4. See H. Lefebvre (1971), *Everyday Life in the Modern World* (London: Penguin).

5. See Stan Karp's article "Equity Claims for NCLB Don't Pass the Test," *Rethinking Schools* (spring 2003). The article provides a cogent explanation about the shortcomings of the act. You can find the article and more information about *Rethinking Schools* online at: www.rethinkingschools. org.

6. See Paulo Freire: *Pedagogy of the City* (New York: Continuum, 1993), *Pedagogy of Hope* (New York: Continuum, 1995), and *Teachers as Cultural Workers* (Boulder, CO: Westview, 1998).

CHAPTER 18

Embodiments

The Art of Soulful Resistance

Art is not a mirror held up to reality, but a hammer with which to shape it.

—BERTOLT BRECHT

Artists throughout history—whether with music, poetry, theater, or visual arts—have used their artistic faculties to create important instances of resistance. Hence, they serve as important cultural workers, creating forms of public pedagogy that speak the unspeakable and challenge us all to evolve our consciousness toward greater freedom and human dignity. However, artists of resistance seek not only to express the individual stirrings of one solitary soul, but to sensually communicate stories of historical suffering and daily endangerments to our collective existence. Their art can be beautiful and political, sublime and powerful, mindful and passionate but also alarming and grotesque if that is what is required to speak the truth of oppression and suffering.

In the United States, as abroad, revolutionary art persists, while examples of the artists' public pedagogy can be found throughout different historical eras in a variety of contexts and forms. During the 1960s, political art within the Black and Chicano movements was paramount to an expression of culture and resis-

Felix Beltrán, 1971[1]

tance to the imperialism and colonization of people of color around the globe. The bright colors and political themes expressed anger, rage, intellect, beauty, and hope of communities, who for so long had remained culturally, racially, economically, sexually, and politically repressed under the thumbs of U.S. capitalism! It is this spirit of resistance that persists, in the contemporary *art of soulful resistance.*

The following are short commentaries and excerpts from and about artists today who recognize the power and responsibility of their craft within the public arena. Their art, driven by a commitment to social justice and human rights, is a collective clarion call of resistance to the destructive impact of economic exploitation and cultural domination in the world today.

Las Krudas: Cuban Revolutionary Hip Hop[2]

La Kruda (being raw) is a way of living,
existing in revolutionary terms, being woman.

Las Krudas is a trio of Cuban female rappers who throw down in Spanish with a powerful political bent. As one of the first groups in the history of Cuban rap music, Las Krudas have received praise for their powerful creativity. Their electrifying performance encompasses their own brand of revolutionary messages, which speaks to the struggle and development of political consciousness—a consciousness tied to the tough realities of economic, gender, sexual, and racialized oppression. Their performances are electrifying! Las Krudas's music is an uncompromising and unapologetic call to struggle and political change in the world.

Margaux Joffe,[3] in a review of the group, writes:

> In their most recent album, *Cubensi*, Las Krudas subvert the typically conservative and sensual feminine presence. Like the blues singers of the 1920s and 1930s, they use bold delivery and powerful voices. As their name implies, their lyrics are raw and direct, as can be seen in the album's opening song, "Vamó a vencer la dificultad."

Sexo femenino, siempre relegado
pero las Krudas el molde han quebrado
vamo' a vencer la dificultad....
Feminine sex, always relegated
But the Krudas have broken the mold
We are going to overcome the difficulty....

Publicity photo of Las Krudas, 2008 U.S. tour

In the song "120 horas rojas," Las Krudas transgress the conventional and address menstruation and feminine biology, with a chorus that starts out, "120 red hours every month." In "Eres bella," Las Krudas rap to "all the women of the world, to all of the women that are fighting with us...to all the sisters; especially the blackest, especially the poorest...."

Eres Bella siendo tú, ébano en flor, negra luz
Eres Bella siendo tú, cuerpo no es, única virtud.
Eres Bella siendo tú, ébano en flor, negra luz
Eres Bella siendo tú, intellegencia es tu virtud.

You are beautiful being you, ebony in flower, black light
You are beautiful being you, your body is not your only virtue.

You are beautiful being you, ebony in flower, black light
You are beautiful being you, your virtue is intelligence.

Favianna Rodriguez: Making Revolution Irresistible!

In her own words:[4]

I was schooled in East Oakland by Chicano political poster artists at a very young age. The free neighborhood art classes of the '80s were a great opportunity that allowed me to learn alongside established third world artists. It is through this training that I became a community poster artist. My art pieces reflect national and international grassroots struggles, and tell a history of social justice through graphics. I am inspired and informed by the stylistic and radical impact of Chicano painters and printmakers. Like the "old-school" artists, my work reflects a growing national consciousness that speaks to the contemporary urban barrios, rebelling against racism, homophobia, sexism and corporate irresponsibility. There has never been a movement for social change without the arts posters, in particular, being central to that movement.

Poster by Favianna Rodriguez

All art is political, but not all art is overtly political. Protest posters flaunt their politics and court discussion. They can deepen compassion and commitment, ignite outrage, elicit laughter, and provoke action. The power of the poster is that it is produced in multiples, and therefore can be easily distributed for all to see.

As a native of Oakland, the home of the Black Panther Party, my work is focused in this community. I am a core member of the EastSide Arts Alliance, a third world artist collective that supports and challenges all its members to think critically about revolution and be accountable to the grassroots. Through the alliance I am also a teacher, and have learned the importance of regeneration, that is, to pass on our skills to the next generation of cultural workers. Our role as revolutionary artists is to define and create a revolutionary culture. To make revolution irresistible! Our role is to undermine the deeply-embedded sickness of this country, to subvert this repressive culture and to build something transformative.

Now more than ever, our protest culture is being co-opted by the mainstream. Counter-culture is in style! But the requirement of study, political debate and practice is absent. We the artists of the people have a responsibility to expose our truths so that we don't become maintainers of this corrupt system. In this age of extreme capitalism, we are surrounded by corporate media that influence our decisions about everything we wear, everything we eat, and everything we buy. We are constantly fed messages to be consumers. I am not in the business of crass commercial advertisement. I am in the business of education and liberation. My subjects are Black, Latino, Asian and Native communities that have been ignored and smashed by this government.

It is in this spirit that I have created artwork: to translate the messages of the frontlines into works of art that can be used to educate and mobilize. I am part of a long tradition of political artists who have used their art to dismantle and expose this fascistic culture.

Anne Feeney: Union Maid, Hellraiser, and Labor Singer

In her own words:[5]

The Vietnam War and the Civil Rights Movement shaped my conscience and served as President of the Pittsburgh Musicians' Union. These days I am living my dream. I'm on the road 200+ days a year...all over the US and Canada, and more recently, Sweden and Denmark. It's my privilege to spend most of my waking hours with people who are trying to make a difference in this world...people on strike, or in a union or community organizing drive, or defending women's rights, the environment, human rights...working to end poverty and racism...consciousness. I worked for a dozen years or so as a trial attorney, and teaching peace.

War on the Workers[6]

Listen up, we've got a war zone here today
Right in our heartland, and across the USA
These multinational bastards don't use tanks and guns it's true

Anne Feeney

But they've declared a war on us, fight back! It's up to you

There's a war on the workers
There's a war on the workers
There's a war on the workers
And it's time we started calling the shots

Going to work could be the death of you and me
But we're not unarmed—Our weapon's solidarity
Jim Beals and Karen Silkwood
The list goes on and on
With every year that passes 60,000 more are gone

There's a war on the workers
There's a war on the workers
There's a war on the workers
And it's time we started calling the shots

When they boost your co-pay (it's a war on the workers!)
don't you know what to say (it's a war on the workers!)
When they talk privatization (it's a war on the workers!)
and co-operation (it's a war on the workers!)
They call it "flexibility" (it's a war on the workers!)
But every working stiff can see (it's a war on the workers!)
When they poison our water (it's a war on the workers!)
We're like lambs at the slaughter (it's a war on the workers!)
When they foul up the air (it's a war on the workers!)
We've got to show that we care (it's a war on the workers!)
Oh, it's a war on the workers—
It's a war on public education, it's a war on child labor protections, it's a war on
the 8 hour day, it's a war on occupational health & safety, a war on social secu-
rity—Now thanks to WTO it's a world wide war—

There's a war on the workers
There's a war on the workers
There's a war on the workers
And it's time we started calling the shots

—ANNE FEENEY

Chola Con Cella: Mapping a Continent without Borders[7]

Maria Elena Gaitan emerged as a performer in the context of the 1992 Los Angeles riots triggered by the acquittal of four Los Angeles policemen who brutally beat an unarmed African American, Rodney King. Los Angeles was in flames; hundreds were arrested. Gaitan was reborn from those warm ashes as a performance artist. What emerged was her continued political commitment to her community, as well as her commitment to establish her voice as an Indigenous Chicana woman and her desire to develop her artistic authority in new ways.

Gaitan fully assumes the power potential of the one-woman show. She is not beholden to any of the established theatrical institutions, which tend to tokenize, trivialize, and censor Raza performance art, allowing only for what she calls "an occasional Beaner Night at the Mark Taper Forum." Her performances are politically and aesthetically motivated. Her political concerns arise from the social crisis generated in California by the passage of xenophobic and anti-immigrant ballot propositions.

Chola Con Cello, for example, was a response to California's Proposition 187, passed by voters in 1992. Proposition 187 sought to deny public education to undocumented immigrant children, while also denying prenatal care to undocu-

Chola Con Cello in performance

mented women immigrants. It was followed in 1998 by Proposition 227, which dismantled bilingual education, and then Proposition 209, which dismantled affirmative action. Various other ballot measures primarily targeting youth of color have also been passed.

John Jennings[8]: Outing the Prison Industrial Complex

John Jennings is a professor of graphic design at the University of Illinois at Urbana-Champaign. His research and teaching focus on the analysis, explication, and disruption of African American stereotypes in popular visual media. His research is concerned with the topics of representation and authenticity, visual culture, visual literacy, social justice, and design pedagogy. His art pushes boundaries, at times overwhelming to the senses, as it transgresses notions of art as simply beauty, and pushes into the realm of public pedagogy. The series below presents powerful messages that clearly speak to the injustices of the prison industrial complex.

Art by John Jennings

Sunaura Taylor: Politics of Seeing and Disability[9]

In her own words:[10]

For many years now my perception of the world has been very much linked to seeing. In many ways I am someone who is obsessed with seeing. And by this, I mean very literally looking. As a painter I have spent hours of my life staring at canvasses, at colors, at pictures, at blank walls. I perceive my world through seeing.

Perhaps I love to see because seeing to me is political. For me, representational painting is about seeing; it is a way of paying attention. As a culture, we are bombarded with millions of images every day, images often intended to manipulate and then disappear. Why, when we almost seem to be growing numb as a consequence of this incessant bombardment, would I feel the need to add more images to this world? I am moved to create work in this vein because I am moved to see.

For me, this process of seeing is at once political and profoundly personal. It is political in its slowness, in its individuality, and its absurd inefficiency. I paint to see in my own way, so that I don't see only what I'm told to see or what I've been given to see. It is this personal and subjective time spent paying attention that is important to me, especially when it is a paying attention to things that are hard to look at, things that we as a culture would rather not see.

So I perceive seeing and painting as political. And politics are deeply important to me. I grew up with the knowledge that I was born disabled due to U.S. military pollution. Thus as a child, the idea that there was this larger world outside myself and my family, that could affect us—and that we in turn could affect through our choices—wasn't strange to me. But although I grew up perceiving myself as an artist and as a political activist, I did not however recognize my own physical body as a site for politics. This changed sometime after Sept. 11th, when it was clear to everyone that we were headed into war and a sense of

Self-Portrait with TCE by Sunaura Taylor

dread and helplessness was all around us. So, I painted *Self-Portrait with TCE* as an anti-war image, an image that I hoped would raise questions of the impact of war pollution and military greed.

People with disabilities confront stereotypes, stigmas, and major civil rights infringements daily due to disability. We are the world's largest minority, the world's poorest, some of the world's least educated, some of the most likely to be abused, and according to a recent report, we are twice as likely to be victims of violence than our able-bodied friends.

Disability is a civil rights issue, but it's a civil rights issue that Americans and even very progressive Americans don't really understand. Being impaired is seen as an individual tragedy. The problem is seen as a medical one versus a social and economic one. Disabled people are constantly confronting a world that tells us our lives are tragic and horrible; tells us, in effect, how to perceive our bodies.

When I was younger, I perceived myself and my 650 million disabled fellow human beings as shameful. As asexual. As incapable. As burdensome. As unnatural. As my politics and critical understanding of society evolved, I came to see that we are far more than what culture, names, and historical discourses tell us we are. I now perceive myself, examine myself, name myself as a member of the disabled community—a community of people deserving of rights, not pity or charity.

Amira Davis: Emancipatory Acts[11]

Amira Davis is an activist, poet, and percussionist, who produced the theater piece *Emancipatory Acts*, which focuses on the struggle of Black women through the years and their efforts to survive the destructive impact of slavery on their lives and the lives of their children and families. Her poetry and scholarly work focus on the notion of Black mothering and critically engages, as does her poetry and music, both the suffering and deliverance that is at the heart of Black women's existence, as they negotiate racism, class inequalities, and patriarchy in their everyday lives. There is no question that her art is one of resistance, as well as an emancipatory act of liberation.

Dead-ication

To my great, great, great mother, Vinnie Banks, great-grandmothers, Priscilla Subtlet, Julia Jones, Carrie May Scott, my grandmothers Millie Jones-Gamble and Fannie Davis, and all those who have returned through my womb.

The circle was drawn
six intersecting lines

—radius bound—
dissected its face
twelve houses, ten planets
four elements, two nodes
three crosses, thirty-six decans
three-hundred and sixty
degrees
"this is your life"
the aging trumpeter,
my musical mentor
said
"you, like most women,
have problems with men,"
his wives,
moving about the perimeter
of our conversation
his trenchant eyes—
framed by the tangle of colors
in a thread worn kufi—
scried my face
"oh," I said
reading him back
"but you see here?
Neptune is elevated
in your tenth house"
I fought his willing me
to plunge headlong
into his particular deep
a Dogon priest on 75th
and Cottage Grove
"what?" I asked
"you give birth
to ancestors."

Amira Davis in performance

Leonard Peltier: Ultimate Sacrifice[12,13]

Born on the Turtle Mountain Ojibwa Reservation in North Dakota, Leonard
Peltier, a member of the American Indian Movement (AIM),[14] has remained incar-

cerated since 1975. Repeated appeals for parole have been denied. While in prison, Peltier emerged as a master of Indigenous art.

Spending time in "the hole," while in the federal prison at Springfield in the 1980s, Leonard watched another prisoner working with pastels and when he got permission to get his own set of pastels and paper, he started working with the images and colors that he has always loved.

Inside the gray walls of the prison, locked away from the natural beauty of Mother Earth and her changes, artists must take their inspiration from books and magazines available to them.

"We are denied seeing Mother Earth and enjoying her, so we use some nice pictures for models and change them around…. I like to express the beauty of my culture to the world—the colors of powwow, dancers, drummers, and crafts. I want to record and share this beauty."

"Painting is a way to examine the world in ways denied me by the United States justice system, a way to travel beyond the walls and bars of the penitentiary. Through my paints I can be with my People—in touch with my culture, tradition, and spirit. I can watch little children in regalia, dancing and smiling; see my elders in prayer; behold the intense glow in a warrior's eye. As I work the canvas, I am a free man."

Ultimate Sacrifice, by Leonard Peltier, retrieved from Google images.

"Sharing my art makes my heart feel good. It's a way, too, of letting people know that I have not been conquered by the oppressor even though I have spent so many years in these iron lodges."

The Message[15]

Silence, they say, is the voice of complicity.
But silence is impossible.
Silence screams.
Silence is a message,
just as doing nothing is an act.
Let who you are ring out & resonate
in every word & every deed.
Yes, become who you are.
There's no sidestepping your own being
or your own responsibility.
What you do is who you are.
You are your own comeuppance.
You become your own message.
You are the message.

—LEONARD PELTIER[16]

Grupo Bayano:
Community Ambassadors of Cultural Democracy

Grupo Bayano is a Seattle community-based Caribbean music and dance group with over twenty years of experience. The group is a project of the Center for Linguistic and Cultural Democracy,[17] a nonprofit community organization, providing educational resources for bilingual and bicultural communities. Named after a Maroon community in what is today Panamá, Grupo Bayano carries out their work in the spirit of community collaboration, strength, and unity. The group collaborates with teachers and community-based organizations to provide arts-based pedagogical projects that are informed by the struggles of formerly enslaved and colonized populations to conserve their languages and cultural values and traditions.

As cultural workers, Grupo Bayano is committed to a public pedagogy of cultural democracy, which supports *the integrity of languages and cultures and supports children, youth, and adults in finding and expressing their bicultural voices.*

Members of Grupo Bayano in community performance

Peter Harris: Inspiration House

Peter Harris, founder and artistic director of Inspiration House, is an African American cultural worker who has since the 1970s has published his poetry, essays, and fiction in a wide range of national publications. He has worked as a publisher, journalist, editor, and broadcaster, and has been an educator and workshop leader for adults and adolescents. His poetry resonates with the unspoken dimensions of Black men's lives, relationships of intimacy and sexuality.

The Ocean Is Ours[18]

don't be foiled or fooled by
the zip code
the ocean is ours
the mountain is ours
the river is ours
the forest is ours
the sky is ours
anything less no
to anything less no
to anything less
than horizons & freedom & justice

Peter Harris

& peace & humanity
day in & day out day in & day out
flooding the calendar with
holidays & democracy & festivals
& meetings & resolution
I'm down with that I'm down with that
don't be tempted or trapped by the zip code
health is ours
wealth is ours
government is ours
law is ours
safety is ours
anything less no
to anything less no
to any murder disguised as deterrence
any whims disguised as policy
any mercenaries disguised as leaders
any theories disguised as gospel
any gossip disguised as science
day in & day out day in & day out
flooding the calendar with
baptisms & rebellion & ceremony
& protection & institutions
I'm down with that I'm down with that
don't be stamped or seduced by the zip code
the second is ours
the minute is ours
the hour is ours
the sun is ours
the galaxy is ours
anything less no
to anything less no
to anything less
than food & shelter & work
& family & life
day in & day out day in & day out
flooding the calendar with
vigilance & fiestas & militance

& dedications & cooperation
I'm down with that I'm down with that

—PETER HARRIS

Kristina Wong: "Brutal but Hilarious"

Kristina Wong is a third-generation Chinese American solo performer, writer, actor, educator, culture jammer, and filmmaker. Described by the East Bay Express as "brutal but hilarious...a woman who takes life's absurdities very seriously," her body of performance work includes short and full-length solo performance works, outrageous street theater stunts and pranks, subversive Internet installations, and plays and sketch comedy.

In her own words:[19]

I believe that as an artist, my job is not to "fix" the wrongs of the world with easy answers, but instead, to further complicate the question by making the invisible—visible, and hopefully, creating some space for public discourse. I would describe my aesthetic at its best as subversive, humorous, and endearingly inappropriate. My non-traditional, multidisciplinary approach logically mirrors

Kristina Wong preforming

my own multi-layered identity that has been influenced by innumerous cultures, religions, political thinking, technology and post-modern performance art. My nebulous identity continues to shift within the communities I live, evolve and interact with. I see my performance work as a humorous and ephemeral response to the invisible and visible boundaries that shape my world, rather than a hermetic declaration of my identity.

I'm interested in guerilla performance as culture jamming—creating performances that subvert the use of space not intended for "performance." I experiment with interactive, improvisational performance that blurs the roles of "artist" and "audience"—recasting unsuspecting bystanders as co-stars to my performance personas—unearthing the masks, disguises and performances hidden in the most mundane of daily life. I adore "culture jammers." Some of my favorites are the street interventions of Michael Moore, the "identity corrections" of the Yes Men, and the feminists who crashed television beauty pageants when I was growing up. Their performances are disguised within daily life to subvert, manipulate, and explode the status quo.

Evan Greer: Radical Queer and Riot Folk

In his/her own words[20]

I am a full-time radical queer singer/songwriter, parent, and community organizer based in Jamaica Plain, MA. my goal is to use my music as a tool that directly supports movements for social and environmental justice, community self-determination, and liberation for all oppressed living beings.

i'm a femme-y genderqueer trans-identified vegan and I'm terribly excited about things like gender liberation, community emergency response, climate justice, anti-racism, Palestinian liberation, reigniting the labor movement, queer parenting, prison abolition, youth empowerment, and growing food!

Never Surrender

it's been raining for a couple of days now
and my dad's pond is overflowing
the orange fish are at the back door

the toxic flood-water is glowing
and we shake our heads
and get in the car
forget those things we said
making love under the stars

i go back and forth daily about us-and-them
and who's really to blame
but i think it's pretty clear who has got the most to gain
from a divided up society that's terrified of honesty
and we can't discern our enemies
so we give them our complicity
they make beer, and we buy it
they make cars, and we drive them
they build walls, we just give in
they build boxes that we live in
they make gods for us to pray to
jobs to give our days to
binaries of gender
but they can't have our surrender

we look at the world around us
and everything we see is crazy
so we drink and we smoke and we watch the tv
they say "don't take your life so seriously"
i say this is the only way i know how to be

'cause we need passion not fashion
we need food not lawns
we need action not factions
we need everyone here to be singing along
we need stories not glory
we need friends not fans
we need guitars not rock stars
we need more than just loud drunk straight white male punk bands
let's destroy out of love
and build out of anger
get our heads out of our asses
and see our lives are in danger

because the world as we know it
is not gonna last forever and these could be the last days
so let's spend them together
and let's never surrender

—EVAN GREER

Aaron Ammons apeaking at the Unity March in Champaign, Illinois

Aaron Ammons: Poet with the People

Aaron Ammons is a poet and community organizer in Champaign, Illinois. With his wife, Carol, and other members of the community, they founded the Champaign-Urbana Citizens for Peace and Justice, a group that has been instrumental in addressing injustices in the area, including the police shooting of Kiwane Carrington, a fifteen-year-old unarmed African American youth, last year. His work as a poet and cultural worker is central to the spirit of his revolutionary politics. SPEAK CAFÉ is a monthly event where Aaron and Carol open the doors to the community to create a place for voice and democratic speech to flourish. Young and old come to share the creations of their souls, as they bear witness to life's agony and beauty.

My Love Poem

Love is a revolution
Properly administered
It produces the solution;
Inclusion, instead of persecution.
We all want love yet we refuse to give it!
This is my love poem...

Volcano

I am a volcano
I'm a typhoon
I'm the beginning winds of a hurricane
The first drops of a monsoon
A tidal wave of emotions
A vortex in the ocean
Siphoned in and sucked out
I am a thunder cloud,
Ready to explode!
To this anger, I speak
I'm scared if it's unleashed
Will it bring back Kiwane?
Will it bring peace to my streets?
How will it empower my peeps?
To stay alive on ice cold streets
Where cops heart beats,
With heat!
Hot lava runs through my veins
I thought we broke free from Massa!
I guess they have us by more than just chains.

—AARON AMMONS

Mujeres Zapatistas en Resistencia

The Zapatistas went public on January 1, 1994, the day when the North American Free Trade Agreement (NAFTA) came into effect. On that day, they issued their First Declaration from the Lacandon jungle and their Revolutionary Laws: a declaration of war on the Mexican government for its longstanding oppression of indigenous people.

From its inception, Zapatista women have been integral, at every level, to the Zapatista movement and the development of autonomous communities in Chiapas and surrounding regions.

The cultural productions of Mujeres Zapatistas are both acts of economic self-subsistence and political

Mujeres Zapatistas with their pottery

resistance. They send their art out into the world both to sustain their lives and as a public pedagogy that invites the world to witness and join them in their struggle for self-determination and the construction of a world that uncompromisingly rejects the greed and ruthlessness of neoliberalism.

Antonia Darder: Speaking Truth to Power

Death by Theory
I have never seen
so many dead folks;
Folks with no heart
or soul showing;
I mean folks who
are breathing,
and talking,
and walking,
but not living
Folks who speak
important things,
using big words,
claiming facts,
spitting out stats,
to flash legitimacy
on their fabricated
hip, slick, cool, or

Keep America Clean, by Antonia Darder

morally ordered
destitute world;
No matter the topic,
they got something
to say; but it never
redefines beyond
their foolish minds,
'cause these folks
don't feel things
with their insides,
they just surmise.
I have never seen
so many dead folks;
Folks walking around
like vacant shells;
Warm flesh robots,
with nothing to say,
except for the same
bullshit lines and
tired out clichés;
Folks who don't
even have dreams;
imagine that;
no dreams.

—ANTONIA DARDER

As a working-class Puerto Rican woman who chose to commit my life to activism and social struggle, my life in the academy has not been an easy one. It has meant, as with so many other artists from racialized communities, contending with marginalization and invisibility—not because of a lack of intellect or talents, but rather because of a message that ideologically disrupts or a manner of speaking that invades the restrictive discursive boundaries of ethnocentric life in the U.S. mainstream. So, for example, even when I speak English, I remain rooted in the passionate discursive style of *Puertorriqueños*.

Many, however, insist on minimalizing or dismissing this embodied expression of cultural identity. It's amazing, for example, to remember all those over the course of my academic life who mightily proclaimed their *celebration of diversity* on one hand, yet would deem me *too emotional* on the other—readily expecting that people like me change in order to accommodate elite, masculine, and racialized sensibilities. Seldom were there genuine efforts to build cultural democracy between us. Years of sustaining the daily weight of this oppressive imbalance in our lives weighs heavily on the soul of oppressed communities.

Hence, art, for so many of the artists featured here, has been an expression of the soul and a mechanism of salvation; it has been the one place where our bodily articulations could freely participate in public, on our own terms. Our art is the one place where our souls can scream, our hearts can laugh, our bodies' sensuality can spill over, or our grief for our sisters and brothers who suffer can flow. Art is one of the few places where we can exist without the imprisonment of bourgeois sensibilities that fly high and mighty within university walls.

Art, as an embodiment of public pedagogy, is imperative to our work as critically engaged intellectuals, community activists, and radically loving human beings. Often existing outside the milieu of capitalist consumption, art as resistance constitutes one of the few political and pedagogical spaces that remains free—where artists everywhere use their soulful imaginations to resist oppressions, to dream of justice, and to speak truth to power.

ENDNOTES

1. www.iisg.nl/exhibitions/chairman/cub25.php

2. Furuhashi, Y. (2006). *Las Krudas: To Be Lesbian, Feminist, and Hip-Hop in Cuba! In Monthly Review* (August).

3. See: http://mrzine.monthlyreview.org/2006/joffe130206.html

4. Se: http://www.favianna.com/statement/index.php

5. See: http://www.annefeeney.com/

6. http://www.soundclick.com/bands/_music_lyrics.cfm?bandid=164922&songID=1119299&keepThis=true&TB_iframe=true&height=530&width=530

7. Excerpt from Broyles-Gonzalez (2003). Performance Artist Maria Elena Gaitan: Mapping a Continent without Borders (Epics of Gente Atravesada, y Entremetida) in *Frontiers.* See: http://findarticles.com/p/articles/mi_qa3687/is_200301/ai_n9201553/pg_3/?tag=content;col1

8. http://www.lulu.com/jayjay

9. See: Taylor, S. (2004) The Right Not to Work: Power and Disability. In *Monthly Review* (March)

10. From Newhouse Awards statements: http://www.wnewhouseawards.com/Artists/sunaurataylor.html

11. Davis, A. (2010). Emancipatory Acts: A Play about Motherhood in the United States. In *International Review of Qualitative Research.* V. 2, N. 4 (February).

12. See: http://www.leonardpeltierart.com/Abouttheartist.html

13. See: http://www.leonardpeltier.net/theman.htm

14. See excellent film about Peltier and AIM, *Incident at Oglala*, narrated by Robert Redford. http://www.amazon.com/Incident-at-Oglala/dp/B000K3H9HE

15. Peltier, L. (2000). *Prison Writings: My Life and My Sun Dance*. New York: St. Martin's Press (216).

16. Leonard Peltier, a member of the American Indian Movement, has spent 35 years incarcerated. He was convicted for the June 26, 1975 murders of two FBI agents on the Pine Ridge Indian Reservation. Many have called for his release, given the questionable tactics, fabricated evidence, and strong-arm tactics used to intimidate witnesses. Four defendants were originally charged before the Grand Jury. Two of the defendants were tried and found Not Guilty by reason of self-defense. Charges were dropped on the 3rd defendant. Peltier, however was tried after a change of venue to North Dakota. In this trial Mr. Peltier wasn't able to put up a self-defense argument. Any evidence that could have proven Mr. Palters' innocence was not allowed in his trial, or if it was allowed it was not allowed in front of the jury. Witness testimony wildly diverged between Grand Jury testimony and trial testimony; further, several of the witnesses recanted their testimony after the trial, claiming perjured testimony because of threats from the FBI. Despite testimony, prosecuting attorneys have stated on several occasions that they don't know who shot the agents. http://www.leonardpeltier.net/theman.htm

17. http://www.culturaldemocracy.org/ The Center is a brain-child of Sharon Cronin, who, in collaboration with bilingual/bicultural educators in Seattle, directs and coordinates the activities of the center.

18. http://www.inspirationcrib.com/poetry.html#ocean

19. http://www.kristinawong.com/about.html

20. http://www.riotfolk.org/?m=evangreer

PART VII.
Public Pedagogy of Dissent

YOU SAY YOU'VE GOT A PROGRAM?

You say you've got a program?
a program to cure all our ills,
a program to stop the violence,
a program to end the drugs,
a program for all abuse,
child beating,
people raping,
and mind fucking;

you say you've got a program?
specially tailored,
custom made
to end all the woes
of our neighborhoods,
put away the criminals,
lock up all the kooks,
reform the juveniles,
and assimilate all those poor
disadvantaged unfortunates;

and i say get lost fool 'cause
i've seen your program
a million times before and
it's nothing but a smoky screen
to hide the blood thirsty
money hungry bastards who
have to masturbate their conscience
for a while so they can go on
believing that god and their
hard work made them rich
and not their disgraceful
and immoral ways;

you say you've got a program
and i say give our people
food to feed our children,
a decent home with no
cockroaches dancing in the aisles,
and a little health and fortitude
to run our own lives,
instead of all your programs
we've been hearing about for
20 years, every time some big
time social scientist gets some
big idea in the laboratory
to cure the ills of the world

you say you've got a program,
well please don't give me
no more of your artificially
processed, date expired,
disgusting excuse for a cheese,[1]
'cause cheese won't buy those
fancy drugs to cure all
the physical woes that pain
my weary fading body and
cheese sure don't give me
no kind of self-respect

you say you've got a program?
and i say, no thank you fool,
'cause i've got a program
that will cure our woes,
it's called liberation,
and when the people find out
you better watch out
—ANTONIA DARDER, 3/9/84

---

1   During the early 1980s, the federal government's response to the increasing poverty and hun-
     ger in the country was to conduct a nation-wide distribution of date-expired, processed cheese
     and butter in low-income communities.

CHAPTER 19

Imagining Justice in a Culture of Terror

Pedagogy, Politics, and Dissent

[U]nder the sign of a timeless war on global terror...dissent as a form of political activism was placed strategically by the rulers of the security state on a continuum of lawlessness leading to terrorism, a continuum in which protest was perceived as disloyal, as the unpatriotic act of the enemy within, as a threat to the safety of the polity—in short, as undemocratic.

—ROBERT L. IVIE (2004)[1]

The attacks on the World Trade Center and the Pentagon on September 11, 2001 stand as a clear demarcating moment in the history of the United States. These attacks on U.S. soil destroyed the comforting illusion of security and invincibility long held as the mainstay of our democracy. No longer would U.S. elites, political officials, and businessmen exist unscathed by the vengeance of the "enemies" that their own greed and imperialist visions helped to produce during the latter years of the twentieth century.

The current international landscape leaves little doubt that we are living in a new era. Steeped in the fears manufactured by a *culture of terror*, dissenting voices are discouraged or repressed, and global protest is rendered impenetrable to neoliberal policies and practices of injustice. Xenophobic pundits denounce the Muslim world, the poor, and the foreign, exploiting the fear of invasion as a clear and present danger. The threat of terrorists, immigrants, and the impoverished now vividly commingle in our psyches. U.S. war acts of aggression persist in Iraq and other parts of the world, while the overwhelming economic, political, and military violence at home has been rendered invisible by the evangelizing patriotism and corporate greed of the last decade.

The political ramifications of this patriotic zeal not only resulted in the passage of the Patriot Act but also condoned the invasion of Afghanistan and then Iraq, orchestrated to protect economic interests and political influences in the Middle East—all in the name of freedom and democracy. This is the same misguided patriotism that has turned a blind eye to the genocide in Darfur, where the U.S. claims no political or economic interests to defend.

On the domestic scene, the rampant incarceration of the poor is justified through the media's barrage of stereotypes that parade as news, reality cop shows, and criminal pseudo-documentaries such as *American Justice* and *Cold Case Files*. Whether at home or in the international arena, U.S. citizens are systematically warned to be afraid of those who are poor or foreign, both major sectors of the population that are rapidly expanding, given the impact of deepening and hardening structures of economic inequality in the U.S. and abroad.

The fear of uncertainty generated by the tragedy of 9/11 led to the formation of The Department of Homeland Security, which initiated a culture of terror and shifted our perceptions of safety on the street and in the air. In its wake, our civil liberties have been vastly compromised in the name of protecting our borders. Through a variety of politically induced media distortions, U.S. citizens are warned repeatedly of "orange alerts" and aroused to question the safety of our own homes. In turn, this has inspired xenophobic sentiments that have given rise to a variety of local, state and federal legislative actions geared toward ridding the country of "illegal" immigrants. At the same time, widespread campaigns for the militarization of the border by both official border patrol agents and border vigilantes prevail.[2]

Today, Muslim and other immigrants have become the scapegoats of the culture of terror, shrouding America's political and economic immorality. For example, a recent *Newsweek* poll, although fairly positive, reported that 25% of Americans would consider putting Muslims in U.S. detention camps if another 9/11-style attack were to occur.[3] Meanwhile, obvious and longstanding determinants of inequality—poor job security, insufficient income, lack of health care, growing poverty, and the wholesale incarceration of the deeply impoverished—are ignored or dismissed as secondary to issues of national protection. As a consequence, trillions of dollars are being poured into Homeland Security and military actions at the border and around the world, while social justice is conveniently redefined to abdicate the State of any responsibility to its distressed citizens. Instead, the free market is touted as the great equalizer of the twenty-first century, leaving those outside the field of its neoliberal global order to fend for themselves or suffer the bitter consequences of its exile

As a leading proponent of the current internationalization of the "war on terrorism," the U.S. remains the world's wealthiest nation, yet one of the most economically unequal. "We live in a society in which 1 percent of the population owns 60 percent of stock and 40 percent of total wealth. The top 10 percent of Americans own over 80 percent of the total wealth."[4] At the same time, the poor are "nickel and dimed" into subsistence by the increasing cost of substandard housing; the lack of health care benefits; expensive transportation and commuting costs; too few and often costly child care options; low-wage employment; and increasing job insecurities tied to outsourcing of well-paying jobs and plant shutdowns.[5] It is disturbing to note that neoliberals often claim that such action are good for the world because it redistributes the wealth, while remaining close-mouthed about the staggering profits gained from employing low-wage workers without benefits and operating their enterprises in environmentally deregulated zones.

Hence, to forge a critical pedagogy within a culture of terror requires us to remain thoughtful about the manner in which neoconservative values and neoliberal policies conflate to protect profits and their stronghold on the economy, through supporting a parallel "terror of dissent." As such, dissenting voices that clamor against current national policies or persistently demand greater democratization of institutional structures are perceived as a danger to the unity of our identity as a nation, justifying the silencing of such dissenters. This is even more disturbing when the politics of neoliberalism, couched in alarmist anti-terrorist rhetoric, is enacted on the international arena, in the name of democracy.

The Hidden Inseparability of Racism and Class Inequality

What tends to disappear from view is the relations of exploitation and domination which irreducibly constitute civil society, not just as some alien and correctable disorder but as its very essence, the particular structure of domination and coercion that is spe-

cific to capitalism as a systemic totality—and which also determines the coercive function of the state.

—ELLEN MEIKSINS WOOD (1995)[6]

Contemporary struggles for democratic schooling do not arise in vacuum.
They are, instead, historically on a continuum with the dissent and struggles of
workers in the early decades of the twentieth century and the anti-war, feminist,
and civil rights struggles of the 1960s and 1970s. However, unlike earlier political
protests, the civil rights movement incorporated a liberal politics of rights, which
prevailed as the common orthodoxy for dissent. Notwithstanding, the presence
of a small cadre of political dissenters, who adamantly argued that any movement
for social justice in the states should be linked to an international, anti-imperialist
agenda, one that clearly challenged the inequalities and social exclusions intrinsic
to a capitalist political economy. In concert with the times, however, the decision
was made to retain a civil rights approach, firmly anchored to a strategy of litigation, to wage dissent and organize communities. This direction in the movement
was to represent a significant political juncture that, unwittingly, left unforeseen
and untouched the unfettered advancement of globalization in the final decades
of the 20th century.

As a result of court gains, movement efforts in schools were chiefly driven
by repeated demands for a multicultural curriculum, bilingual education, ethnic
studies programs, and affirmative action efforts to diversify students and faculty,
and create a greater link between schools and communities. Dropping earlier progressive strategies of dissent tied to class struggle, most movement efforts of the
period, principally founded on identity politics, pushed aggressively against traditional institutional boundaries linked to "race" inequality. Although such forms of
dissent most certainly served to initiate and marshal a new population of "minority" professionals and elites into a variety of fields and professions, it did little
to change the larger structural conditions of inequality most prevalent in poor,
working class, and racialized communities. The "race relations" paradigm, unfortunately, failed to challenge the fundamental contradictions of capitalism, that
continued to misinform the policies and practices of schools and society—contradictions that both conserve and disguise assymetrical relations of power.

Key to this discussion is an understanding of racism that acknowledges class
and capitalism as inextricably linked, in ways that do not apply to other categories of exclusion. Class inequalities encompass the State's cultural and political-
economic apparatus, which functions systematically to retain widespread control
and governance over material wealth and resources. As such, racism operates in
conjunction with other ideologies of exclusion (whether cultural, political, class,

gendered, sexual or racialized) to preserve the hegemony of the modern capitalist state, engendering its capacity to appropriate even revolutionary projects born of dissent and strip them of their transformative potential.

A major study, conducted by Gary Orfield[7] at the Civil Rights Project at Harvard University, for example, concluded that although progress toward school desegregation had peaked in the late 1980s—with the courts concluding that the goals of *Brown v. Board of Education* had largely been met—the current trend is moving rapidly in the opposite direction. Concerns regarding segregation, therefore, still have tremendous political saliency today, particularly with respect to questions of academic achievement and the failure of U.S. schools to educate Latino, African American, Native American, and other racialized and working class student populations. In fact, as Latinos became the largest minority population in the U.S., hegemonic forces at work in the reproduction of racialized class inequalities have rendered Latino students (dubbed the "new face of segregation") more segregated today than their African American counterparts.

This study points to the inseparability of racism and economic inequality. Accordingly, contemporary theories of segregation, as an outcome of racialized and class reproduction, must be grounded in a politics of class struggle. This is to say that racism, as a significant political strategy of exclusion, domination, marginalization, violence, and exploitation, cannot be separated from its economic imperative. Thus, it should be no surprise that over 90 percent of segregated African American and Latino neighborhood schools are located in areas of concentrated poverty.[8] In fact, students who attend segregated minority schools are 11 times more likely to live in areas of concentrated poverty than students (of all ethnicities) who attend desegregated schools.

Hence, when problems of schooling are racialized, deep-seated questions of economic injustice are often deceptively camouflaged. For example, poor students labeled "white" exhibit comparatively similar social and academic difficulties as their counterparts of color. This is most visible in rural schools of the Midwest or the South, where poor "white" students are generally the majority. However, this phenomenon in the United States has been effectively masked and obscured through the racialized portrayals of youth of color in the media and the social sciences. It is interesting to note that this process of racialization became most pronounced, following the protests of African American, Latino, Asian American, and Native American students of color in the 1960s and 1970s. It was at this historical juncture that the media shifted from commonplace portrayals of "white" youth as juvenile delinquents or hoodlums to the racialized depictions of gang-bangers as urban terrorists. The point here is that the impoverished conditions that prevail in segregated communities are inextricably tied to the reproduction of racialized class formations—not some biological or cultural predisposition. Hence, racism can only be ameliorated through a vision of social justice and a politics of dissent firmly rooted in a redistribution of wealth, power, and privilege.

So, although much good has been attributed to the politics of *Brown v. Board of Education*, we find ourselves in a new historical moment that warrants a critical rethinking of emancipatory solutions and strategies of dissent rooted in another time and place. Given the lessons of the last fifty years, many solutions anchored in the "race relations" paradigm of the civil rights era have been called into question by today's context. For instance, there are researchers who contend that the "race relations" paradigm actually functions, unwittingly, to obscure the phenomenon of racism and hence, the hegemonic forces at work within the sociopolitical construction of segregation. [9] Instead, they contend that the process of racialization, with its reified commonsense notions of "race," fails to challenge fundamental structural inequalities of an internationalized capitalist mode of production.

Contemporary society has become entrenched in the language of "race" as destiny, with an implicit dictum that membership in particular "races" enacts social processes, rather than ideology and material conditions of survival. Today, political discourses of every kind are structured by attaching deterministic meaning to social constructs of physical and cultural characteristics, although the racialized landscape has become far more complex. Interestingly, this same myopic lens is often reflected both in liberal advocates of identity politics and in those conservatives who espouse xenophobic views of "foreigners" or the "other." In stark contrast, critical pedagogy must seek to reinforce an understanding of democratic vision and dissent, beyond dichotomies of black and white. In the absence of a more complex vision of ethnic, religious, and political differences, the outcome is the absolutizing of all social and political relations, with little room for the formation of a heterogeneous U.S. national identity in the United States. Instead of waging dissent across our differences on issues and concerns that impact all communities (i.e., health, income, education, environment, etc.), all political interests are categorically racialized. As such, the notion of "race" becomes both absolute and instrumentalized by even well meaning theorists and policy makers who seek to analyze the difficulties and concerns of racialized populations. Accordingly, the malignant ideologies of oppression that sustain necessary capitalist inequalities and result in segregation and other forms of social exclusion [10] are left unattended or reputed irrelevant.

A key point to be made here is that the ideology that informs how we define a social or institutional problem will also determine our choice of political strategies, potential solutions, and ultimately the outcome. The busing solution of the 1970s is a useful example. Busing was one of the predominant integration solutions chosen to wage protest against segregation—a solution anchored in a "race relations" paradigm. But to the chagrin of many African American and Latino communities, this solution actually functioned to destroy the strength, cohesion, and coherence of community life. Some would further argue that it was, in fact, the already more economically privileged minorities (who, incidentally, defined the problem and chose the predominant means for dissent) who made the greatest gains. And, despite the interventions of the civil rights movement, forty years later the class composition of U.S. society based on control of wealth has failed to improve, becoming, in fact, more polarized between the rich and the poor, across all population groups. That is to say, members of the ruling class, of all ethnicities, are wealthier today than they were in the 1960s. Hence, the expansion of an elite, professional class of African Americans and Latinos ultimately failed to dismantle the oppressive economic and racialized policies and practices of the Capitalist State. Instead, hegemonic practices of economic exploitation and the hardened structures of racialized inequality became further camouflaged behind neoliberal aspirations.

Such was also the fate of multiculturalism, which, falling prey to both the politics of identity and state appropriation, became an effective vehicle for further depoliticizing the remnants of political dissent rooted in the civil rights era of the 1960s and 1970s. Notwithstanding its original emancipatory intent, the politics of multiculturalism was from its inception flawed by its adherence to the language of "race relations" and its rejection of class struggle. Moreover, the well-meaning celebrations of difference and the hard-fought battles of a variety of identity movements for representation failed to generate any real or lasting structural change, beyond liberal proposals such as affirmative action, for instance, that more often than not served the interests of the more privileged. In the final analysis, multiculturalism became an effective mechanism of the state, used to manage, preserve, and obscure racialized class divisions, while in the marketplace the new multiplicity of identities generated new products for global consumption.

Beyond the Domestication of the Culture of Terror

> Also familiar are the effects of the large-scale violence undertaken to ensure the welfare of the world capitalist system...
> [while] the culture of terror domesticates the expectations of the majority. People may no longer even think about alternatives different than those of the powerful, who describe the outcomes as a grand victory for freedom and democracy.
>
> —NOAM CHOMSKY[11]

In the midst of empire-building abroad and the tightening of individual civil liberties at home, radical educators attempt to make sense of the world, through our practice and our theoretical reflections. It is in response to the current culture of terror, along with the everyday fears and uncertainties of old, that many embrace critical pedagogy to provide direction and inspiration to move their teaching beyond the growing inequalities that function to domesticate the vitality of students' lives and their dreams.

Unfortunately, however, critical pedagogy's promise to contend with growing oppressive conditions within schools and to develop a consistent project of dissent has often fallen short. This has been as much due to the repressive conditions within schools as to its depthless and misguided use. In the latter instance, critical pedagogy has been reified into simplistic fetishized methods that are converted into mere instrumentalized formulas for intervention, discouraging dissent and leaving untouched the inequities and assymetrical power relations in schools today. But, in truth, a critical pedagogy cannot be realized as merely a classroom-centered pedagogy. Instead, it must reach beyond the boundaries of the classroom, into communities, workplaces, and public arenas where people congregate, reflect, and negotiate daily survival. In the absence of such a public project, critical pedagogy cannot support dissent nor advance an emancipatory vision for the eradication of political and economic enslavement. Moreover, its revolutionary potential for contending with uncertainty and despair must be grounded in the material conditions that give rise to oppression. It is the power of this perspective that enhances the capacity of educators to read power effectively and thus, enact political and pedagogical interventions in the interest of cultural and economic democracy.

Many educators in poor communities express a deep sense of powerlessness in their efforts to teach marginalized students. In the midst of a culture of terror, with its vitriolic rhetoric of terrorism and deceptive justifications, this sense of powerlessness is intensified, particularly in regions where the population is increasingly poor, diverse, and immigrant. School issues related to academic failure, student delinquency, or classroom inattentiveness are generally addressed in superficial or alienating ways. The objective becomes solely to eliminate the immediate symptom, masking the underlying social malaise. Meanwhile, the deeply serious problems students face within schools and in their private lives are ignored carte blanche, swept under the carpet of institutional efficiency and classroom control.

Yet still, the Jeffersonian ideal of educating citizens for participation in a democratic society continues to be widely expressed, even by the most conservative educators and policy makers. Meanwhile, poor, working class, and racialized students are socially and politically exiled within schools, resulting in their academic demise. As teachers intentionally embrace or unintentionally internalize a belief in the neutrality and benevolence of schooling, students are simultaneously tested, labeled, sorted and tracked, while simplistic bootstrap platitudes of self-reliance warp ideals of social justice and institutional equality. These misguided notions undergird the policies and practices of No Child Left Behind (NCLB). With NCLB's intensely conservative agenda, pedagogical authoritarianism with its instrumentalization of knowledge is translated most violently within public schools that serve the most disenfranchised students. As such, public schooling in an age of terror works to effectively trump the development of critical consciousness, civic sensibilities, and political empowerment.

In the interest of capitalist accumulation, schooling in the United States socializes the majority of students to accept the betrayal of their civil rights in exchange for a fantasy of accumulation and security that can never be guaranteed. The construction and control of knowledge are at the heart of this phenomenon. Despite democratic claims, conditions within public schools reproduce inequalities and social exclusions through pedagogical relationships that reinforce repression and deny most students and faculty, for that matter, their freedom and autonomy to think and express themselves without undue fear of retaliation. Consequently, marginalized populations are terrorized daily by policies and practices systematically designed to limit their imaginations and participation in social transformation, while the dissonance existing in the culture of the school and that of students' lives is often dismissed as irrelevant to their schooling and academic success.

Unfortunately, even well-crafted programs which claim to be committed to social justice tend to sabotage student autonomy and cultural integrity, compelling them to adopt prescribed ways of knowing and manufactured identities that prove false when brushed across their daily experiences.[12] Here, well-meaning teachers use their authority and privilege to invalidate, intentionally or unintentionally, students who become involved in the construction of oppositional knowledge, thus reinforcing students' silence and self-doubt. Unfortunately, many teachers who are able to recognize the violence of injustices within other instructional settings are less willing to accept that they themselves might need to make fundamental changes in their classroom teaching in order to support democratic practices—including political dissent.

Critical ideas and practices in the interest of democratic schooling must remain central to our efforts to confront the concealed alienation and powerlessness so prevalent in schools and society today. To challenge the repressive tendencies of the culture of terror, educators must stretch the boundaries of critical educational principles, in order to infuse public contexts with critiques that counter the violence of both neoconservative values and neoliberal solutions. It is a moment when emancipatory theories of schooling must be put into action, in an effort to counter a repressive national educational agenda that renders teachers, students, parents and communities voiceless and devoid of social agency. There is an urgent need for civic courage that challenges the contemporary rhetoric of rugged individualism and neo-Darwinian self-reliance, which shamelessly undermines difference and dissuades dissent.

Through authoritarian educational practices and the imposition of a hidden curriculum of the market place, the ideological practices of public schooling uncritically nourish patriotic zeal, defend the violence of war as necessity, and justify the violation of our civil rights in the name of national security. Simultaneously, strident individualism and backlash politics destroy historical memory and impose an *official public transcript* (an apolitical, ahistorical, and, at moments, blatantly dishonest spin) on events, in concert with the imperatives of neoliberalism. Namely, the expansion of the "free" market, the deregulation of environmental policies, the corporatization of all bureaucratic institutional functions, the monopoly of the media, and the wholesale privatization of every human need.

In response to the current political climate, an important role of critical educators, then, is not only to unveil the hidden curriculum of terror in schools and society but also to work toward the reinstitution of a multiplicity of historical memories tied to disenfranchised communities and their survival. In these repressed histories is often found the collective possibility to wage protest through the opportunity to imagine a different world. As such, this constitutes an essential dimension in forging a critical pedagogy that challenges civic domestication, opens the ground for political engagement, and welcomes the heated passion of dissent.

Imagination and Dissent

Imagine all the people
Sharing all the world...

You may say I'm a dreamer
But I'm not the only one
I hope someday you'll join us
And the world will live as one

—JOHN LENNON

To use imagination is to...enable us to break with the one-dimensional vision, to look towards what might or what ought to be.
Clearly, this is troubling to those who seek the comfort of the
familiar. For others, however, it signifies an end to submission,
to the taken-for-granted, to what has seemed inescapably "given"

—MAXINE GREENE[13]

The culture of terror disrupts our critical powers to imagine a different world—
a world in which our shared humanity is central to our politics. This neoliberal
culture of terror, steeped in the shadows of paranoid delusions, thrives on "cynicism, fear, insecurity, and despair."[14] And, since it is precisely the ability to imagine beyond the status quo that opens the door to a new vision of politics and the
world, neoliberalism renders unfettered imagination at best suspicious and, at
worst, terrorism. Hence, the voices and participation of those who refuse to extend
their consent to its treachery are rendered invisible or marked for subjugation. The
crackdown on civil liberties, including the right to information, movement, and
dissent, has rapidly intensified over the past decade.

However, it is important to note that the current efforts of the Department
for Homeland Security did not just materialize overnight. Since the late 1980s, an
increasing number of men and women from working class and racialized communities have lost their civil rights, as a consequence of felony convictions and massive rates of incarceration. The level of surveillance within many public schools,
including armed personnel, has made them paragons of the Security State. In addition, a plethora of federal, state and local policies have been proposed and many
enacted to repress the movement of people (but not capital) across U.S. borders.

More recently, actions have been instigated against anti-war protestors, critics of globalization, and other political dissenters. In 2005, for example, a Flag
Amendment was passed that made burning the American flag a felony. In 2002,
Joseph Frederick unveiled a 14-foot paper sign declaring "Bong Hits 4 Jesus."
Although he was on a public sidewalk outside his Juneau, Alaska, high school, he
was suspended. His civil rights case reached the Supreme Court, where the court's
decision drew a fuzzy line between advocacy of illegal conduct and political dissent, ultimately limiting student rights.[15] The *Democracy Now!* Archive is replete
with news stories of peace and anti-war dissidents who have been spied on, jailed,
or fired from their workplaces, including longtime progressive columnist Robert
Scheer, who was fired by the *L.A. Times* in 2005.[16] And, most recently, Ward
Churchill, a professor of Ethnic Studies at the University of Colorado Boulder
was fired for his political views, despite the ostensible protections of academic freedom. Meanwhile, private groups such as the Minuteman Civil Defense Corps[17] at

the U.S./Mexico border and internet terrorist hunters like Shannon Rossmiller[18] are the new millennium's self-appointed vigilantes, drenched in the moralistic rhetoric of the culture of terror.

Much of this commotion has been fueled by the hysteria of the war on terrorism and The Uniting and Strengthening America by Providing Appropriate Tools Required to Intercept and Obstruct Terrorism Act of 2001, better known as the Patriot Act. In response, Michael Steinberg, Legal Director of the American Civil Liberties Union, encouraged political dissent saying, "in times of crises, it is even more important for citizens to dissent when the government is doing wrong.... Dissent is not antipatriotic."[19] Given the repressive context illustrated by these examples, it is imperative that critical educators take on publicly issues of social justice in a serious, forthright, and sustained manner. To accomplish this requires that we remain ever cognizant of the political nature of education and its inextricable relationship to the larger societal and economic forces that govern our lives.

Historically disenfranchised populations who have borne the brunt of political and economic policies of exclusion, for example, must find within public schools and communities an opportunity to develop their critical faculties and political awareness. This demands pedagogical conditions that tend to the free development of intellectual formation, respect the sovereignty of cultural identities, support solidarity of collective action, and foster faith and confidence in political dissent. The educational neglect of such overarching pedagogical and political needs in a democratic state, coupled with an unmerciful emphasis on assimilation and the dispossession of rights, constitutes an act of covert political terrorism waged against disenfranchised communities through the hegemonic mechanism of schooling.

The relationship between pedagogy, politics and dissent must intermingle with emancipatory principles of an engaged public life, making it impossible to deny that dissent, though not synonymous with democracy, is an essential political ingredient for the evolution of a just and democratic society. Dissent is, in fact, absolutely necessary to the enactment of democratic principles, particularly within a nation so tremendously diverse (e.g., ethnic, gender, class, culture, language, sexuality, etc.) as the United States. Politics stripped of dissent leaves the powerful unaccountable, to run roughshod over the interests, needs, and aspirations of the majority of the world's population, irrespective to any expressed principles of freedom and democracy.

Nowhere has this been more evident than in the manner in which the voices and concerns of millions of anti-war protesters around the globe have been flagrantly ignored, in order to assure that the war interests of neoliberal enterprise would not be daunted by large-scale popular dissent. In the face of the recent devastating events in Iraq, it is evident that the Bush administration should have heeded the concerns and warnings of informed protesters who imagined a different world and assumed their civic responsibility as citizens of the international community to raise their voices of discontent.

Imagining justice requires an ability to rethink the world anew. What this points to is the pedagogical importance of imagination to both critical formation and political development. Unfortunately this is an aspect of education that seldom receives the attention that it merits, particularly within an ostensibly democratic society. Yet, the capacity to imagine the world beyond our current social conditions, with a confidence in our ability to enact change through individual and collective efforts is central to any transformative process. However, it is the power of imagination that opens the field for students to simultaneously reflect on what is, as well as what might be. As students are supported in efforts to grapple with what they find beyond the present conditions, they are "midwifed," so to speak, into critical social insights that unveil the hidden ideologies and material conditions that repress their freedom. By so doing, imagination compels students to break through the silences of injustice and speak the unspeakable. Once spoken, new ideas of the world can be shared in dialogue and critically engaged. It is through the organic regeneration of such a pedagogy of imagination that we become empowered to forge a collective vision of social justice, founded on a politically moral and ethically grounded understanding of public life.

In line with a radical philosophical tradition of education, both Paulo Freire and Maxine Greene spoke often in their work about the importance of imagination to the forging of an emancipatory political vision. They similarly linked the notion of imagination to our capacity to step back from a set of familiar circumstances or conditions in order to enter into a different understanding of the world. By opening up to a variety of tested and untested possibilities of knowing and experiencing the world, we are better able to understand how students from different cultural traditions come to think or act differently in the world. Unlike the narrow rationality and ethnocentrism of conservative identity politics, critical imagination can exist only within a realm where plurality of thought and practice resides. This is so, for critical thought requires an open-mindedness and expansiveness of vision that can only be found through our willingness to confront fear as a normal aspect of everyday life, consistently countering, individually and collectively, values and practices that seek to terrorize or pathologize dissenting views. To nourish imagination, then, is to fuel one of the most indispensable qualities inherent to the practice of transformative dissent. For without imagination, the injustice of an exploitive status quo is rendered intractable. As is often the case in schools where bureaucratic power, in direct contradiction to democratic rights and principles, represses creativity, fosters dependency, and coerces consent.

In contrast, a critical pedagogy cultivates imagination and seeks to create opportunities to insert students into new and unfamiliar contexts, so they can grapple with the cognitive dissonance and ambiguity, intrinsic to a highly diverse society. Moreover, such imagination is important to the process of critical dissent, because it not only centers its focus on undoing but also is attentive to critically rethinking conditions of inequality and offering "solutions that arise from collaboration and consensus."[20] Rather than simply entering into dissent and conflict with wholesale antagonism, critical educators must recognize the complexity of both human relations and human existence, to thus enter into conflict with not only clear values and vision but also with humility.

Humility, anchored in a politics of love, provides the open-mindedness to listen to an adversary, without stripping the person of dignity and respect.[21] In the absence of such political imagination, any possibility of dialogue is stifled. Generally, this is so because the communication becomes stonewalled and oppositional. Once this happens, the two sides of a conflict become mired in the ego-pursuit of winning the battle and being right rather than remaining focused on a collective democratic intent. Righteousness and moralism seem to be by-products of such a contentious process, limiting the possibility of critical compassion and revolutionary solidarity in the course of political struggles.

A critical pedagogy, through invigorating critical discourse with imagination and faith in our humanity, supports students in building sound epistemological and ontological pursuits, in resonance with universal principles of emancipatory life. It is here where often there is a departure between postmodernists and those who remain committed to the belief in the salience of class struggle and the anti-capitalist project. Just as it was for Marx, the struggle against capitalism today and its culture of terror is indeed a fiercely moral one. Undoubtedly, the ferocity of Marx was as much a part of his political convictions as his ability to imagine the limitless capacity of human beings to continuously make, unmake, and remake the world.

At a time when the culture of terror seems hell-bent on the disintegration of our civil rights and the relentless immorality of global capital threatens environmental collapse, we need a critical pedagogy that is unapologetically political and moral. A critical pedagogy for the classroom and our daily lives that can help us to unearth the virulent structures of power that limit our dreams, incarcerate our bodies, and defile the meaning of democracy and freedom. We need a revolutionary pedagogy of love that embraces our civic responsibility as critical citizens of the world and fully authorizes our kinship as human beings. All this, so that we might thoughtfully and passionately voice, labor, dissent, struggle, hope, and imagine a future, where "all the world can live as one."

NOTES

1. R.L. Ivie, "Prologue to Democratic Dissent in America," *Javnost/The Public* 11, no. 2 (2004): 19–36.

2. See A. Darder, "Radicalizing the Immigration Debate: A Call for Open Borders and Global Human Rights," *New Political Science* 29, no. 2 (2007).

3. B. Braiker, "Americans and Islam," *Newsweek*, July 20, 2007; available at: http://www.msnbc.msn.com/id/19874703/site/newsweek/.

4. A.J. Noury and N.C. Smith, "Bye, Bye American Dream," *Political Affairs* (December 2004): 26.

5. See: B. Ehrenreich, *Nickel and Dimed* (New York: Turtleback Books, 2002).

6. E. Meiksins Wood, *Democracy against Capitalism* (New York: Cambridge University Press, 1995), 256.

7. See: G. Orfield, *Schools More Separate: Consequences of a Decade of Resegregation* (Boston, MA: Civil Rights Project, Harvard University, 2001).

8. Ibid.

9. See: R. Miles, *Racism after "Race Relations"* (London: Routledge, 1993); and A. Darder and R.D. Torres, *After Race: Racism after Multiculturalism* (New York: New York University Press, 2004).

10. See: P. Gilroy, *Against Race: Imagining Political Culture Beyond the Colorline* (Cambridge, MA: Harvard University Press, 2000).

11. N. Chomsky, *Profit over People: Neoliberalism and Global Order* (Seven Stories Press, 1998), 24.

12. R. Butson, "Teaching as a Practice of Social Injustice: Perspective from a Teacher," *Radical Pedagogy* (2003); available at: http:radicalpedagogy.icaap.org/content/ Issue 5_1/10_butson.html.

13. M. Greene, "Metaphors and Responsibility," *On Common Ground: Partnerships and the Arts* 5 (fall 1995); available at: http://www.yale.edu/ynhti/pubs/A18/greene.html.

14. H.A. Giroux, "Public Pedagogy and the Politics of Neoliberalism: Making the Political More Pedagogical," *Policy Futures in Education* 2: no. 3-4 (2004): 494.

15. B. Mears, "'Bong Hits for Jesus' Case Limits Student Rights," CNN Washington Bureau (2007); available at: http://www.cnn.com/2007/LAW/06/25/free.speech/index.html.

16. See *Democracy Now!* (November 14, 2005); available at: http://www.democracynow.org/ article.pl?sid + 05/11/14/1447244.

17. To see the Minuteman website, go to: http://www.minutemanhq.com/hq/.

18. B. Harden, "In Montana, Casting a Web for Terrorists," *Washington Post*, June 4, 2006, A03; available at: http://www.washingtonpost.com/wp-dyn/content/article/2006/06/03/AR2006060300530.html.

19. S. Chang, "ACLU Encourages Political Dissent as a Patriotic Action," *Michigan Daily*, April 12, 2002.

20. J. Hart, "Meet the New Boss: You: How and Why the People Are Taking Charge," *Utne Reader*, May–June 2007, 42.

21. See: A. Darder, *Reinventing Paulo Freire: A Pedagogy of Love* (Boulder, CO: Westview Press, 2002), for an extensive discussion of Paulo Freire's pedagogy and the indispensable characteristics that he identifies within a revolutionary understanding of love.

CHAPTER 20

Radio and the Art of Resistance

A Public Pedagogy of the Airwaves

The time has come for educators to develop more engaged systematic political projects in which power, history, and social
movements can play an active role in constructing the multiple
and shifting political relations and cultural practices necessary
for connecting the construction of diverse political constituen-
cies to the revitalization of democratic public life.

—HENRY GIROUX (2003, 13)

The revitalization of public democratic life, as articulated in these words by Henry
Giroux, speaks to the heart of all critical pedagogical efforts within and outside
classroom life. In contrast, it is through both the silencing and dismantling of democratic participatory rights that we are rendered most vulnerable to the destructive
impact of neoliberal forces in the world today. At a time when public mainstream
discourse touts its self-congratulatory "post-racial" declarations, the policies
and practices of the State continue to harshly impact the lives of poor African
Americans and Latinos, as well as other working-class people in the United States
and abroad. Moreover, their disempowering impact within the public sphere is

particularly felt among those who can find little relief for the poverty, surveillance, and injustice what thwarts their community participation.

In Champaign-Urbana, the twin-city Midwest university town where I live and teach, community participation is further complicated by the rhetoric of corporate interests that effectively shroud neoliberal objectives of small university town governance. Within this context, efforts calling for institutional change and municipal reform must be waged by community residents who depend on nomadic, albeit progressive, student and faculty participation. This aspect unfortunately serves as a double-edged sword, in that there is a transient quality to public life and the body politic of this Midwest community. Such a politically unstable context requires creative pedagogical interventions by those who will eventually move on, in concert with those who call these twin cities home. In an effort to support the tenuous nature of community relationships within the confines of a neoliberal university agenda, public pedagogical projects can serve as alternative venues for supporting civic participation and a critical form of public engagement.

Critical public interventions are of particular importance, within an increasingly conservative culture of scholarship, where neoliberal interests are neatly concealed within an academic rhetoric that furiously prioritizes global concerns over the needs of local communities. This is the case, particularly, in the current climate of "economic decline," where university "shock doctrine" solutions conveniently signal retrenchment among administrators, faculty, and students, through institutional reliance on "color-blind" neoliberal policies that effectively reinforce traditional structures of privilege and power.

The Media in the Age of Neoliberalism

Understood as one of neoliberalism rather than simply globalization, the current era seems less the result of uncontrollable natural forces and more as the newest stage of class struggle under capitalism.

—ROBERT MCCHESNEY (2001)[1]

It is impossible to speak of the media in the age of neoliberalism without engaging their power to exercise a homogenizing impact on social, political, and economic relations at a global level. McChesney insists that *neoliberalism* is a more accurate explanatory term from which to discuss the overwhelming control of the corporate sector over the public sphere. From this standpoint, "governments are to remain large so as to better serve the corporate interests, while minimizing any activities that might undermine the rule of business and the wealthy.... The centerpiece of neoliberal policies is invariably a call for commercial media and communications markets to deregulate" (McChesney 2001). Moreover, given its privatizing propensity, ownership of the airwaves has become consolidated among a few corporate giants, including General Electric, Time Warner, Univision Communications, and Viacom, that now monopolize the ideological architecture and design of U.S. radio programming.[2,3]

This power over the airwaves was consolidated following the passage of the Telecommunications Act of 1996, which was the first major reform in the telecommunications law since the act of 1934. Supposedly, the law was to create greater access to the communications industry by fostering increased market competition for the airwaves. But in reality, the act radically restructured regulations in such a way as to intensify the market's rule rather than benefit consumers, as its proponents claimed. As large corporations fought behind the scenes over the wording of the act, citizen consumers were left completely out of the picture, the majority unaware of the corporatized politics that threaten the democracy of telecommunications in this country. So, although it is true that the Telecommunications Act, indeed, required a radical overhaul, given the dramatic changes in digital technology since 1934, McChesney (1998) argues that the act of 1996 was a complete disaster.

The Telecommunications Act, with its relaxation of ownership restrictions to promote competition across sectors, was supposed to produce competition, a far-fetched notion in view of the concentrated nature of these markets, but in fact the law has paved the way for the greatest period of corporate concentration in U.S. media and communications history. The seven Baby Bells are now four—if the SBC Communications purchase of Ameritech goes through—with more deals on the way. In radio, where ownership restrictions were relaxed the most, the entire industry has been in upheaval, with four thousand of the eleven thousand commercial stations being sold since 1996. In the fifty largest markets, three firms now control access to over half the radio audience. In twenty-three of those fifty markets, the three largest firms control 80 percent of the radio audience. The irony is that radio, which is relatively inexpensive and thus ideally suited to local independent control, has become perhaps the most concentrated and centralized medium in the United States.[4]

In line with this unprecedented corporate control of the airwaves, radio in conjunction with other media outlets delivers the hidden curriculum of a de facto neoliberal public pedagogy. One that, Giroux (2004a) contends, "has become thoroughly reactionary as it constructs knowledge, values, and identities through a variety of educational sites and forms of pedagogical address that have largely become the handmaiden of corporate power, religious fundamentalism, and neo-conservative ideology" (497). Hence, in contrast to the old belief that the media should function as a neutral sphere in which different ideas and perspectives can be engaged and interrogated within a democratic context, the mainstream media now, more than ever, is a powerful hegemonic tool that functions in the overriding justification and legitimation of societal inequalities, political exclusions, and environmental demise.

Efforts to counter the pervasiveness of oppression—whether tied to racism, class, and gendered inequalities, or stifling homophobic representations—must contend with neoliberal distortions that create confusion and contradictions among even well-meaning people. In the homogenizing script of neoliberal existence, bootstrap accountability returns as a central value of the "good society." Therefore, the stories that move across the mainstream airwaves embrace again notions of self-reliance and self-made individualism. Accordingly, a "rugged individualism" is venerated and social action, outside the marketplace or neoliberal dictates, is deemed either suspect or the product of the weak and whining.

Moreover, Giroux (2004b), in *Dissent Voice*, condemns neoliberal ideology for its dehistoricizing and depoliticizing of society, and says that "in its aggressive attempts to destroy all of the public spheres necessary for the defense of a genuine democracy, neoliberalism reproduces the conditions for unleashing the most brutalizing forces of capitalism. Social Darwinism has been resurrected from the ashes of the 19th century sweatshops and can now be seen in full bloom."[5] As such, neoliberal sensibilities turn a blind eye to the suffering of the oppressed through a systematic denial of its dehumanizing propensities—propensities that privilege profit and material gain over even the essential human needs of the most vulnerable. The stories of the disenfranchised are systematically silenced and maligned, while their truths are relegated to the political wastebasket of corporate dominion. This consistent denial or maginalization of stories that unveil injustice prevents any possibility of truly becoming a democratic society, in that the strength, knowledge, and wisdom of those subjugated are rendered unavailable or nonexistent. This further prevents the genuine integration of disenfranchised populations into the decision-making life of the community. Instead, neoliberalism leaves us all at the mercy of the marketplace, restricting the nature of our very existence, as it unmercifully seeks to shrink and contort our definitions of self and humanity.

In response to the limiting neoliberal priorities of both public universities and municipalities, many communities have begun to explore the use of community radio, in an effort to both counter the silences and revitalize solidarity across cultural, class, gendered, and sexual differences. Early proponents for the use of community radio include the founders of Pacifica in California, which later merged with KPFK, one of the strongest public radio stations in the western United States.[6] KPFK has been a leader in the use of the airwaves as public pedagogy, regularly airing programming produced by David Barsamian[7] of *Alternative Radio* and Amy Goodman and Juan Gonzalez of *Democracy Now!* KBOO community radio in Portland, Oregon, has been broadcasting to diverse communities for over forty years.[8] In a city that is predominantly white, the station focuses its programming by and for marginalized communities in the area. Since 1979, WMNF has brought alternative music, arts, and public affairs programming.[9]

Independent media centers around the country have also played an important role in championing more democratic access and control to media resources, including the establishment of low-wave radio stations to serve their local and surrounding communities. One excellent example is the work of Grand Rapids Media Consortium,[10] which for over twenty-five years has maintained technology tools and created media services and community venues to benefit the larger community. Here in the Midwest—just as with the Zapatistas "Voice of the Voiceless" and other community-based radio projects around the world—the use of alternative media has shown the potential to enhance communication and social action among disenfranchised communities. WRFU,[11] a project of Champaign-Urbana Independent Media Center,[12] has been an important resource for the airing of alternative voices.

An important thread that weaves through the mission of most community radio stations is an emphasis on critical engagement with controversial, neglected, and nonmainstream perspectives, as well as an expressed commitment to social justice and democratic life. No doubt without community stations such as these, the airwaves would remain completely in the hands of corporate media moguls, eliminating the possibility for alternative programming and dissenting views. Moreover, in light of the growing international consolidation of control over the media, community radio creates an important political space where hegemonic belief systems can be challenged and alternative views can be mobilized for social action. Eronini R. Megwa (2007) asserts, in his writings about community radio in South Africa,

> Community radio gives listeners a sense of community and identity and creates action space for people to have both direct and indirect link with community power structures as well as to have access to resources. Community radio is an integral part of the community in which it is located. It is acceptable to the community as a development tool. Community radio can mobilize communities to act as change agents by engaging groups and organizations to direct their resources in order to actualize strategies at individual, group, and organizational levels (53).

Community Radio as Public Pedagogy

I attended to the public pedagogy of the free radio airwaves.... Between belting out oldies lyrics along with the station disc jockeys who populate the dial, I listened to National Public Radio in its various forms across two time zones. Within one 13-hour jaunt, I learned four lessons that make me a modern American:

Lesson One: Consume above all else, consume,

Lesson Two: Believe experts,

Lesson Three: Romanticize the past, and

Lesson Four: Civic life is boring.

—PATRICK SHANNON (2007)[13]

In 1941, twenty years after the first radio news program was aired, George V. Denny, executive director of the League for Political Education, enthusiastically declared that *radio builds democracy*. As a device designed to attract attention and stimulate interest in social and political problems, he surmised that radio could function as an effective medium of public instruction within a democratic society. Hence, the interrogation of radio as a public sphere for democratic participation has a long history within the educational field. However, initial perspectives were generally grounded upon a modernist assumption that a "neutral" discourse, which presented a variety of sides, was in the best interest of genuine democracy.

Peter G. Mwesige (2009), who studied the promise and limits of radio programming in Uganda, strongly disagrees with any view that essentializes radio as a democratizing public sphere. He argues instead that

> radio also appears to peddle misinformation and distortions; to invite adulterated debate that excites and inflames rather than informs; to give the public the illusion of influence; and, arguably, to lead to political inertia. At the group level, talk radio may have created an illusion of competition to the extent that it provided voice to oppositional political groups that were otherwise not fully free to participate in the political process. What we have, then, is an imperfect public sphere—but a sort of public sphere nonetheless (221).

Similarly, critical education theorists (Giroux 2004a; Apple 2004; McLaren 1997; Kellner 1995; Freire 1993) have indeed shattered the assumption of neutrality attached to public media production. Instead, they unveil the hidden curriculum of wealth and power, embedded in discourses of neutrality and meritorious solutions thought to "naturally" arise from the "fair airing" of all sides. In concert, the four lessons garnered by Patrick Shannon during his thirteen hours of "free" radio listening shed light not only on the overwhelming adherence of radio to values that bolster neoliberal society but also the deceptive manner in which the notion of neutrality operates amid the public airwaves. And, despite claims that listeners are not passive agents, constant repetition of embedded values appears to erode the human agency of unsuspecting audiences, while simultaneously conditioning and priming the mind (Croteau and Hoynes 2002, 1994), as Shannon (2007) notes, to equate consumption with freedom, believe in the power of experts over one's own knowledge, objectify the past as romantic ideal, and readily abdicate our right to civic participation in search of pleasure and entertainment. In the midst of convoluted discourses that legitimatize and perpetuate the interest of the powerful and wealthy, critical educators and community activists are challenged to establish spaces for counterhegemonic dialogue and alternative public engagement. This entails the development of a critical public pedagogy in which social agency is nurtured and critical faculties of political discernment are activated and stretched, in the interest of social justice and public democratic life.

With this intent, the Liberacion![14] Radio Collective was established in 2005 as a means to apply critical academic knowledge to the practice of a public pedagogy within the public sphere of radio programming. Critical public pedagogy is defined here as a deliberate and sustained effort to speak through a critical lens of society, in such a way as to inform (and transform) mainstream public discourses and community political practices in the interest of the disenfranchised. This is of particular significance, as previously noted, within the contemporary neoliberal context in which we struggle to live and resist the market forces of privatization and "accountability" ever encroaching upon our daily lives. More specifically, the work here points to a political process within the public life of a small rural university town in the Midwest—a context in which the power of conservative ideologies push forcefully against the forces of difference—forces that call for systematic and structural institutional change, predicated upon the politics of social justice, human rights, and economic democracy.

Nowhere is the battle to control the minds and hearts of the populace ever so contentious and strained as it is within small rural communities, where notions of "tradition" and "insider" entitlement are given reign over political and cultural forces that seek social inclusion within the fabric of democratic life. This means, more specifically, to engage from *within* a community context where neoliberal values and the rhetoric of impending economic collapse now offer a respite from what many deem the "bothersome" politics of diversity. Within this deeply entrenched conservative public arena, community radio plays a significant role in countering the official transcript of "whiteness," privilege, and conserving ideals of tradition, so blindly embedded in the dominant relationships and discourses of both the university and the larger municipal landscape.

It is precisely in the midst of such a politic that critically engaged radio pedagogy, with an eye toward participation within the public sphere, has been forged. This entails a pedagogical process that makes central the significance of public life and recognizes the importance of creating alternative venues for democratic participation, especially for those who have been historically silenced and relegated to the margins of municipal existence. Through a sustained commitment to combining graduate intellectual formation, collective media production, and critical community engagement, the Liberacion! Radio Collective was born. Its impetus emerged from an acceptance that democracy is never guaranteed and that inherent in its possibilities is the need for ongoing interaction and engagement with public issues that require the silences to be broken and the voices of the voiceless and unattended to find themselves at the center of the airwaves.

Hence, progressive, independent media production, tied foremost to the needs of the disenfranchised and oppressed within neoliberal society, encompasses a counterhegemonic alternative for community expression and dialogue as well as political engagement. That is, a form of public engagement that places public media "at the heart of a democratic society" (Aufderheide and McAfee 2005), one that "treats people as active learners in and builders of society...[where] people can assert themselves not only as individuals but also, if they work with others, as decision-makers and mobilizers of the public will."[15]

It is with these key elements in mind that the radio collective was established to function principally as an avenue for alternative readings of the world as well as a means to document ongoing political struggles—struggles that, although they might seem unrelated and disparate, are fundamentally interconnected with the subordination of populations deemed disposable and problematic to neoliberal capitalist dictates. Within small communities, such efforts are especially significant in that fewer public pedagogical venues are available for challenging the distortions and false readings that flourish about the "other," who remain underserved and only minimally acknowledged within the public life of the twin cities.

This is important, here, in that the radio collective exists within a context in which the airwaves, just as the streets, are dominated and policed through a racialized victim-blaming rhetoric that belies the impoverished conditions and lack of opportunities available to marginalized populations in the region. This home of the diehard Indian mascot "tradition" is also home to poor Black and Latino families who contend daily with the impact of poor schooling, high unemployment, lack of health care, poor housing, and increasing homelessness and incarceration. Moreover, it is the site where racialized policing has led, for example, to numerous police shootings of unarmed Black youth; where corporate-inspired relationships permitted a twenty-year cover-up of an abandoned toxic waste site in a poor Black community; and where a deep homophobic culture has resulted in violent attacks of working-class gay and transgendered people in the campus town area.

A recent incident serves as an illustration of the difficulties and tensions at work in this small rural college town. In October 2009, police shot to death Kiwane Carrington, a fifteen-year-old poor Black youth who had lost his mother to cancer two months earlier. The youth, who had forgotten his key to the house in which he was staying, was apprehended when attempting to enter the home through a rear window. Within minutes of the arrival of an officer and the chief of police, the boy was gunned down, allegedly for trying to flee from the scene. Although Kiwane was unarmed and there was no evidence of the youth resisting arrest, police entered the scene with pistols drawn—an action that is considered a violation of their own protocols for handling juvenile encounters. Official actions taken after the death of Kiwane and the arrest of the other youth that accompanied him were met with community outcry.

A community coalition formed in response to the shooting circulated and then presented to the city with over seventeen hundred signatures from individuals calling for an investigation into the death and the dismissal of a criminal case filed against the other youth. Despite this and a variety of other concerted community efforts, the shooting was ruled "accidental" by the state's attorney (whose husband is a Champaign police officer). During the months that followed the shooting, the local "news" venues ran stories that seem to both support police actions in the case and belittle community participation in the matter. One editorial that appeared in the *News Gazette* on March 3, 2010, again, maligned the community coalition's persistent public involvement. It read,

> The incident is a tragedy both for Carrington's friends and family members as well as the community, and *the event has become a cause celebre for local residents* who feel the shooting reflects an institutional bias by police against members of minority groups. So they have taken up [the arrested youth's] cause, insisting that the charge against him be dismissed. But the [state's attorney], quite correctly, refused to do so, *explaining that public opinion plays no role in prosecuting cases*.... The justice system would be a shambles *if the prosecution of criminal cases became the subject of popularity contests*...That's why the petition drive... is not just naive, but *an assault on the entire concept of the rule of law*....[The youth being charged] is represented by a lawyer who is working with [the state's attorney's] office to resolve this case *based on its merits*. That is how it has to be. To handle it any other way would turn the entire concept of the judicial system upside down (my emphasis).

As an active independent community radio project, members of the *Liberacion! Radio Collective* gathered to produce and air two community radio programs on the Kiwane Carrington case, as a contribution to the collective action and efforts to bring alternative voices to bear on the official transcript being circulated by the mainstream media, the courts, and the police department. The radio segments were archived on the *Liberacion!* website[16] and copies were made and distributed within the community as part of an educational campaign. It is important to note, at this juncture, that the effectiveness of the *Liberacion!* radio efforts on this issue was only possible given preestablished working relationships with community residents, members of the Urbana Champaign Independent Media Center's newspaper, the Champaign Urbana Citizens for Peace and Justice,[17] and the Solidarity Committee of the Graduate Employees Organization (GEO)[18] on campus.

Key to this discussion is the impact of the radio production. The two segments on the case were played on both community radio stations and on a variety of other public affairs programs. Information provided by *Liberacion!* stimulated further dialogue on the issue at community meetings. The radio program, in combination with many coordinated community efforts of CUCPJ, the GEO Solidarity Committee, the *Public I* (community newspaper project of the UCIMC),[19] the local Ministerial Alliance, and others serve to expand community awareness about the case and to consolidate the voices of community members in calling for fundamental change to the policing of African American youth. Central to the demands of community groups working on the case was the termination of Police Chief R.T. Finney, who was on site during the actual shooting.

Despite a Champaign County coroner's jury ruling the police shooting as accidental,[20] an independent community review of all documents and statements of those interviewed cast suspicion upon the testimony of the officer who allegedly shot the youth. One of the most troubling aspects of the case was the manner in which, Kiwane's young friend, who was with him that ill-fated day, was held in custody by the Champaign police for "aggravated resisting a police officer," remaining silent, until recently. On October 6, 2010, a civil suit was filed on behalf of the youth and his mother, Laura Manning, alleging that Champaign police chief R.T. Finney, and not Officer Daniel Norbits, "fired a shot downward into the chest of Kiwane Carrington, killing Carrington." The suit charged the City of Champaign and Finney with "intentional infliction of emotional distress" to Manning-Carter.[21]

Although the charges were dropped several months later, the law suit caused a major stir in the community, with the chief of police not only adamantly denying the allegations—"I categorically deny that I was the shooter in this incident, and I look forward to presenting the obvious facts of the case in court"[22]—but also asserting in the *News Gazette* that

> activist groups are using the Manning family to further an agenda against me and the police department. My family and I believe this suit…is libelous, slanderous and defamatory as well as without merit, and that private legal action will be forthcoming against all

who are found to be involved.... Blatant unsubstantiated lies that affect my reputation are actionable and will come at a price to Mr. Ivy.[23]

Given the enormous controversy that has surrounded the shooting death of Kiwane Carrington, it was the coordinated public pedagogical efforts within the community that ensured that the youth's death was not swept under the carpet, as has occurred over the years with similar cases across the country (Kumeh 2010).

What must be overwhelmingly underscored, here, is that the art of public pedagogy—whether radio, visual art, music, poetry, or theater—is most powerful and effective when linked to larger social movement efforts, which support and sustain one another in collective endeavors to create public spaces, where alternative political discourses are urgently needed to counter powerful hegemonic structures. And although the theoretical lens that best informs the praxis of the radio collective is that of a critical public pedagogy, the production process by which mainstream airwaves are disrupted and redefined is firmly anchored in the art of resistance, with its multiplicity of voices and methods for naming and renaming the world.

The Art of Resistance and Multidimensionality

We chose the title "The Art of Resistance" as a way of communicating to fans and listeners to stop and think about their lives and the world around them.... I'm not a teacher or a politician; I'm an artist, writer and musician, and this is my way of expressing what's on my mind and how I think I can impact people's lives. I've learned over the years that music can be as powerful a force as politics to bring out issues that need to be addressed, and the things like what we touch on here, like the prison industry and the way children are being raised, will open eyes.

—CALEB CUNNINGHAM (2009),
Hip-Hop Collective Project Lionheart[24]

The art of resistance, as described by the Project Lionheart band member Caleb Cunningham, is shaped by struggles to address in multidimensional ways the underbelly of economic and cultural domination as it manifests within disenfranchised communities, while simultaneously seeking critical solutions that might potentially disrupt its negative impact. There's no doubt that the art of resistance encompasses a deep faith in humanity and the profound capacity of human beings for creativity and resilience, even in the face of suffering and adversity. The art of community resistance, then, implies that there is an organic and collective quality to the manner in which issues are undertaken and the participatory processes by which the design of Liberacion! radio programs are carried out. This posits a formulation of community resistance that inherently redefines the potential power of the airwaves within the public arena from that of solely entertainment to that of public pedagogical significance for democratic life. In the Gramscian sense, then, this public media production by the radio collective functions, uncompromisingly, as a counternarrative to hegemonic discourses of the neoliberal State. It is precisely this quality of counternarration that supports a space in which dominant political, economic, cultural, and ideological interests and their consequences can be interrogated, unveiled, and potentially transformed.

True to its critical foundation, Liberacion! radio segments focus consistently on emancipatory themes and issues raised by community participants themselves, in which multidimensional aspects of social issues can be engaged by a variety of spokespersons, representing both academic and nonacademic praxis. Hence, for example, an interview with a professor who can provide a critical theoretical analysis of incarceration is woven together with an interview of a parent of an incarcerated youth, with a commentary of an educator who teaches in a prison program, with the poetry of inmates, and the music of Dead Prez that challenges the politics of incarceration in the Black community. Through the use of what I term a *multiintellectual design*, this form of community resistance as public pedagogy is shaped, simultaneously, through multidimensional discursive forms, which break with the tradition of isolated, one-dimensional approaches generally utilized even among progressive radio programmers.

This form of multidimensional community engagement is important to building greater fluidity and a more expansive understanding of political participation and community resistance. Thus, a capacity to willingly and legitimately integrate vastly different perspectives and different articulations of similar societal mechanisms and oppressive structures cannot be undermined or ignored within critical media production or community resistance efforts. Through multiple discursive engagements with a variety of social and political issues, new public discourses organically emerge to forge new avenues and possibilities for dissent.

From the experiences of the radio collective, new avenues for dialogue, solidarity, and dissent are best achieved through dismantling false competing perspectives that privilege either academic knowledge over community or community knowledge over the academic. This calls for releasing the objectifying strictures perpetuated by anti-intellectual views of disenfranchised community members, as well as debilitating criticisms of elitism projected onto formally educated comrades. Moreover, it is only through the courage to enter into such a multidimensional praxis of public pedagogy, with humility, dignity, and respect, that new relationships of solidarity can be built, anchored upon ongoing genuine exchanges of both lived and formally studied knowledge, technical skills, historical understandings, and community resources—all deeply valuable and vital to the interrogation and transformation of racialized inequalities, class and gendered formations, heterosexist ideations, and other forms of social exclusions in the world.

This is the kind of public pedagogy that embraces an integrated and communal understanding of knowledge, one that is guided by life-affirming principles of social justice, human rights, and economic democracy. The intentionality behind this public pedagogical approach with students is fundamentally linked to creating the conditions, through dialogue, reflection, and action, for the development and evolution of political consciousness—a consciousness grounded in organic community relationships and joint political labor. To effectively integrate public pedagogical projects, such as the Liberacion! Radio Collective, into the intellectual formation of graduate students demands that our teaching be rooted in a political process of critical academic praxis.

Within this perspective, the privilege of an education is not predicated upon competing against one another for individual rewards or privileged institutional status. Rather, university education is a politicizing context in which faculty and students must consistently (re)learn together to read the shifting cultural landscapes of power, so that we might sharpen our understanding of institutional constraints that thwart community self-determination. Such formation also challenges deeply held bourgeois notions of "professionalism"[25] tied to traditional academic preparation and, instead, asks students to consider how their intellectual preparation will function in the service of justice.

Within such a context, academic "success" is no longer attached to the material ambitions of individuals and their contribution to bolstering capitalist democracy but rather to generating academic resources and technical skills that can be shared and utilized in the collective interest of community solidarity and democratic participation. And all of this can be generated and sustained only through the unambiguous cultivation of a revolutionary love—a love that enhances our solidarity and commitment to one another, as kin and comrades in our struggle to overcome the debilitating forces of human oppression through the daily revitalization of democratic public life.

REFERENCES

Apple, M.W. (2004). *Ideology and Curriculum*. London: Routledge and Kegan Paul.

Bledstein, B.J. (1978). *The Culture of Professionalism*. New York: Norton.

Croteau, D., and W. Hoynes (2002). *Media Society: Industries, Images, and Audiences*. Los Angeles/ London: Pine Forge Press.

Croteau, D., and W. Hoynes (1994). *Invitation Only: How the Media Limit Political Debate*. Monroe, ME: Common Courage Press.

Denny, G. (1941). "Radio Builds Democracy," *Journal of Educational Sociology* 14, no. 6 (Education Turns the Dial): 370–77.

Freire, P. (1993). *Pedagogy of the City*. New York: Continuum.

Giroux, H. (2003). "Public Pedagogy and the Politics of Resistance: Notes on a Critical Theory of Educational Struggle," *Education Theory* 35, no. 1: 5–16.

Giroux, H. (2004a). "Public Pedagogy and the Politics of Neoliberalism: Making the Political More Pedagogical," *Policy Futures in Education* 2, nos. 3–4.

Giroux, H. (2004b). "Neoliberalism and the Demise of Democracy: Resurrecting Hope in Dark Times," *Dissent Voice*. Available at: http://dissidentvoice.org/Aug04/Giroux0807.htm.

Kellner, D. (1995). *Media Culture: Cultural Studies, Identity, and Politics between the Modern and the Postmodern*. London: Routledge.

Kumeh, T. (2010). "When Police Shoot and Kill Unarmed Men," *Mother Jones* (July 14). Available at: http://motherjones.com/mojo/2010/07when-police-shoot-unarmed-man-oscar-grant-verdict-Mehserle.

McChesney, R. (2001). "Global Media, Neoliberalism, and Imperialism," *Monthly Review* 52, no.10. Available at: http://www.monthlyreview.org/301rwm.htm.

McChesney, R. (1998). "Making Media Democratic," *Boston Review* (summer). Available at: http://bostonreview.net/BR23.3/mcchesney.html.

McLaren, P. (1997). *Revolutionary Multiculturalism: Pedagogies of Dissent for the New Millennium*. Boulder, CO: Westview Press.

Megwa, E.R. (2007). "Community Radio Stations as Community Technology Centers: An Evaluation of the Development Impact of Technological Hybridization on Stakeholder Communities in South Africa," *Journal of Radio Studies* 14, no. 1: 49–66.

Mwesige, P. (2009). "The Democratic Functions and Dysfunctions of Political Talk Radio: The Case of Uganda," *Journal of African Media Studies* 1, no. 2 (May): 221–45.

Shannon, P. (2007). "Pedagogies of the Oppressors: Critical Literacies as Counter Narratives." Speech presented at the Rouge Forum, March 2. Available at: http://www-rohan.sdsu.edu/~rgibson/rouge_forum/shannon.htm.

NOTES

1. See: http://www.monthlyreview.org/301rwm.htm.
2. "Who Owns the News Media," available at: http://www.stateofthemedia.org/2010/media-ownership/dashboard.php.

3. "Fear and Favor in the Newsroom," produced by Beth Sanders and Randy Baker in 1996 and narrated by Studs Terkel, provides one of the most powerfully incisive critiques of corporate control of news reporting in the United States. Unfortunately, the documentary was "turned down by virtually every entity in the PBS system. *Frontline, Point of View,* PBS's independent documentary series, and PBS itself all refused to give the show a national broadcast. Indeed, after viewing an early sample clip of the show, Mark Weiss, the Executive Producer of *Point of View,* told us P.O.V. would not be interested, because the show would not be well received in venues such as *Redbook.*" To learn more about the story of the documentary, see: http://www.albionmonitor. com/9804b/copyright/fearfavor.html and listen to a *Democracy Now!* segment about the film: http://www.democracynow.org/1997/11/18/fear_and_favor_in_the_newsroom.

4. See: http://bostonreview.net/BR23.3/mcchesney.html.

5. See: http://dissidentvoice.org/Aug04/Giroux0807.

6. Pacifica was established in the late 1940s out of the peace movement surrounding World War II. In 1949 KPFA went on the air from Berkeley, California. KPFK, in Los Angeles, was the second of what would eventually become five Pacifica stations to go on the air. See: http://www.kpfk. org/aboutkpfkpacifica-.html.

7. Alternative Radio, established in 1986, is dedicated to the founding principles of public broadcasting, which urge that programming serve as "a forum for controversy and debate," be diverse, and "provide a voice for groups that may otherwise be unheard." The project is entirely independent, sustained solely by individuals who buy transcripts and tapes of programs. See: http:// www.alternativeradio.org/.

8. See: http://kboo.fm/node/34.

9. See: http://www.wmnf.org/station/about.

10. To learn more about the work of the Grand Rapids Media Center, see: http://www.grcmc.org/.

11. See: http://www.wrfu.net/.

12. The Urbana-Champaign Independent Media Center is a grassroots organization committed to using media production and distribution as tools for promoting social and economic justice in the Champaign County area. See: http://www.ucimc.org/content/about-uc-imc.

13. See: http://www-rohan.sdsu.edu/~rgibson/rouge_forum/shannon.htm.

14. I established the Liberacion! Radio Collective with graduate students and community members. The intent was to create a space where students could be involved in the practice of public pedagogy, in conjunction with community members. For more information on the program and our radio archives, see: http://www.radioliberacion.org/.

15. See: http://www.current.org/why/why0517aufdermcafee.shtml.

16. To access the radio segment of "The Police Shooting of Kiwane Carrington," parts 1 and 2, see: http://www.radioliberacion.org/audio/Kiwane.mp3 and http://www.radioliberacion.org/ audio/Kiwane2.mp3.

17. See: http://www.facebook.com/group.php?gid=216465429114.

18. See: http://www.uigeo.org/.

19. See: http://publici.ucimc.org/.

20. See: http://www.news-gazette.com/news/courts-police-and-fire/2010-02-19/teens-fatal-shoot-ing-police-ruled-accident.html.

21. See the story filed by Brian Dolinar: http://ucimc.org/content/civil-suit-alleges-chief-finney-killed-kiwane-carrington.

22. See: http://www.news-gazette.com/opinions/editorials/2010-10-15/shooting-allegation-way-over-top.html.

23. Ibid.

24. See: http://www.prlog.org/10436445-seattlebased-hiphop-collective-project-lionheart-makes-sound-records-debut.html.

25. For an excellent historical discussion and critique of "professionalism" see: *The Culture of Professionalism: The Middle Class and the Development of Higher Education in America* by Burton Bledstein (1978).

CHAPTER 21

Political Grace and the Struggle to Decolonize Community Practice

With Zeus Yiamouviannis

[Political grace] is an act of seeking not to participate in structures that profit one but not another, to not profit at the expense of others, but to be part of that which changes the structure, that is, to be redemptive, penitent, reconciliative, revolutionary.

—WES REHBERG (1995)

Decolonization involves both engagement with the everyday issues in our own lives so that we can make sense of the world in relation to hegemonic power, and engagement with collectivities that are premised on ideas of autonomy and self-determination, in other words, democratic practice.

—CHANDRA TALPADE MOHANTY (2003)

In the midst of national and international economic malaise and its consequences, disenfranchised communities everywhere are forced to contend with conditions of political, economic and social alienation as they struggle to survive the erasure of history, the erosion of dignity and obstructions to community self-determination. Unfortunately, even within the context of well-meaning community practice, there persists a tendency toward mechanistic approaches that render the poorest and most marginalized sectors of the population silent and passive in the face of their own historical and contemporary suffering. Experiences of debilitating democracy, and the manner in which these resonate with many of the problems experienced by poor and racialized working-class communities who seek greater horizontal relationships of self-determination, serve as the impetus for this reflection on the need for a decolonizing community practice—one that cultivates political grace among those who aspire to create both social and material change.

In the U.S. today, the negative consequences of globalized neoliberal policies are devastating. The concentration of wealth and power held by the international elite is staggering. The Bush administration alone spent over $650 billion on the war in Iraq. We face unparalleled pollution of our waters and lands. Poor communities around the globe are forced to contend daily with the horrific impact of environmental destruction. Unprecedented surveillance of the population persists. An alarming consolidation of the mainstream media infuses new meaning to the old 'culture industry' thesis of the Frankfurt School. The U.S. incarceration rate—over two million—is the highest of any industrialized nation. Working-class populations across the country are experiencing the intensification of economic apartheid and resegregation of their communities. Economic safety nets for the poor are all but extinguished. Forty-five million are without health-care benefits. The disappearance of jobs in the last decade has left millions unemployed.

These conditions signal the urgent need for fundamental political change at both the structural and communal levels. But change in today's world seems especially difficult, given the manner in which corporations and public and private institutions remain entrenched in political processes of narcissistic proportions that obstruct democratic life. But all this is more that just about a bad president; it is about a bankrupt philosophy of power and its exercise within public life. This suggests pathology of power, with its elitism, arrogance and privilege that brazenly justifies and rationalizes both foreign and domestic policies of domination and exploitation, in the name of democracy and national security. And as such, its agents (whether astute or naive) arbitrate dominance and aggression as worthy and legitimate strategies that, wittingly or unwittingly, preserve the status quo. The result is the perpetuation of social and material conditions that reproduce social estrangement, human suffering and wholesale abandonment of those who pay the greatest price for the excesses of capital. Even so, capitalism fails not only because of its morally wretched impact on the poor but also its alienation of those it allegedly benefits.

Hence, it should be of no surprise that many of the ideas utilized to make sense of this phenomenon are inspired by Paulo Freire, the world-renowned Brazilian educator and the decolonizing reflections of Frantz Fanon, whose efforts sought to address the impact and limitation of social dynamics between those with power, privilege and access and those who exist as disenfranchised subjects of history. Much has transpired since Freire (1971) first wrote his seminal text, *Pedagogy of the Oppressed*, or Fanon (1952) penned *Black Skin, White Masks*, yet what seems to remain constant are the structures and politics of inequality that breed poverty and human suffering. And, despite the recent election of Barack Obama to the presidency of the United States, impoverished populations, here and abroad, will continue to face the dreadful consequences of intensifying economic exclusion for years to come. Many of these communities are also subjected to the dehumanizing effects of serving as quasi-laboratories for the benefit of corporate experiments, university researchers and professional organizers. And, although some of these efforts may have positive outcomes, more times than not, the gains are short lived, as professional community organizers take on single issue campaigns in ways that paradoxically disempower those most in need. Given rising impoverishment around the globe, there is a serious need to nurture radical organizing strategies that embody the courageous power of political grace to support both acts of resistance and revolutionary transformation.

Disrupting Community Practice

It is on the assumption—that [humans] are sheep—that the Great Inquisitors and the dictators have built their systems. More than that, this very belief that [humans] are sheep and hence need leaders to make decisions for them, has often given leaders the sincere conviction that they were fulfilling a moral duty— even though a tragic one.

—(ERICH FROMM, 1964)

Despite an espoused rhetoric of social justice in community practice, many conflicts prevail that disrupt efforts to ameliorate symptoms of inequalities within disenfranchised communities. This phenomenon is often tied to the way both "dominance" and "empathetic" approaches (Yiamouyiannis, 1998) function to disrupt community dialogue, solidarity and grassroots actions to transform conditions of poverty and alienation. Recently, for example, a number of activists and organizers came together in a small mid-western university town to work on an environmental justice project that involved a historically marginalized black working-class community.

Twenty years earlier, a major power utility plant shut its doors, leaving behind a flimsy fenced-off contaminated toxic site in this community. Over the years, a growing number of what seemed to be toxic related cancers begun to erupt all along the perimeter of the toxic waste site. In response, an official campaign was initiated by a community coalition that included a non-profit organization, some university faculty and students, and members of a grassroots community group. Unfortunately, despite an expressed commitment to the community's welfare and empowerment, it did not take long before major conflicts erupted between community organizers, over conflicting views about the best approach to contend with the issue.

The leadership of the non-profit organization (an established professional change agency) favored attacking the problem from the standpoint of a human rights campaign. Several university students working with the organization proceeded to interview residents of the area, hoping to get them on board with their particular vision. In concert, the organization's leadership publicly focused on their past successes with other health related campaigns, thereby highlighting their extensive knowledge and expertise.

However, not all of the members of the coalition were necessarily impressed by the often-touted resume of accomplishments. Instead, grassroots community members advocated for a very different approach. That is, given the long history of problems faced by this community, there was a desire to create a community-centered and decolonizing approach to carrying out the work. Grassroots community organizers called for a dialogical or (de-objectifying) approach, anchored in the individual and collective histories of the residents. This would require greater time and space for the area residents to become involved in an active process of participation and decision making. The activists and organizers who held this perspective felt that, despite the blanket of urgency draped over the toxic waste issue by the non-profit organization, it was absolutely necessary to use this opportunity for community members to establish greater political confidence and collective empowerment among themselves.

The grassroots organizers expressed an unwavering desire to bring together community concerns related to toxic waste with other significant issues of environmental racism—namely, severe unemployment, police brutality, the miseducation of children, the instrumentalizing of community by academic researchers and historical government neglect of the area. Moreover, it was deemed vitally important to recover people's histories of struggle, from which to enhance community self-determination (Darder, 2002). The hope, of course, was that community members would become better armed not only to contend with the negative impact of the utility plant on the lives of the residents and their children but to struggle together on community issues that would persist once the toxic waste issue was mediated and rectified.

The deep fundamental differences in defining both the issue and organizing approach resulted in a major rupture in the relationship of the coalition's community practice. Distrust over unilateral decisions by the non-profit organization's leadership to define the campaign as a "rights" movement intensified the debate, creating an environment in which critical dialogue was almost non-existent. To make things worse, a racializing division also resulted, with the white leadership of the non-profit organization choosing to sever its organizing relationship with several key members of the grassroots community group, who all just happened to be of color.

Objectifying "Rights"

I came into the world imbued with the will to find a meaning in things, my spirit filled with the desire to attain to the source of the world, and then I found that I was an object in the midst of other objects.

—FANON, 1967

The non-profit organization aggressively pushed for a "rights" approach, insisting this was the most effective strategy for contending with environmental issues. Their track record as an advocacy organization was used to legitimate their entitlement in directing (or controlling) the actions and decision-making of the coalition. There was no question that the nonprofit organizational leadership and staff felt comfortable and safe in their grand task as advocates of the poor. Unfortunately, the power and privilege they wielded, through the control of organizational networks and nonprofit resources, remained hugely unacknowledged even when grassroots community members objected to the disparities in power. Meanwhile, their universalizing attitudes towards human rights conveniently allowed them to "ignore the localities, particularities and daily manifestations of the oppression in their midst" (Rehberg, 1995: 85).

Another objection by grassroots organizers to an approach they saw as individualistic and objectifying was that of legal actors being prematurely summoned to take on the case of the toxic site, without community residents ever having an opportunity to come together to consider their priorities and strategies for contending with the twenty-year-old problem. In this community, longtime residents knew that legal matters had seldom favored their needs or priorities; often signaling only greater discrimination in the application of legal decisions. Hence, grassroots organizers conveyed their objections to this decision, by explaining that a "rights" solution was actually foreign to the community, and the premature implementation of its requirements could easily function to thwart other creative and more empowering solutions that could be build upon the strengths of existing communal relationships. These sentiments are summarized by Jaime Martinez Luna (2006) in his reflections on Oaxacan indigenous communities, autonomy and self-determination. "One always reasons in terms of the individual right, one never thinks of the communal right; that is to say, one always reasons in terms of the interests of an individual and it is understood that all positions derive from an individual interest. One never incorporates the possibility of understanding that the attitude is the result of a social fact, and better said communal fact, that thus merits a different treatment."

From a marginalized perspective, all "rights," including civil rights, must be social (collective) rights, since any individual right can be taken away and any individual singled out, without committed community support to protect that person. Therefore, it is the strength, acknowledgment, and dialogue of the community, which provides the protection, not abstract or legal guarantees. When, for example, a black community member is lynched by a white mob (despite laws to the contrary) and the perpetrators are exonerated by a jury of their peers, protection from further injustice and restitution of practical justice emerges from the black community's own organization, action and resistance, not external "expertise," sentiment or abstract principle. These things only have purchase when attached to a structure of power. If that power structure is embedded or invisible, as it is often with the dominant culture, it can lead its members to believe that they somehow enjoy "natural rights" or privileges. Those subordinated to the power structure know better and are in a far better position to construct rigorous, effective strategies of resistance and creativity, unclouded by liberal romanticism. This is so, because their concerns are born from a raw, more intimate, and less mediated or processed experience with the world.

From a dominant perspective and experience, "rights," even civil rights take on the character of individual rights, precisely because members are led to believe that their favored positions are a natural feature of the world. This sets up not only a discourse of "do-gooding" for liberal dominant members but one in which some kind of fault or deficiency must be imputed to the marginalized, so-called "underclass" of society. One sees this constantly in discourses in educational environments around "closing the achievement gap," whereby usually white enthusiastic young idealists try to bring hope, a joy of learning, and a prep school curriculum to transform and lift out the disadvantaged from their dire social, economic, or familial straits. If rights are an individual possession, then they become easily conflated with one's individual identity, fanning the prevalence of identity politics and single-issue voting; this further compartmentalizes and debilitates civic public action around shared concerns.

Given these concerns, insistence on a "rights" approach by the non-profit organizational leadership (more interested in accomplishing an "organizing product" than community empowerment and self-determination) served to disrupt the ability of the coalition to construct a "site of resistance" or a space of political grace (Rehberg, 1995). More specifically, this disrupted the necessary relational space for community organizers and residents to join together, across their differences, to co-create the transformation not only of the toxic site but of the community they called home. This reinforces the notion that the meanings co-created within community practices are always partial and must be understood as contingent on the lived conditions that inform their production. What this example of interrupted solidarity clearly demonstrates is the unfortunate temptation to reinscribe dominance within community practice unto those who resist mainstream definitions and solutions.

Given this discussion, it should not be surprising that a politics of expediency, prone to expert quick-fix and task driven solutions, functions as one of the cornerstones of liberal strategies to community "intervention" (the word itself connotes a "platooning" in from the outside). Rather than to seek organic opportunities for voice, participation, and social action among community members themselves, the premature leap into a well-defined "rights" campaign leads to a "true-and-tried" solution. What cannot be ignored here is that mainstream solutions anchored in a "rights" approach are often much more compelling to mainstream (often "white") community organizers, since it allows them to feel far more secure, competent, and comfortable in leading the charge. This, despite their lack of lived knowledge about how generations of racism and poverty can disable community empowerment, through contradictions, conflicts, dependencies and despair (Darder, 2008). With this in mind, both Freire and Fanon's writings reinforce the need for establishing decolonizing dynamics that instill a sense of intimacy and openness or "authentic conversation," in grappling with class, cultural, gendered and racialized differences within the context of community struggles.

In this light, our responsibility to a decolonizing practice must be connected to a consistent commitment to remain ever vigilant of self and the social and material conditions that challenge our privilege, entitlement and certainties of efficacy. This is particularly so where communities have been subjected to long-term abuses, predicated on historical legacies of genocide, slavery and colonization—with their lasting impact on both the oppressed and the oppressor. Given its emancipatory purpose, revolutionary community practice requires the exercise of an integral process—one in which the mind, heart, body and spirit are welcome in the active service of liberation. This integral dynamic generates the conditions for political grace to touch our communal exchanges. In its absence, our community practice can easily, albeit unwittingly, degenerate into acts of dominance and debilitating empathy that ultimately thwart dialogue, empowerment and social transformation.

Shattering Oppressive Economic Norms

The system we are fighting is not merely structural; it's also inside us, through the internalization of oppressive cultural norms that define our worldview. Our minds have been colonized to normalize deeply pathological assumptions.
—PATRICK REINSBOROUGH, 2004

The struggle to decolonizing community practice must unquestionably abandon mindless practices that adhere to the "American Dream." This begins with a critical interrogation of unexamined assumptions and commonsense notions about why people are poor, homeless, or unemployed, as well as challenging pre-packaged and recycled solutions to poverty based on ignorance. Such interrogations are important, given assumptions about poverty based on oppressive myths—myths which ascribe superiority, entitlement or privilege to those granted full subjecthood under norms that conserve racialized, patriarchal and capitalist desires. A decolonizing approach, on the other hand, requires that we confront misguided loyalties to economic values that normalize abject poverty, unprecedented incarceration, war policies and a host of other economically-instilled conditions of human suffering.

With this in mind, a political vision that can inform a decolonizing community practice must work to dismantle those values and assumptions that normalize colonizing dynamics. It is impossible to consider these norms effectively without attributing their stubborn persistence to the reproduction of class formation and the vastly unequal distribution of wealth. The growing gap between the rich and the poor, generated under neoliberal policies around the world, is consonant with the imperialist features of advanced capitalism.

In the U.S., we live with the overriding capitalist myth: "Free market is equal to democracy." Hence, any sort, of regulation by the public sphere is considered in the current neoliberal climate as a detriment to democratic life. The reign of the marketplace is responsible for the commodification of almost every aspect of human life. Nothing that can be converted into exchange value is sacred, leaving all up for grabs to the highest bidder. Alongside, all welfare programs have been put on the chopping block, as they are shamelessly called "a drain on the economy." Over the last twenty years, Keynesian economics, with its belief in government responsibility for its most vulnerable, has systematically eroded, as neoliberal rule intensified both nationally and internationally. The abandonment of poor racialized communities is felt in a variety of ways—gross unemployment, absence of adequate healthcare, poor education, and environmental injustices that have left many communities living in the time-bombs of toxic waste and land erosion. And when, for example, neglect of the environment results in major disasters, such as Hurricane Katrina in New Orleans, corporate pirates immediately swoop down. Inspired by their narcissistic greed, they offer a fraction of land worth to area residents, still dazed from the shock of devastation (Klein, 2007).

Speculative economic pursuits coupled with deregulation of major corporations across the country have left millions of working people in dire straits—many who at another moment in history lived the "good life." Today, the myth of the "good life" tied to consumption still gains traction in the corporate media, but the promises of neoliberal speculative schemes fall flat for the majority who became prey to the "prosperity" glitz.

In "Decolonizing the Revolutionary Imagination," Reinsborough (2004) argues that a "key to debunking the neoliberal myth of growing prosperity" is to understand through our community practice that

> None of the money circulating in the speculative economy feeds anyone, clothes anyone, nor does it provide anyone with meaningful jobs. Rather, the speculative economy is mostly just a way for rich people—through their corporate institutional proxies—to use the money they already have to make more. Moreover, this massive speculative economy is a powerful destabilizing force that threatens local economies and ecosystems, since speculation is the opposite of sustainability and encourages a deeper disconnect between ecological realities. (p. 213)

Characteristic norms of economic inequality are often enacted within community relationships that inadvertently affirm the very system they seek to challenge. The centralization of power is generally embraced at the expense of community autonomy and self-determination. People enamored by the "little kingdom" they establish become easily competitive and threatened by community people who challenge their arbitrary authority. The consequence here is that authoritarian views are preserved, reinforcing reliance on both physical and ideological relationships of dominance and control. Often media-fabricated stereotypes of "the other," fuel distortions and delusions which seep into the organizing arena, potentiating false, racialized attitudes and beliefs that further fragment community relationships, rendering cultural knowledge as irrelevant.

The far-reaching web of capital has cleverly eclipsed the relational significance and relevance of subordinate cultures, by way of messages that reinforce materialism and blind consumption as well as an unwarranted faith in the power of technology. There is no question that capitalism has effectively driven the planet closer to ecological collapse, as important support systems have been undermined by pathologies of power and hopelessly flawed values that seek to homogenize the very meaning of being human.

Most unfortunate here is the manner in which the "overconsuming class" fails to connect their affluence to the brutal poverty of three quarters of the world's population. In stark contrast, those who live in the shadows of monstrous affluence know only too well that the world remains in an economic vise (Reinsborough, 2004; Darder & Torres, 2004). By naturalizing the notion of life as toil and dreariness from which one must escape, rather than life as a blessing that inspires infinite creativity and connection, capitalist norms provide fodder for its structural and ideological machinery. If I cannot partake of political grace, deep relationships and authentic dialogues with others in community, then I am easily colonized by notions of dreariness, whose respite is fantasy and escape, either to a tropical island for vacation, or of "saving the world," or to a homogenous "American dream" peddling mechanistic formulas of consumption and work. How can I challenge the status quo if I depend upon it for my very identity, worth and sense of value? How can I say no to a system, which insists that I age and make decisions according to my exploitability—where my productivity and retirement are tied to my ability to generate quantitative profit?

There is little doubt that the Western mind is largely conditioned to enact dominion and mastery over all life, in its search to reach beyond human confusion, emotional anxieties and corporeal disruptions—including the sweaty, burping, farting, lusty body. This misguided yearning for transcendence from the earth into the heavens engenders mystifications and authoritarian fantasies of absolute control that alienate and interfere with organic relationships and ecological respect. In contrast, decolonizing approaches work to shatter social norms that displace the body and emotions in the act of knowing, in order to support communal relationships of embodied solidarity, trust and faith, shared responsibility for the welfare of the community and respect for the sacredness of all life. Within such a context, love as a vital revolutionary force infuses political grace into our community struggles, guiding us toward new possibilities for a more just world.

Political Grace and Decolonizing Community Practice

> [The human being] this vast and complex combination of pain and joy; solitary and forsaken, yet creator of all humanity; suffering, frustrated, and humiliated, and yet endless source of happiness for each one of us; this source of affection beyond compare, inspiring the most unexpected courage; this being called weak, but possessing untold ability to inspire us to take the road of honor; the being of flesh and blood and of spiritual conviction— this being is you!
>
> —THOMAS SANKARA (1990)

Paulo Freire consistently sought to ask, as should we, how those who enter oppressed communities can labor in ways that respect the wisdom, cultures and histories of the oppressed. This is particularly significant, given the mainstream culture of "expert" intervention, with its emphasis on profit, product or quick-fix solutions. Too often such efforts, inadvertently, splinter and uproot community self-determination (albeit unintentionally), as community members become colonized objects of study or organizing pawns to be instrumentalized for purposes beyond their own interests. Rather than supporting the creation of conditions for greater democratic life within oppressed communities, often practices and relationships utilized in grassroots political organizing only serve to further intensify subordination and harden inequalities. The outcome is mistrust and isolation—not just for disenfranchised communities, but also for those "experts" who in their unexamined ignorance miss precious opportunities to support collective transformation.

Hence, decolonization is necessary for all participants in a community, including those who occupy a dominant or privileged social position. One cannot effectively exorcise damaging social beliefs and habits on the personal level without practically and theoretically identifying and challenging the collective structures that give rise to their production. In this process of decolonization, both oppressor and oppressed must reclaim and reassert the primal and central value of human life. This is made more difficult by privileging a rationality which has been narrowed to exclude "subjective" qualitative experience, as simply a luxury, a diversion or a matter of inconsequential taste. This subjectivity is counter-posed with an authoritative objectivity that pretends it exists only as natural law, without human roots. Again the alienation is evident.

The rationality that sustains such alienation is by necessity emotionless and spiritless. Those that would inscribe exploitation as human nature or as necessary means to desirable "profit" must find a way to deny that suffering or other qualitative states of being or experience have any value. Indeed, these attributes might otherwise be contemplated and weighed as costs, against the supposed benefits of exploitation. In the light of full examination, many, if not most, community members would judge the personal and social costs of exploitation too high and the systems that run on them (i.e., unrestrained capitalism) as invalid. So a kind of conceptual disciplining is enacted to exclude those costs from consideration. Love, for example, is made suspect, worthless or mere grist for fantasy; uncertainty an invitation to nihilism. Trespassing into subjective or uncertain realms are discouraged or prohibited (particularly for those seen as "other"), otherwise the larger claims to order, control, and predictability might be exposed as charades, along with the authority occupying "objective" structures. Fear of difference becomes the sentinel, denial a means of self-protection. Vulnerability becomes a kind of crime or, at the very least, an act of an irrational or naive person. While, systematic cynicism reinforces hopelessness and despair.

The empowered community, embodied by political grace, threatens to undo all these pretensions. Hence, it is no wonder that systems of exploitation, including unrestrained capitalism, function to deny those collective practices which inspire political grace. Even assistance to the marginalized must reinforce dependency and resist challenges to this system—becoming a form of projection and fantasizing, whose aim is to fulfill individual narcissistic perceptions or identity about how the helper (i.e., organizer, teacher, community leader, etc.) wishes to be regarded, rather than on changing the structural problems and conditions that give rise to voicelessness, suffering or exploitation.

Hence, what gives the concept of political grace its significance in decolonizing community practice is its relational power as a catalyst for resistance and transformation. To better reckon with what this means requires us to comprehend all people as full human beings. That is, an understanding of humanity as predicated on the intersections of physical, intellectual, emotional and spiritual life. Key to this perspective is an abandonment of Western scholarly traditions that relegate to inferior status or popular metaphysics anything that cannot be directly seen and measured. In its place, a decolonizing view of life embraces all aspects of our humanity, within the relational encounters that are essential to our participation as full subjects of history (Darder, 2002).

In fact, Rehberg (1995) in *Political Grace: The Gift of Resistance* affirms, "that the gift of political grace is the offer of full participation" (p. 26) and characterizes its presence and function as a decolonizing force in the following way:

> It is an "other" which refuses categorization and systemization, rationalization, yet which phenomenally appears to assemble in ways that privilege the unprivileged. This "other" offers itself as another dimension to the …"wretched of the earth." Though it defies naming, it discloses itself while its divine aspect remains partially unrecognizable….This is grace that definitively sides with the impoverished, that impels alternative possibility from its own radical alternative, that only has power of becoming material when people act in accordance with its gift. It infuses. It interrupts. It creates coincidence. It calls, yearns, struggles to be "visible," yet cannot entirely be so because of the limitations of the phenomenal realm. (p. 22).

Political grace, then, can best be understood as an integral human experience that is the collective outgrowth of decolonizing dynamics. It constitutes an embodied force that is ever-present and exchanged freely, through relationships that embody respect and faith in the participants' capacity to name their world and, through this process, participate in transformative acts of co-creation. As a revolutionary force, shared political grace enables the establishment of "sites of resistance" where community members can reflect on their social and material conditions and grapple to find solutions, solidly anchored upon their histories, the priorities of their daily lives, and self-determined emancipatory dreams. It speaks to the enhancing power of communal experiences, which emerge freely through open, interconnected, and grounded relationships of decolonizing struggle within the process of political transformation.

Within such an understanding of community practice, all lives are acknowledged as subjects to those who live them and, thus, have the potential of inspiring and transforming others. No one is expected to be sidelined in order to assuage the narcissistic whims of another. Political grace in this context is enhanced by collective heartfelt relations that promote more equitable distribution of time, attention, material resources—and the decision-making power attached to these—is among those most affected by the structures that reproduce injustice.

At this juncture, it is helpful to note that decolonizing relationships that inspire the exchange of political grace are not necessarily neat and orderly. They often are forged within radical moments of suffering that establish on-going contexts where affirmation, challenge, critique, resistance, disagreement, anger, joy, frustration, confusion, confidence and other human expressions of naming the world are welcomed and expected, in the course of passionate engagement as responsible citizens of the world. Within the process of decolonizing community practice, both passive and active articulations of power are recognized as necessary parts of any dynamic that promotes democratic life. Unlike the "professional,"

"safe," comfortable, and carefully manicured rules of engagement of "group relations," a decolonizing dynamic supports a sacred place of convening, enlivened by
passion, desire, activity, movement, fluidity, change, fears, tensions, rage, laughter, joy, noise and tears. Accordingly, participants find "breathing room" to be, to
offer, to examine who they are—all from the authority of their lived experiences
and their process of unearthing subjugated memories.

This encompasses a collective presence that coheres and transforms not by
way of domination but by way of political grace, generated freely within all present.
In the absence of practices that humiliate and shame, freedom to exist flourishes,
as participants accept greater responsibility for naming and renaming the world—
a precious gift of life that we collectively nurture with humility and respect. In
the presence of collectively inspired power, possibilities beyond our wildest imaginings emerge, to speak, to act, to be known; for also found in the experience of
political grace is the radical courage necessary to risk the collective embrace of
life-affirming love.

Political grace is, thus, generated within recognition of the comprehensive
damage done to all members of a community when any participant is objectified.
To objectify other persons in this space is to harm them, to reduce their subjectivity to an instrument for one's own pleasure or profit. However, objectification also
precludes the humanity of the participant doing the objectifying, creating alienation and isolation. For in the process of eliminating the self-expressed subjectivity of the other and replacing it with one's own design, one eliminates relationship
and the possibility of authentic dialogue. One is walled into one's own perceptions,
desires, falsehoods acted out in a world of objects with no true human beings,
merely projected representations of humans. Therefore one becomes an object of
one's own gaze, driven by unexamined and unchallenged ideas, emanating from
a preserving self-reference to one's own humanity, obligation, and contingencies,
made void of the capacity to care or love that which resides outside the narcissistic
realm (Fromm, 1964).

Through human connections bathed in political grace, a liberatory sense of
love is generated, which is neither projection, domination, romanticism, or ideology but rather more like the sustenance water, sun, and soil give a seed. This signals
a sense of support that retains and honors the creative tension, as a precondition of
human relationships. This kind of support, in both individual and communal relationships, respects and honors the presence of an organic space of "betweeness"—
a generative gap, between our commonalities and differences—necessary for the
emergence of transformative possibilities and collective co-creation to take root
(Yiamouyiannis, 1998). In this light, our community accomplishments are collective works in the art of living, where the fuel for our co-creation is generated by

the spiritual dialectic of our multiple encounters. Community practice from this vantage point is fundamentally decolonized when we acknowledge freely that no human endeavor is ever truly the product of a sole creator.

Last but not least, a decolonizing community practice must also be tied to our capacity to bear witness to life, not as passive spectator, neutral observer, or jaded critic, but as full participant in a revolutionary process to save ourselves and each other from the hellish conditions of alienation and greed. Herein, we bear witness to suffering and beauty, to war and peace, to anguish and joy, to the living and the dying. As such, political grace emerges and regenerates through the power of our connections to one another and to the earth; to life and our inner being. Ultimately, it is this powerful force that inspires our life commitment, beyond our alienated and fractured self-absorptions; to bear witness to the wonder of our sisters and brothers; and in solidarity with them, take back the dignity, freedom and self-determination that are our only birthrights as integral human beings.

Youth Speaks! Decolonizing Community Practice in Action

Even after a document was signed proclaim we were free
You still raped our women and hung men from the trees
And yes we were strange fruit
But you'll never take our roots
We will continue to create
And maybe you will continue to hate
But that too will end up on my pen and paper
I let everyone know you are a hater

—YOUTH SPEAKS POET

The word speaks to culture, struggle, education, politics, Hip-Hop and community...informing potential...continuing our oral tradition.

—YOUTH SPEAKS WEBSITE SEE:
WWW.YOUTHSPEAKS.ORG

The communal tradition of spoken word summons the two-fold nature of resistance, which encompasses the communal embrace of political grace and new articulations of power as co-creations of new possibilities and transforming histories. First words become tools of resistance, which unmask the contradictory notions of law and justice—the gap between the legal and cultural image of justice and the practical lived reality of marginalized groups. Secondly it confirms a collaborative and horizontal empowerment, generated internally by the community and the lived experiences of its members. Radiating outward and onto the creative act, such resistance is not conferred by an orthodox hierarchical authority. Instead, it asserts its own kind of moral and historical authority to put "the system" itself on trial and under a microscope, to be probed and observed, subverting colonial dynamics of power.

The creator and cultural worker of the lyrics above, and many others like her, is part of a growing creative and collaborative movement known as *Youth Speaks*. The organization is a community, youth-inspired space (see:www.youthspeaks. org), that generates offerings of "slam poetry," a penetrating, incisive expression of lived perspectives, which challenge the gauzy fantasies peddled to youth by the commercial, economic, and political status quo. What makes this movement unique is its commitment to supporting the creative production of knowledge among its members rather than simply the typical creative space of reception/ rejection. *Youth Speaks* attempts to "shift perceptions of youth by combating illiteracy, alienation, and silence to create a global movement of brave new voices... [challenging] youth to find, develop, publicly present and apply their voices as creators of social change." What started as a community effort to involve youth has now evolved into established efforts to create a 'history department' in the Living Word Project, "using the model of performed ethnography to develop a consciousness around the social impact of historical elements that are somehow 'missing' from traditional educational texts."

The personal transformative effect this has on the *Youth Speaks* community, as well as the social effects it has for those who participates as witnesses of these co-creations is striking. Mateo, a twenty-seven-year-old Filipino American, *Youth Speaks* participant, who was recently profiled in the *San Francisco Chronicle* (Vigil, 2008), (grew from a seventeen-year-old participant of the program to a mentor and director of one of the community programs. As he puts it: "It's hard to know where I would be without poetry, but I know where I am with it....Through words, poetry has the power to change the world. You make your parents laugh and cry by the words you share with them. You vote for your president by the words they speak."

Community members of all ages, who witness the spoken word events, gain a palpable understanding of the powerful ways in which the messages, habits, and philosophies of capitalist exploitation, in particular, are experienced and challenged by the courage of transgressive youth to speak the unspoken. Where capitalism accentuates ignorance and inspires insularity—for the purposes of maximizing profit—*Youth Speaks* brings together co-creating young poets in order to deepen their awareness of self and others. They find solidarity, not just from their camaraderie but through the ways in which each is the other's witness. Through their communal relationships of affirmation and challenge, their shared passion and honesty help participants to reach more deeply into the well of their integral humanity, so they can experience the fluidity of political grace among them in order to create and express that which is most hidden and vulnerable, but often most meaningful.

Where capitalist norms engender emotional holes, deficits, doubts, insecurities, plastic pleasures, and fabricated needs to be filled by neurotic consumption, *Youth Speaks* participants explicitly challenge these manipulations, name the holes and deficits they create, and call into poetic account the personal and collective damage perpetrated upon the oppressed. For example, one poet expressed through his spoken word how body images in magazines assault his girlfriend, encouraging her to hold unhealthy attitudes about herself and affecting his ability to form deeper connections with her. What makes these young people critically conscious is that beyond their individual concerns, they know that their struggles are collective and involve the well-being of their communities. It is a sense of community wellness and health that extends beyond individual concerns into the realm of collective empowerment.

Where capitalism requires a zero-sum, homogeneity of value—a fabricated "single scale scarcity"—*Youth Speaks* promotes heterogeneity and abundance as a necessary precondition of good spoken word. There is a sense of understanding that the word is born long before it is spoken (as Freire so rightly claimed) and encompasses the interconnectedness of communal distinctions. Different voices, different subjects, different ethnicities, different experiences, different sexualities, all express value as they are shaped and experienced coherently, through a free and ever-changing poetic medium of spoken word. No matter the source, a poem's ability to evoke and call into reality powerful truths that transcend the individual poet is not only what creates value and meaning but what enhances the communal relationships that dialectically nurture political grace.

Inherent in capitalist relations is treatment of members from disenfranchised communities as mere recipients, hardened passive objects at the service of capital rather than sentient and actively engaged citizens of the world. *Youth Speaks* supports youth as co-creators, as sensual subjects of history, through enacting their collective power and capacity for co-creation and collaboration within a dynamic process of community life. The *Youth Speaks* community is composed of passionate initiators and active witnesses, in stark contrast to community projects that favor the passive spectators and referential servants.

The norms inspired by capitalism emphasize physical and/or quantitative material as holder and arbiter of value. *Youth Speaks* emphasizes the emotional as the holder and channel of value. Where capitalism feeds on fear, secrets, and privileged, surveilled access, the community of *Youth Speaks* poets and participants feeds on courage and transparency, in the process of revealing their hidden truths, struggles, hopes and dreams within the human condition. Where capitalism promotes a splitting apart of the public and private, in its effort to privatize and shatter the public, *Youth Speaks* stridently encourages the sacred alliance of public and private, in its bold public offerings of searing and poignant insights, traumas and triumphs.

The spoken word of *Youth Speaks* poets shatters those myths of capital that deceptively promote leisure and untroubled neutrality as exemplars of the "good life." Instead, the *Youth Speaks* community offers troubled waters of nitty-gritty realities that bare witness to our complex humanity, incited by revolutionary imaginings inspired by passion and purpose. This is a courageous community of youth that seeks to remain vigilants, rather than to escape into fantasy and magical thinking as the "medium" for coping or deriving pleasure. They reject capitalism's relational investment in producing remoteness from bourgeois assumptions about a cruel, dreary, or boring world. Decolonizing communities like *Youth Speaks* thrive on intimacy and presence; moving closer to the subject and one another, not farther. Inherent here is an intuitive impulse within this community of youth that sparks them to fend off their objectification and alienation, by delighting in the power of communal presence and the precious gift of being alive.

Political Grace and the Courage to Love

> The Master's tools will never dismantle the Master's house.
>
> —AUDRE LORDE

Youth Speaks, as a "site of resistance" exemplifies one of the most salient contemporary responses to Audre Lorde's often recited dictum. Youth in these communities, along with those who witness and support their efforts, re-assert the communal power of oral tradition in their own cultures and, as such, the transformative potential of political grace, unavailable to the oppressed in the "Master's house." *Youth Speaks*, Oaxaca's indigenous people, independent media groups, and many other community-grounded communities and organizations around the world recognize that liberation is neither a process that can be guaranteed nor an object that can be possessed. Instead, it demands our full presence and the collective courage of political grace born from resistance and struggle. Only in this way might we, together, forge the wisdom, faith, and strength of revolutionary consciousness to leap into the fire of human anguish and suffering, so that we might liberate ourselves and one another from the colonizing legacy of Western imperialism.

Just as young cultural workers of *Youth Speaks* reach out to one another, utilizing the tools of their own histories and lived experiences, we too must find the courage to struggle in solidarity to break with the alienating morass of capitalism that deadens our lives and betrays our revolutionary dreams. Our collective struggles to decolonize community practice are, intimately, tied to our personal struggles to liberate and awaken our minds, bodies, hearts, and spirits to the communal dance of life—a dance inspired by political grace and our renewed commitment to the power of love.

REFERENCES

Darder, A. (2008). "Pedagogy of the Oppressed Revisited in Public I." Urbana, IL: CU Independent Media Center, 11.

Darder, A. (2002). *Reinventing Paulo Freire: A Pedagogy of Love*. Boulder, CO: Westview.

Darder, A., and R.D. Torres (2004). *After Race: Racism after Multiculturalism*. New York: New York University Press.

Fanon, F. (1967). *Black Skin, White Masks*. New York: Grove.

Fanon, F. (1952). *Peau Noire, Masques Blancs*. Paris: Seuil.

Freire, P. (1971). *Pedagogy of the Oppressed*. New York: Seabury.

Fromm, E. (1964). *The Heart of Man*. New York: Harper and Row.

Klein, N. (2007). *The Shock Doctrine: The Rise of Disaster Capitalism*. New York: Metropolitan Books.

Martinez Luna, J. (2006). "Communality and Autonomy: A Compilation of Three Essays and Two Declarations by Indians of the Northern Sierra of Oaxaca." Translated by G. Salzman and N. Davies. Available at: http://site.www.umb.edu/faculty/salzman_g/Strate/Commu/index.htm.

Mohanty, C.T. (2003). *Feminism without Borders: Decolonizing Theory, Practicing Solidarity*. Durham, NC, and London: Duke University Press.

Rehberg, W. (1995). *Political Grace: The Gift of Resistance*. Ph.D. dissertation, State University of New York at Binghamton.

Reinsborough, P. (2004). "Decolonizing the Revolutionary Imagination: Values Crisis, the Politics of Reality, and Why There's Going to Be a Common-Sense Revolution in This Generation." In D. Solnit (ed.), *Globalize Liberation*. San Francisco: City Lights, 161–211.

Sankara, T. (1990). *Women's Liberation and the African Freedom Struggle*. New York: Pathfinder.

Vigil, D. (2008). "Youth Speaks Encourages Young Poets," *San Francisco Chronicle*, March 30. Available at: http://www.sfgate.com/cgi-bin/article.cgi?f=/ c/a/2008/03/30/PK4TVMO2S. DTL.

Yiamouyiannis, Z. (1998). *tt* Doctoral dissertation, Cultural Foundations of Education and Curriculum, Syracuse University (UMI No. 9842213).

From Madness to Consciousness

Redemption through Politics, Art and Love

Carmel Borg and Peter Mayo

In times of crisis, we summon up our strength. Then, if we are lucky, we are able to call every resource, every forgotten image that can leap to our quickening, every memory that can make us know our power.

MURIEL RUKEYSER[1]

An Interview with Antonia Darder

Antonia Darder is professor of Educational Policy Studies and Latino/a Studies at the University of Illinois, Urbana-Champaign. Her current work focuses on comparative studies of racism, class and society. Her teaching examines cultural issues in education with an emphasis on identity, language, and popular culture, as well as the foundations of critical pedagogy, Latino studies, and social justice theory. Over the years, Professor Darder has also been active in a variety of Latino/Chicano grassroots efforts tied to educational rights, worker's rights, bilingual education, women's issues, and immigrant rights. Her interview touches on some of her personal and community-oriented struggles.

Excavating one's life experiences could be a very painful endeavor. Why did you decide to answer our questions?

I was not born to a family where questions of social struggle or deep critical reflections fuelled the din of dinner conversations. Instead, I was a child born of the "underclass." It is not a place that can easily or honestly be romanticized—not if one has known the anguish and torment of its shadows. Or lived the mounting tensions of an everyday where surveillance in a million different forms is commonplace. It is a prison of another sort, camouflaged behind the white sheet of political scriptures proclaiming "all men are created equal" and "justice and liberty for all." It is a place of tremendous fear and despair, where daily survival is at best dubious. A place that we may be tempted to recall as more benign, so that we need not return to the pain, even as memory. In this no-person-land, chaos and anguish are the direct outcome of contentious social, political, and economic forces that exert their brutal pressure upon the impoverished, while all along, as William Ryan so rightly attested, employing self-righteous moralism to blame the poor for their absence of wealth, power and knowledge. Yet, it cannot be forgotten that the madness that ensues from the oppressed and forgotten, as Frantz Fanon so eloquently argued, is nothing more than the normal psychological response of people driven to the edge.

I pronounce these words not as one who has been a good reader of theory, or one blessed with compassion to empathize, but rather a woman who has known the edge of American life. So it is, that my story is about a long struggle to decolonize my mind and liberate my body from the internalized maladies of childhood. But it is about much more. It is an unlikely tale about a displaced woman's tenacious confrontation with the contradictions of U.S. liberalism and capitalist greed. Indeed, my rage clamored first to enter, then to shatter, and finally to dissolve all inkling of oppression that crossed my path. Naively, I often forgot the power of loyal institutional gatekeepers, men and women of every color and persuasion, who safeguard the doors of the empire, refusing to surrender the unrighteous power wielded over the lives of so many.

This response is a first attempt to mine the recesses of a life filled with so much conflict, pain and disappointment—but still much love. How much do I expose? What do you want to know? What do I have the courage to say, despite the humiliating critics perched on the wall of disdain? Can I step fully into the jagged and gritty humanity of a woman who loves, hates, cries, envies, despairs, fights, hopes in the everyday? How exactly do I begin to make sense of my life and my evolution as an activist scholar? How did I move from madness to consciousness?

It is difficult for me to say if I chose my life as an activist or if my life as an activist chose me. Yet, for some of us, there is no choice, if we are to find our dignity and persevere. Perhaps, it is best to say that my life has been a true dialectic—choosing each step as it was choosing me. For many years, I was too young or naive to be cognizant of this powerful relationship. But today I embrace my life fully knowing, as did Karl Marx, that we make history as much as we are made by history—which requires us to remain ever vigilant and yet humble. No doubt, Antonio Machado's often-recited mantra "el camino se hace al andar,"[2] resonates well with my life, although the path upon which I've walked has seldom been entirely of my own making. I say this in recognition that our personal histories are always tied to the larger social, political and economic realities of the time. None of us lives in a vacuum. Mine is a history of struggle and resistance, in which the politics of colonialism, capitalism, migration, racism, and sexism have been instrumental to my understanding of the world and my emancipatory efforts as a working-class feminist, living the many contradictions of the Puerto Rican Diaspora. As such, mine is a life often betrayed by translation.

Where and when did your life journey begin?

They say that witches are born on days when the sun is shining in the sky, while the rain showers down on the earth. I was born, on such a day, in Vega Baja, a poor rural community in Puerto Rico, in the midst of the McCarthy era and the Korean War. My birth in 1952 was the result of a liaison between a poor nineteen-year-old woman from Vega Baja and a 52-year-old wealthy, married man from Arecibo. The story goes that my poor grandmother and wealthy father entered into a financial agreement in which my mother was "sold" to him as his mistress in exchange for a monthly stipend to support my mother's family.

Just prior to this transaction, my mother had lost her fiancé in the Korean conflict. He was a young, nineteen-year-old, Puerto Rican man who had been deployed immediately after his enlistment into combat. Sad and despondent over her lover's death, my mother fought with my grandmother over the transaction. Eventually, she acquiesced, seeing few alternatives for her life. Hence, her relationship with my elderly father were initiated purely on economic terms for the exchange of sexual favors. The loss of her early romance and the resulting mismatched liaison with my father were to leave an enduring mark on my mother's life.

The 1950s were the era of "Operation Bootstrap" on the island, a U.S. public policy initiative. A primary objective of the initiative was to reduce poverty in Puerto Rico. Overpopulation was deemed the culprit of the island's problems, while the disastrous impact of U.S. economic policies was left virtually unaddressed. Two state-sponsored tactics were widely enacted. The first was the mass migration of Puerto Ricans to large U.S. urban centers. So successful was this effort that by the 1960s one-third of the colony's population had been relocated to the mainland. The legacy of this mass migration is obvious today, with as many Puerto Ricans living in the Diaspora, as on the island. The second tactic was the mass sterilization of Puerto Rican women. By the 1970s, over thirty-five percent of all Puerto Rican women of my mother's generation had been sterilized.

So it came to pass that my mother at twenty-one was sterilized immediately following my sister's birth—a procedure orchestrated by my well-connected father, who already had no intention of continuing his relationship with my mother. Unwilling to leave his wife, my father once again used his government connections to obtain inexpensive airfare tickets for my mother, my sister and me to leave the island. With our departure, we left behind not only our extended family but all the familiar sounds, sensations, and beingness of a cultural milieu in which we belonged, along with a lived connection to a history that was to elude me throughout most of my life.

What were your first years of the Diaspora like?

We arrived in Chicago during the winter of 1954, remaining in the area less than six months. The inhospitable cold of the Midwest winter and difficulty finding full-time employment caused my mother much unhappiness with our conditions in Chicago. Hoping that things would improve on the West Coast, my mother desperately pulled together the money to purchase one-way airline tickets to Southern California, where two years earlier my grandmother had migrated.

Life in East Los Angeles, however, also proved to be a hardship. We lived off and on with my grandmother or moved from room to room for years, as my mother tried to find a place to settle down. My mother alternated between living on welfare and working in the sweatshops of Santee Street in the Los Angeles garment district. When on welfare, we lived in fear that the county social worker would show up unexpectedly and discover my mother was living with a man or that she was making a little extra money sewing for the neighbors—both "justifiable" reasons for terminating all welfare benefits from the State. When working in the factory, my mother spent long hours hunched over a sewing machine in a dirty, dusty, and crowded warehouse. In this way, she earned the piecework tickets that would be added up at the end of the week to determine her pay—pay without benefits of any kind. Occasionally in the chaos of her life, she would lose or misplace the little tickets. Pandemonium would strike! My knees would shake, as I watched my mother anxiously ransack the house. Furiously, she would fling things about, cursing loudly, her rage oozing from her eyes—no tickets meant no pay.

It was common for my mother to arrive home tired and angry at the exploitation and degradation she felt at the factory. "I'm nothing but a slave chained to a machine," she would yell. She thought of herself as the mule of the boss who made the money and paid the workers pennies for their hard labor. Yet in spite of these conditions, I recall several occasions when the union tried to organize workers in the factories where my mother worked. The workers, who were mostly women and undocumented, were intimidated by the bosses who threatened them with loss of their livelihood or a call to immigration. Unfortunately, on every occasion, the workers acquiesced, leaving them with a greater sense of powerlessness.

Along with the exhaustion and frustration felt at work, my mother's romantic relationships were tumultuous, with a long string of men coming and going throughout my childhood. The unfortunate conditions of poverty and her many troubled romances contributed greatly to my mother's disabling anxieties. Her pains and maladies are consistent with those of so many disenfranchised people—namely, depression, alcoholism, diabetes and emotional and mental instability. Yet despite her difficulties and emotional suffering, my mother was unable to secure treatment for her alcoholism or for her violent outbursts against her children or anyone that happened to cross her path. Hers was a miserable existence—an ambitious, intelligent girl forced to drop out of school to help support her family. Like so many oppressed women, she found herself imprisoned by the futility of underclass hopelessness, discouragement, and despair.

The conditions of poverty and injustice were marked on my mother's body—her sallow swollen skin, the ceaseless tension in her face, the dark circles around her eyes, and the brusque and impatient manner of interacting with others. Her features became emblazoned in my mind. Her uncontrollable rage and violence terrified me. Yet, the abuse I endured at the hands of my mother was the same violence she had received from her mother. If all this was not bad enough, both my sister and I became victims of child sexual abuse, perpetrated by several of my mother's lovers. I was molested for three years, from ages six to nine, and my sister was molested once when she was eleven.

My sister's molestation was to mark a pivotal moment in my life. During the years that I was molested, I had been too terrified to speak. I lived those years silently imprisoned in a surreal existence, in which I felt dirty, violated, isolated and unprotected. So, when my sister told me she had been molested, I felt my fury surge and I jumped to her defense. At thirteen years old, I summoned all the courage that my fury could harness to tell my mother—who I deeply feared—that her boyfriend had sexually molested my sister. Unable to save myself when I was younger, I now felt a sense of vindication. For the first time, I took a stance against my mother's blazing emotional fortress. Unfortunately, it was a very short-lived victory.

Sadly, for my sister and me, my mother regrouped quickly. She let the man back into our house and intimidated us into "forgiving" her boyfriend, because this was the Christian thing to do. Simultaneously, she began to send us off to a Seven Day Adventist Church (although we were Catholic) with a co-worker on Saturdays for religious instruction—as if my sister and I were in need of salvation. In the absence of my mother's protection, my sister and I grappled for footing. The scars of violence and emotional neglect in our childhood, not surprisingly, followed us into adulthood. It took decades before I could talk with my mother frankly about the physical and sexual abuse of those early years. For my sister, this was never to happen.

What does early schooling mean to you?

In the midst of the instability and isolation of our experience as Puerto Rican migrants living far from the majority of our extended family, school represented a mixed bag. Upon entering school, I felt more lost than ever. I only spoke Spanish and was unable to understand the teachers. Only my fellow classmates spoke Spanish, but this was the 1950s and we were prohibited from speaking Spanish in school—a linguistically oppressive practice that in U.S. schools seems to be gaining popularity. Consequently, I began to develop a terrible ambivalence about my language and my identity as a Puerto Rican. Constantly moving from school to school, I remember the humiliation I felt when I tried to speak English and the teacher would harshly correct me or the other children would laugh. Even my last name, Darder, became an issue. It was always mispronounced and I hated the sound. Even when I tried to correct my teachers, they insisted on anglicizing the pronunciation, which made it seem that I didn't even know how to pronounce my own name. This made me feel stupid and unwelcome.

Yet, school also represented a sort of respite from the pain and confusion at home. School was a place where I didn't have to worry about being beaten or sexually molested. As I learned English, I worked hard to adapt to the expectations of my teachers and peers. On a couple of occasions, I had teachers who took interest in my learning and my abilities. However, despite my enthusiasm, I often felt out of sync with teacher expectations. So, in many ways, I lived two lives. One of the eager child anxious to learn at school, while contending with the racialized attitudes of my teachers who knew little about (im)migrant Spanish-speaking children. The other of the very frightened and insecure child at home, fending off the attacks of a mother completely unprepared to ward off the hostility and brutality of a deeply racialized and unequal society.

This duplicity, however, actually served as an effective survival mechanism to withstand the cognitive dissonance of a child barely able to critically decipher the world around me. This tactic worked until middle school. In primary school, I worked to excel and did well. During recess and lunchtime, I loved to play kickball and basketball. The movement of my body released my anxieties and, for a moment, let me feel free. However, conditions in my life began to deteriorate at home during my early adolescence. My mother was hospitalized several times for schizophrenia. The more demanding curriculum of middle school required more concentration. The opportunities for running loose in the schoolyard disappeared. I became depressed and my grades suffered. Yet, no one in the school seemed to notice. No one ever asked about my home life nor inquired into the changing quality of my academic work. In many ways, I felt invisible and without direction.

In eighth grade I was assigned to an art class. I was excited by the possibility that I would learn to paint and draw. In kindergarten, painting was my favorite time. In third grade, a teacher asked us to draw a picture of ourselves in the future. I drew myself as a painter in Paris. I don't even know where this image came from. Maybe an old movie I had seen somewhere. My mother, however, did not approve of my interest in art. When ready to sign my middle school eighth-grade course list, she became undone when she saw I was assigned an art class. In her mind, we were poor and I had to learn something that would help me get a job. This was the first and last time that I remember my mother actually calling the school. In her deeply accented English, she cursed out the counselor and demanded that I be changed to a typing class. Needless to say, I hated typing class and to this day can only peck away at the keyboard.

How did you "awake to politics"?

It is important to note that some of the tensions and frustrations of this period of my life were also linked to what was happening on the streets. At age ten, we moved from East Los Angeles to an area now known as South Central Los Angeles. The face of poverty was present everywhere—children and adults in worn tattered clothing, tired drawn faces, drunks visible on the street, youths fighting in the alley, and even a junkie on the stairwell shooting up.

On television, civil rights and Vietnam War images were juxtaposed. In 1964, the Watts riots erupted around us. African-American organizers came knocking at our door warning us that the riots were going to happen and that we should remain indoors. We were afraid but survived the burning and the closure of businesses in our neighborhoods. Again, we watched on television the images of burning buildings and the convulsion of people on the streets. Through it all, I found silence at home and silence at school. Few conversations provided us with a real understanding of what was happening in our community. We just knew that we were suddenly afraid, and then the fear dissipated as life re-normalized. And, in spite of all the official promises made following the Watts Riots very little seemed to change in our tiny corner of the world.

Overall, my family was politically invisible and powerless. In fact, the only presidential election in which my mother voted was that of John F. Kennedy. Of all the national political campaigns, Kennedy's was the only one in my childhood that inspired the wide participation and support of disenfranchised people. For a moment, that campaign touched and inspired poor, uneducated people of color like my mother to believe that another world was possible—a world where their presence would count. The fact that Kennedy was a member of the ruling elite seemed overshadowed by a campaign of vitality and a glimmer of hope that life in the barrios and ghettos could be transformed. Along the same vein, when Kennedy was assassinated everyone around me mourned, but for many their grief turned into political cynicism and despair—a despair that my mother was to carry with her to her grave. Not only had she lost hope in electoral politics, she felt duped and betrayed by a political system that she saw working for the rich, while leaving those most in need to fend for themselves.

By the late 1960s, my mother's rejection of all political activism echoed the fatalism that Paulo Freire so poignantly described in many of his writings. With the deaths of Martin Luther King Jr., Malcolm X, and Robert Kennedy, along with the atrocities of the Vietnam War, my mother's contempt for all political activism solidified. Not surprisingly, my early involvement in community politics was discouraged and maligned at home. To my mother, politics and art were a complete waste of time—neither could pay the rent nor relieve our poverty. Perhaps, it was no coincidence that later in my rebelliousness I readily embraced both political work and art as a way to deal with the pain and anguish in my life.

Unhappy in a home filled with constant turmoil and chaos, I turned my attention to a boyfriend who was six years older and who my mother forced me to marry at sixteen, for fear that I would become pregnant. Although a coerced and misguided action, this proved to be an effective escape from the insanity of my mother and the futility of life on Magnolia Street. But shortly after my wedding, I became pregnant. Eager to continue my studies, I stayed in school and managed to earn my high school diploma before my son was born. I attended Whitney High School, a continuation program for students with behavioral problems and pregnant teens.

The control of a poor woman's reproductive rights in the U.S. was not unlike the colonial legacy of my mother's generation in Puerto Rico. For example, when seeking contraceptive advice, I was simply prescribed birth control pills, without clear information. When the pills caused nausea, I stopped taking them and immediately became pregnant. After the birth of my second child, an IUD was inserted at the county clinic, to prevent conception. I experienced much bleeding and discomfort. Yet when I complained, the doctor told me that it was "normal" and to just take a couple of aspirin for the pain. Within a month, I had become pregnant again. Upon examination, the doctor was unable to find the device. Rather, than carry out further examination, he insisted that it must have been expelled without my awareness despite my efforts to protest his conclusion. Three years later, when I was suffering from pain and distension in the abdomen, a simple X-ray revealed that the IUD had perforated my uterus and become lodged in the abdominal cavity. This now required major surgery. The attending physician at the time treated me like an idiot. How could I have not known that the IUD had become dislodged? Upon the birth of my third child, I was lectured in the hospital about either staying on birth control pills or being sterilized. Given my mother's history, I refused a tubal ligation and accepted the pills. It was in nursing school that I learned about natural means for contending with unwanted pregnancy. However, even in this female-dominated training context, there was an implicit message that poor women were not to be trusted with control of our bodies, and hence this method was heavily criticized and discouraged.

Although by age 20 I had given birth to three children, my hope of attending college remained an ever-burning desire. I still believed that education was the only path out of the poverty that I had known all my life. In fact, in the only letter I was ever to receive from my father, he urged me to get an education because it was "lo unico que nadie te puede quitar."[3] My mother repeatedly urged me to get an education so that I would "not be a slave" like her. I decided education would provide me with the tools to help myself and to struggle for change. There is no question that the liberating messages and actions attributed to the student walk-outs in Los Angeles, the growing antiwar movement, and the civil rights initiatives across the nation had an enormous impact on my aspirations and dreams as a young woman. Unfortunately, my aspirations were not shared by my husband, a working class Mexican-American man, who although kind, manifested recalcitrant patriarchal expectations—a wife should take care of the home, cook the meals, and tend to the children. This conflict caused me much frustration and anger. I acted it out by becoming involved with a college student and separating from my husband of six years. Hence my academic dreams and immaturity to contend with our difference led to a divorce, and thus began my life as a single parent and full-time student.

Your profile as an academic is complemented by a life dedicated to community activism. What were the highs and lows of your experience within different communities?

At 21, I enrolled into a community college with the hope of becoming a medical doctor in the community. I was quickly discouraged, however, by a counselor who authoritatively pronounced to me that "You people do much better in vocational programs," urging me instead to earn a certification as a licensed vocational nurse. Yet another counselor advised me to consider the registered nursing program because I was a single parent and ten years of medical school would be too difficult for my children to endure. Taking his suggestion, I completed the registered nursing program at a community college. While a student there, I became involved in student and community activism and worked as a peer counselor for students with personal histories similar to my own. Community college was, indeed, a blessing. For given my economic conditions and lack of knowledge regarding higher education, it served as an important entry point to begin my academic journey.

After graduation from nursing school, I worked as a pediatric nurse with children and their families in a hospital setting. Unhappy with the racism and cultural insensitivity I both experienced and witnessed among the medical staff, I opted for a pay cut, left the hospital, and went to work for the Head Start Program. At Head Start, a federally funded educational preschool program for low-income children, I provided basic health assessments and educational information for Latino children and their parents. I believe it was during this time that my community activism deepened, an activism rooted in my struggle to create options for families with scant resources—families very similar to my own. I also became acutely aware of the manner in which the early childhood curriculum and assessment tools used were actually complicit with the program's inculcation of middle-class, market values upon young impressionable minds. Through my practice at Head Start, I came to recognize how the middle-class values of parent education program were unrealistic and inappropriate for poor working-class Latino families, as they unwittingly reinforced a message of cultural deficit. This stirred me to begin advocating in new ways, recognizing my interventions demanded greater attention to cultural and class issues if my efforts were to create the conditions for families to empower themselves.

Within a few years, I began working towards a degree as a marriage and family therapist, while employed at a community mental health centre. As part of my duties, I counseled Spanish-speaking clients who came to the clinic and worked in the community with immigrant children and their families. My emphasis was to reconstruct parent education programs to meet the needs of working class

Latino families. During that time, I conducted "rap groups" in public schools with Spanish-speaking children, as they struggled to integrate themselves into the mainstream of classroom life. I also became active in anti-racism work, conducting workshops for counselors, teachers, and community workers. Outside of my practice as a therapist, I served on the staff of an alternative community newspaper and was involved with an anti-nuclear organization, organizing and demonstrating against the proliferation of nuclear arms and power plants, with my three children in tow.

There is no doubt that my children played a significant role in my development as a woman and an activist. As a young mother, they anchored me and kept me focused. With them, I hoped to redeem my life, by working to change the course of our destinies. When my children were born, I made a deliberate decision that the child abuse that I had known would not be repeated. However, to keep such a promise would take more than my resolve—I would have to face the madness from which I was running. So not surprisingly, in an early relationship, I saw the physical and emotional abuse being reproduced in front of my eyes by a partner. Again, the fear of an earlier time consumed me. It took me several years to completely extricate myself from this destructive liaison—something that I was able to accomplish only with therapeutic intervention. In the process, I set out very consciously to create an atmosphere of open communication, one in which my children might experience the love and security that I had never known. As I struggled to be a good mother, I came to learn so much from my children about human resiliency and the meaning of unconditional love—a love where intimacy, honesty, and commitment are central. Moreover, it was my children who gave me the strength to struggle internally with my personal demons and gave me the impetus to struggle politically out in the world. Fighting against the suffering and injustices I witnessed all around me became a very personal affair. I wanted a different world for all children but most tangibly for my own.

Meanwhile, my work with community organizations and schools revealed more clearly how racialized, gendered, and homophobic class relations were inextricably linked to the reproduction of inequality and social exclusion, particularly in poor communities. More importantly, I began to understand the manner in which "professionals" not only manage and control working class populations but also buffer and mask the manner in which ruling class interests reproduce economic and political impoverishment. As I attempted to challenge and change the mental health practices of the organization, I experienced much resistance from the Anglo director and clinical supervisors. Agency officials insisted that I follow traditional protocols dictated by institutional mental health practices— approaches that were not only inappropriate but proved to be further oppressive to the lives of poor Latino men and women. Latino bilinguals and Spanish-speaking clients who came to the center were generally court-referred for alcoholism, child abuse, or domestic violence. Unfortunately, the treatment protocols utilized by mainstream therapists at the clinic often did little to build on the existing cultural knowledge and strengths of Latino clients. Rather, their interventions further alienated Latino clients from the very therapists who supposedly were there to "help" them. During my tenure at the mental health center, I consistently urged officials to hire more Spanish-speaking mental health workers with an intimate understanding of Latino cultural values and knowledge of the immediate community.

After several years of struggling vociferously over these issues, I found myself marginalized by the administrative and clinical staff. Although initially praised for my therapeutic prowess, when I began to question the legitimacy of mainstream intervention strategies used with Latino families, I was not only characterized as a political radical, my mental stability was called into question. Upon completing my Master's degree and receiving my license as a therapist, I decided to leave the mental health center to seek employment where my knowledge, skills and sensibilities would be more welcomed. In an effort to channel my energies into community work, I took a job at a family support center in East Los Angeles that focused on mental health intervention for child physical and sexual abuse. Although Latinos directed the organization and attempted to conduct culturally appropriate intervention practices, major difficulties existed in the center's advocacy efforts within schools and the courts. This led me to critically question if mental health practice was the most effective political venue for working toward minority community empowerment. Hence, my concern for Latino community empowerment led me to accept a new position with a Latino non-profit organization working for the rights of Latino and immigrant Spanish-speaking populations.

How do you reconcile politics with art and spirituality?

This was an enormously creative and vibrant moment in my life. In fact, it was during these years that I began painting, writing poetry, and learning music through a completely organic process. My artistic expression proved to be my salvation through many difficult personal and political moments. I became immersed in the poetry of Jose Marti, Julia Burgos, Pablo Neruda, Nikki Giovanni, Maya Angelou, Rumi and others. I began to develop as a poet through my participation in a weekly barrio writers' workshop for Chicano/ Latino activist writers in Los Angeles organized by Luis Rodriguez and the late Manazar Gamboa. Music was always a mainstay in my life, since my early years dancing, singing, or lip-syncing to the music of Celia Cruz, the Grand Combo, Tito Puente, The Temptations, Martha and the Vandelas, the Beatles, Janis Joplin, the Rolling Stones, and later Bob Marley and Peter Tosh. With friends, I learned a little percussion and began writing simple songs of struggle and love. My painting literally began after my first visit to the La Casa Azul, the Frida Kahlo museum in Coyoacan. As I walked through the house, I became completely swept away by her paintings and the stories of her life. Similar to Kahlo, my deep anguish found in painting a medium in which to project my fears, angers, hopes, and political vision. From that time on, my artistic expression became central to my survival and to how I came to experience my aesthetic relationship to the world, as an educator and political activist.

My conscious spiritual quest also began during the early 1980s. As a child I had reached beyond our immediate tangible existence, to find solace in my loneliness. But catechism classes at Resurrection Parish had rung hollow in the midst of the turmoil at home. Perhaps the memories of that time prevented me from discovering real meaning in the Catholic Church. Now as a young adult, I sought more earnestly to explore spirituality and its role in both my daily life and political work. I read books on Zen Buddhism, Taoism, shamanism, Santeria, and indigenous spirituality. Over the next twenty years, I would become involved with a variety of spiritual traditions, searching to reconcile the anger, pain, conflict, and anguish within. I attended prayer circles, sun dances, moon meditations, vision quests; I danced, I prayed, I sat alone in the dark. But just as earnestly, I sought to integrate my intellectual, emotional, physical and spiritual faculties in my revolutionary practice and political vision of society—a daunting project in the midst of radical political ideas that rejected the legitimacy of such a quest.

Politics, art and spirituality evolved as parallel dimension within me. Art and spirituality teachings gave me an inward focus, politics an outward focus; all providing me with the sustenance to interrogate the contradictions, to speak the unspeakable, to persist even when all seemed lost. In many ways, this intermingling gave the artist and poet a place to exist. From my outrage and anguish, I struggled to create beauty and possibility. The spiritual cast a light within. The political cast a light on the world. These interacting forces, now, exist dialectically. Politics, art and spirituality intermingle in my life, rooting out my inconsistencies and humbling me to see the poet in every life—keeping my life supple and fluid, even in the most disheartening times.

Your passage to academia followed a period of political conflict and strife. Can you describe the period in question?

As director of the community agency, I worked with others to develop a popular education program for children and adults, while simultaneously learning to raise funds to expand the organization. I became more politically involved with efforts related to worker rights, bilingual education, women's rights, and immigrant rights. I participated in a multitude of political projects, from street demonstrations against U.S. intervention in El Salvador and Nicaragua to community forums on education and cultural festivals that celebrated Latino community life and political solidarity. We organized the Latino community against land developers, in support of bilingual education, and to demand health services for impoverished residents in the city. For several years my work with the organization seemed tremendously successful. I felt happy and extremely fulfilled. However, in the third year of my tenure all hell broke loose!

In 1985, the organization lost several important sources of funding which required the difficult task of cutting programs and reducing the staff. Upset by how the crisis was handled, some of the staff became disgruntled and broke off, staging a series of protests. I was shocked by the actions taken against me and felt tremendously betrayed. Suddenly, all that I had worked so hard to accomplish for the organization and the community appeared to be in ruins. A campaign of harassment was launched against me, using the Spanish media and the local newspaper (which quickly obliged). Wherever I was asked to speak or perform my poetry, the event organizers received phone calls slandering my personal and political integrity and threatening a boycott of the event. This was probably one of the darkest moments in my life. In retrospect, I recognize that given the difficulty of what was occurring within the organization, I became immobilized with fear and failed to create the conditions for sufficient dialogue among the staff before decisions were made regarding the crisis—an error in judgment that I will always regret.

Nevertheless, there is little doubt that the viciousness with which I was persecuted and attacked, by people whom I considered to be my comrades, was equivalent to a witch-hunt. This caused me great turmoil and anguish and its negative impact on my self-esteem and confidence, given my personal history, took years to overcome. Over time, many comrades that were initially swept up by this vendetta returned to apologize. Some actually spoke of both the inherent sexism (a woman in leadership in a traditionally male-dominated arena) and the sectarianism (a Puerto Rican working in a predominantly Chicano community) utilized to fuel the campaign against my work. They noted that I had been attacked in a manner that seldom is experienced by men. In fact, the campaign never targeted any of the men who were also involved in the decision-making process of the organization. In an effort to assist the organization to regain some equilibrium and to personally recover from the blows, I decided to remain for another year trying to pick up the pieces of the fiasco, while beginning a doctoral program in education.

From 1982–1986, I taught courses in Chicano literature, bicultural development, and anti-racism as an adjunct professor in a variety of colleges. In 1986, I decided to leave the organization and accepted a full-time faculty position. The first year at the college was exhilarating but also frustrating. While attempting to incorporate my knowledge of community into my teaching, I encountered, among some faculty and students, significant resistance to engaging more critically with issues of social justice, particularly those related to racism and poverty. Suddenly without notice, I was again embroiled in controversy. I was given notice that my contract would not be renewed in the middle of my second semester.

The dean often seemed uncomfortable when interacting with me, perhaps disturbed by both an ideology that made power explicit and a communication style that was more direct and intense than her own. Nevertheless, following a protest by students against my firing and a threat of a lawsuit against the institution—pointing to the lack of due process, since no warning or evaluation was ever issued to substantiate the decision—I was offered a contract renewal. I accepted the contract with the understanding that my bicultural development program would become an independent specialization within the larger curriculum. Accordingly, I went on to establish the first human development program in the country that was specifically grounded in the contexts and realities of subordinate communities and, thus, central to the core curriculum of the program.

Who were your key intellectual mentors?

As a Master's student in the early 1980s, I was strongly influenced by the work of Carol Phillips and Louise Derman-Sparks. Their work critically examined human development and schooling in terms of sociopolitical context that included culture, race, class and gender. Carol Phillips, an African American professor, particularly influenced not only my conceptual understanding of these issues but inspired me to believe in my own intellectual capacity. Louise Derman-Sparks, a longtime radical activist, feminist, and educator grounded my initial understanding of capitalism and mentored my teaching for several years. In addition, writers such as Paulo Freire, Frantz Fanon, Albert Memmi, Kenneth Clarke, Angela Davis, Rodolfo Acuna, Mario Barrera, Gloria Anzaldúa and Cherrie Moraga influenced my thinking.

During my doctoral program, I again returned to the writings of Paulo Freire. In 1987, I had the good fortune of attending a critical pedagogy conference where Freire and many of the major critical educational theorists of the time were presenting their work. This experience fundamentally changed my life, as I came to know personally many of these thinkers. Freire opened his heart to me as a teacher, mentor, and friend. He was to become my father in the struggle. For the first time, I had discovered critical principles that provided me with the theoretical tools for engaging in a more systematic examination of education—an approach that brought together history, culture, politics, and economics to formidably challenge class and racialized inequalities.

Paulo Freire's *Pedagogy of the Oppressed* was a particularly significant text to my intellectual formation as both an educator and political activist. His capacity to politically embrace the concept of love as our vocation and as a fundamental ingredient in the struggle for liberation has underscored my work and my own writings in the field ever since. Over the next few years, I also became immersed in the work of Karl Marx, Antonio Gramsci, the Frankfurt School, as well as the critical pedagogy literature of Henry Giroux, Michael Apple, Peter McLaren, Ira Shor, Donaldo Macedo, bell hooks and others. My dissertation, which focused on culture and power in the classroom, was greatly influenced by my reading of these powerful texts, which I combined with my knowledge as a therapist, educator, cultural worker, and community organizer.

My teaching practice in both the classroom and community has been not only a central aspect of my political work and a source of great joy but an important site for my intellectual formation. Whether within the community or university classroom, students have been instrumental to my political understanding of the world and the pedagogical needs of students. Recognizing my authority within the classroom and my power to use this authority in the interest of my students, I worked with them to develop innovative democratic approaches to create ongoing intellectual spaces for dialogue and reflection. They taught me the power of listening and being present to students as a collective learning community, as well as individuals with particular needs for their development of consciousness. More importantly, in my relationship with students I discovered the power of intimacy and love in the act of teaching. Hence, to teach critically was not an act of political indoctrination but rather the liberating of public space for dialogues that brought the alliance of theory and practice to the centre of our learning together.

However, there is no denying that my consistent focus on issues of racism, sexism, class inequalities, and other forms of exclusion has also made teaching a challenge. Students often enter the classroom with many conditioned notions that move contrary to emancipatory ideals. Yet like all of us, they generally are unable to recognize readily their own internal contradictions. Efforts to enliven consciousness and to engage authentically are not easy tasks, particularly, since we can seldom leave our life experiences (good or bad) out of our interactions with students. Many times this caused me great emotional upset when working diligently in the classroom to examine conditions of oppression—many conditions that I had personally endured during my lifetime.

It is only honest, at this juncture, to note that at times I responded to my students' comments too personally, feeling the pain too acutely, and inadvertently pushing them too quickly with my own political urgency. This led me to not only approach my work from a commitment to a larger political vision, but also, unwittingly, from emotionally self-righteous anger, frustration and rage over the oppression I had witnessed and experienced in my own lifetime. So although, in such moments, I may have been politically correct, I was pedagogically ineffectual. My brashness and tendency towards an indulgence of my victimization, unwittingly, displaced the needs of students and pushed them away from engagement. This shortcoming in my teaching and political practice has proved to be one of my greatest challenges: to move beyond the arrogance and ego-driven survival mechanisms I learned as a child to a place of greater compassion and critical understanding as an activist scholar. This demands not only critically comprehending emancipatory theories and revolutionary practices but also contending forthrightly with my internal contradictions in clear and open ways. Sometimes I do this well and sometimes not.

Your academic life is also marked by political struggle.

Yes, very much so. After years of fighting with the ravages of oppression in my private and public life, I found myself within a privileged university context. The dissonance I experienced during my beginning years as a Latina, working-class, female professor in an all-Anglo department is a feature of junior faculty life that is seldom discussed in any substantive manner within the academy. There were many personal doubts and insecurities I faced in my efforts to find a place for myself in the university. Patriarchy, class, and racism within the university function nearly invisibly to those immersed within the contours of privilege. But this is not so for activist scholars, particularly women, from historically disenfranchised populations. Given the trajectory of our uneven development, we are often acutely aware of the racism and elitism that underscores university relationships, even with the most supportive of colleagues.

Hence, as a working-class, Latina professor I often felt acutely aware of the racism, sexism, and elitism of administrators, faculty and even students. In essence,

I found the academy to be, on the surface, hospitable, while in practice a brutally political arena where the oppressive structures of the larger society were systematically reproduced. More disheartening has been the politics of silence, where faculty members deem major ideological differences within a department to be simply a matter of competition. The primary concern here is to steer themselves free of conflict, despite the most unjust conditions. In short, there is an absence of lived moral courage. Even esteemed progressive colleagues can become more concerned about not tainting their reputation, in order to preserve the power or influence they feel they've garnered along the way. Hence, on more than one occasion I found myself completely isolated and alone, surrounded only by the echoes of liberal social justice rhetoric and books filled with lovely radical ideas by colleagues-authors missing in action. This may help to explain one of the reasons why the structures and practices that reproduce inequality remain intact. All social change requires the insertion of the body into the struggle; our ideals are thwarted by inaction.

The struggles within the academy were to become central to my work as a professor. For example, the university I joined proved to be very supportive during my early years as a junior and associate professor at the institution—perhaps partly spurred on by a multimillion-dollar lawsuit for discrimination filed by an African American professor against the department. However when I became a senior professor, the faculty and administration did not appear to respond as positively to the influence that my teaching and writings were having within the university and the larger community. Tensions began to ensue with faculty members who held more conservative notions of education and who feared the loss of control over the curriculum, student formation, and the intellectual direction of the department. As I attempted to challenge and vie for changes in a department that was quickly moving from a more progressive to a more conservative educational agenda, I found myself under fire once more.

When a group of graduate students protested curricular changes that portended a more conservative teacher education curriculum, I extended my support in a brief email that later was circulated. This public support for a more critical curriculum became the tangible act necessary to orchestrate a faculty hazing, where I was falsely accused of trying to destroy the department and damage the reputation of the university. Colleagues contended that I had proven myself to be noncollegial and could never be trusted again. Following the meeting, I learned that covert actions were taken by some faculty members to work toward forcing my removal. I was alerted that those in power had gone to university attorneys to discuss the possibility of rescinding my tenure, an action that was discouraged since there were insufficient legal grounds to carry out such an action.

I learned quickly that the marginalization I had experienced from my colleagues in the past was only child's play compared to the fallout I now faced. A group of students were organized to meet with the dean and the president of the college regarding the injustices at work in my case. I made repeated efforts to discuss the matter with the provost, dean and colleagues. All efforts were to no avail. Eventually, most of the students became confused by what they were told by other faculty members, who wished to keep matters under wraps. Legitimate concerns and important ideological differences were reduced to personality conflicts. After 10 years of superior university, department and student evaluations, suddenly my research was questioned and maligned. The tension was thick enough to cut with a knife. Finally, in an effort to step out of the eye of the storm, I asked for a leave of absence. Supportive colleagues at another university were able to create a visiting appointment for me, which provided the space I needed to recuperate from the assaults of this unexpected attack.

You give a lot of importance to personal community

Personal community—family, friends, comrades and colleagues—has played an important role in my life and my scholarship. For example, despite the hardships I endured in my early years, I continued to make efforts to reconcile my relationship with my mother. Although it took many years to make peace with those early years, our relationship blossomed during the last 10 years of her life. I learned to see and appreciate my mother as the suffering soul she was and from there began to accept her history as also part of mine. In the process, I discovered who my mother was and grew to understand more fully the impact of racialized and gendered class oppression upon an individual life. I also found the room to let my mother be herself, to enjoy her raunchy humor, to appreciate her skill as a seamstress and cook, and to recognize that in spite of her personal demons, she loved my sister and me dearly and was haunted by enormous shame and remorse.

Given my difficulties with intimate relationships, the power of community has been a saving grace. Yet, I don't want to leave the impression that my intimate relationships and love affairs with men were bad. For, in fact, I was quite fortunate to be in the company of many intelligent and creative men. However, it is not surprising that oppressed souls find one another. And in the midst of intimate relationships, we often act out the most irrational and violent aspects of our violated bodies. For some of us, it takes a very long time to grapple with the disowned rage and grief that sits just beneath the mask of social niceties. For me, it has been only very recently, that I have found the strength and wherewithal to begin actually enjoying my life with respect to men. It has required facing my shame for all the mistakes that I have made and embracing each relationship as a moment in which I learned something new about myself. None was a failure. Yet, it is not surprising that a history of four marriages easily opens one to humiliation and brutal judgment, particularly from those who would commingle their moralism with their envy. This speaks to a colonizing shame rigidly constructed by social conventions that disregard the alienating impact of capitalist society and the hardships of just staying alive. To struggle for liberation then requires that we disrupt the tyranny of shame in our own lives, so that we will not repeat it in our relationships with others. My personal community is comprised of individuals who also aspire to such a politics of human emancipation.

My friends and comrades over the years have also been key to my development and sustenance as an educator, political activist, and scholar. They encouraged and challenged my work, inspired me to persevere, and embraced me during hard moments with their love and solidarity. Although too many to mention here, my friend and comrade Rudy Torres is an example. His intellectual prowess and extensive knowledge of Marxism filled an important theoretical gap in my scholarly formation. Through our dialogues, I came to interrogate more deeply my constructions of "race" and more firmly anchor my understanding of political economy. We worked on a variety of scholarly collaborations that contributed to the field of Latino studies and helped to carve an argument for a critical theory of racism. The latter writings sought to shatter reified notions of "race," which function to stifle the formation of political solidarity across class and cultural differences. It was in my relationship with Rudy that I learned much about constructing healthy working boundaries, while struggling in concrete ways with the sexual politics so prominent in relationships between women and men. At times we fought over ideas or personal differences. Yet, our friendship and scholarship, grounded in our shared political commitment to the struggle for economic democracy and social justice, have withstood the test of time. Moreover, our intimate familiarity with poverty and its devastation and the painful histories of our childhood could not help but become inextricably inscribed in our work together.

My personal community has been my lifeline during moments of extreme personal and political turmoil. They have seen me through political struggles, broken relationships, job difficulties, major illnesses, my house burning, and my mother dying. They are my extended kin of the heart and through them I have found the way to stay open and alive. These are the people that have known me at my best and my worst, yet continue to love and appreciate me for the woman I am. They support and challenge me to live my life in concert with my values and beliefs. Yet, when I falter, they never expect or require more from me than I am able to give. These relationships are lifelong, nourished by politics, food, conversation, notes, books, music, art, dance, love, and the knowledge that we are growing old together in a history we share. But more importantly, this comprises a personal network of relationships that is not anchored in repressive interpretations of reality or the unrelenting drive for material gain. Instead, our anchor is our love for the world, which drives our revolutionary dreams.

How do you see your future?

Well, in 2002, unable to return to the politically strained environment of my former university, I began a job search and was offered a faculty position at a university in the Midwest. I now entered a department in a large public institution with a very diverse faculty working on many of the issues that were close to my heart. Yet, even within this more hospitable context, many of the same concerns I found in a small private institution continue to be at work but with an enlarged bureaucracy. Despite very gracious interactions among the faculty, there clearly exist contesting notions of identity politics, "race" and racism, the political economy, gender differences, and the role of activism in graduate education. Yet, seldom are tough intellectual issues engaged in any substantive manner among the faculty. As is so common within university environments, there exists little time for sustained dialogues. This is generally coupled with an unspoken competition over ideas, which unfortunately is indirectly waged through the mentorship of students—making scholarship an issue of personal loyalties, rather than of the larger intellectual and practical concerns of emancipation.

Furthermore, despite the large number of faculty of color in the department, questions of elitism and sexism continue to go unaddressed, and we have been unable to establish a consistent democratic governing practice, although the majority espouse democratic empowerment and hold expressed commitments to social justice. However, in this instance, these concerns seem less about unwillingness or resistance. Here the issues are more tied to institutional expectations of productivity, university service, and external professional contributions. These expectations ultimately result in placing major time constraints on faculty—time constraints that subsume collective interrogation of academic ideas, structures, and practices, as well as the building of a solid intellectual community. The key to making a change in the university requires surrendering our proclivity to chase after new intellectual experiences for the mere sake of obtaining individual professional recognition or reward. Instead, the faculty would need to link collectively our labor within universities to actual community conditions and events, with the very clear purpose and intent of transforming these conditions in concrete and meaningful ways. After 20 years in the academy, I've come to firmly believe that the fundamental structures of inequality that shape university life make it next to impossible to construct an emancipatory political practice, even in the presence of radical scholarship. For what is necessary is a critical mass of scholars at a university who embrace emancipatory ideals in practice and, this, unfortunately, is very difficult to find. The structures of individualism, competition, and rewards within the academy work effectively to counter such a phenomenon. Hence, the obdurate structural reality of the university challenges us, as radical intellectuals, to wrestle with what at times seems the futility of our context. What exactly is the contribution of university professors to an emancipatory political vision? How do we contend with the complicity of our faculty role? What are the limits and possibilities of radical scholarship in these times? How do we link our scholarship to the everyday realities of oppressed people's lives? And how can we even measure the extent of our contribution to the ongoing struggle for social justice, human rights and economic democracy? Important questions in the midst of the internationalization of capital, the fascism of the media, the current evangelizing campaign of the Right, and the deceptive political repression of dissenting voices.

It is also important here to speak for a moment about the link between the scientism and racism of the academy. There is no question in my mind that the penchant for employing scientific paradigms of precision and objectivity for interpreting human conditions works to harden consciousness. We are taught (and teach our students) to accept a static science and the static vision it affords. As an abstraction of life, our research freezes everything, including the motion of our imagination and all social relationships. Struggling to disrupt this hardened consciousness has been one of the most difficult tasks of my labor as a professor. Colleagues and students educated in the "classical traditions" are often more resistant to a pedagogy that shifts the centre of power from elite traditional readings of society to a critical understanding of the world.

My efforts to crack disciplinary borders and counter static scientific methodologies within the academy have closed many doors. For example, as a visiting instructor at a very prestigious northeastern university, I asked to meet with the chair of the department to discuss the possibility of my remaining once my contract ended. Within moments of beginning the meeting, the chair told me, in no uncertain terms, that "not even in my dreams" should I think that I could remain for another year. His contempt and disdain were spurred by my efforts to "politicize the curriculum with multicultural rhetoric." In his eyes, this "weakness signaled a deep flaw in my scholarship." It took me some time to recover from the condescending manner in which he spoke to me. As a loyal gatekeeper of the institution, he deployed his power and influence to protect the tradition of positivism, a tactic I have seen repeated in a thousand ways, throughout my tenure in the academy.

Hence, despite my accomplishments, I must confess that I am terribly disheartened with my work as a professor. I seek a life where books are not the primary source for making meaning but rather where relationships nourish and sustain our capacity to live fully the dialectics of our existence. Yet, I know that in my effort to renew my work, I'm forced to confront my contradictions and acknowledge how the economic advantage and privileges of university life are the carrot that keeps me on course with the university's hegemonic function in the larger world. It is the price I pay for my stressed-out, always-so-busy life, lived isolated and alienated from the vitality of the streets and just outside of the suffering and anguish of so many. It is the reward that keeps my eyes seeking the elusive prize—being deemed an important radical intellectual of our time. All this, while I am supposedly tearing down the master's house? Isn't this the fallacy that Audre Lorde warned us about? Didn't she say that we couldn't dismantle the master's house using the master's tools? In my misguided zeal and arrogance, I guess I thought I could.

So, after so many years of dedicating myself to what now seems a futile endeavor, I must extricate myself from academia and reenter the world that, unbeknownst to me, I tried to escape by dancing with ideas in my head. Instead, I need to be more outward in the midst of nitty-gritty commonplace problems. Where will this lead me? I can't really say. But it must be toward a life where happiness, even in the midst of struggle, becomes revolutionary purpose. And where the freedom to express my humanity, as I am, is welcomed—whether in the company of people or on a blank sheet of paper—where my voice can flow freely and the colors of my being explode into a million shades of love.

How do you envisage the struggle for greater social justice from now onward?

Over the years, my struggle for consciousness has always brought back home to me the body. This is particularly true for those of us who exist, as Henri Lefebvre contends, in a world where every aspect of our daily life—birth, death, marriage, family, school, work, leisure, parenthood, spirituality, and even entertainment—has been colonized. Under such a regime of power, our bodies become alienated, disconnected and compartmentalized, leaving us unmercifully vulnerable to the whims of capital. Meanwhile, the marketplace fools us into believing that democracy equals capitalism and consumption equals happiness. As our consciousness becomes more and more abstracted, we become more and more detached from our bodies. The consequence is a deep sense of personal and collective dissatisfaction generated by a marketplace that cannot satisfy authentic human needs— human needs that can only be met through relationships that break the alienation and isolation we live.

Throughout my life, I have seen how injustice, both personal and institutional, blocks, disrupts and corrupts the free and fluid participation of subordinated bodies within society. In a myriad of forms, oppression reifies exclusion in the interest of economic imperatives, without regard for the violated bodies left behind. When human needs such as food, shelter, meaningful livelihood, healthcare, education and the intimacy of a community are not met, bodies are violated. Violated bodies easily gravitate to whatever can provide a quick fix to ease the pain and isolation of an alienated existence. I witnessed this in my own life. For years, I repeatedly tried to erase the pain and grief with temporary quick fix solutions. But illicit drugs, excess food, and a multitude of troubled relationships only dug me deeper into the hole of my despair, making it more difficult for me to participate fully in coherent struggles out in the world. We need, instead, fully integral bodies expressing our humanity from a place of wholeness and love, rather than fear and uncertainty, if we are to transform our personal and political madness.

When I recall my mother's life or the lives of many students and comrades, I can't help but conclude that to summon the power of consciousness requires the development of a moral and ethical understanding that can safeguard the dignity and integrity of all human differences. Moral here should not be confused with moralism. Being moral means exploring and being self-vigilant of all our sensations, ideas, and practices. This is a process that is impossible to accomplish by abstracting our current conditions from our ideologies and histories of survival. It requires that we bring together the moral and political, as well as the particular and the universal, acknowledging that all life exists interconnected.

This entails an understanding of politics that begins with the needs of the body. For without our bodies to enact the principles we embrace, any notion of an emancipatory democracy is meaningless. Moreover the origin of emancipatory possibility and human solidarity resides in our bodies. Terry Eagleton reminds us that it is the moral, fragile, suffering, ecstatic, needy, dependent, desirous, and compassionate body which furnishes us the basis for all moral thought; and it's moral thought that places our bodies back into the political discourse. Yet, discourse here extends beyond the notion of voices; for genuine democracy is about the body's interaction with the world. Thus, it must exist as a practice, in which human beings interact as equals in order to contribute to the world the best of what we have to offer. And it all must take place within unfettered human interaction—the organic medium for struggle and the development of consciousness. Throughout my life as an activist scholar, I have worked to embrace the tradition of revolutionary love as did Che Guevara, Paulo Freire, and others in the past. This is a love that compels us to become part of an emancipatory politics and pedagogy that cultivates human connection, intimacy, trust and honesty. Here again, Eagleton provides us the direction. Revolutionary love means to comprehend that the moral and the material as inextricably linked. And as such, our politics must recognize love as an essential ingredient of a just society. Love as a political principle motivates the struggle to create mutually life-enhancing opportunities for all people. It is a love that is grounded in the interdependence of our human existence—that which we share, as much as that which we do not. This is a love nurtured by the act of relationship itself. It cultivates relationships with the freedom to be at one's best without undue fear. Such an emancipatory love allows us to realize our nature, in a way that allows others to do so as well. Inherent in such a love is the understanding that we are never at liberty to be violent, authoritarian, or exploitive.

My life has shown me that love is revolutionary when it is empowered by consciousness. And the power of our consciousness exists within our bodies. It is in our freedom to speak and act collectively that our power commingles with one another. It is this commingling of emancipatory consciousness that oppression seeks to contain or halt altogether. However, once our freedom to exist is unleashed, the beauty and power of the decolonized cannot be pimped by the whims of political tyranny or the greed of capital. Instead consciousness sustained becomes human energy to produce change in the existing conditions which shape our lives, as both individuals and social beings.

Most importantly, it is through such collective struggle that consciousness is born. The poet Muriel Rukeyser said that "a true consciousness is the confession to ourselves of our feelings; a false consciousness disowns them."[4] This disowning leads to the corruption of the mind and the body. Often, it is the outcome of seductive sounding images—via a celluloid screen, a third grade teacher, a social worker, a college counselor, a doctor's diagnosis, a "beauty" magazine, the evening news—colonizing images in disguise that tell us our lives, as they exist, are worthless, or at best deficit. Consciousness distracted by the false yearning and desires of the marketplace corrupts our political will. With promises of an easier life, we are rendered passive citizens of the empire.

Hence, the struggle for me has always been to fight against the inertia of passivity inspired by capitalism, so that I might find the moral courage required to voice dissent, even when standing alone. In the mining of my own grief, I have heard the grief of our humanity. With great effort I have fought to contend with the blinders of complacency, the indulgence of my victimhood, and the political righteousness of my oppression. In so doing, I have found that the path to a revolutionary struggle must be grounded in shared kinship, political self-determination, and economic justice. It is a struggle that holds no guarantees or promises yet finds in our collective consciousness the seeds of our liberation and in our buried histories, the quickening of our power. Oppression would love them to remain forever hidden; perhaps this is why it takes madness, something of the insane, to redeem the power from all that we have lived.

NOTES

1. M. Rukeyser, *The Life of Poetry* (Ashfield, MA: Paris Press, 1996), 1.
2. "We make the path by walking."
3. "What no one can take from you."
4. Rukeyser, *The Life of Poetry*, 49.

Index

D

M

Studies in the Postmodern Theory of Education

General Editor
Shirley R. Steinberg

Counterpoints publishes the most compelling and imaginative books being written in education today. Grounded on the theoretical advances in criticalism, feminism, and postmodernism in the last two decades of the twentieth century, Counterpoints engages the meaning of these innovations in various forms of educational expression. Committed to the proposition that theoretical literature should be accessible to a variety of audiences, the series insists that its authors avoid esoteric and jargonistic languages that transform educational scholarship into an elite discourse for the initiated. Scholarly work matters only to the degree it affects consciousness and practice at multiple sites. Counterpoints' editorial policy is based on these principles and the ability of scholars to break new ground, to open new conversations, to go where educators have never gone before.

For additional information about this series or for the submission of manuscripts, please contact:

Shirley R. Steinberg
c/o Peter Lang Publishing, Inc.
29 Broadway, 18th floor
New York, New York 10006

To order other books in this series, please contact our Customer Service Department:

(800) 770-LANG (within the U.S.)
(212) 647-7706 (outside the U.S.)
(212) 647-7707 FAX

Or browse online by series:
www.peterlang.com